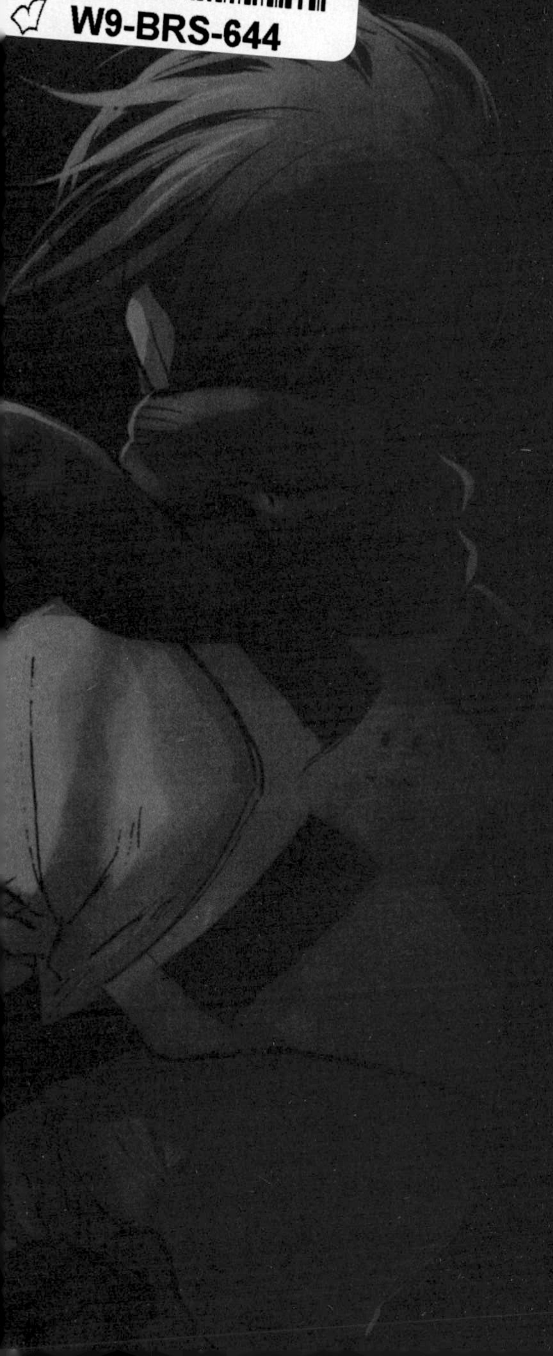

ATTACK ON TITAN 31

HAJIME ISAYAMA

THE CHARACTERS OF ATTACK ON TITAN

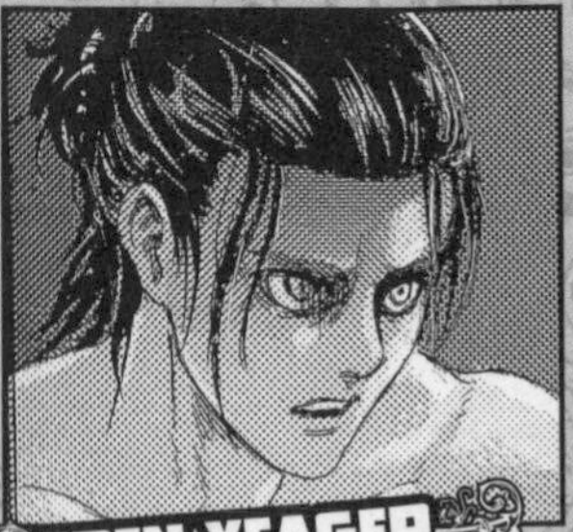

EREN YEAGER

FROM THE 104TH TRAINING CORPS; NOW IN THE SURVEY CORPS. HOLDS THE POWER OF THE ATTACK TITAN AND THE FOUNDING TITAN. BOLDLY INFILTRATED MARLEY ON HIS OWN.

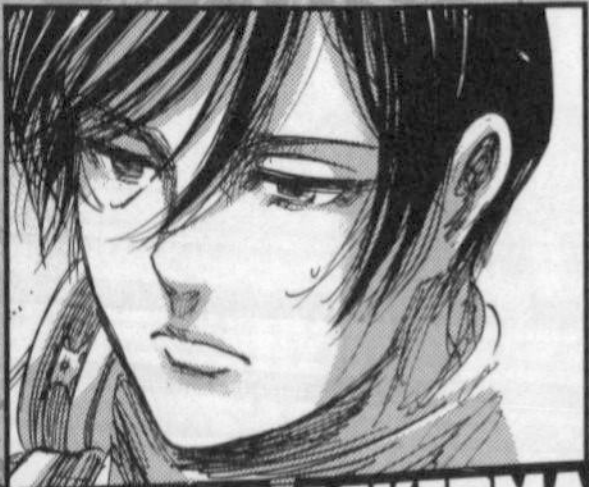

MIKASA ACKERMAN

FROM THE 104TH TRAINING CORPS; NOW IN THE SURVEY CORPS. SHE HAS SHOWN INCREDIBLE COMBAT ABILITIES EVER SINCE SHE WAS A RECRUIT. SHE SEES PROTECTING EREN AS HER MISSION.

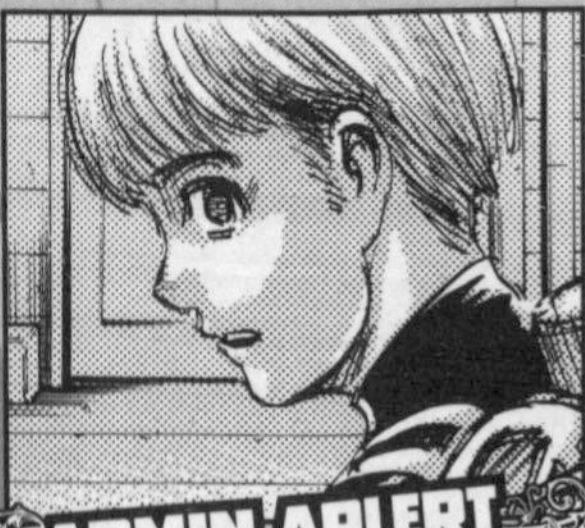

ARMIN ARLERT

FROM THE 104TH TRAINING CORPS; NOW IN THE SURVEY CORPS. HOLDS THE POWER OF THE COLOSSUS TITAN. HE HAS SAVED HIS COMRADES COUNTLESS TIMES WITH HIS SHARP INTELLECT AND BRAVERY.

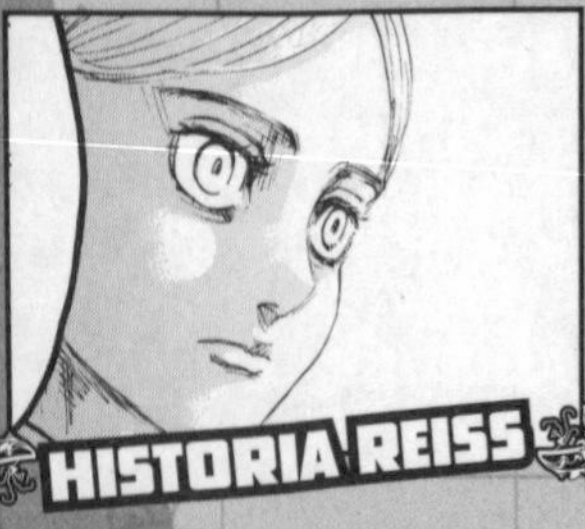

HISTORIA REISS

A DESCENDANT OF THE REISS FAMILY, THE TRUE ROYAL BLOODLINE, HISTORIA HAS ASCENDED TO THE THRONE AS QUEEN. SHE ONCE BELONGED TO THE SURVEY CORPS UNDER THE NAME KRISTA LENZ.

THE NATION OF ELDIA [THE ISLAND OF PARADIS]

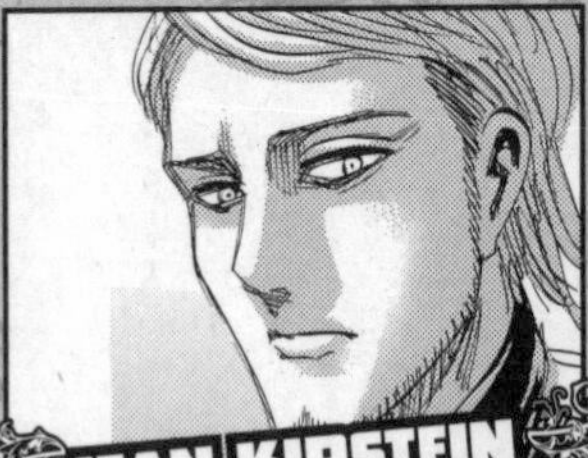

JEAN KIRSTEIN

FROM THE 104TH TRAINING CORPS; NOW IN THE SURVEY CORPS. ONCE KNOWN FOR HIS SARCASTIC PERSONALITY, HE HAS SINCE GROWN INTO A LEADER.

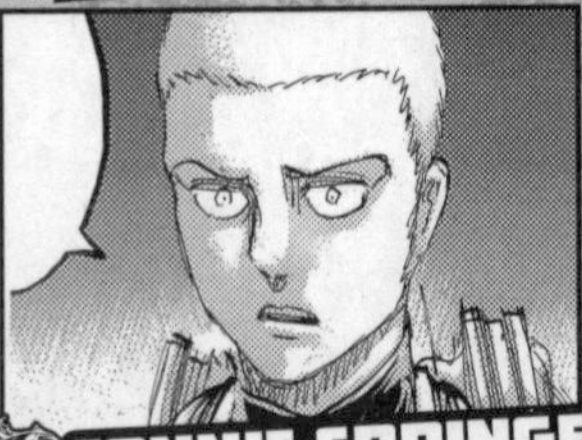

CONNIE SPRINGER

FROM THE 104TH TRAINING CORPS; NOW IN THE SURVEY CORPS. HE IS CHEERFUL IN PERSONALITY, BUT FINDS HIMSELF LOSING EVERYONE IMPORTANT TO HIM... ORIGINALLY FROM RAGAKO VILLAGE.

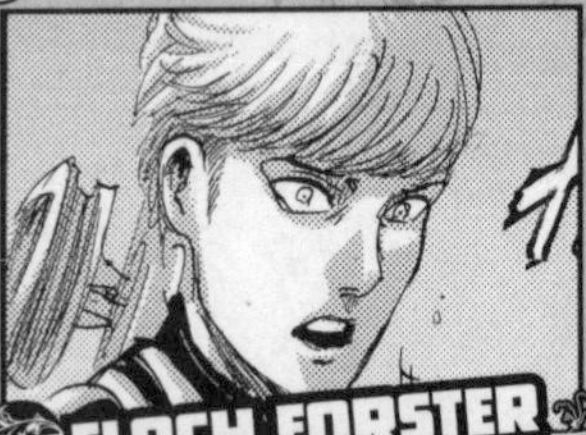

FLOCH FORSTER

A MEMBER OF THE SURVEY CORPS. A SURVIVOR OF THE DECISIVE BATTLE FOR SHIGANSHINA DISTRICT, WHICH CLAIMED MANY LIVES, INCLUDING ERWIN'S.

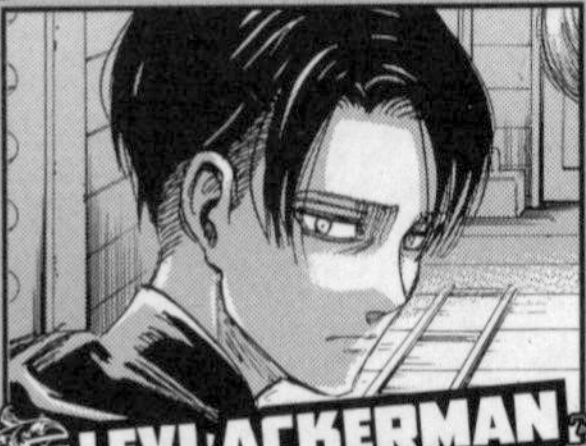

LEVI ACKERMAN

CAPTAIN OF THE SURVEY CORPS. KNOWN AS "HUMANITY'S STRONGEST SOLDIER." HE FIGHTS THROUGH HIS STRUGGLES IN ORDER TO CARRY ON HIS GOOD FRIEND ERWIN'S DYING WISHES.

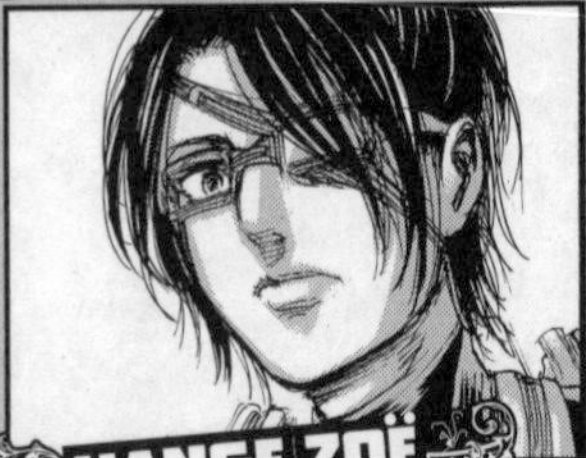

HANGE ZOË

COMMANDER OF THE SURVEY CORPS. KEEN POWERS OF OBSERVATION LED ERWIN TO NAME HANGE HIS SUCCESSOR DESPITE OBVIOUS ECCENTRICITIES.

THE ELDIAN WARRIORS OF THE MARLEYAN ARMY

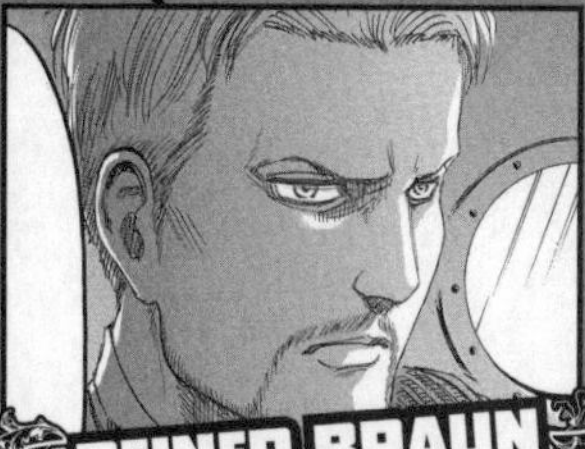

REINER BRAUN

HOLDS THE ARMORED TITAN WITHIN HIM. SINCE HE WAS THE ONLY ONE TO MAKE IT BACK FROM THE MISSION ON PARADIS, HE SUFFERS FROM A GUILTY CONSCIENCE.

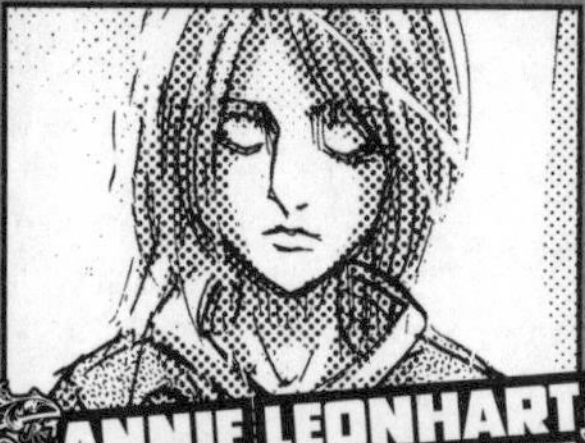

ANNIE LEONHART

HOLDS THE FEMALE TITAN WITHIN HER. A MEMBER OF THE 104TH. SHE HAS BEEN SLEEPING WITHIN A HARDENED CRYSTAL EVER SINCE HER TRUE IDENTITY WAS DISCOVERED.

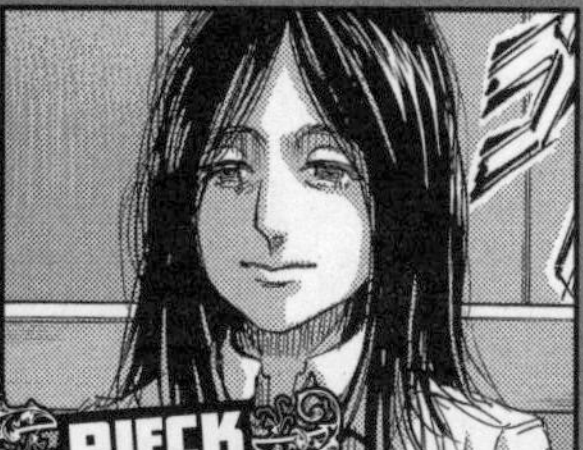

PIECK

HOLDS THE CART TITAN WITHIN HER, CARRYING THE PANZER UNIT ON THE BACK OF THE "CARTMAN" TO FIGHT. HIGHLY PERCEPTIVE.

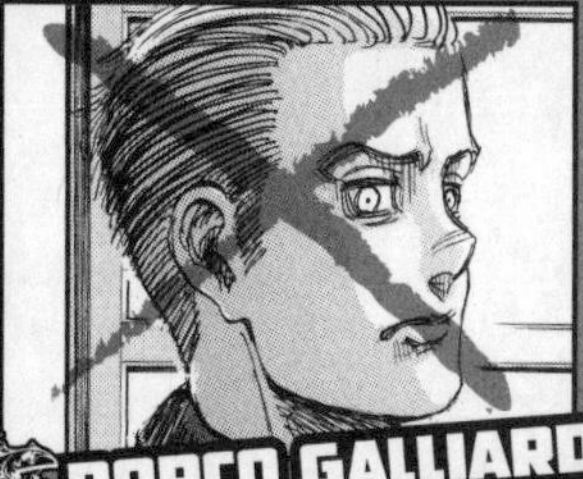

PORCO GALLIARD

HOLDS THE JAW TITAN WITHIN HIM. THERE IS STRIFE BETWEEN HIM AND REINER OVER BOTH THE INHERITANCE OF THE ARMORED TITAN AND THE DEATH OF HIS OLDER BROTHER, MARCEL.

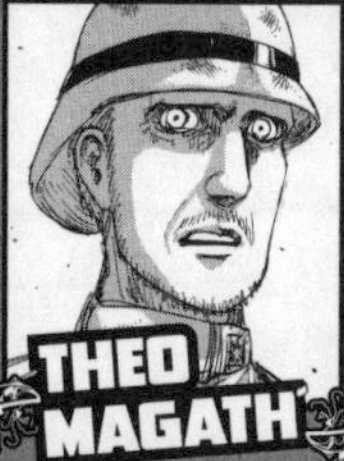

THEO MAGATH

A MARLEYAN WHO LEADS A UNIT OF ELDIANS. PROMOTED TO GENERAL.

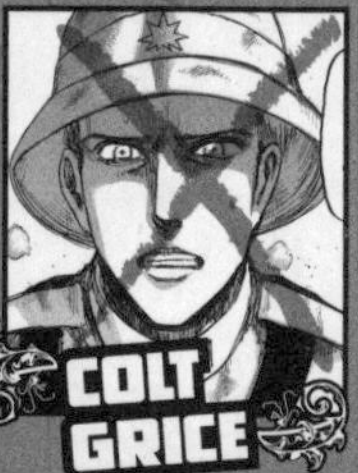

COLT GRICE

FALCO'S OLDER BROTHER. THE OLDEST OF THE WARRIOR CANDIDATES, AND, IN EFFECT, THEIR LEADER.

THE ANTI-MARLEYAN VOLUNTEERS

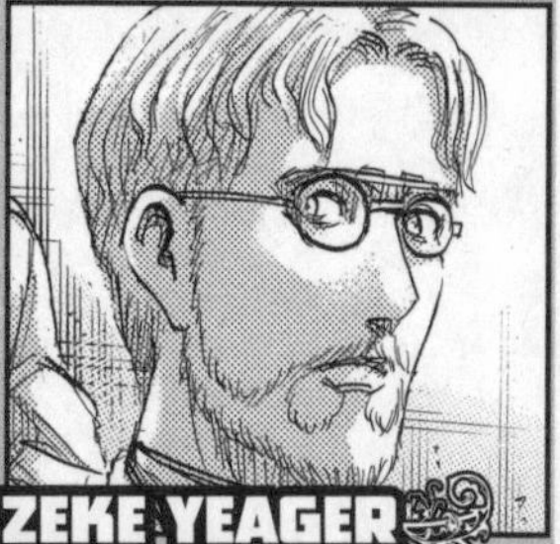

ZEKE YEAGER

HOLDS THE POWER OF THE BEAST TITAN. A LEADER OF THE WARRIORS, HE WAS ONCE KNOWN AS THE "WONDER CHILD." HIS MOTHER IS A DESCENDANT OF THE ROYAL BLOODLINE. HE IS ALSO EREN'S HALF BROTHER.

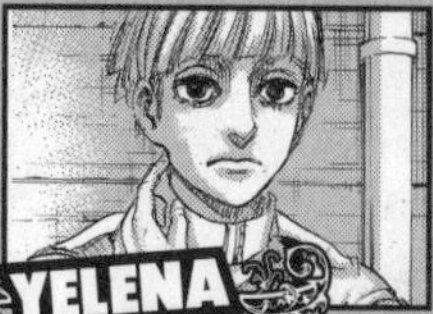

YELENA

YELENA COMMANDS THE VOLUNTEERS AND FOLLOWS ZEKE. SHE DRESSED AS A MAN DURING THE EXPEDITION TO MARLEY IN ORDER TO WORK IN SECRET.

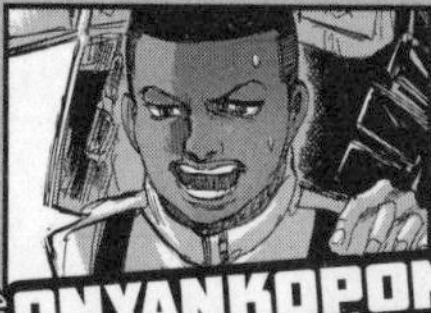

ONYANKOPON

AFTER TRAVELING TO PARADIS WITH YELENA, HE TELLS ITS INHABITANTS OF MARLEY'S ADVANCED CULTURE.

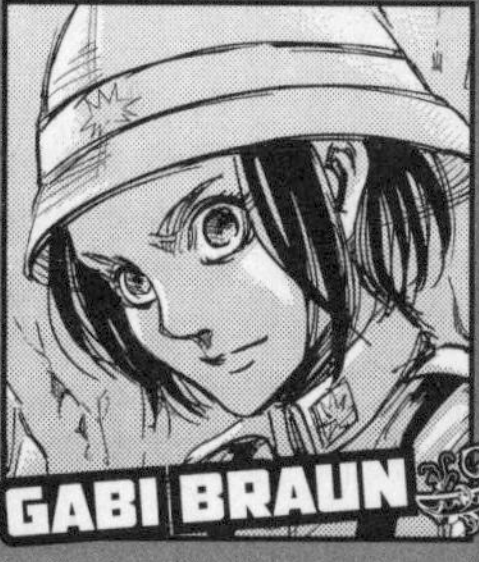

GABI BRAUN

BOLD DESPITE HER SMALL SIZE, GABI IS A DYNAMIC WARRIOR CANDIDATE. HER GOAL IS TO EVENTUALLY INHERIT THE ARMORED TITAN. REINER'S COUSIN.

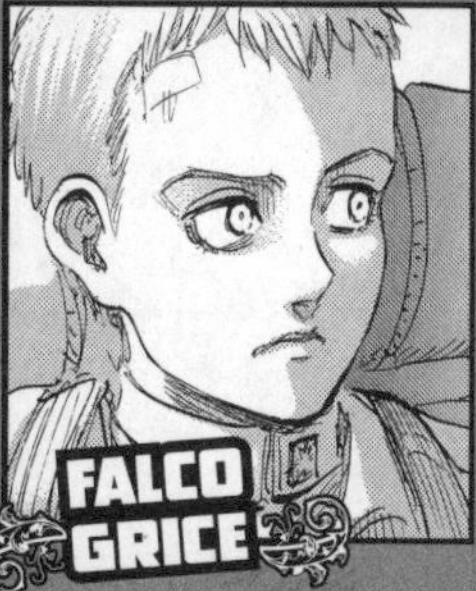

FALCO GRICE

A WARRIOR CANDIDATE. HE HAS AFFECTION FOR GABI AND WANTS TO PROTECT HER. DURING EREN'S TIME INFILTRATING MARLEY, FALCO CAME IN CONTACT WITH EREN WITHOUT REALIZING HIS TRUE IDENTITY.

ATTACK on TITAN

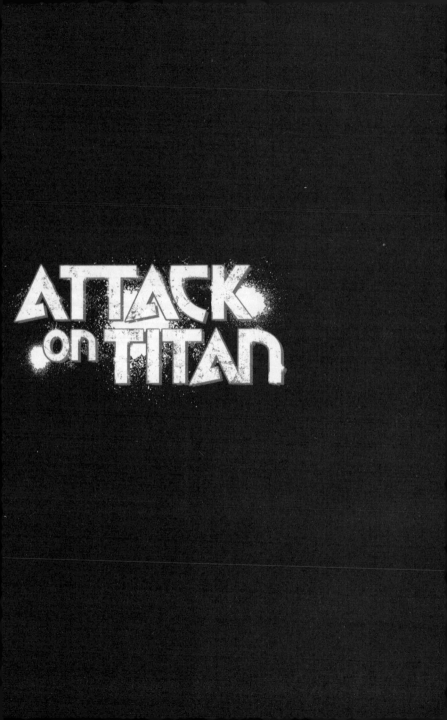

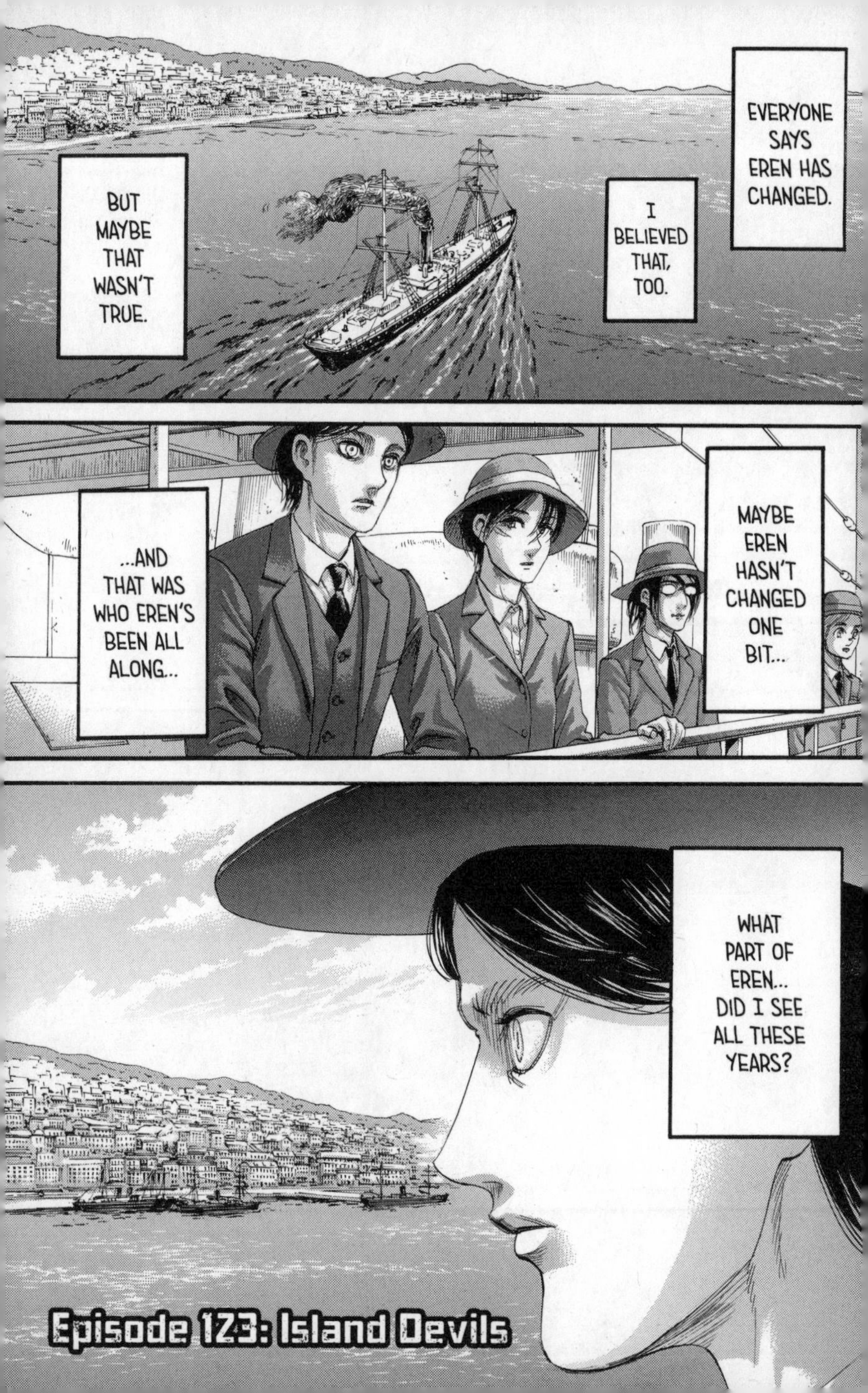
EVERYONE SAYS EREN HAS CHANGED.
I BELIEVED THAT, TOO.
BUT MAYBE THAT WASN'T TRUE.
MAYBE EREN HASN'T CHANGED ONE BIT...
...AND THAT WAS WHO EREN'S BEEN ALL ALONG...
WHAT PART OF EREN... DID I SEE ALL THESE YEARS?
Episode 123: Island Devils

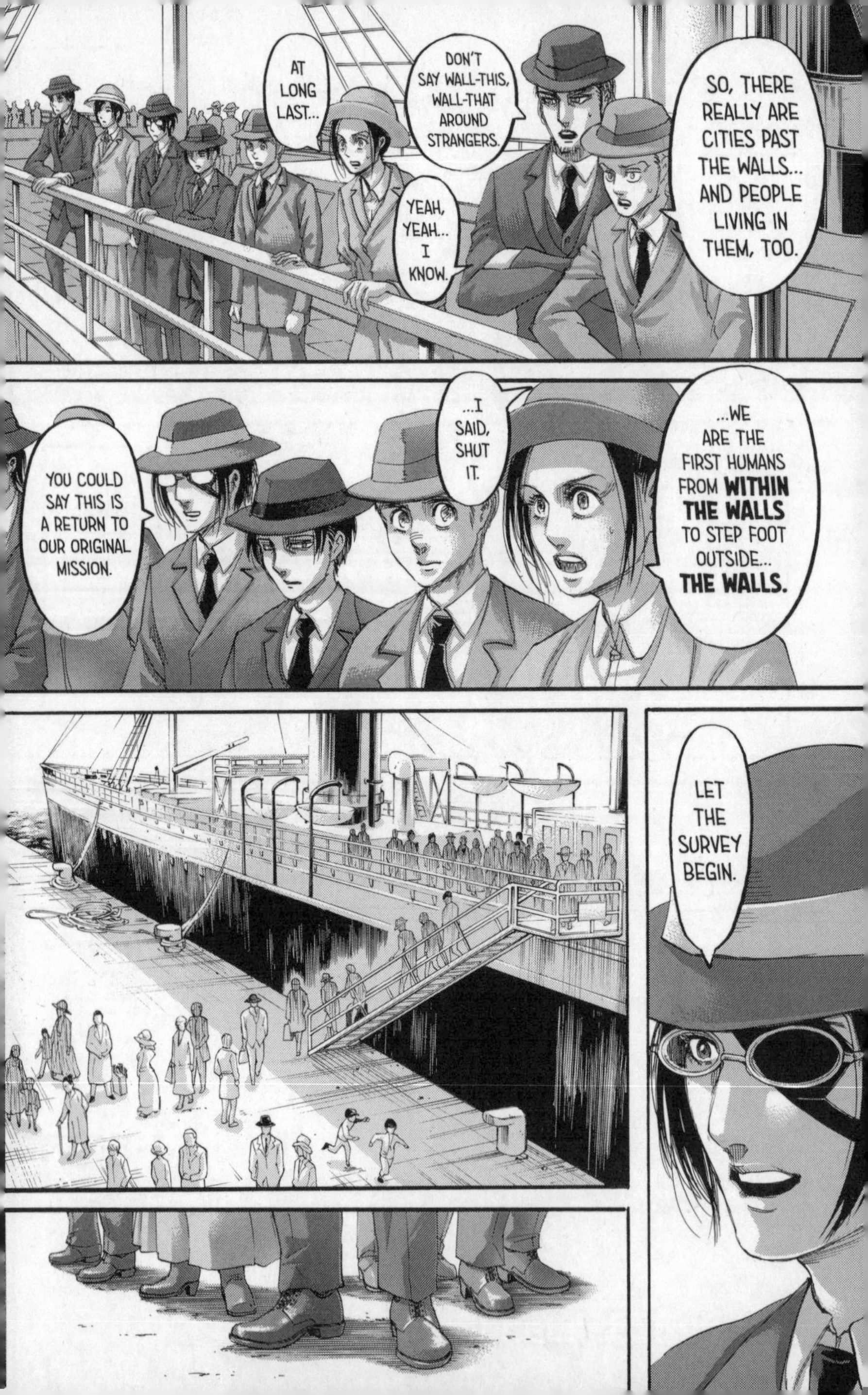
SO, THERE REALLY ARE CITIES PAST THE WALLS... AND PEOPLE LIVING IN THEM, TOO.
DON'T SAY WALL-THIS, WALL-THAT AROUND STRANGERS.
YEAH, YEAH... I KNOW.
AT LONG LAST...
...WE ARE THE FIRST HUMANS FROM **WITHIN THE WALLS** TO STEP FOOT OUTSIDE... **THE WALLS.**
...I SAID, SHUT IT.
YOU COULD SAY THIS IS A RETURN TO OUR ORIGINAL MISSION.
LET THE SURVEY BEGIN.

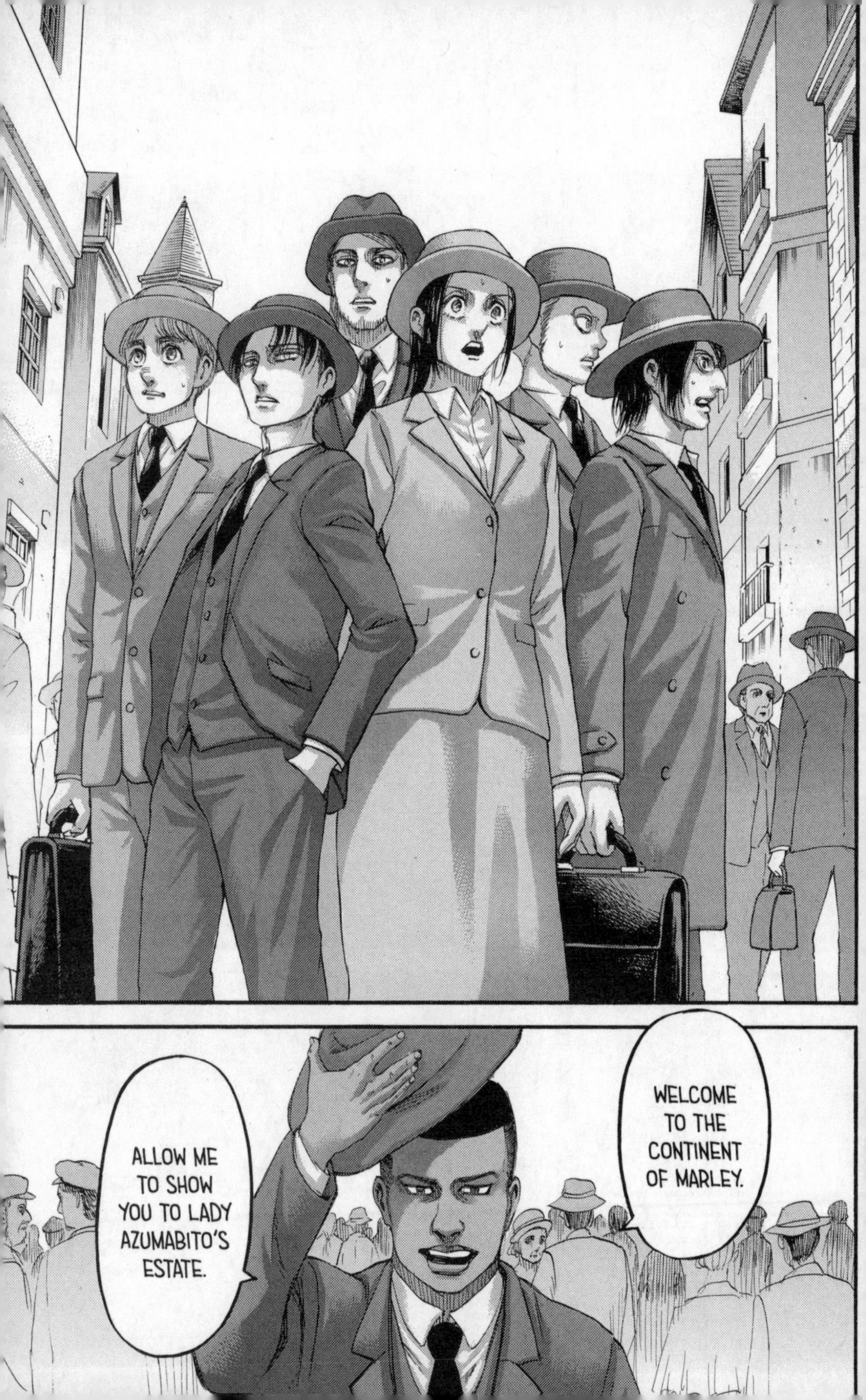
WELCOME TO THE CONTINENT OF MARLEY.
ALLOW ME TO SHOW YOU TO LADY AZUMABITO'S ESTATE.

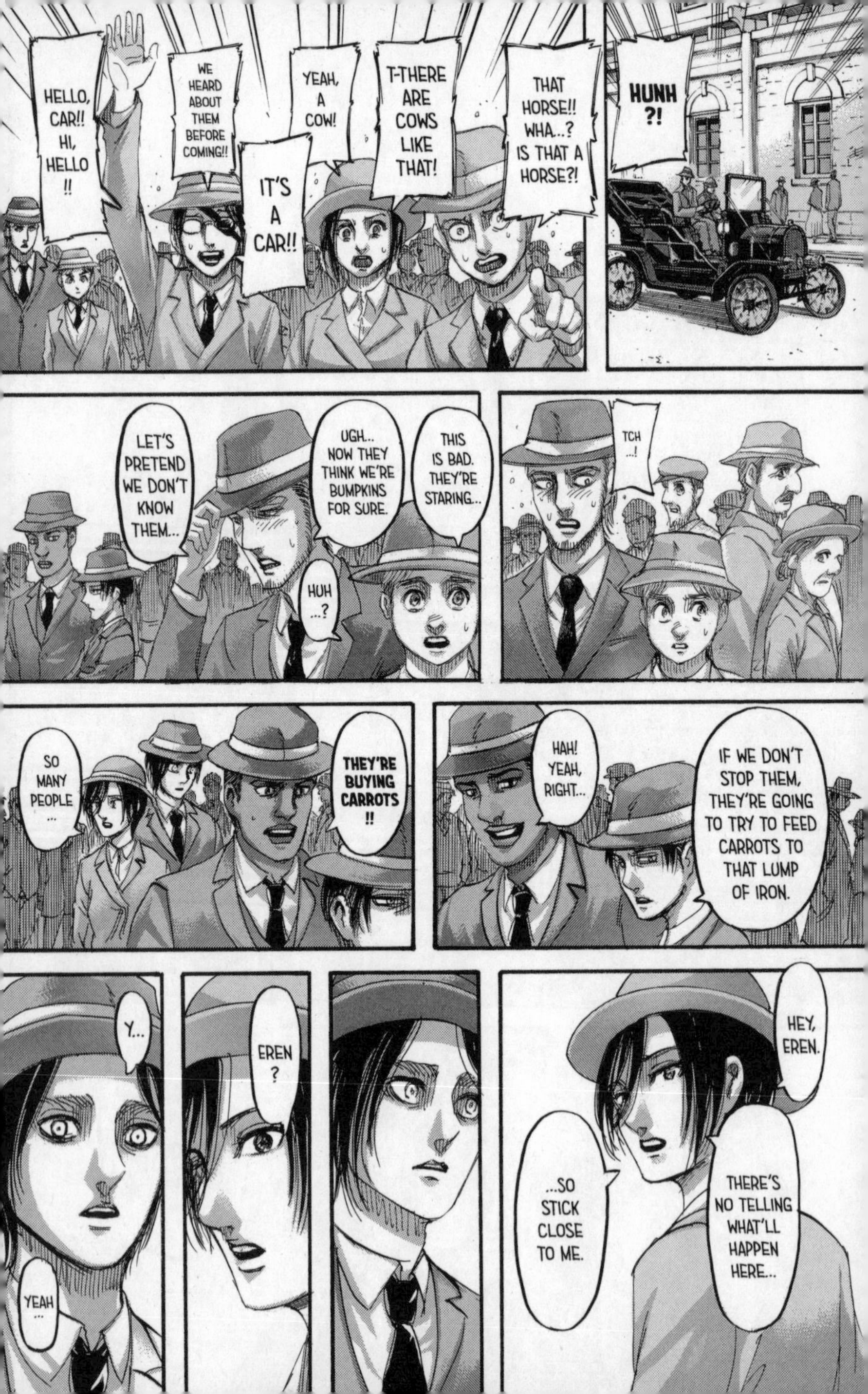
HUNH ?!
THAT HORSE!! WHA...? IS THAT A HORSE?!
T-THERE ARE COWS LIKE THAT!
YEAH, A COW!
IT'S A CAR!!
WE HEARD ABOUT THEM BEFORE COMING!!
HELLO, CAR!! HI, HELLO !!
TCH ...!
THIS IS BAD. THEY'RE STARING...
UGH... NOW THEY THINK WE'RE BUMPKINS FOR SURE.
HUH ...?
LET'S PRETEND WE DON'T KNOW THEM...
IF WE DON'T STOP THEM, THEY'RE GOING TO TRY TO FEED CARROTS TO THAT LUMP OF IRON.
HAH! YEAH, RIGHT...
THEY'RE BUYING CARROTS !!
SO MANY PEOPLE ...
HEY, EREN.
THERE'S NO TELLING WHAT'LL HAPPEN HERE...
...SO STICK CLOSE TO ME.
EREN ?
Y...
YEAH ...

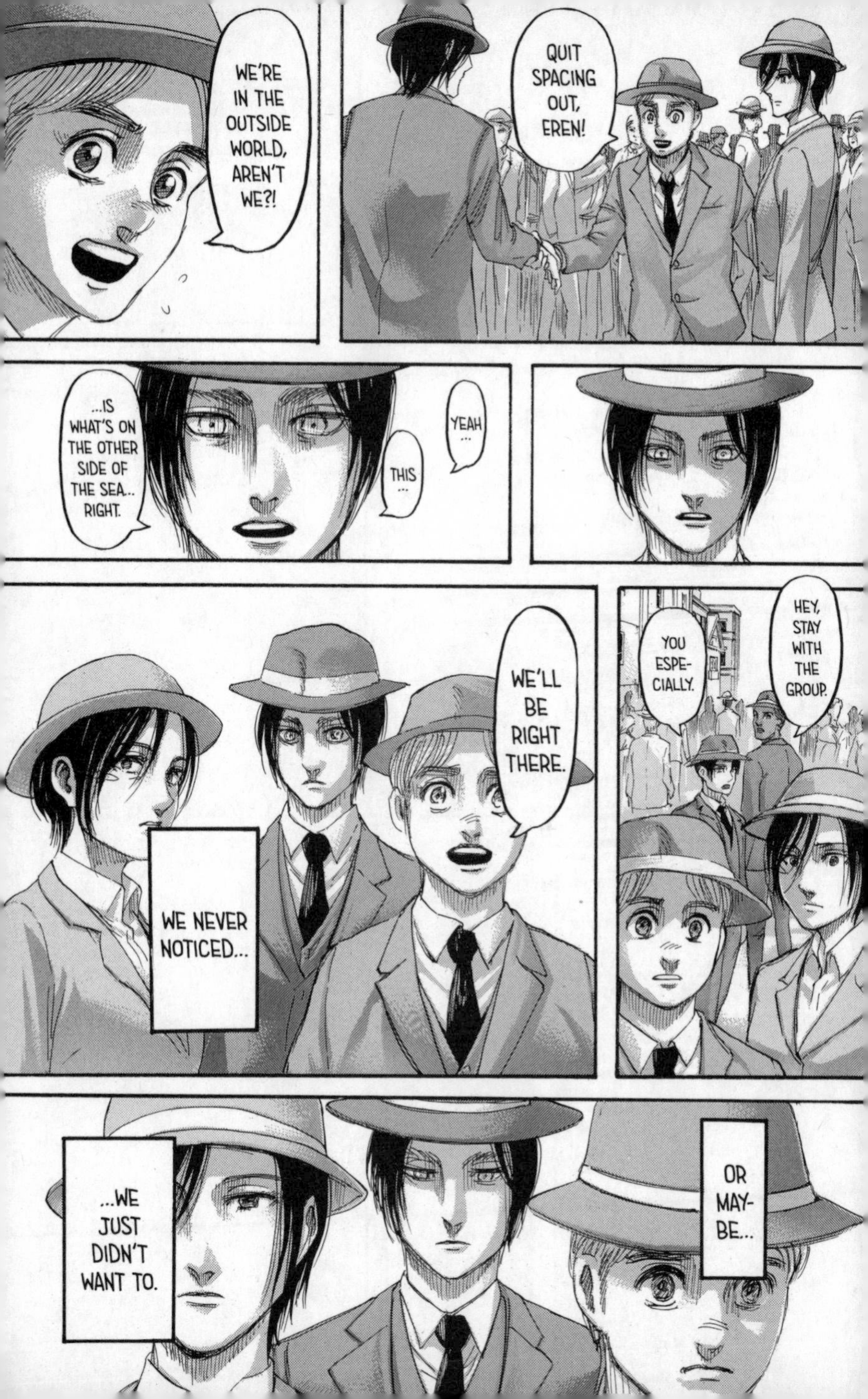
QUIT SPACING OUT, EREN!
WE'RE IN THE OUTSIDE WORLD, AREN'T WE?!
YEAH...
THIS...
...IS WHAT'S ON THE OTHER SIDE OF THE SEA... RIGHT.
HEY, STAY WITH THE GROUP.
YOU ESPE-CIALLY.
WE'LL BE RIGHT THERE.
WE NEVER NOTICED...
OR MAY-BE...
...WE JUST DIDN'T WANT TO.

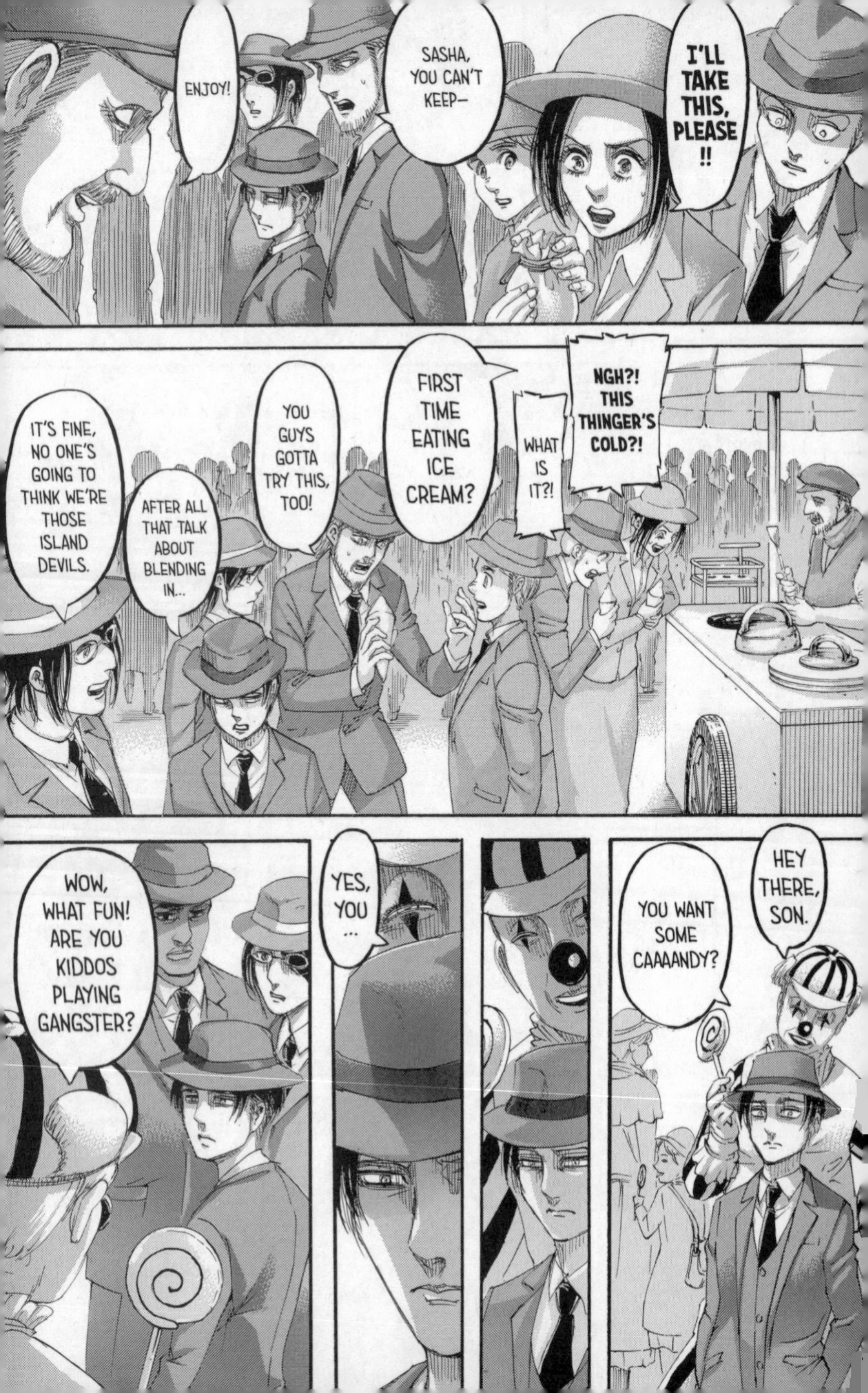
I'LL TAKE THIS, PLEASE!!
SASHA, YOU CAN'T KEEP—
ENJOY!
NGH?! THIS THINGER'S COLD?!
WHAT IS IT?!
FIRST TIME EATING ICE CREAM?
YOU GUYS GOTTA TRY THIS, TOO!
AFTER ALL THAT TALK ABOUT BLENDING IN...
IT'S FINE, NO ONE'S GOING TO THINK WE'RE THOSE ISLAND DEVILS.
HEY THERE, SON.
YOU WANT SOME CAAAANDY?
YES, YOU ...
WOW, WHAT FUN! ARE YOU KIDDOS PLAYING GANGSTER?

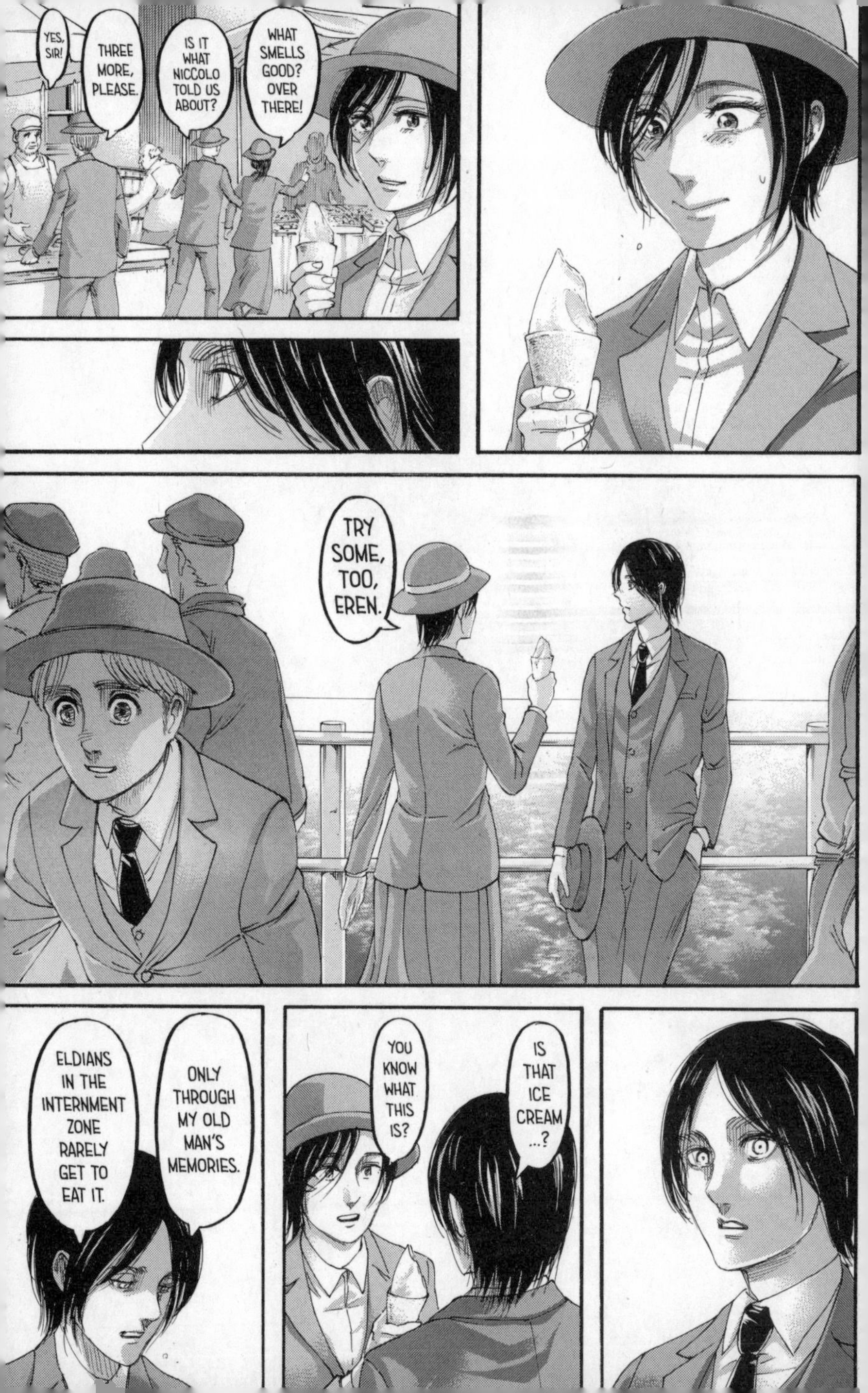
WHAT SMELLS GOOD? OVER THERE!
IS IT WHAT NICCOLO TOLD US ABOUT?
THREE MORE, PLEASE.
YES, SIR!
TRY SOME, TOO, EREN.
IS THAT ICE CREAM ...?
YOU KNOW WHAT THIS IS?
ONLY THROUGH MY OLD MAN'S MEMORIES.
ELDIANS IN THE INTERNMENT ZONE RARELY GET TO EAT IT.

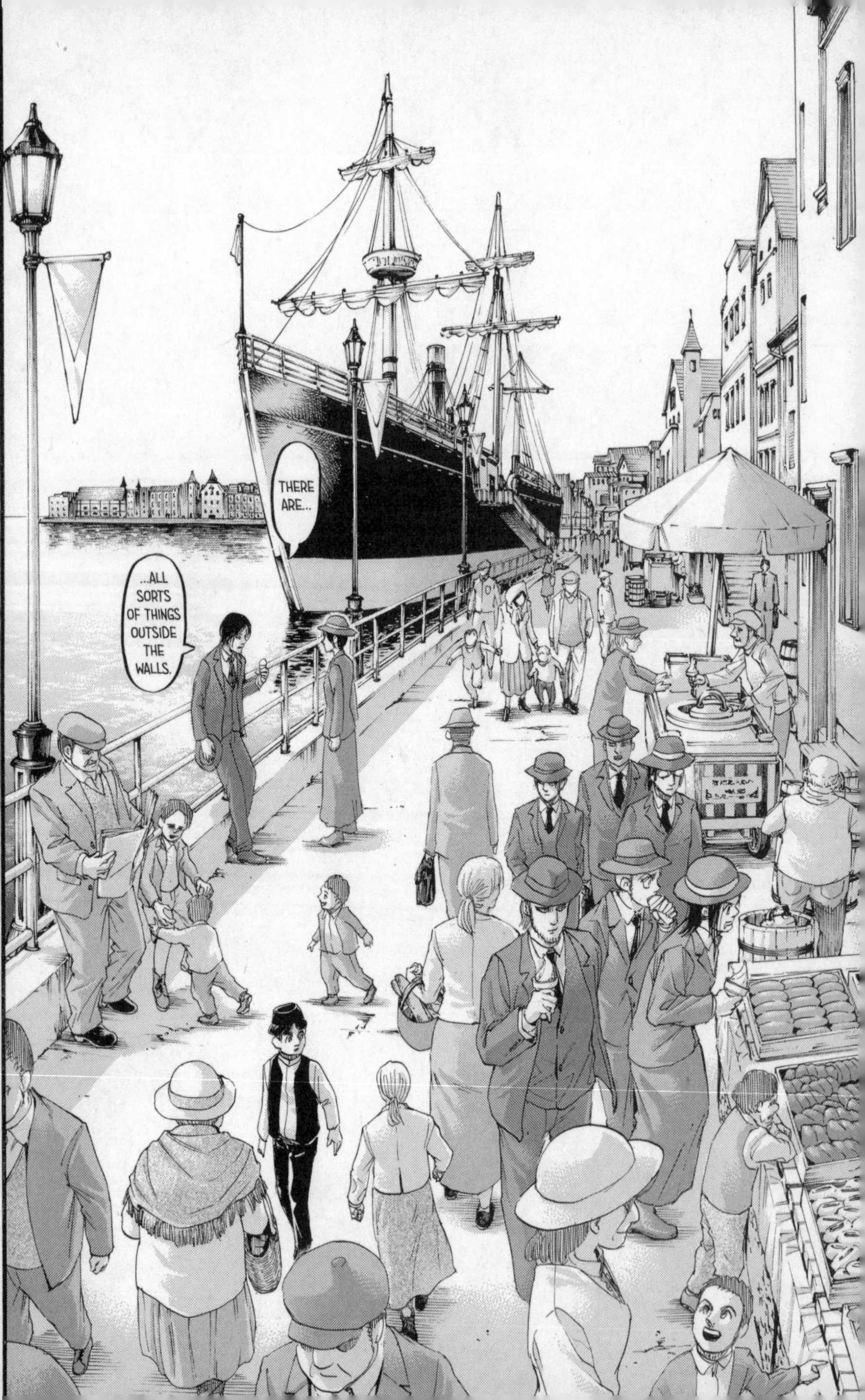
THERE ARE...
...ALL SORTS OF THINGS OUTSIDE THE WALLS.

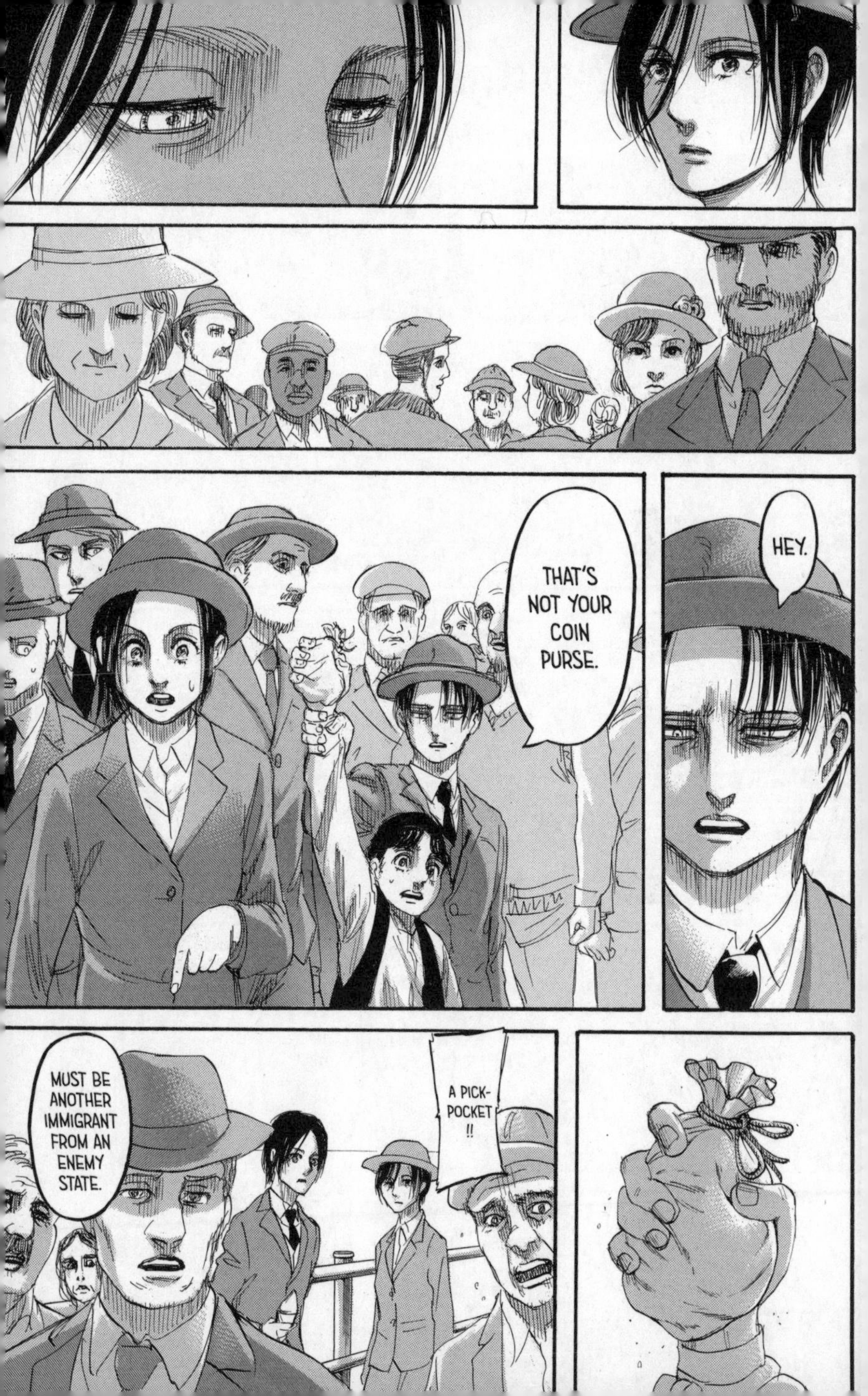
HEY.
THAT'S NOT YOUR COIN PURSE.
A PICK-POCKET!!
MUST BE ANOTHER IMMIGRANT FROM AN ENEMY STATE.

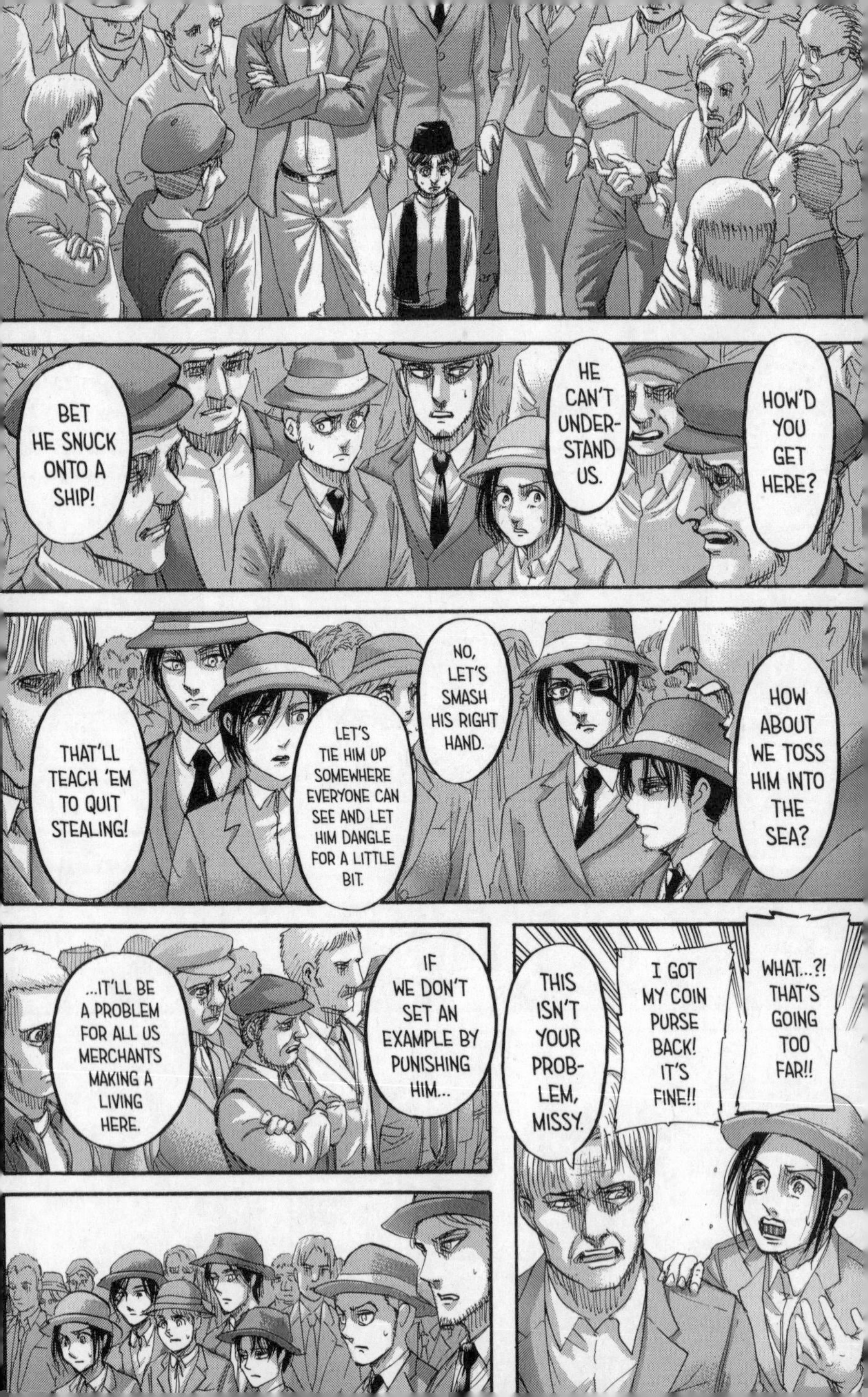
HOW'D YOU GET HERE?
HE CAN'T UNDERSTAND US.
BET HE SNUCK ONTO A SHIP!
HOW ABOUT WE TOSS HIM INTO THE SEA?
NO, LET'S SMASH HIS RIGHT HAND.
LET'S TIE HIM UP SOMEWHERE EVERYONE CAN SEE AND LET HIM DANGLE FOR A LITTLE BIT.
THAT'LL TEACH 'EM TO QUIT STEALING!
WHAT...?! THAT'S GOING TOO FAR!!
I GOT MY COIN PURSE BACK! IT'S FINE!!
THIS ISN'T YOUR PROBLEM, MISSY.
IF WE DON'T SET AN EXAMPLE BY PUNISHING HIM...
...IT'LL BE A PROBLEM FOR ALL US MERCHANTS MAKING A LIVING HERE.

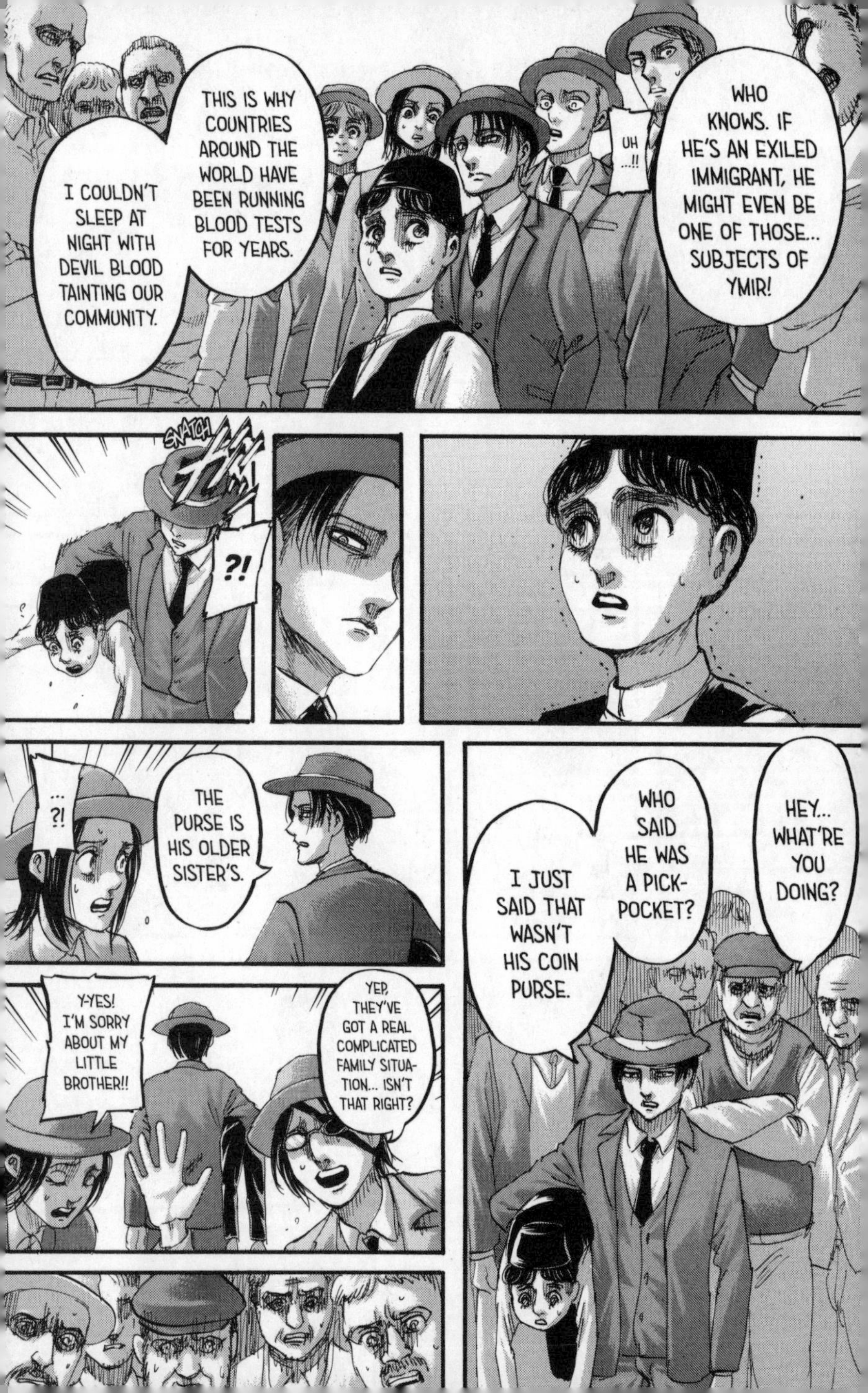
WHO KNOWS. IF HE'S AN EXILED IMMIGRANT, HE MIGHT EVEN BE ONE OF THOSE... SUBJECTS OF YMIR!
UH ...!!
THIS IS WHY COUNTRIES AROUND THE WORLD HAVE BEEN RUNNING BLOOD TESTS FOR YEARS.
I COULDN'T SLEEP AT NIGHT WITH DEVIL BLOOD TAINTING OUR COMMUNITY.
SNATCH
?!
HEY... WHAT'RE YOU DOING?
WHO SAID HE WAS A PICK-POCKET?
I JUST SAID THAT WASN'T HIS COIN PURSE.
THE PURSE IS HIS OLDER SISTER'S.
... ?!
YEP, THEY'VE GOT A REAL COMPLICATED FAMILY SITUA-TION... ISN'T THAT RIGHT?
Y-YES! I'M SORRY ABOUT MY LITTLE BROTHER!!

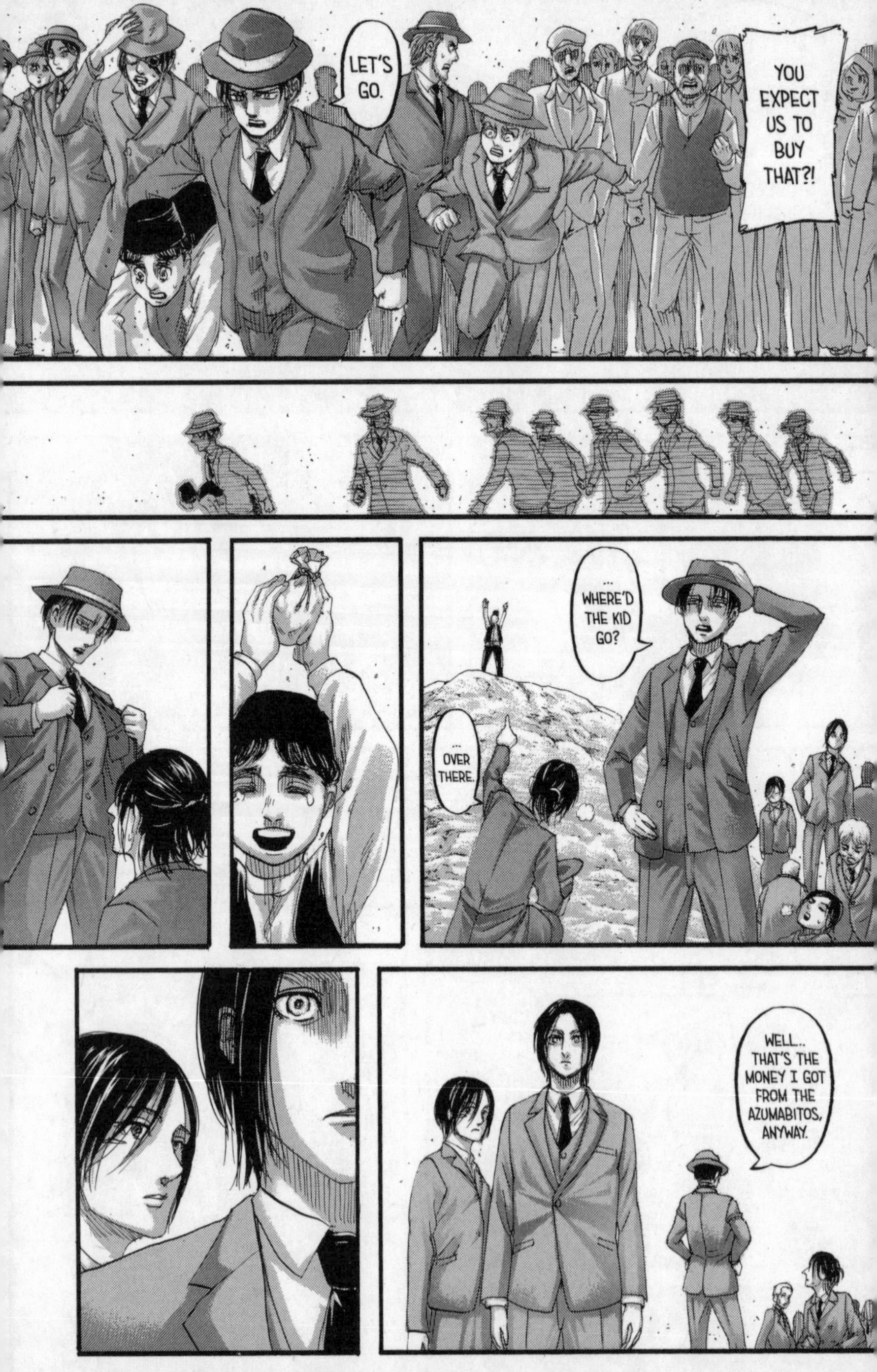
YOU EXPECT US TO BUY THAT?!
LET'S GO.
... WHERE'D THE KID GO?
... OVER THERE.
WELL.. THAT'S THE MONEY I GOT FROM THE AZUMABITOS, ANYWAY.

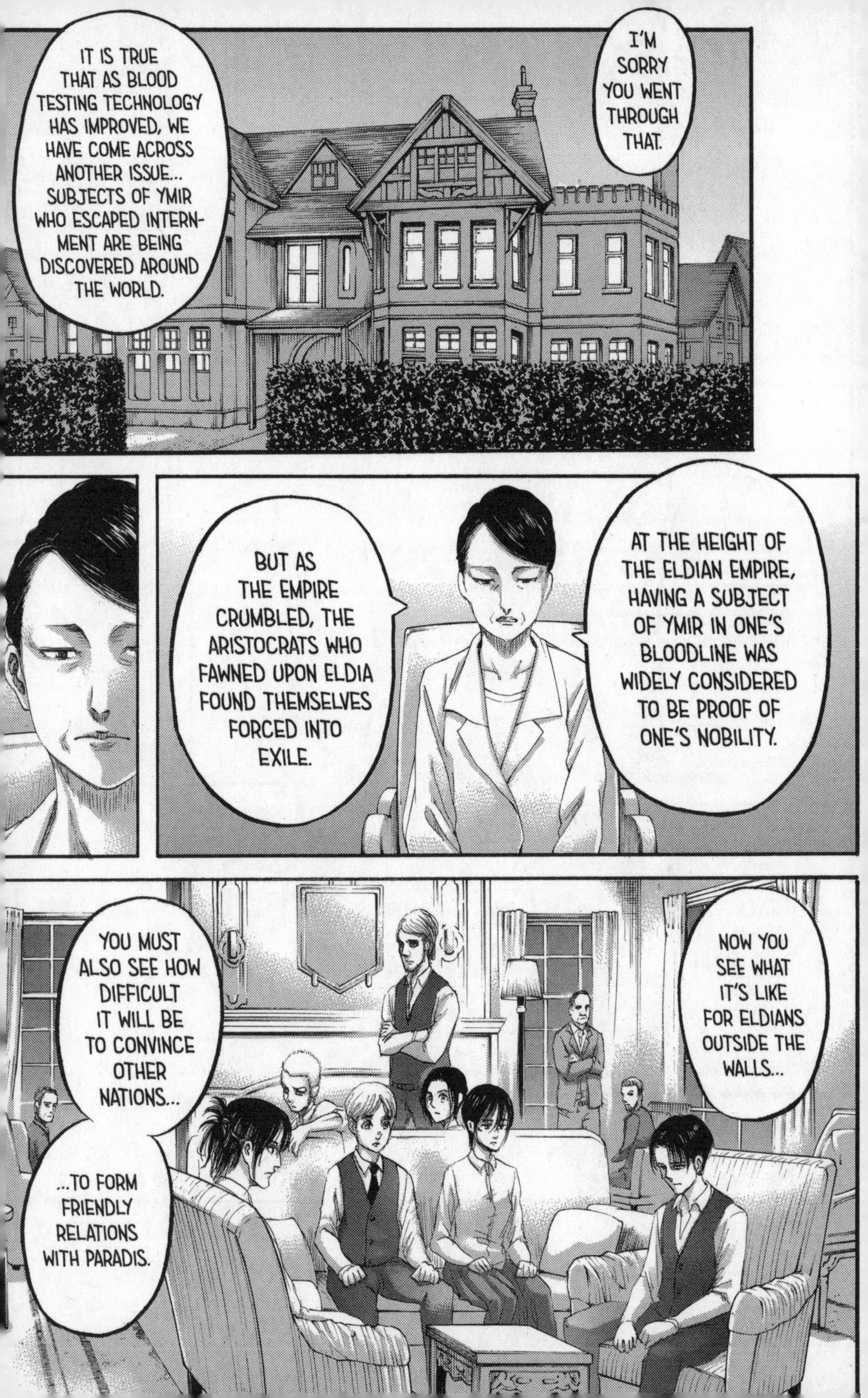
I'M SORRY YOU WENT THROUGH THAT.
IT IS TRUE THAT AS BLOOD TESTING TECHNOLOGY HAS IMPROVED, WE HAVE COME ACROSS ANOTHER ISSUE... SUBJECTS OF YMIR WHO ESCAPED INTERN-MENT ARE BEING DISCOVERED AROUND THE WORLD.
AT THE HEIGHT OF THE ELDIAN EMPIRE, HAVING A SUBJECT OF YMIR IN ONE'S BLOODLINE WAS WIDELY CONSIDERED TO BE PROOF OF ONE'S NOBILITY.
BUT AS THE EMPIRE CRUMBLED, THE ARISTOCRATS WHO FAWNED UPON ELDIA FOUND THEMSELVES FORCED INTO EXILE.
NOW YOU SEE WHAT IT'S LIKE FOR ELDIANS OUTSIDE THE WALLS...
YOU MUST ALSO SEE HOW DIFFICULT IT WILL BE TO CONVINCE OTHER NATIONS...
...TO FORM FRIENDLY RELATIONS WITH PARADIS.

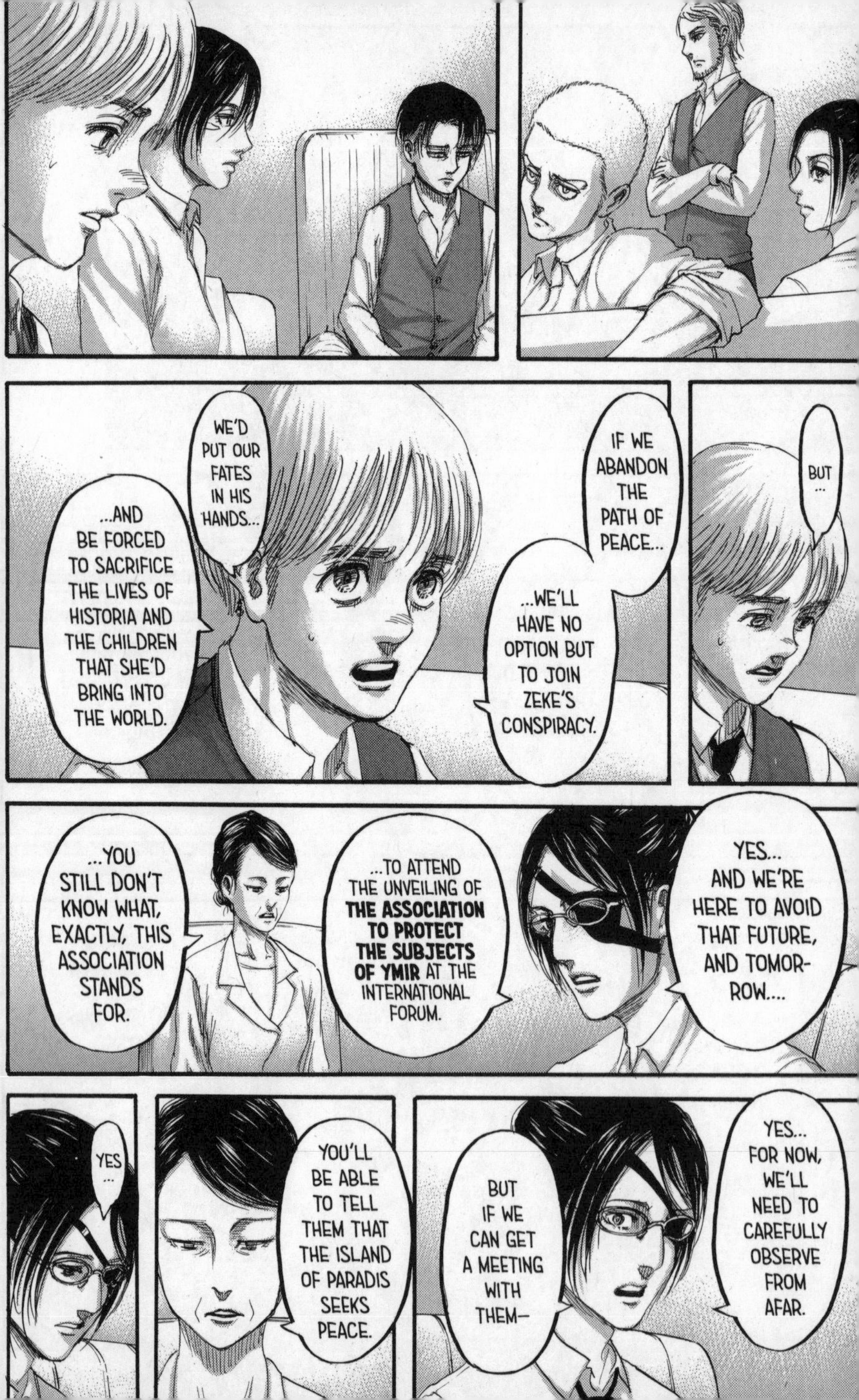

BUT...
IF WE ABANDON THE PATH OF PEACE...
...WE'LL HAVE NO OPTION BUT TO JOIN ZEKE'S CONSPIRACY.
WE'D PUT OUR FATES IN HIS HANDS...
...AND BE FORCED TO SACRIFICE THE LIVES OF HISTORIA AND THE CHILDREN THAT SHE'D BRING INTO THE WORLD.
YES... AND WE'RE HERE TO AVOID THAT FUTURE, AND TOMOR-ROW....
...TO ATTEND THE UNVEILING OF **THE ASSOCIATION TO PROTECT THE SUBJECTS OF YMIR** AT THE INTERNATIONAL FORUM.
...YOU STILL DON'T KNOW WHAT, EXACTLY, THIS ASSOCIATION STANDS FOR.
YES... FOR NOW, WE'LL NEED TO CAREFULLY OBSERVE FROM AFAR.
BUT IF WE CAN GET A MEETING WITH THEM—
YOU'LL BE ABLE TO TELL THEM THAT THE ISLAND OF PARADIS SEEKS PEACE.
YES...

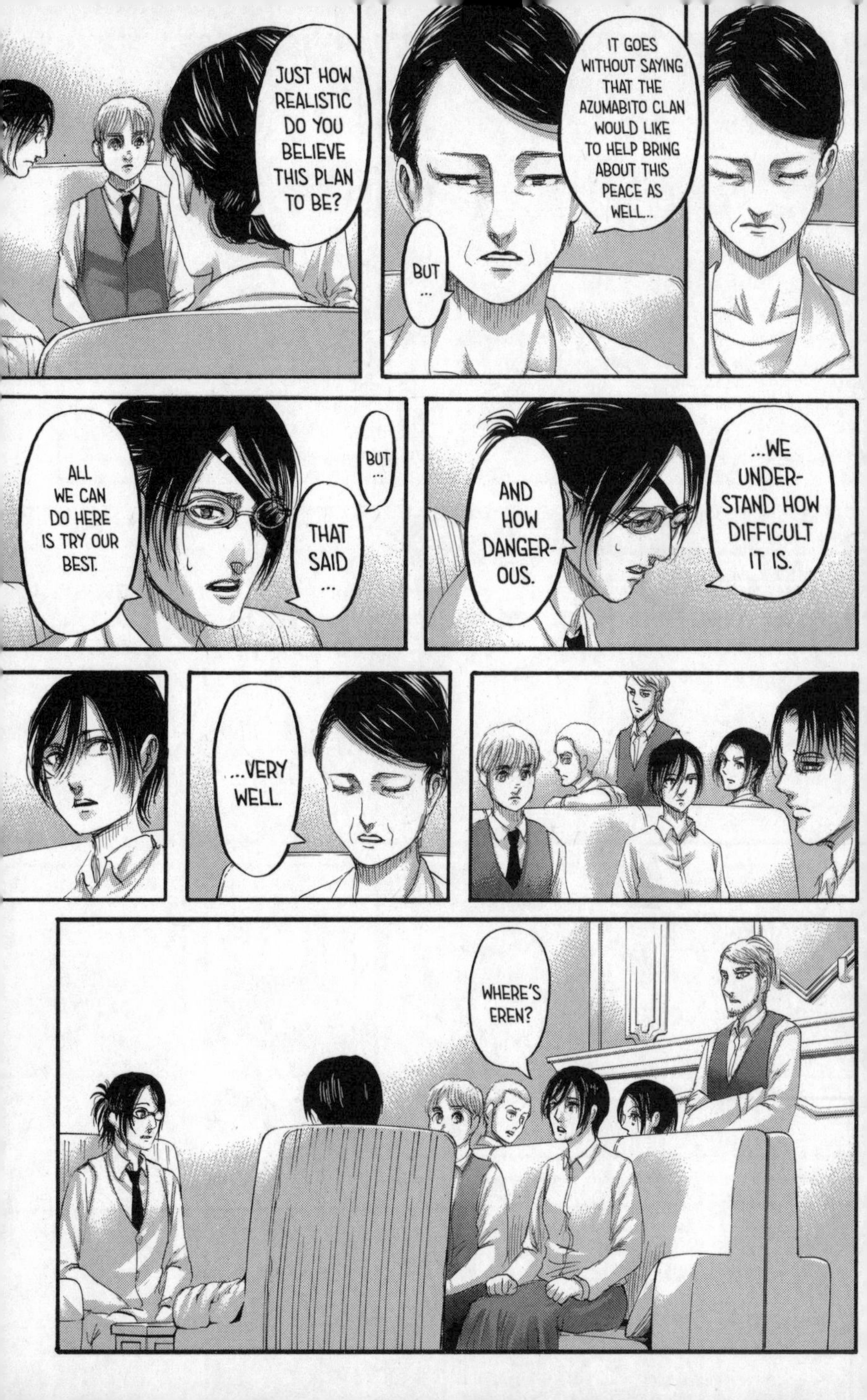
IT GOES WITHOUT SAYING THAT THE AZUMABITO CLAN WOULD LIKE TO HELP BRING ABOUT THIS PEACE AS WELL..
BUT ...
JUST HOW REALISTIC DO YOU BELIEVE THIS PLAN TO BE?
...WE UNDER-STAND HOW DIFFICULT IT IS.
AND HOW DANGER-OUS.
BUT ...
THAT SAID ...
ALL WE CAN DO HERE IS TRY OUR BEST.
...VERY WELL.
WHERE'S EREN?

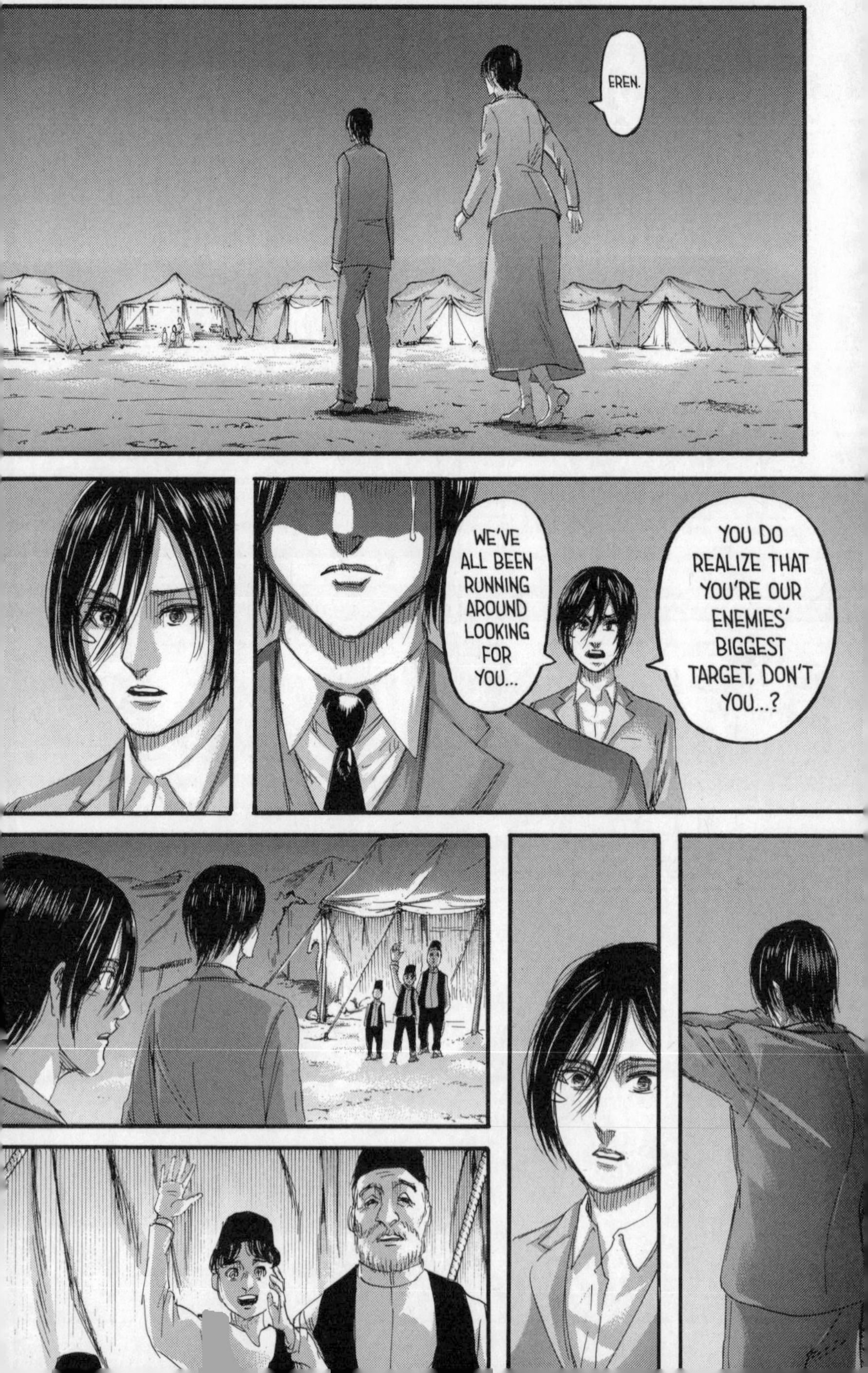
EREN.
YOU DO REALIZE THAT YOU'RE OUR ENEMIES' BIGGEST TARGET, DON'T YOU...?
WE'VE ALL BEEN RUNNING AROUND LOOKING FOR YOU...

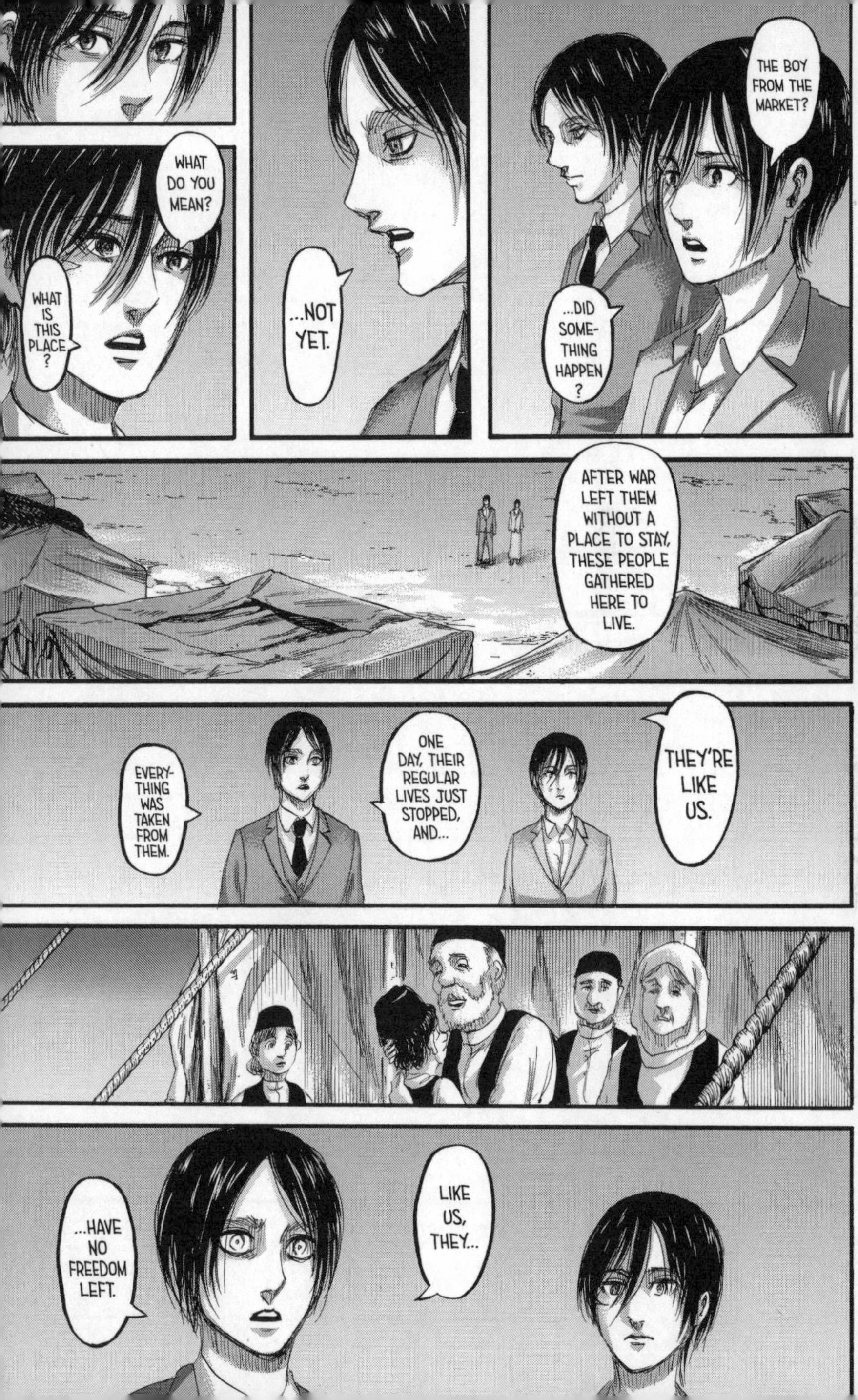
THE BOY FROM THE MARKET?
...DID SOMETHING HAPPEN?
...NOT YET.
WHAT DO YOU MEAN?
WHAT IS THIS PLACE?
AFTER WAR LEFT THEM WITHOUT A PLACE TO STAY, THESE PEOPLE GATHERED HERE TO LIVE.
THEY'RE LIKE US.
ONE DAY, THEIR REGULAR LIVES JUST STOPPED, AND...
EVERYTHING WAS TAKEN FROM THEM.
LIKE US, THEY...
...HAVE NO FREEDOM LEFT.

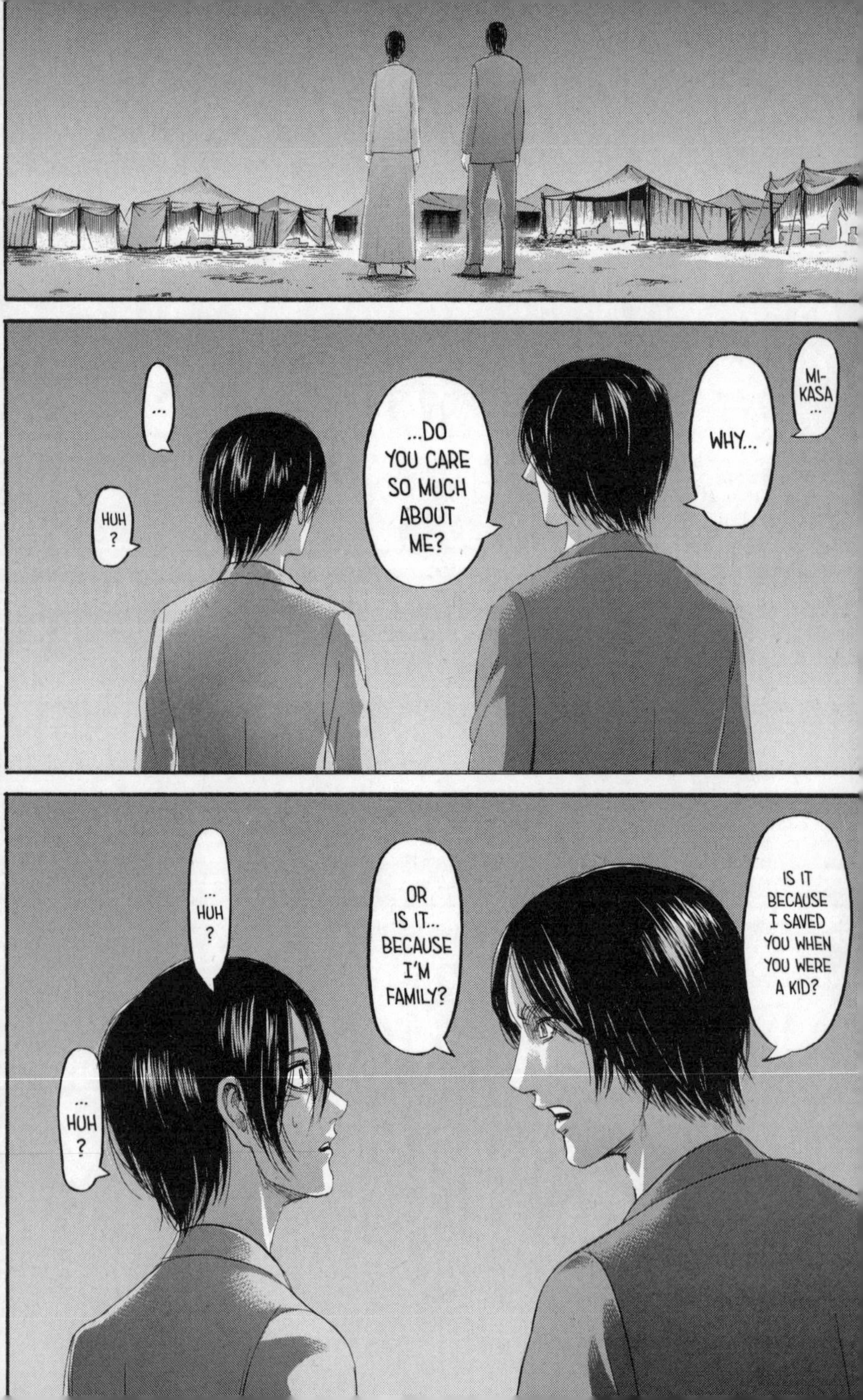
MI-KASA...
WHY...
...DO YOU CARE SO MUCH ABOUT ME?
...
HUH?
IS IT BECAUSE I SAVED YOU WHEN YOU WERE A KID?
OR IS IT... BECAUSE I'M FAMILY?
...HUH?
...HUH?

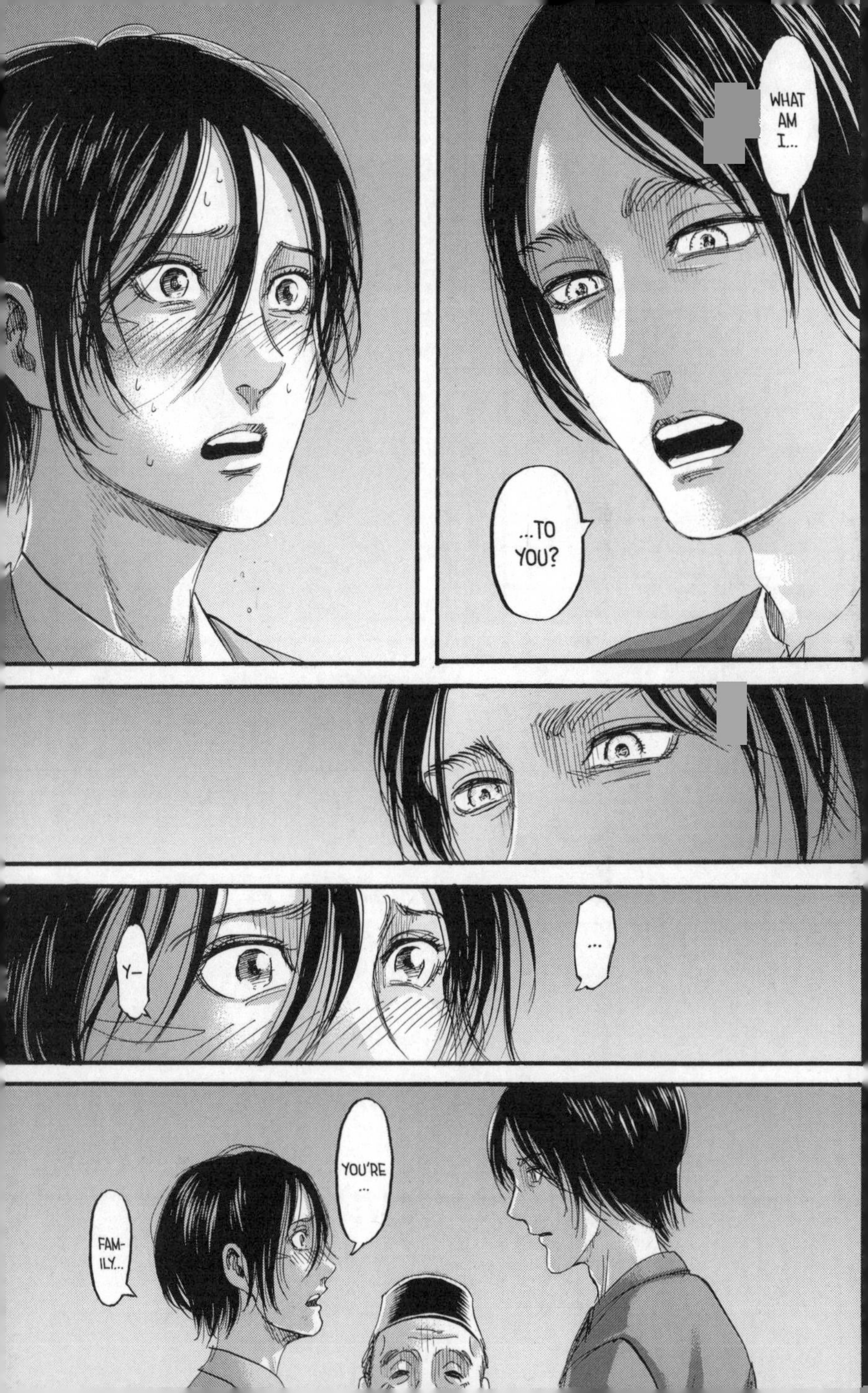
WHAT AM I...
...TO YOU?
...
Y—
YOU'RE ...
FAM-ILY...

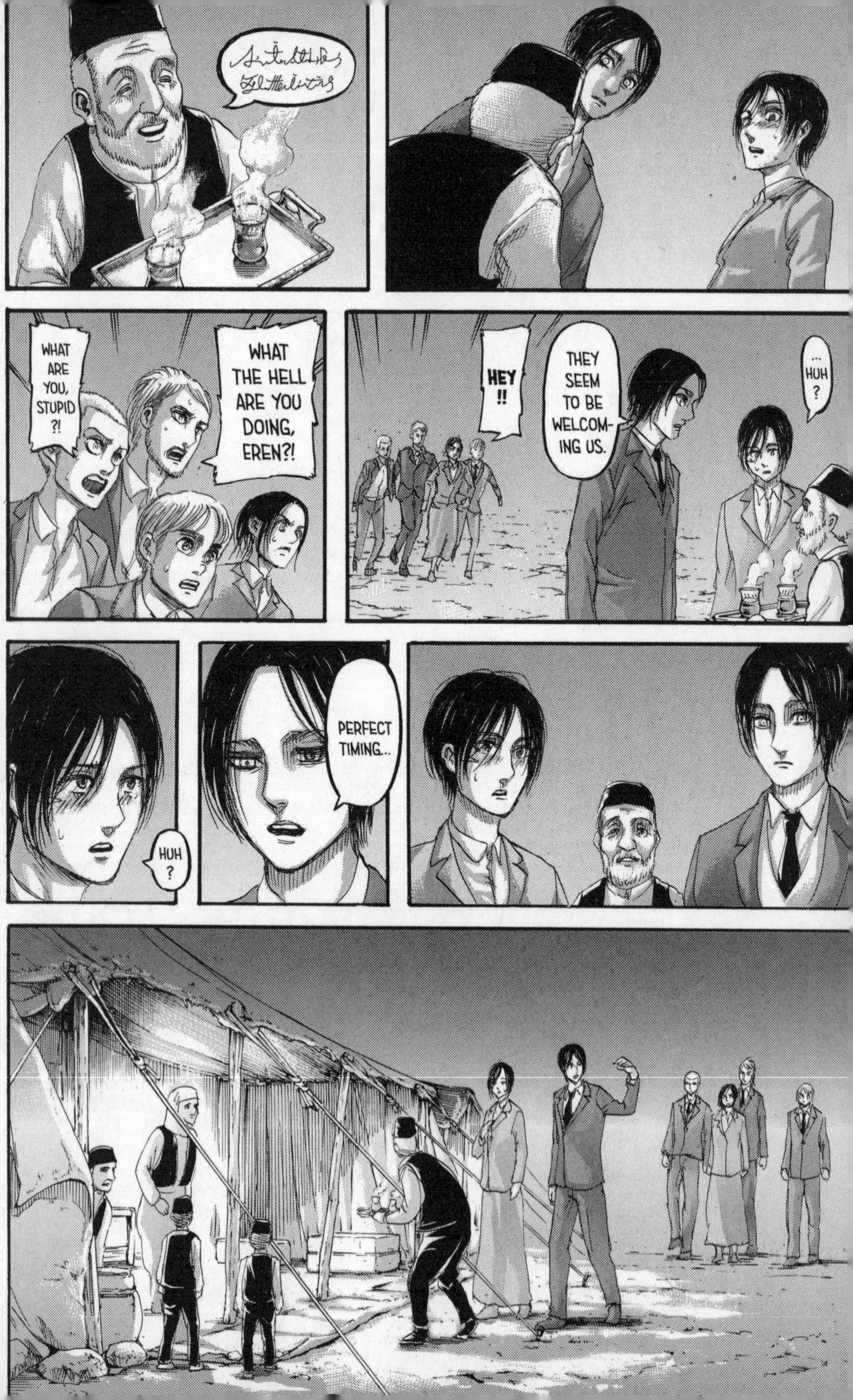
...HUH?
THEY SEEM TO BE WELCOMING US.
HEY!!
WHAT THE HELL ARE YOU DOING, EREN?!
WHAT ARE YOU, STUPID?!
PERFECT TIMING...
HUH?

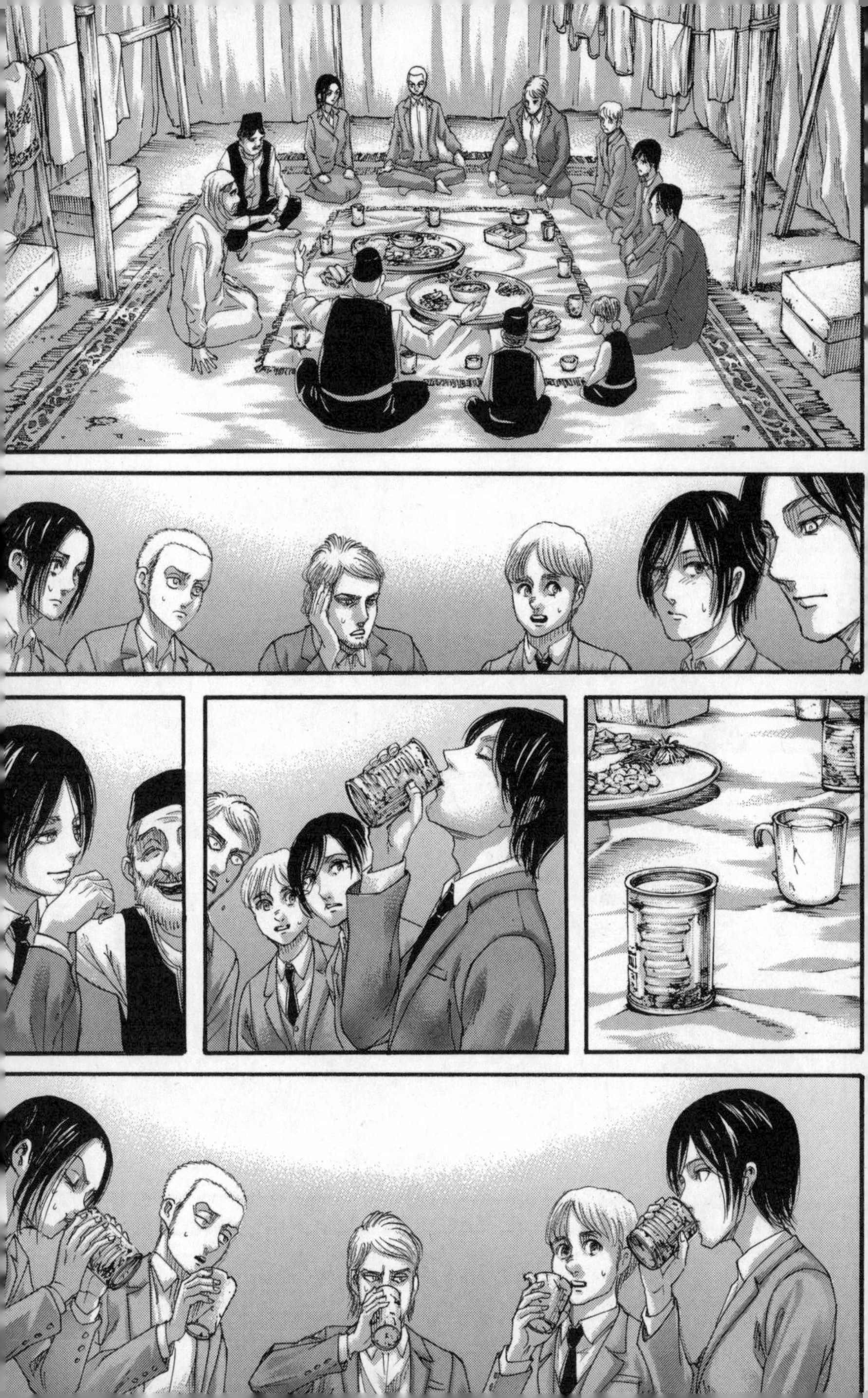

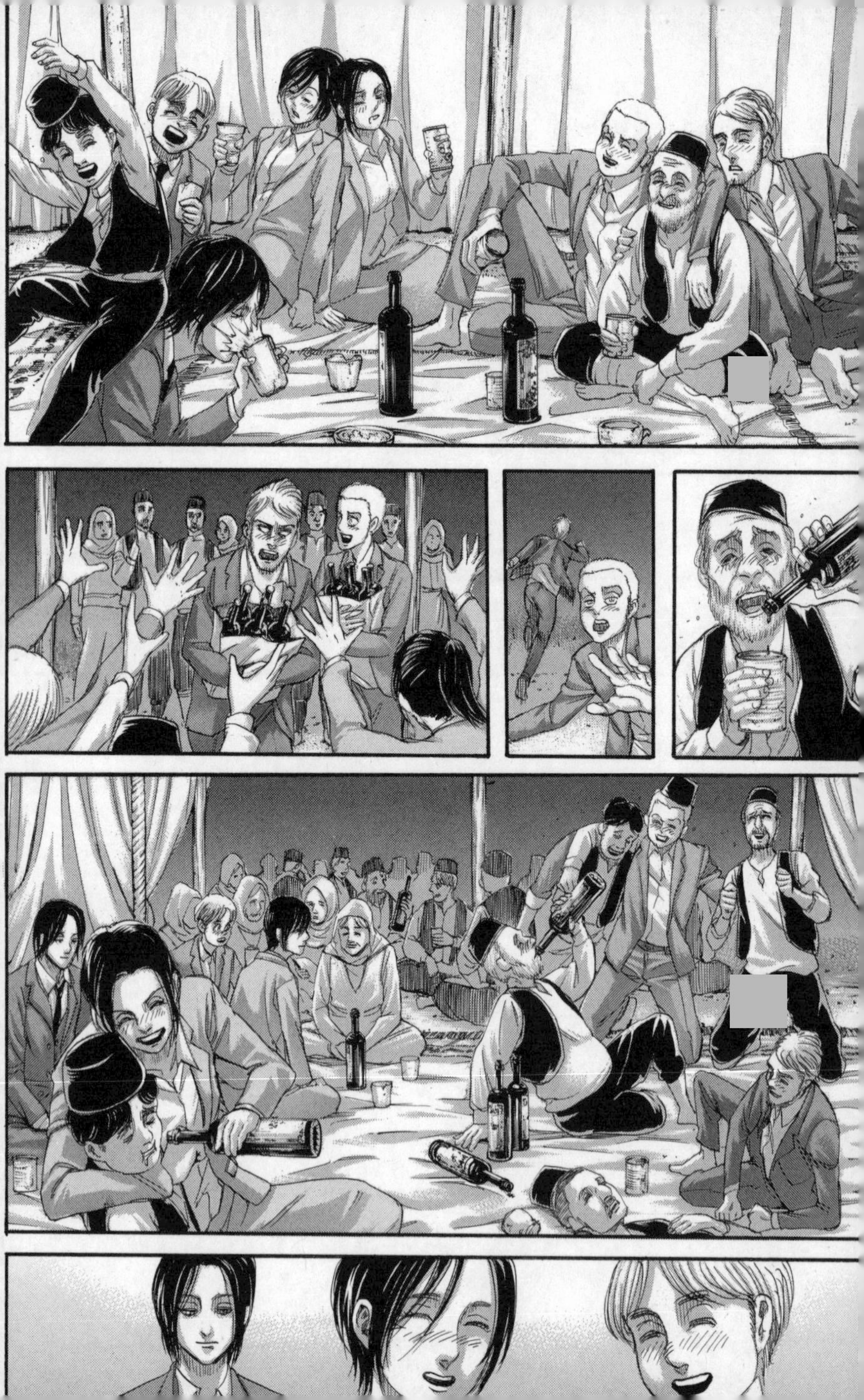

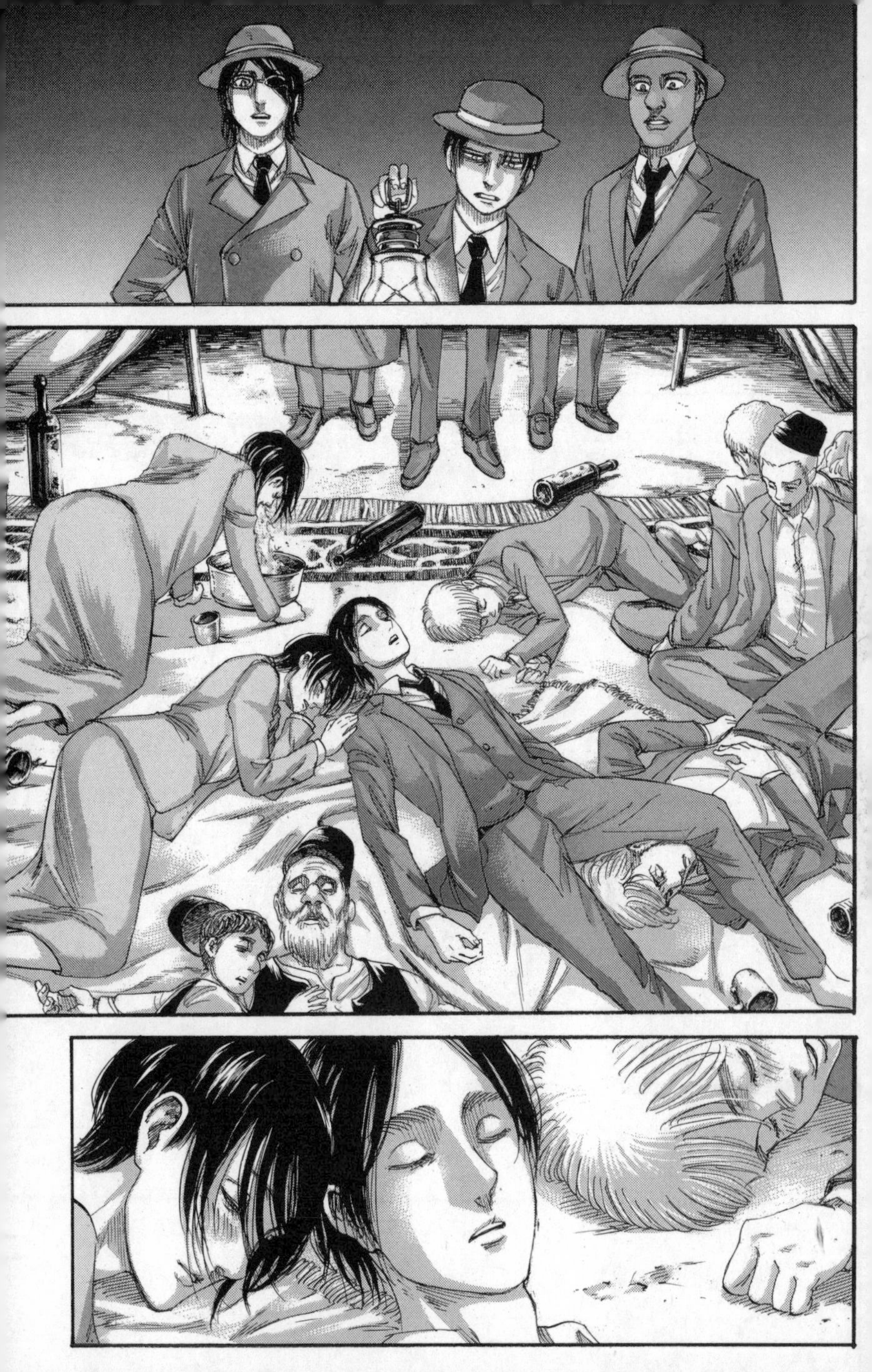

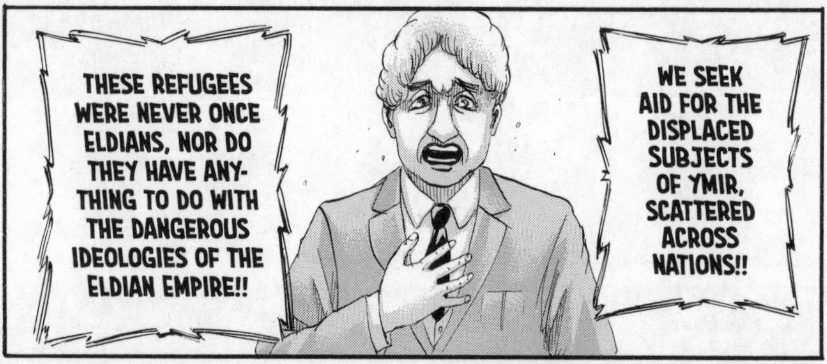
WE SEEK AID FOR THE DISPLACED SUBJECTS OF YMIR, SCATTERED ACROSS NATIONS!!
THESE REFUGEES WERE NEVER ONCE ELDIANS, NOR DO THEY HAVE ANY-THING TO DO WITH THE DANGEROUS IDEOLOGIES OF THE ELDIAN EMPIRE!!

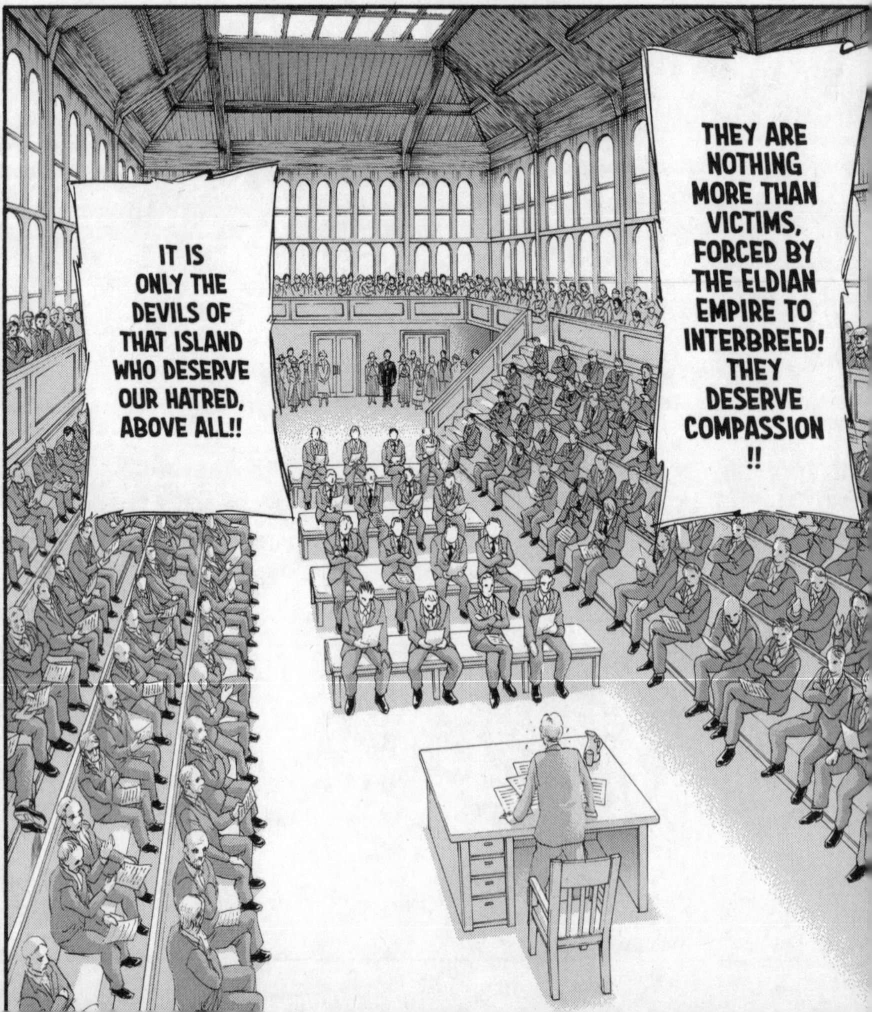
THEY ARE NOTHING MORE THAN VICTIMS, FORCED BY THE ELDIAN EMPIRE TO INTERBREED! THEY DESERVE COMPASSION!!
IT IS ONLY THE DEVILS OF THAT ISLAND WHO DESERVE OUR HATRED, ABOVE ALL!!

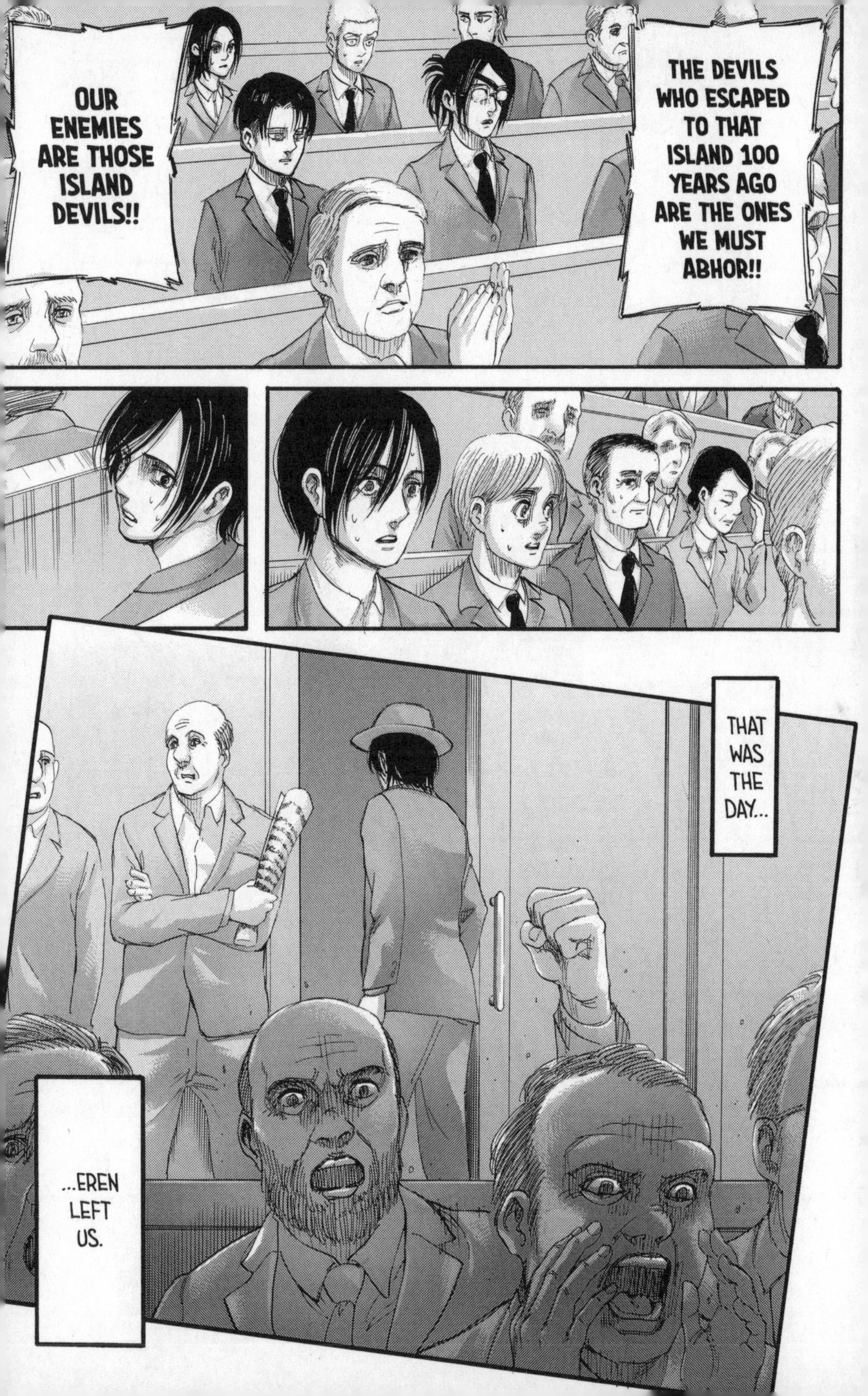
THE DEVILS WHO ESCAPED TO THAT ISLAND 100 YEARS AGO ARE THE ONES WE MUST ABHOR!!
OUR ENEMIES ARE THOSE ISLAND DEVILS!!
THAT WAS THE DAY...
...EREN LEFT US.

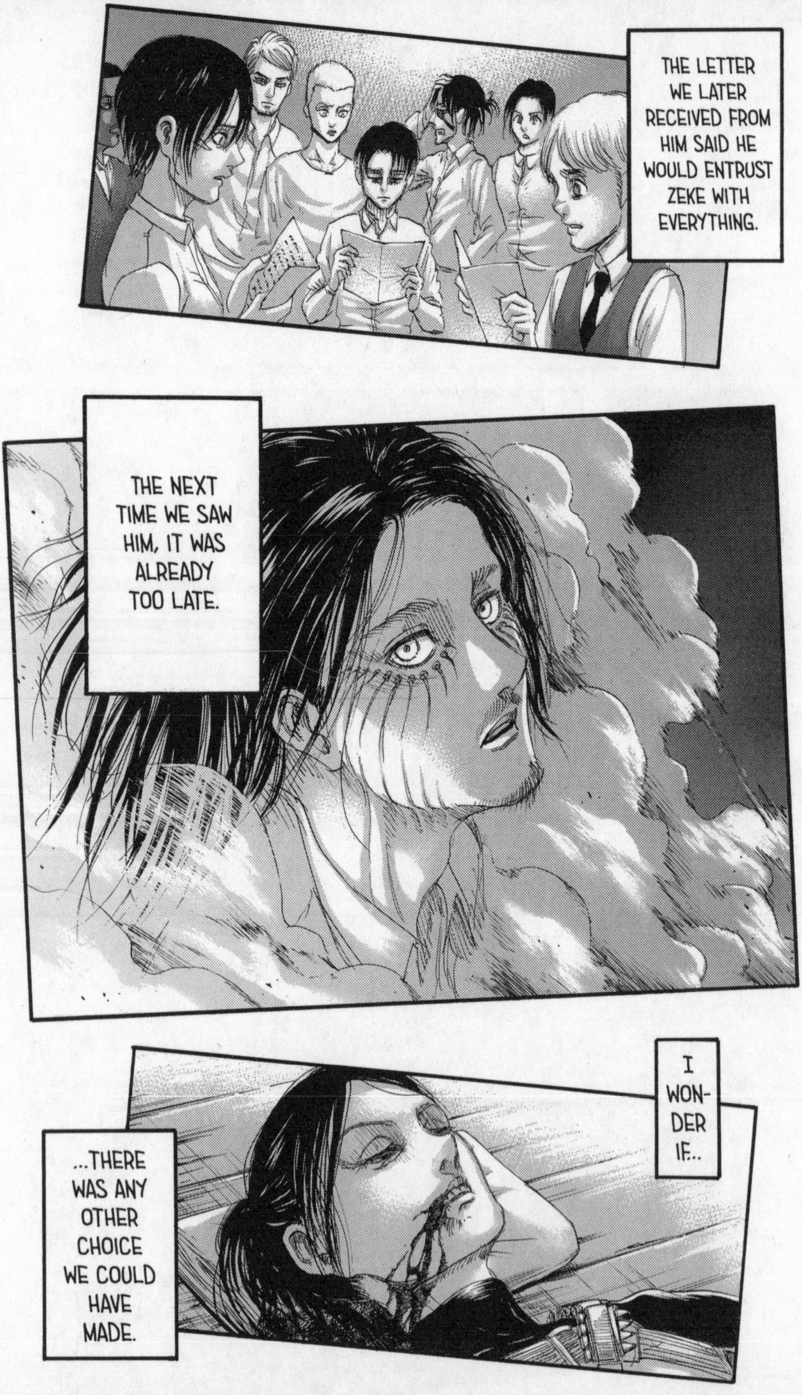
THE LETTER WE LATER RECEIVED FROM HIM SAID HE WOULD ENTRUST ZEKE WITH EVERYTHING.
THE NEXT TIME WE SAW HIM, IT WAS ALREADY TOO LATE.
I WON-DER IF...
...THERE WAS ANY OTHER CHOICE WE COULD HAVE MADE.

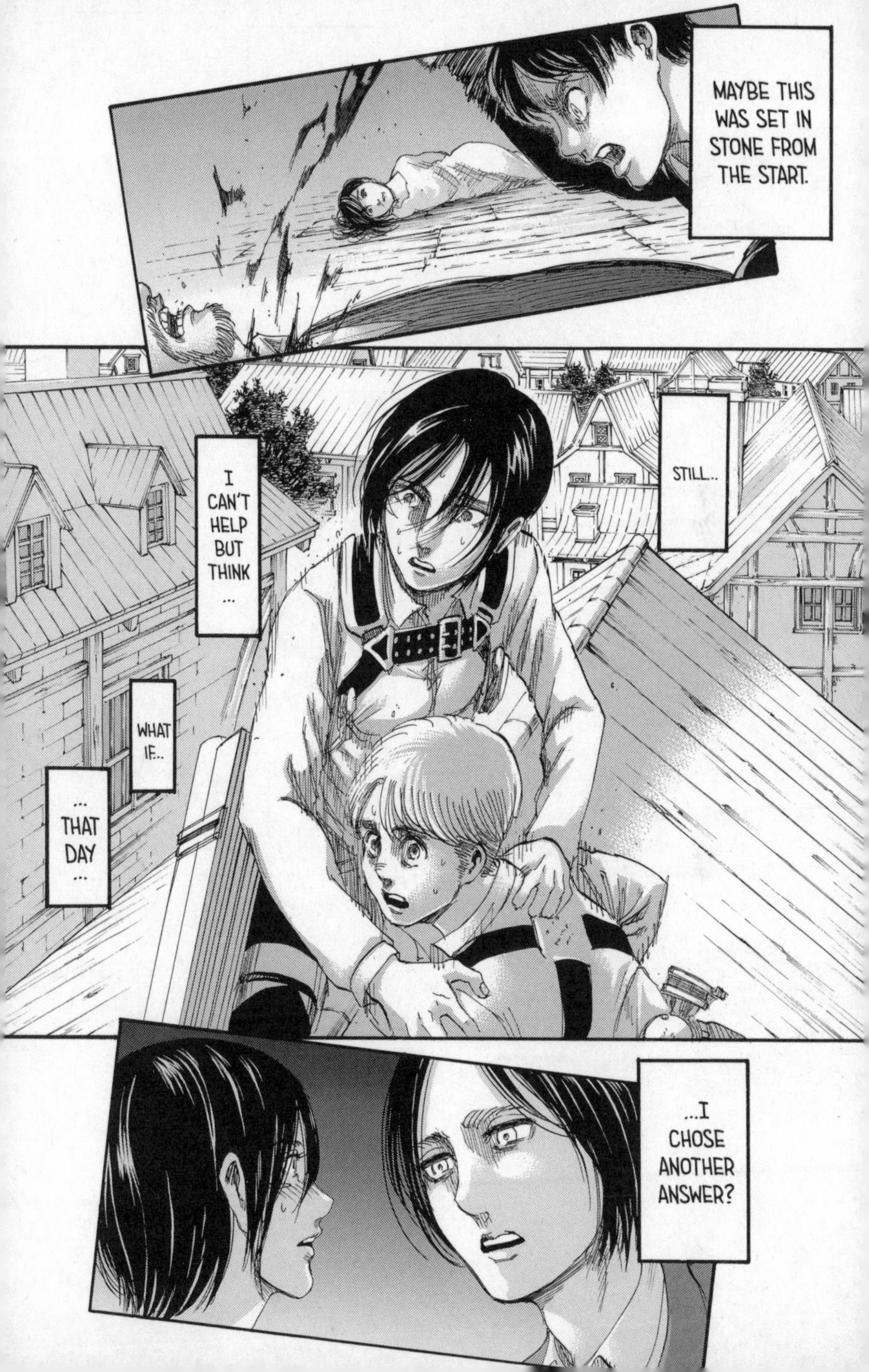
MAYBE THIS WAS SET IN STONE FROM THE START.
STILL...
I CAN'T HELP BUT THINK ...
WHAT IF...
... THAT DAY ...
...I CHOSE ANOTHER ANSWER?

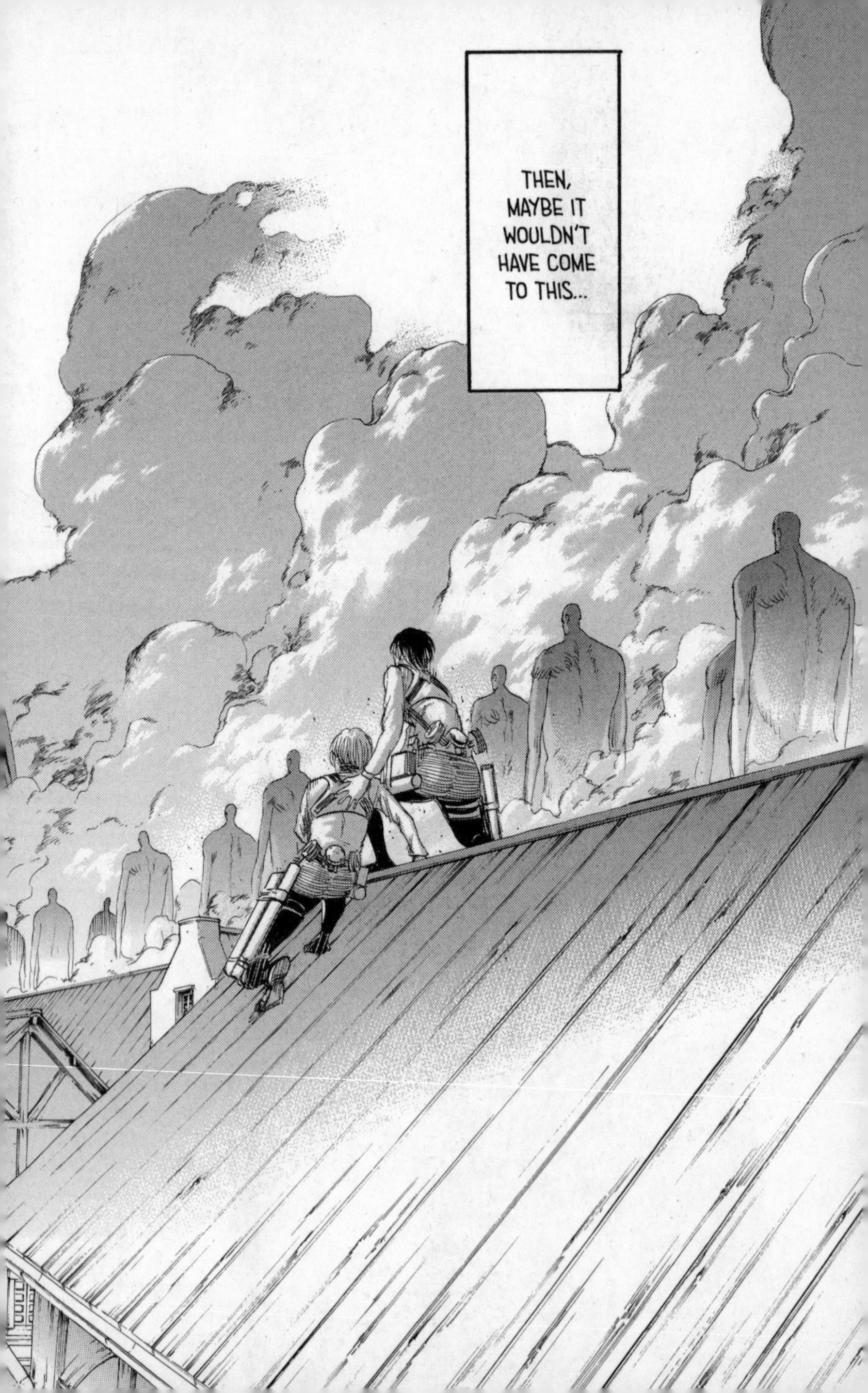
THEN, MAYBE IT WOULDN'T HAVE COME TO THIS...

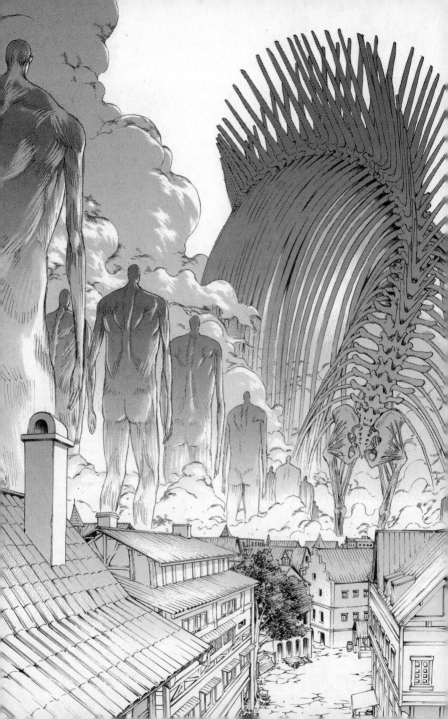

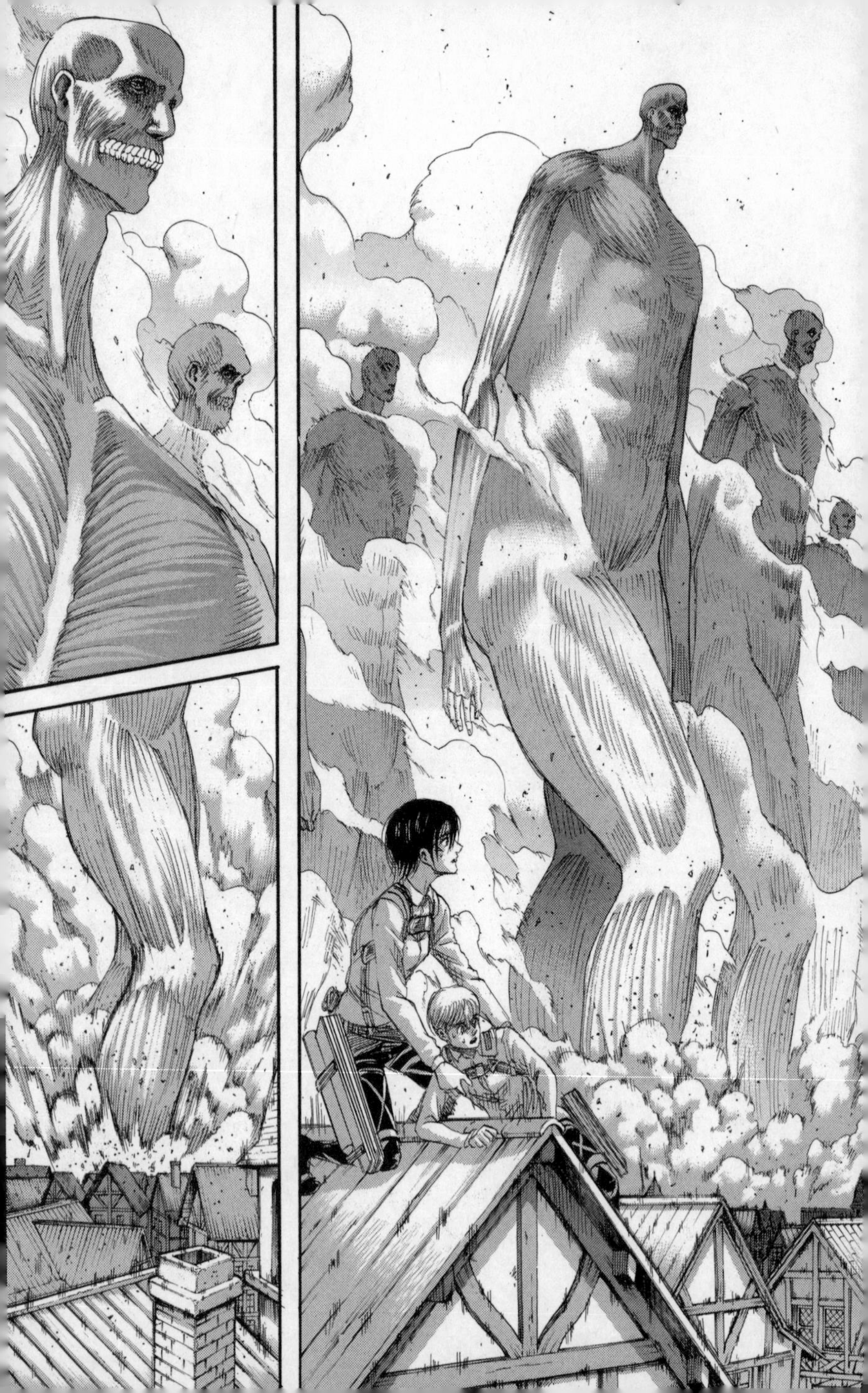

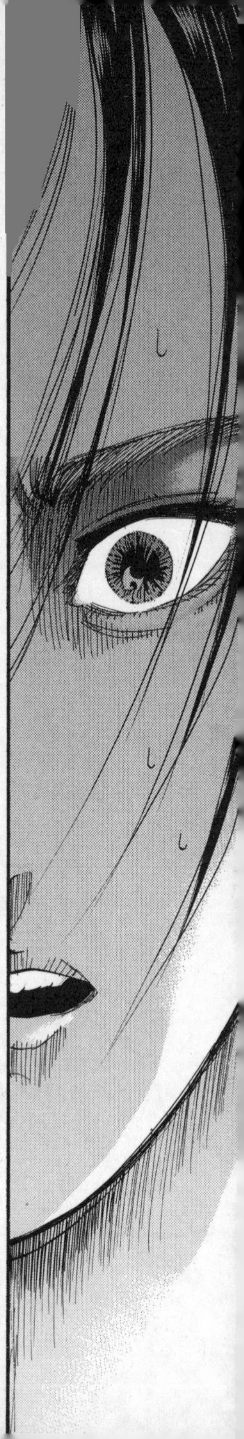

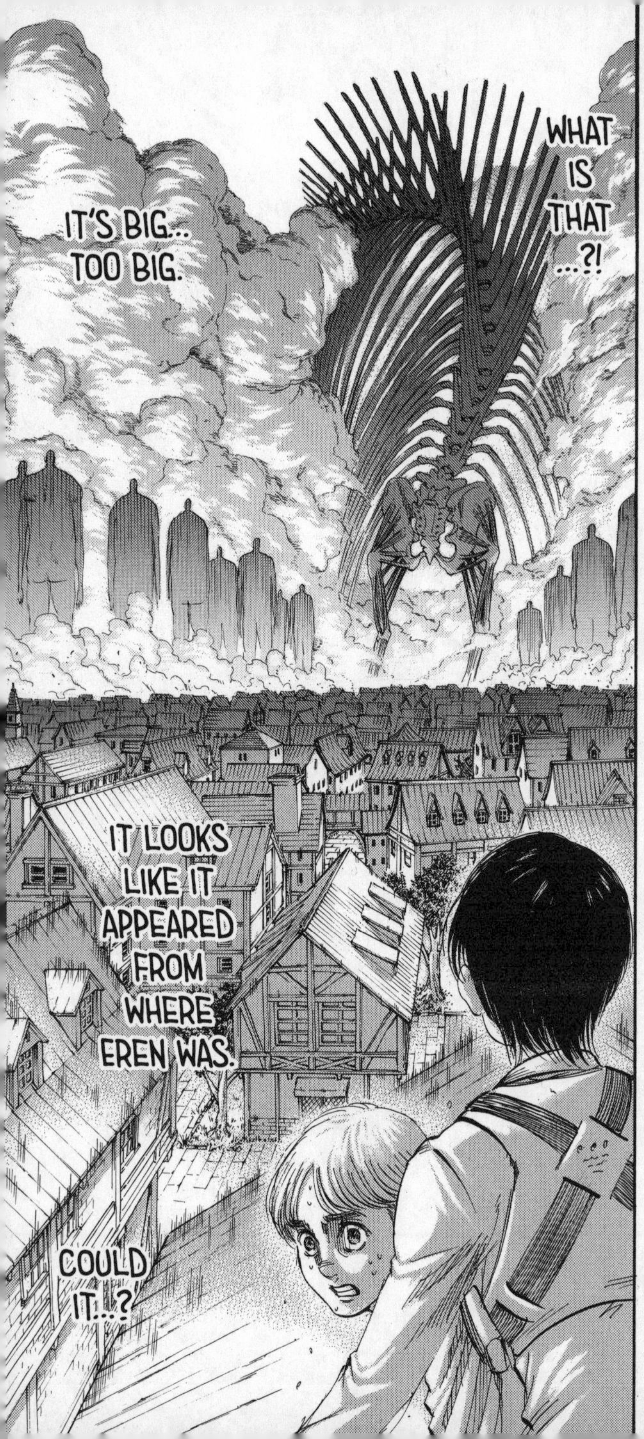
WHAT IS THAT ...?!
IT'S BIG... TOO BIG.
IT LOOKS LIKE IT APPEARED FROM WHERE EREN WAS.
COULD IT...?

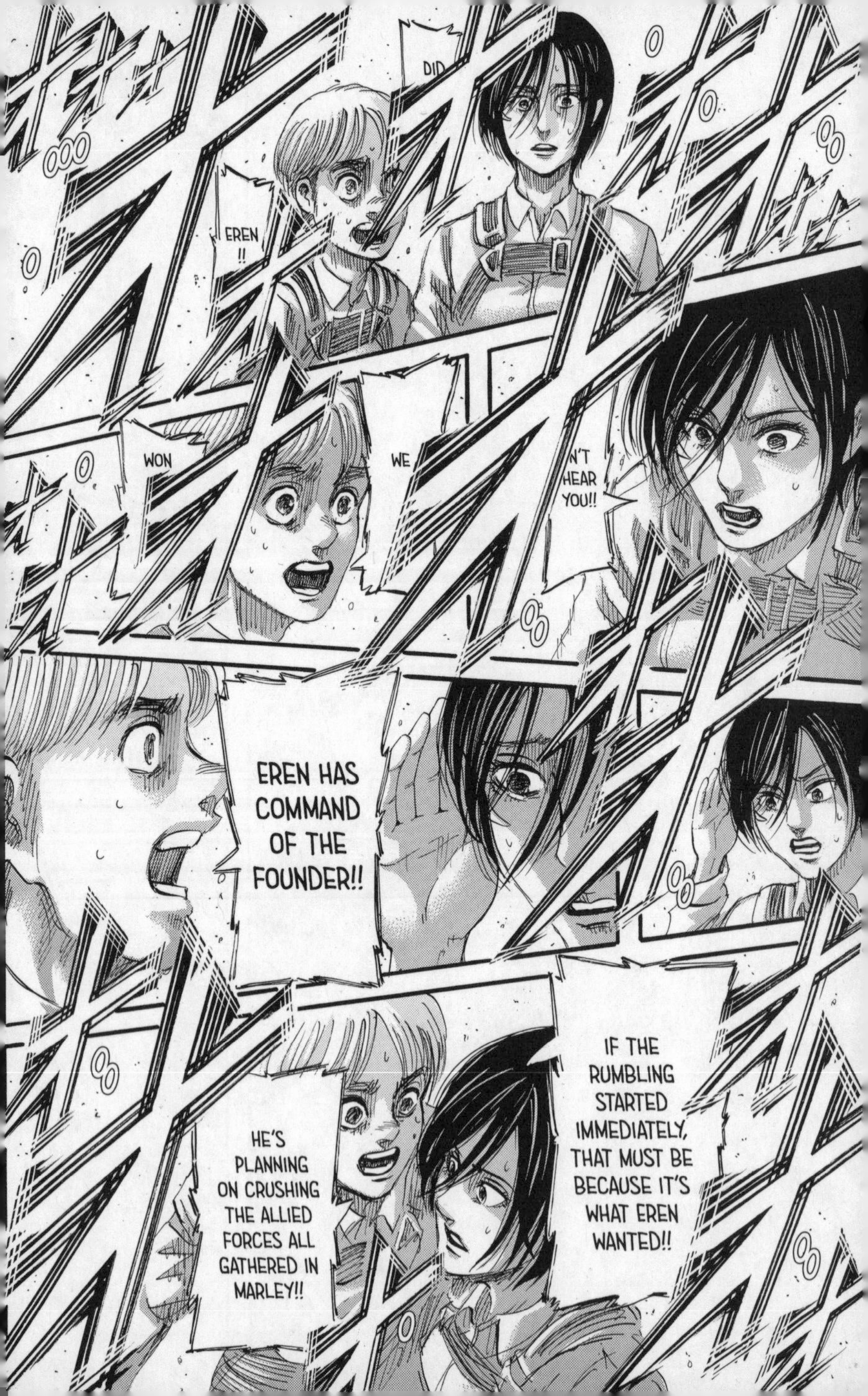
DID
EREN !!
N'T HEAR YOU!!
WE
WON
EREN HAS COMMAND OF THE FOUNDER!!
IF THE RUMBLING STARTED IMMEDIATELY, THAT MUST BE BECAUSE IT'S WHAT EREN WANTED!!
HE'S PLANNING ON CRUSHING THE ALLIED FORCES ALL GATHERED IN MARLEY!!

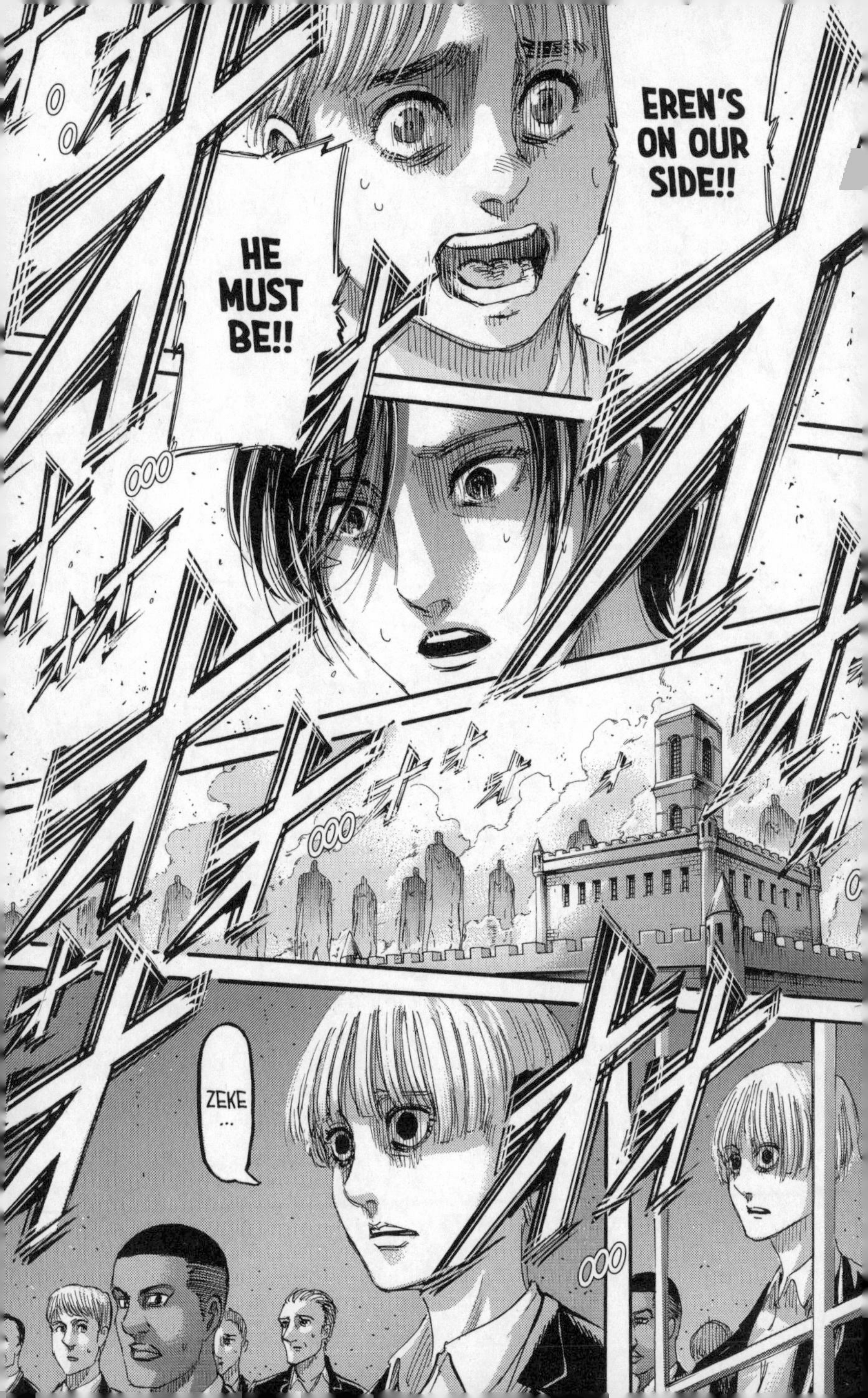
EREN'S ON OUR SIDE!!
HE MUST BE!!
ZEKE ...

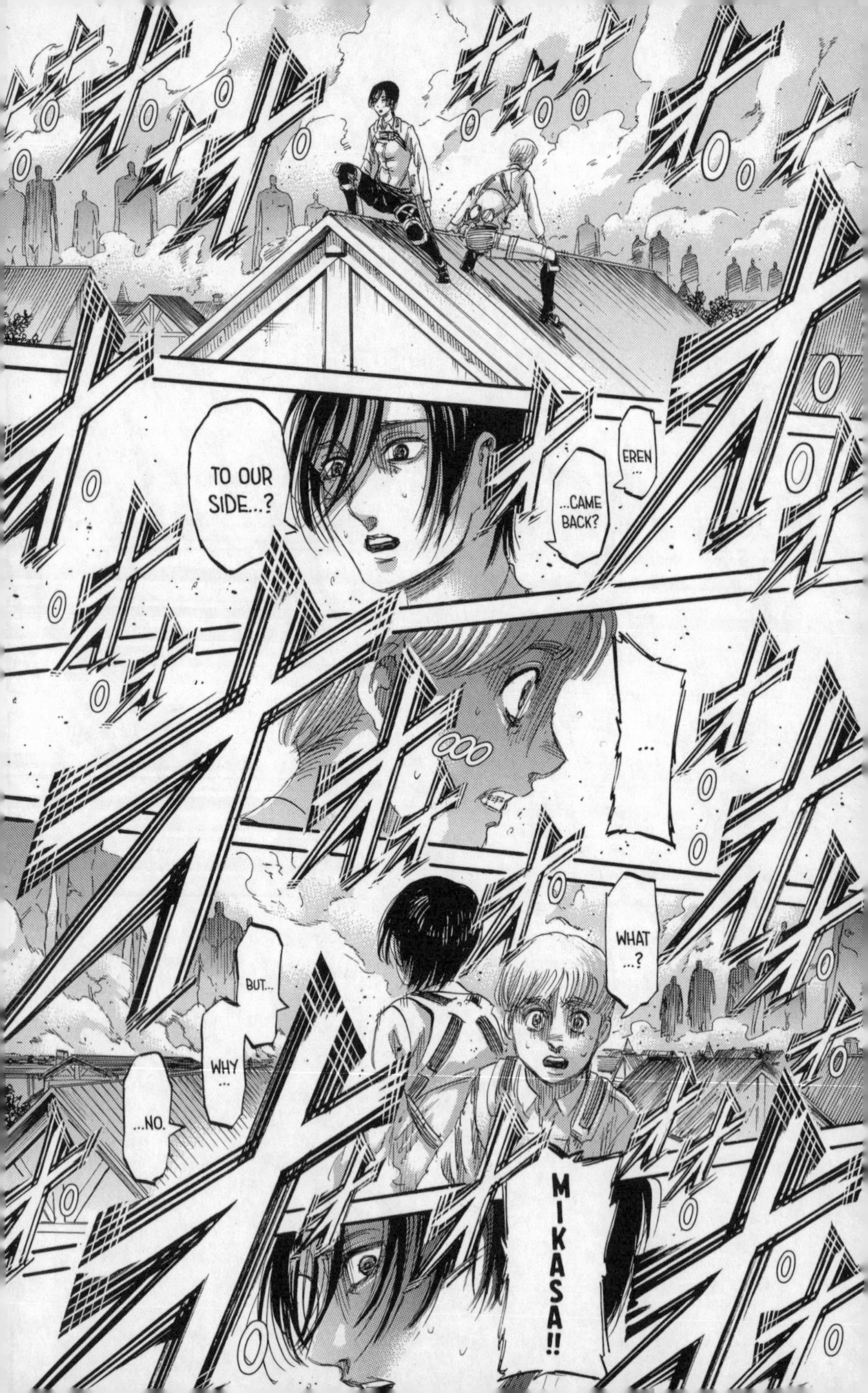
EREN ...
...CAME BACK?
TO OUR SIDE...?
...
WHAT ...?
BUT...
WHY ...
...NO.
MIKASA!!

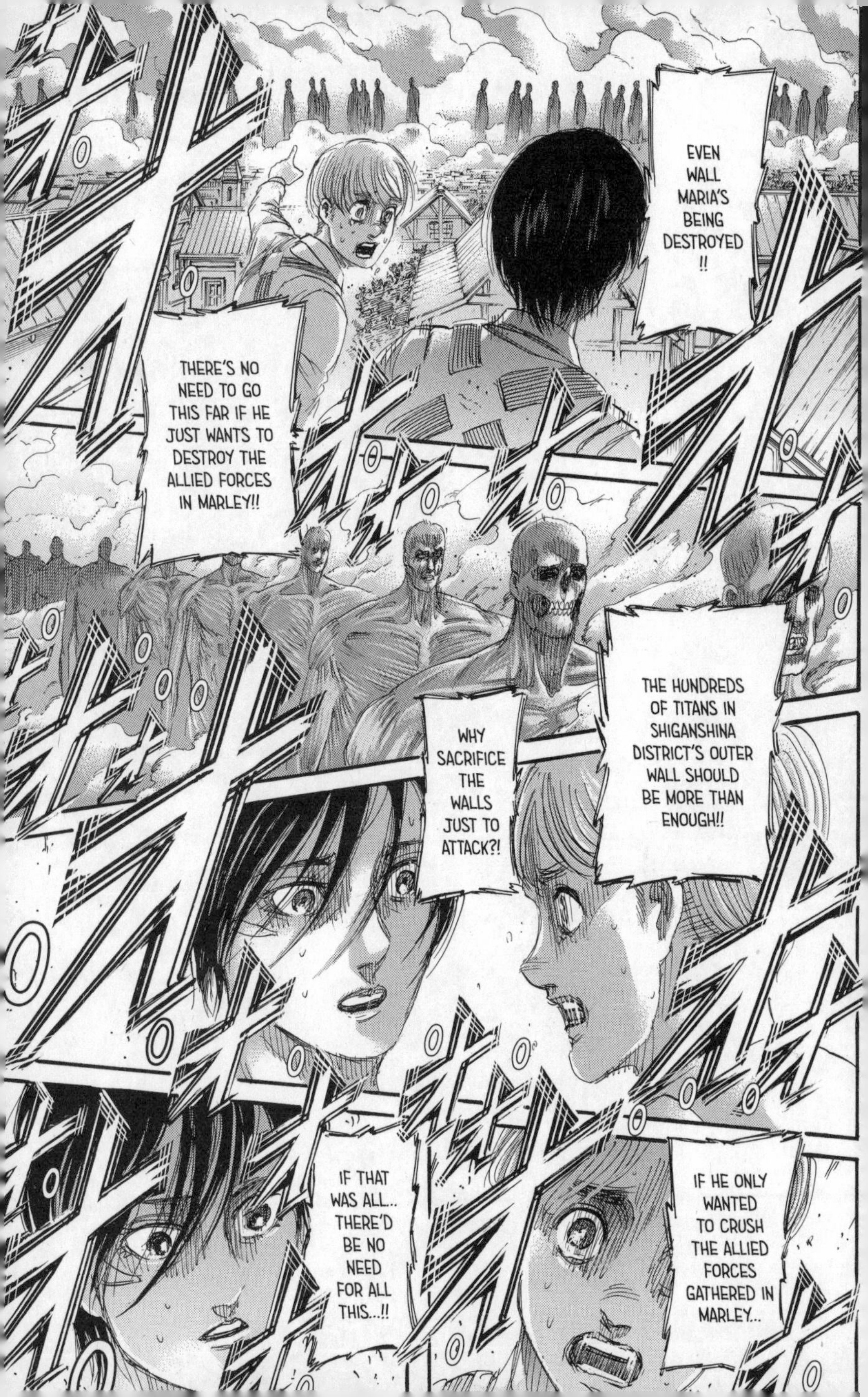
EVEN WALL MARIA'S BEING DESTROYED!!
THERE'S NO NEED TO GO THIS FAR IF HE JUST WANTS TO DESTROY THE ALLIED FORCES IN MARLEY!!
THE HUNDREDS OF TITANS IN SHIGANSHINA DISTRICT'S OUTER WALL SHOULD BE MORE THAN ENOUGH!!
WHY SACRIFICE THE WALLS JUST TO ATTACK?!
IF HE ONLY WANTED TO CRUSH THE ALLIED FORCES GATHERED IN MARLEY...
IF THAT WAS ALL.. THERE'D BE NO NEED FOR ALL THIS...!!

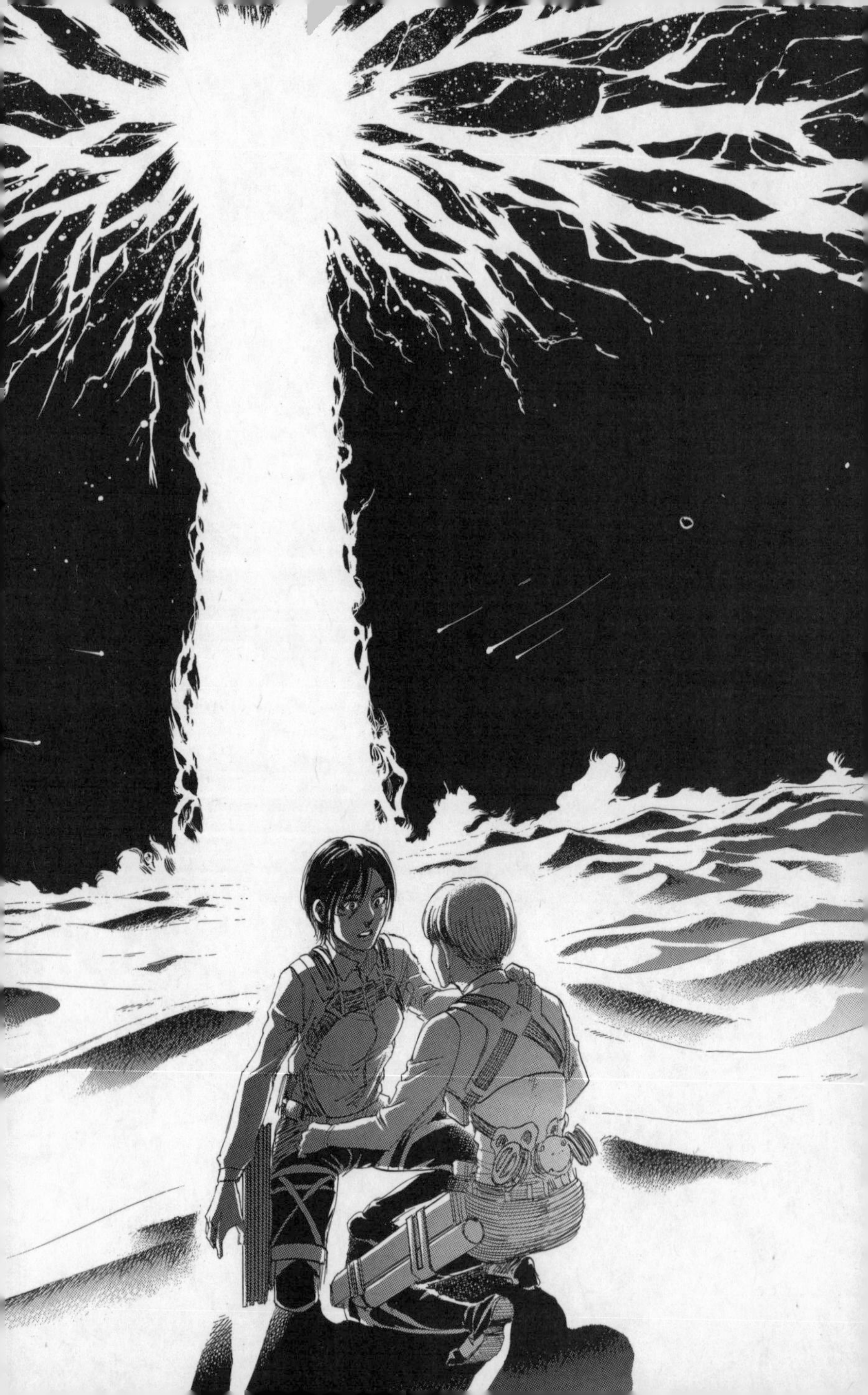

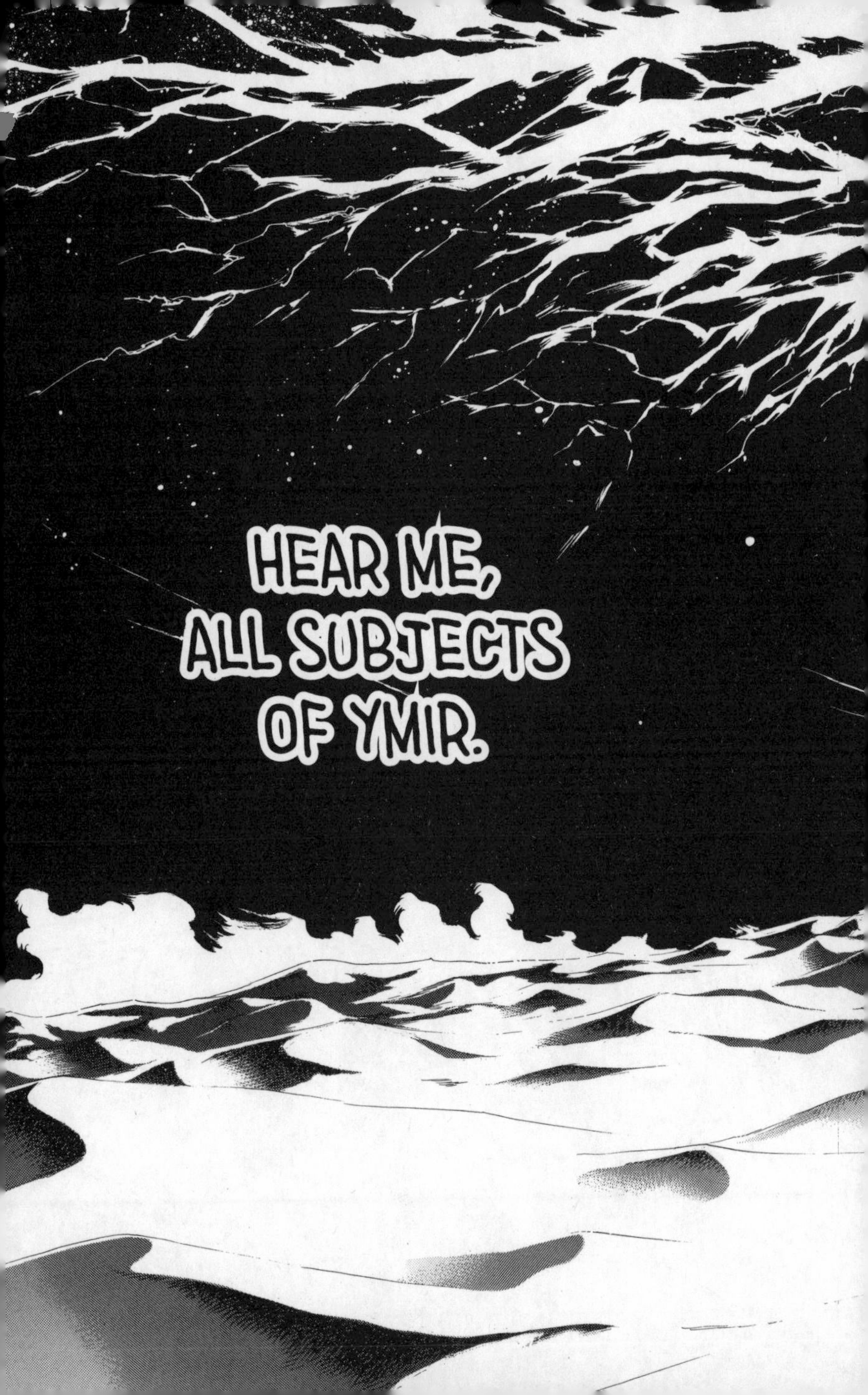
HEAR ME, ALL SUBJECTS OF YMIR.

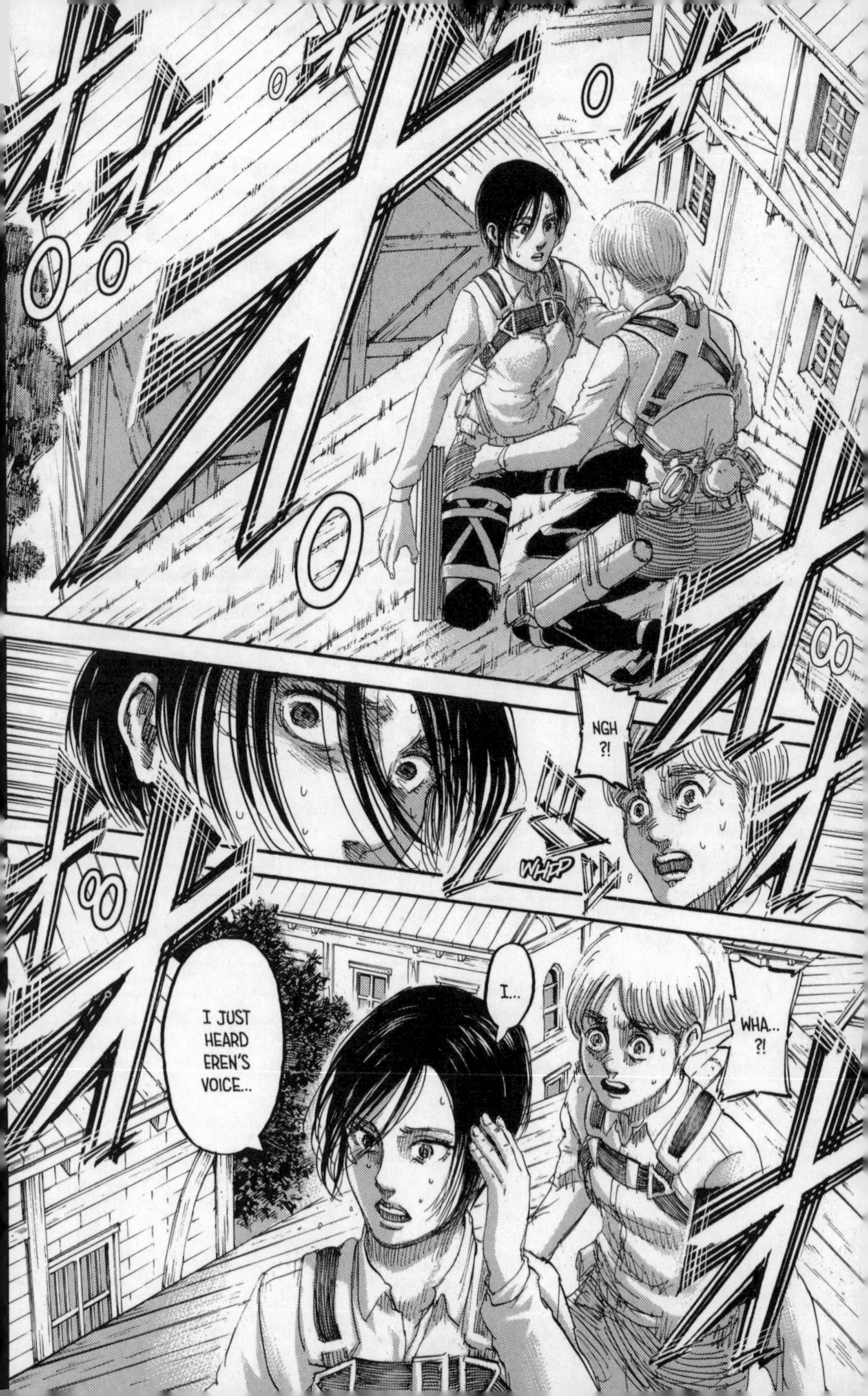
NGH ?!
WHIP
WHA... ?!
I...
I JUST HEARD EREN'S VOICE...

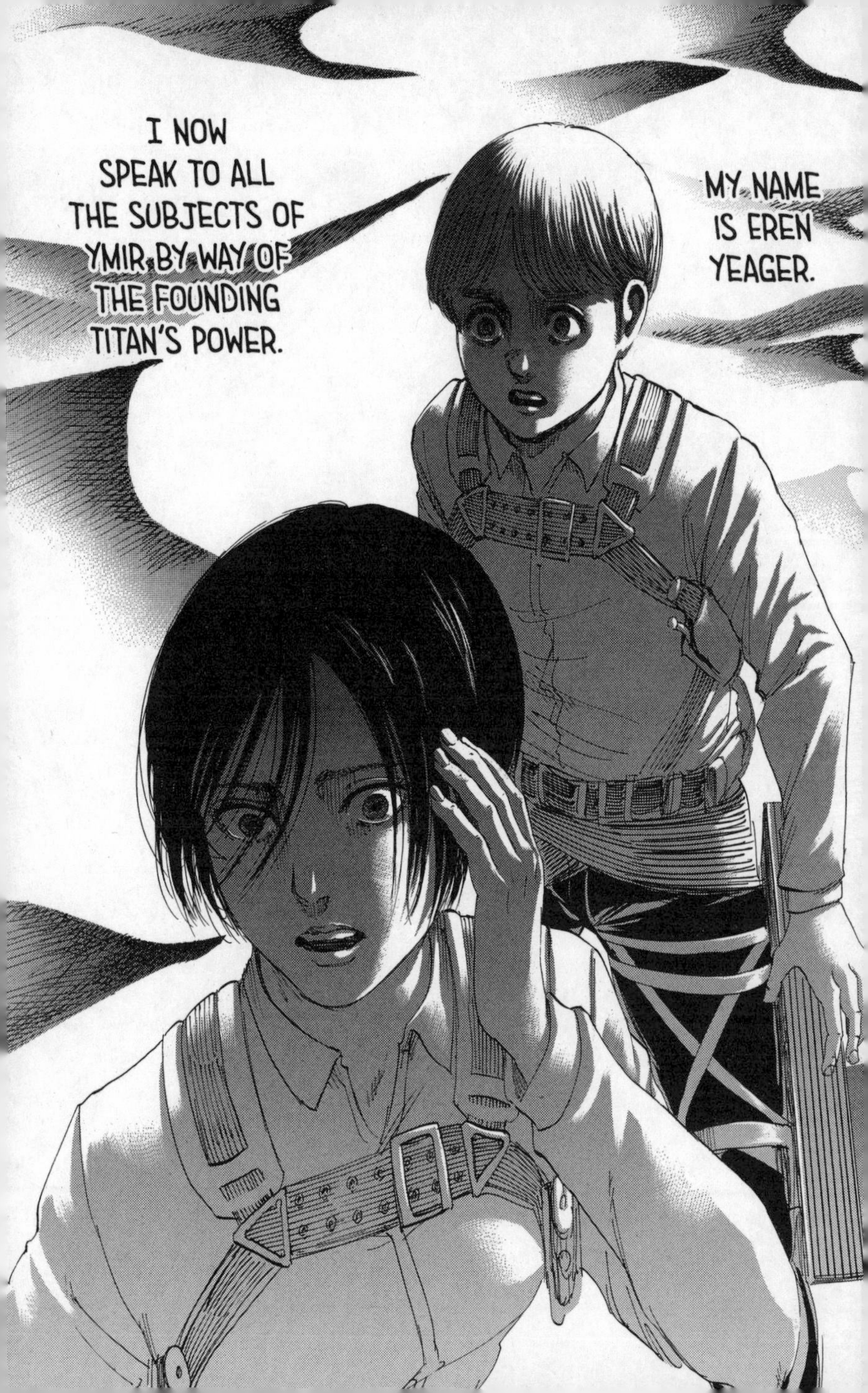
MY NAME IS EREN YEAGER.
I NOW SPEAK TO ALL THE SUBJECTS OF YMIR BY WAY OF THE FOUNDING TITAN'S POWER.

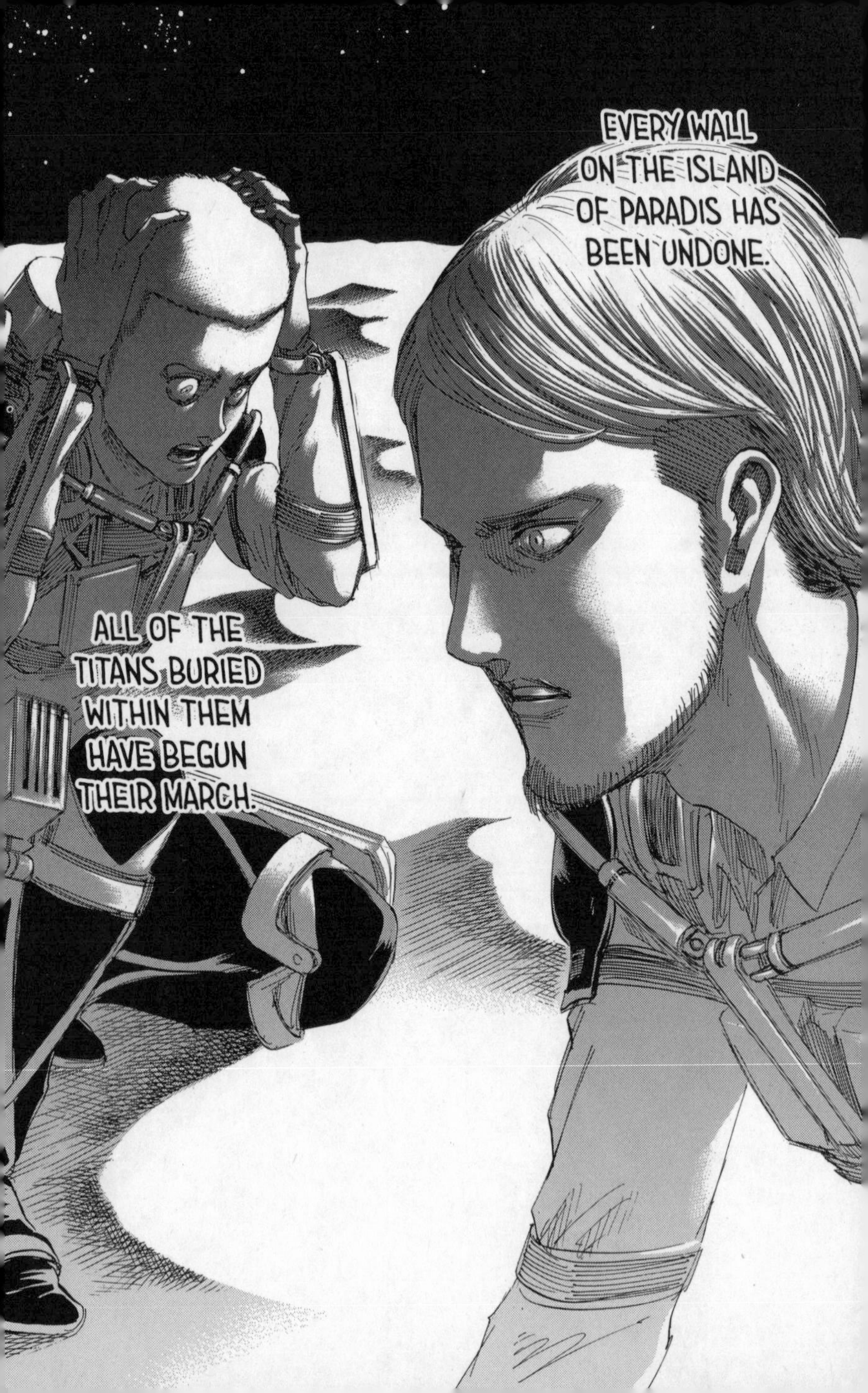
EVERY WALL ON THE ISLAND OF PARADIS HAS BEEN UNDONE.
ALL OF THE TITANS BURIED WITHIN THEM HAVE BEGUN THEIR MARCH.

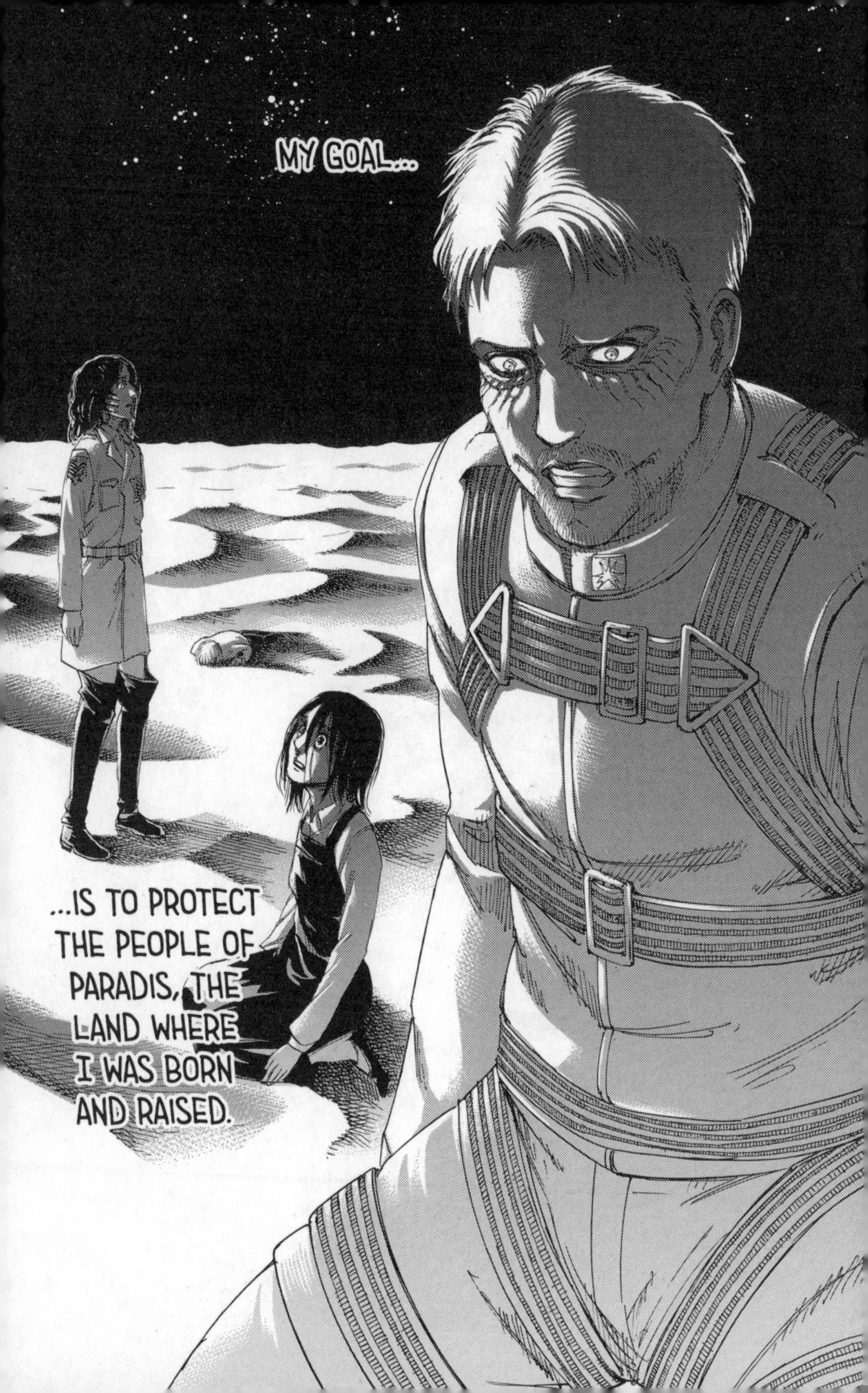
MY GOAL...
...IS TO PROTECT THE PEOPLE OF PARADIS, THE LAND WHERE I WAS BORN AND RAISED.

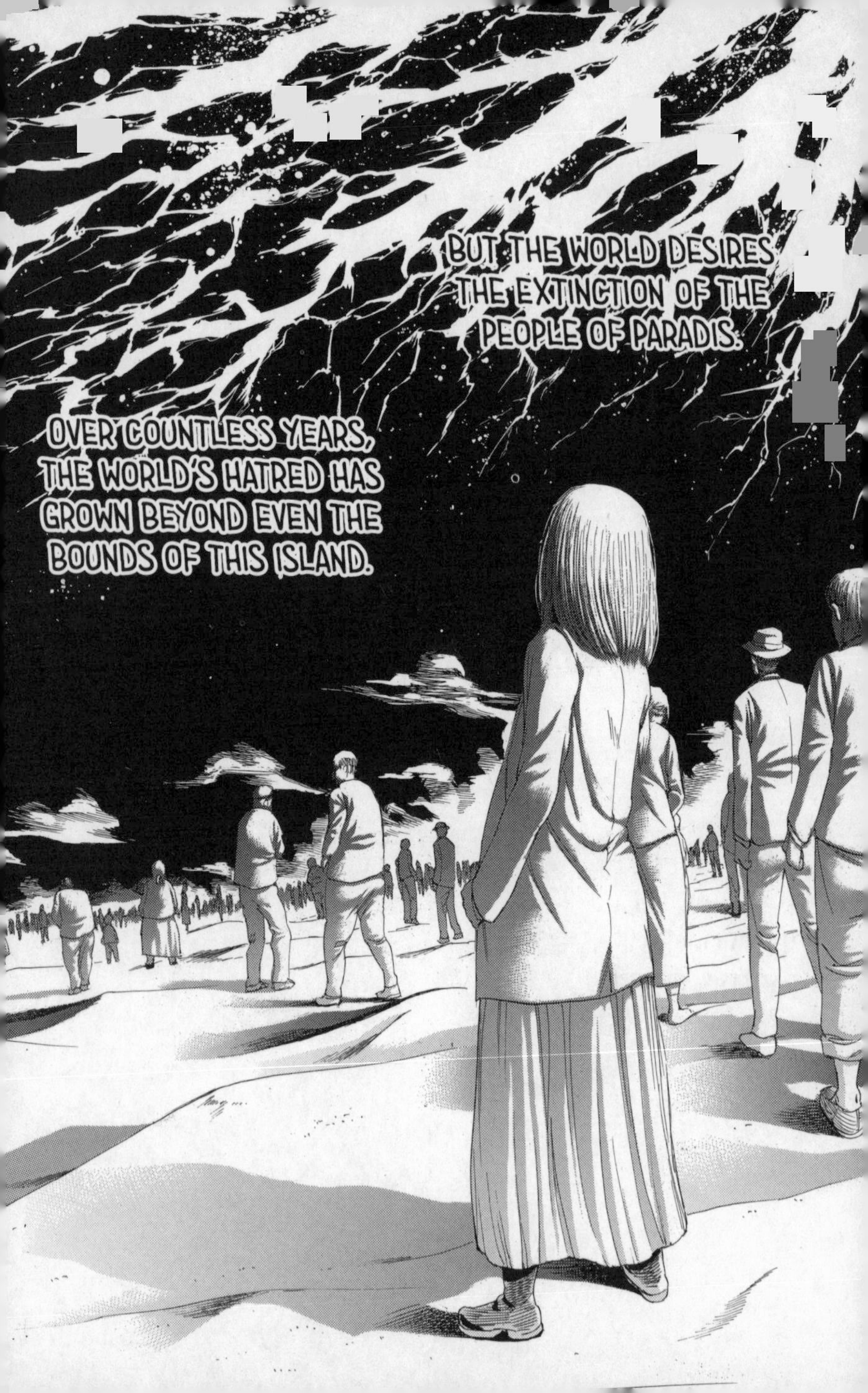
BUT THE WORLD DESIRES THE EXTINCTION OF THE PEOPLE OF PARADIS.
OVER COUNTLESS YEARS, THE WORLD'S HATRED HAS GROWN BEYOND EVEN THE BOUNDS OF THIS ISLAND.

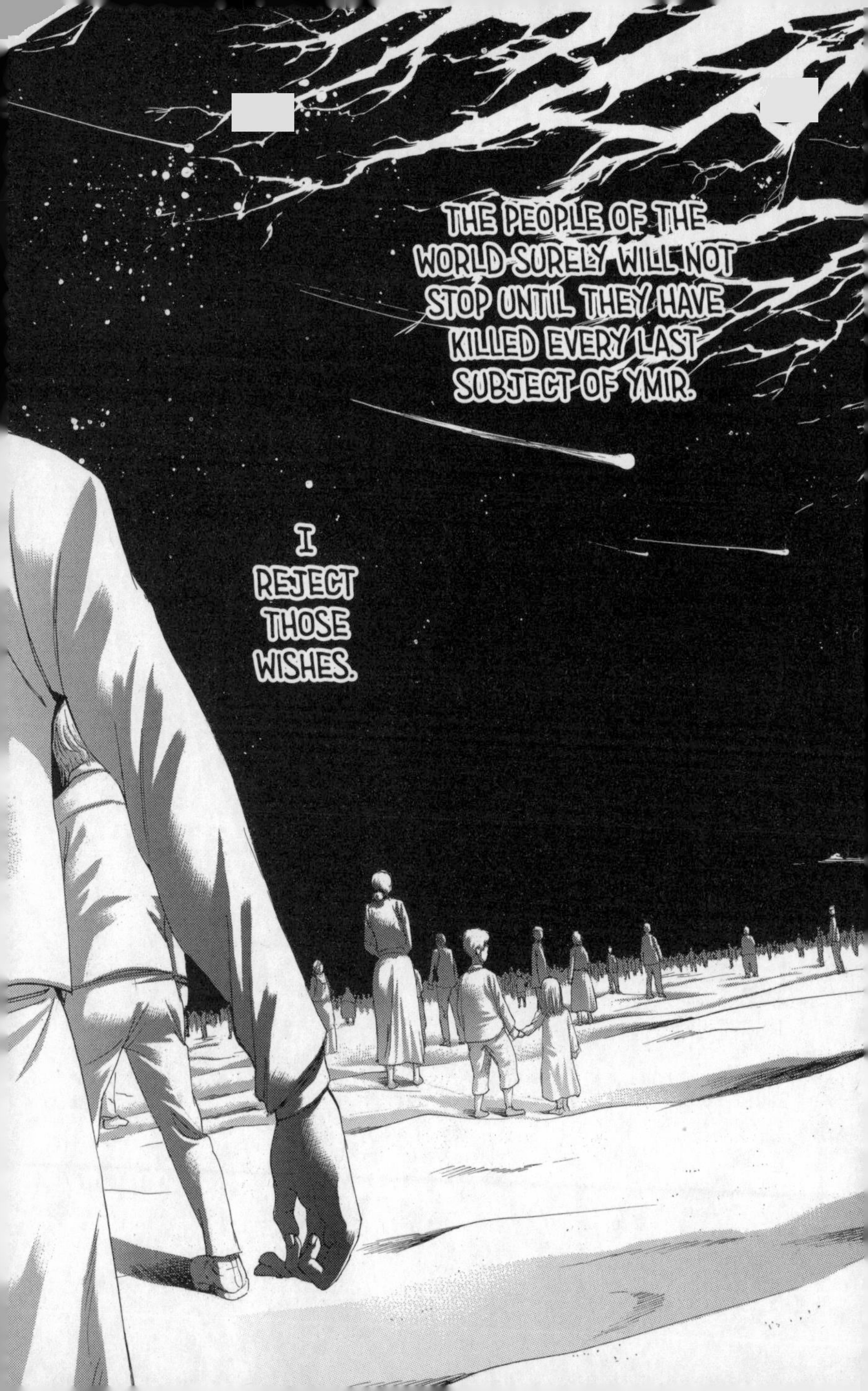
THE PEOPLE OF THE WORLD SURELY WILL NOT STOP UNTIL THEY HAVE KILLED EVERY LAST SUBJECT OF YMIR.
I REJECT THOSE WISHES.

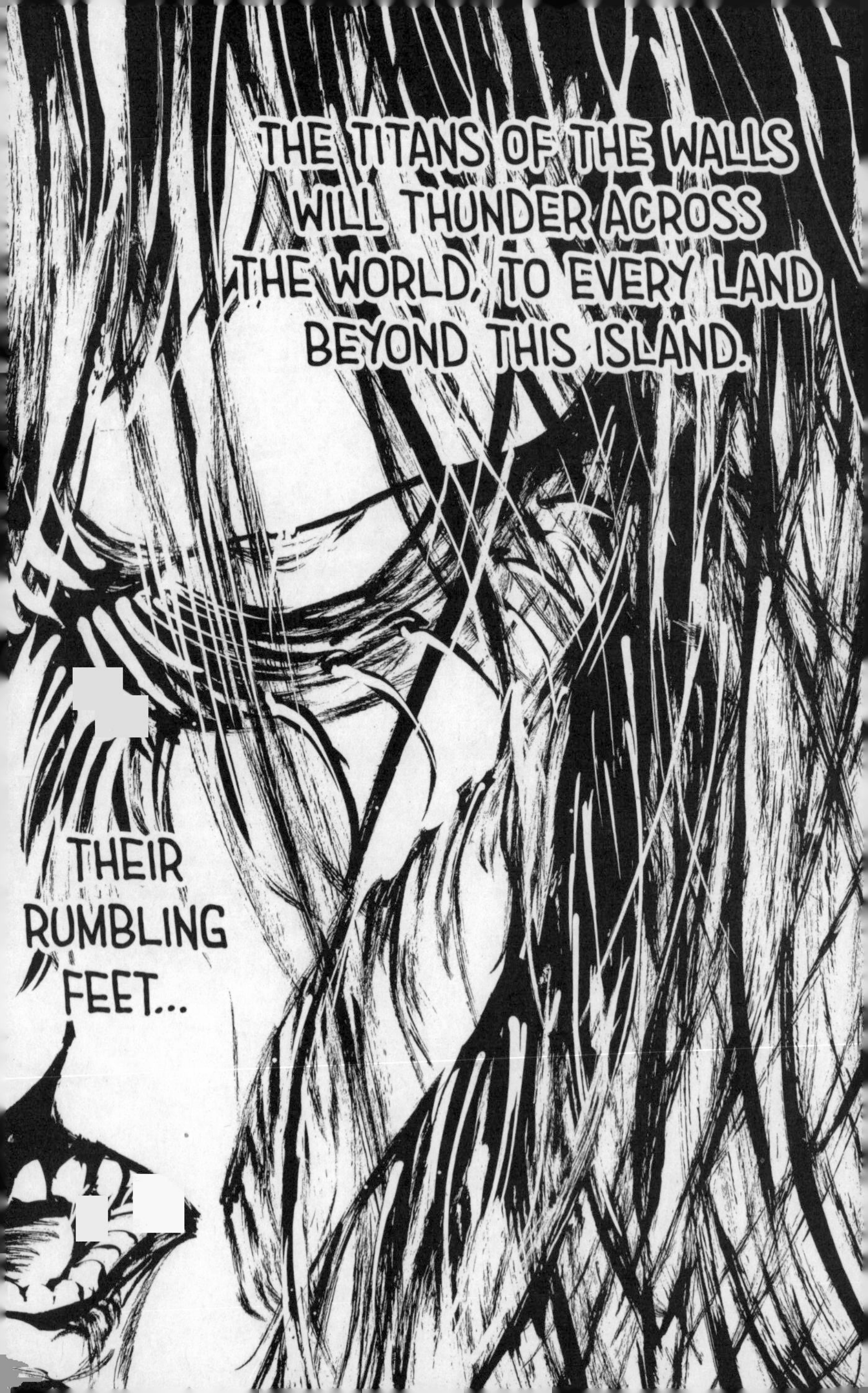
THE TITANS OF THE WALLS WILL THUNDER ACROSS THE WORLD, TO EVERY LAND BEYOND THIS ISLAND.
THEIR RUMBLING FEET...

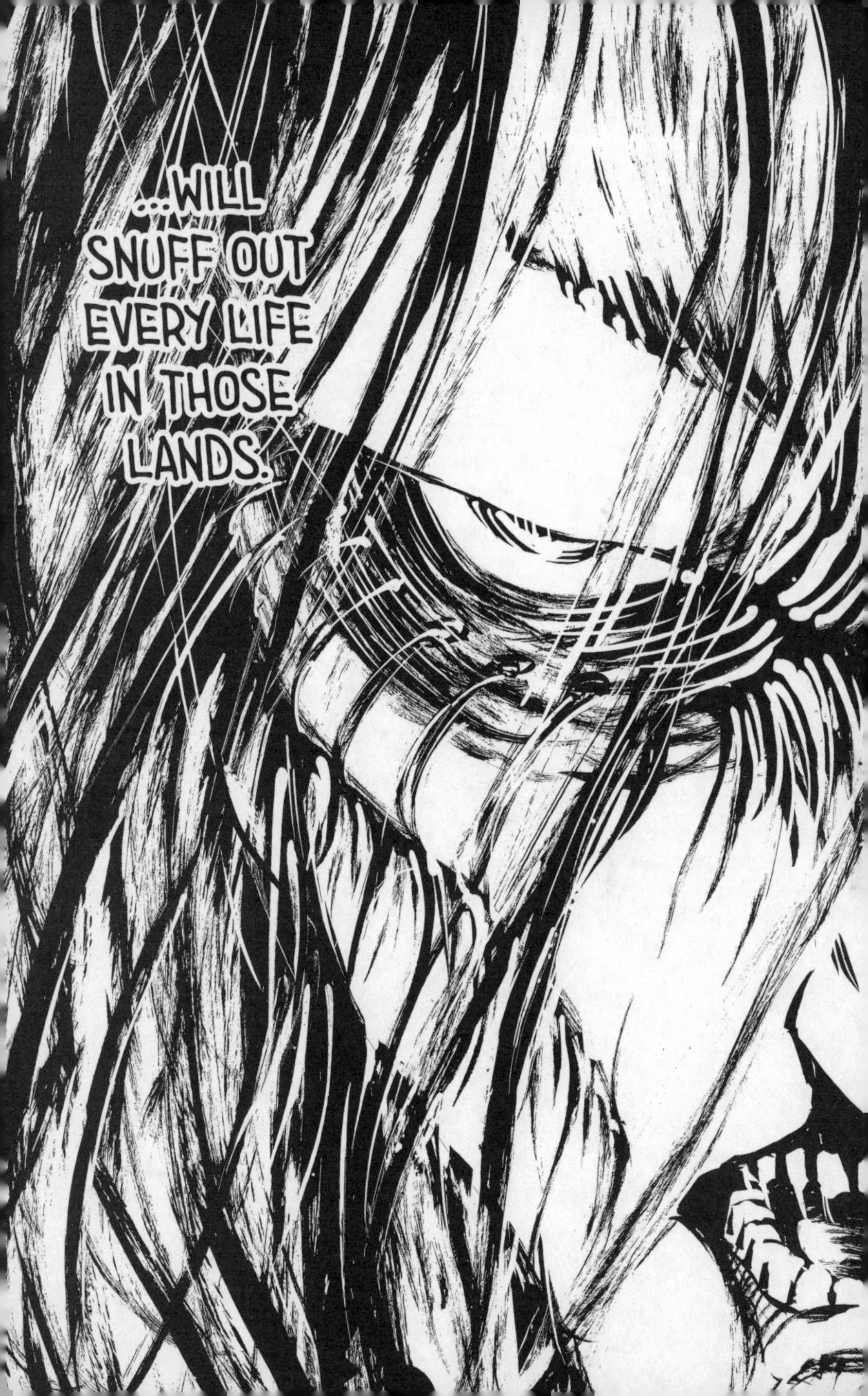
...WILL SNUFF OUT EVERY LIFE IN THOSE LANDS.

ATTACK on TITAN

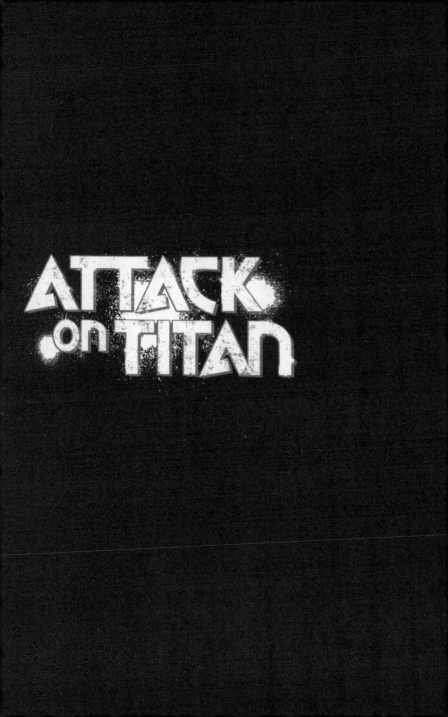

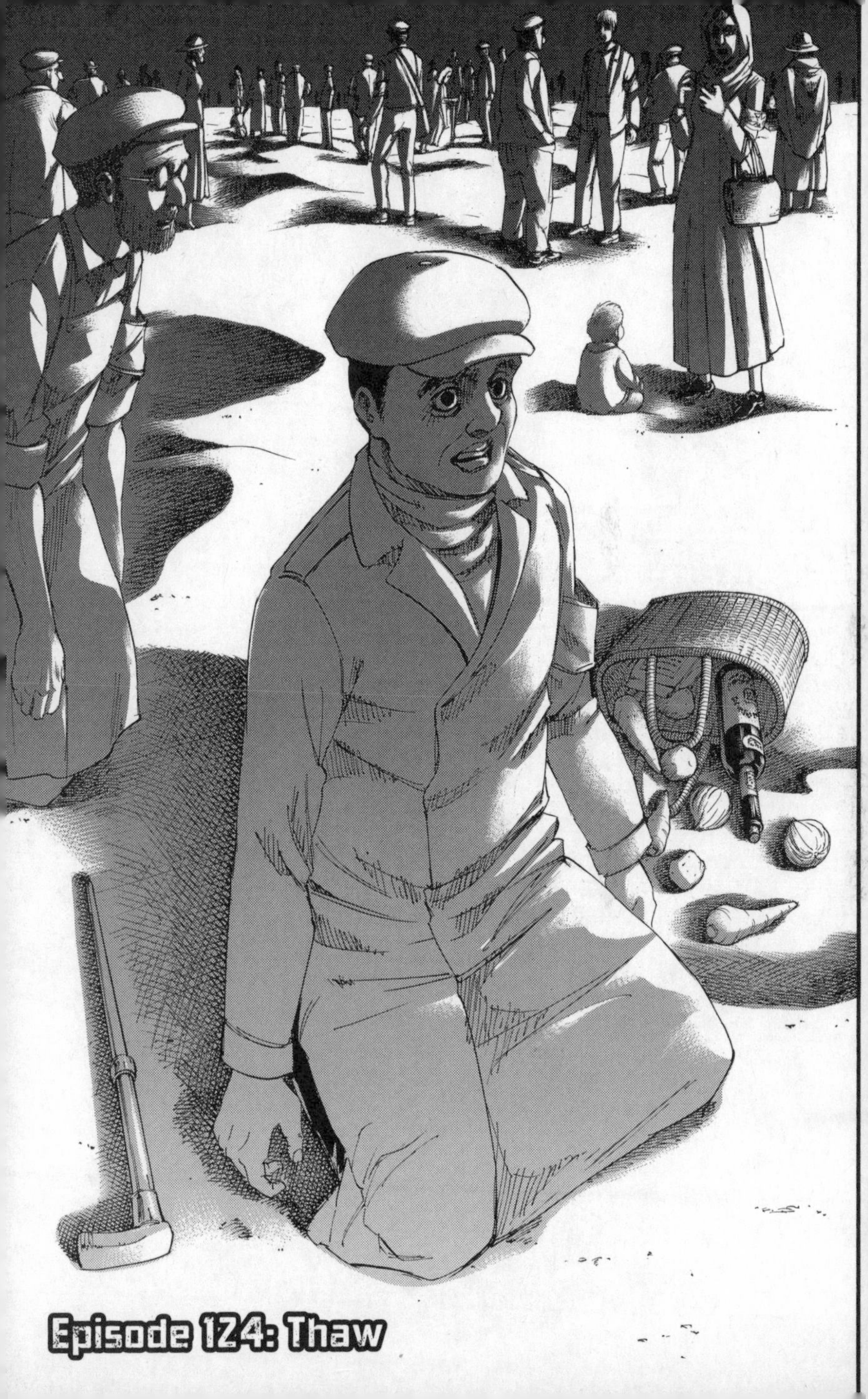
Episode 124: Thaw

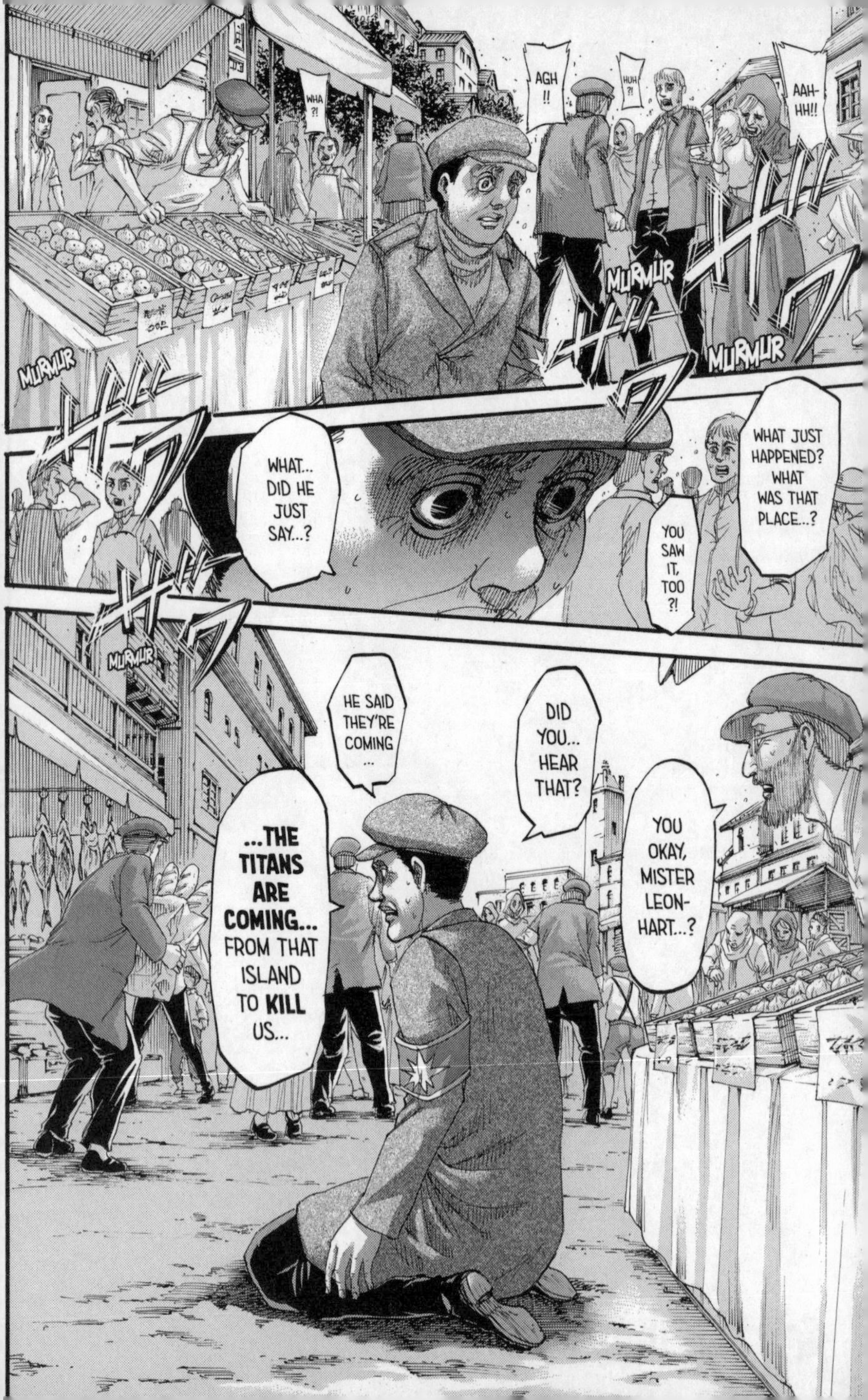
AAH-HH!!
HUH ?!
AGH !!
WHA ?!
MURMUR
MURMUR
MURMUR
WHAT JUST HAPPENED? WHAT WAS THAT PLACE...?
YOU SAW IT, TOO ?!
WHAT... DID HE JUST SAY...?
MURMUR
YOU OKAY, MISTER LEON-HART...?
DID YOU... HEAR THAT?
HE SAID THEY'RE COMING ...
...THE TITANS ARE COMING... FROM THAT ISLAND TO KILL US...

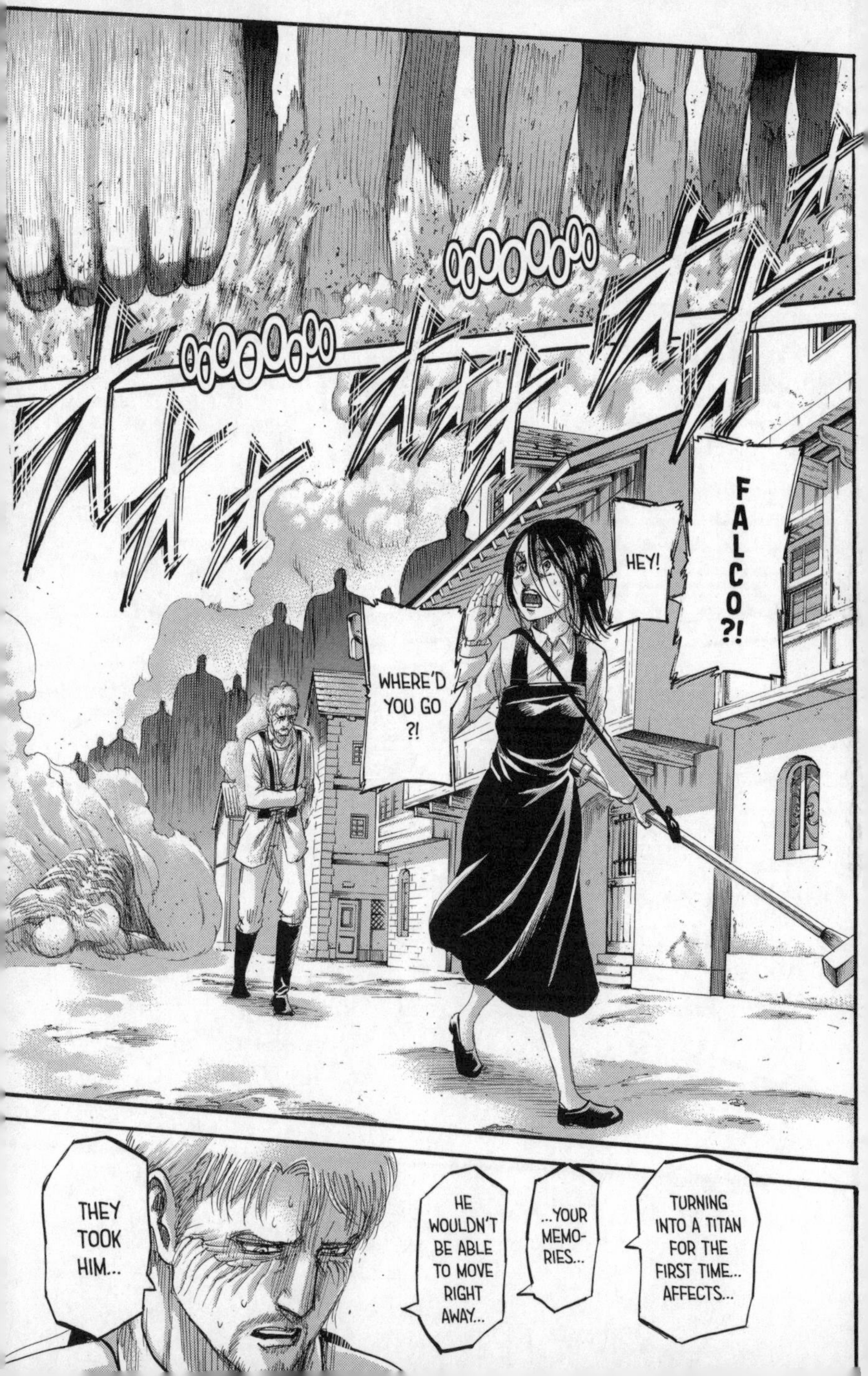
OOOOOOOO
OOOOOOOO
FALCO?!
HEY!
WHERE'D YOU GO?!
TURNING INTO A TITAN FOR THE FIRST TIME... AFFECTS...
...YOUR MEMORIES...
HE WOULDN'T BE ABLE TO MOVE RIGHT AWAY...
THEY TOOK HIM...

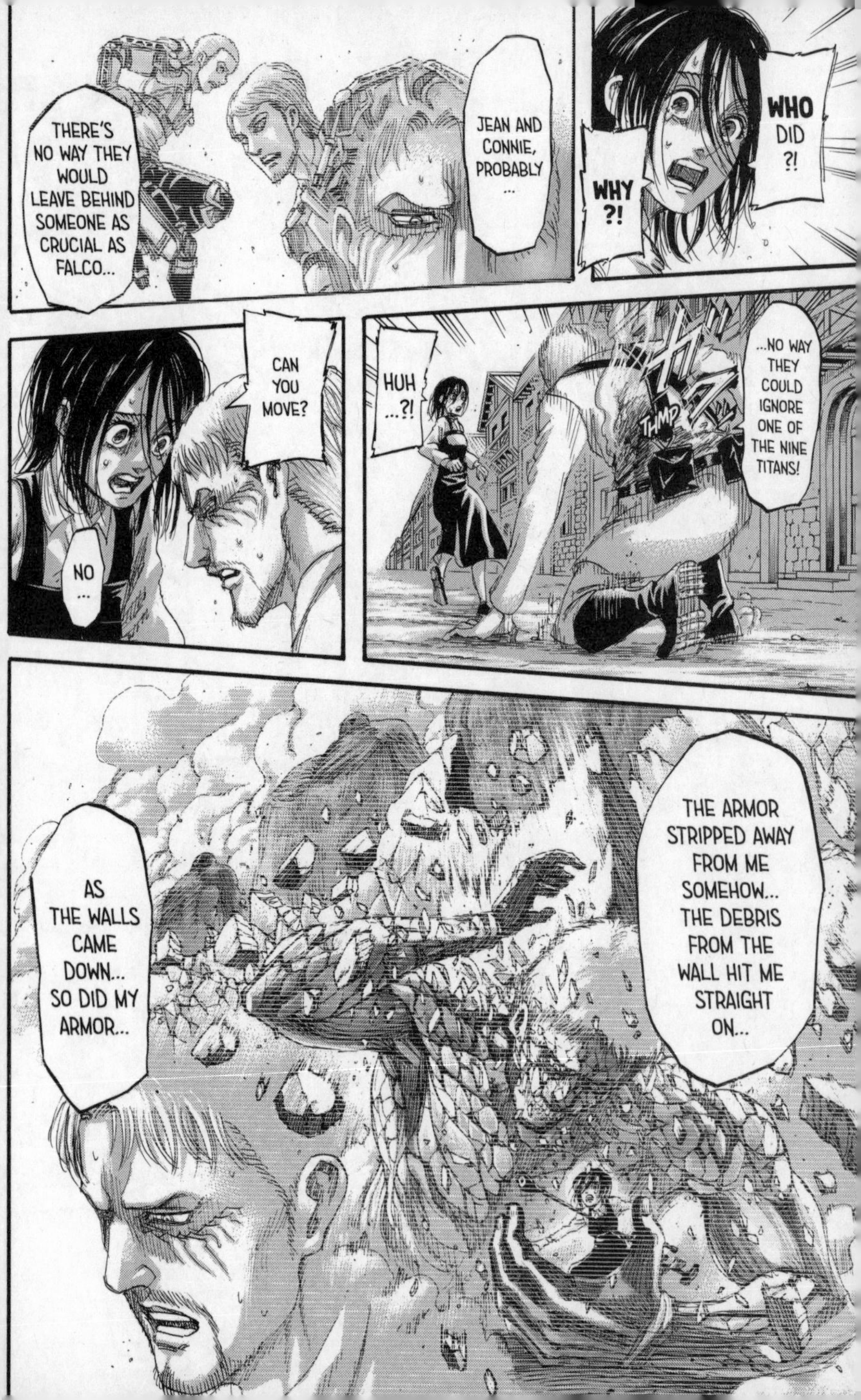
WHO DID ?!
WHY ?!
JEAN AND CONNIE, PROBABLY ...
THERE'S NO WAY THEY WOULD LEAVE BEHIND SOMEONE AS CRUCIAL AS FALCO...
...NO WAY THEY COULD IGNORE ONE OF THE NINE TITANS!
THMP
HUH ...?!
CAN YOU MOVE?
NO ...
THE ARMOR STRIPPED AWAY FROM ME SOMEHOW... THE DEBRIS FROM THE WALL HIT ME STRAIGHT ON...
AS THE WALLS CAME DOWN... SO DID MY ARMOR...

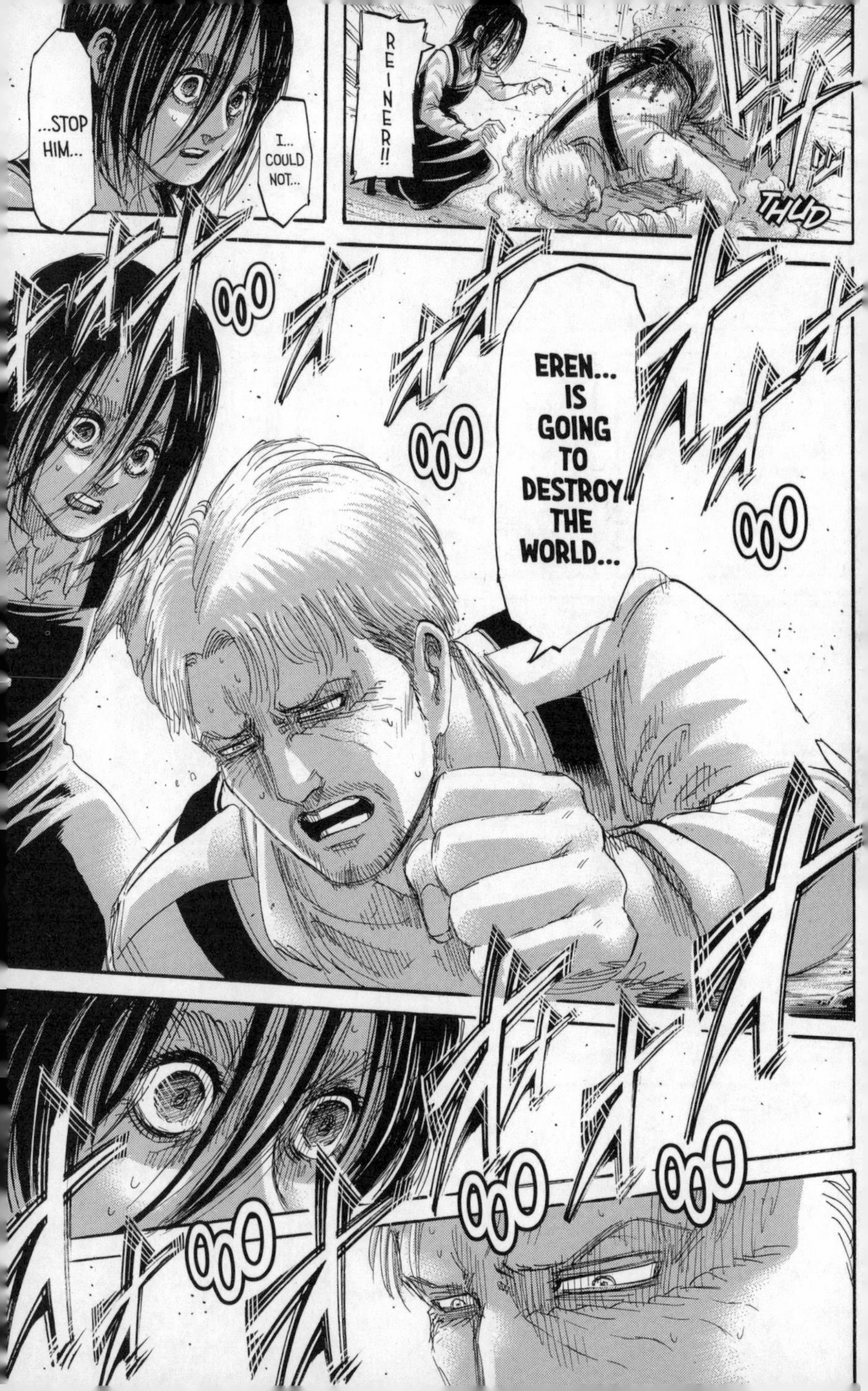
THUD
REINER!!
I... COULD NOT...
...STOP HIM...
OOO
OOO
EREN... IS GOING TO DESTROY THE WORLD...
OOO
OOO
OOO
OOO

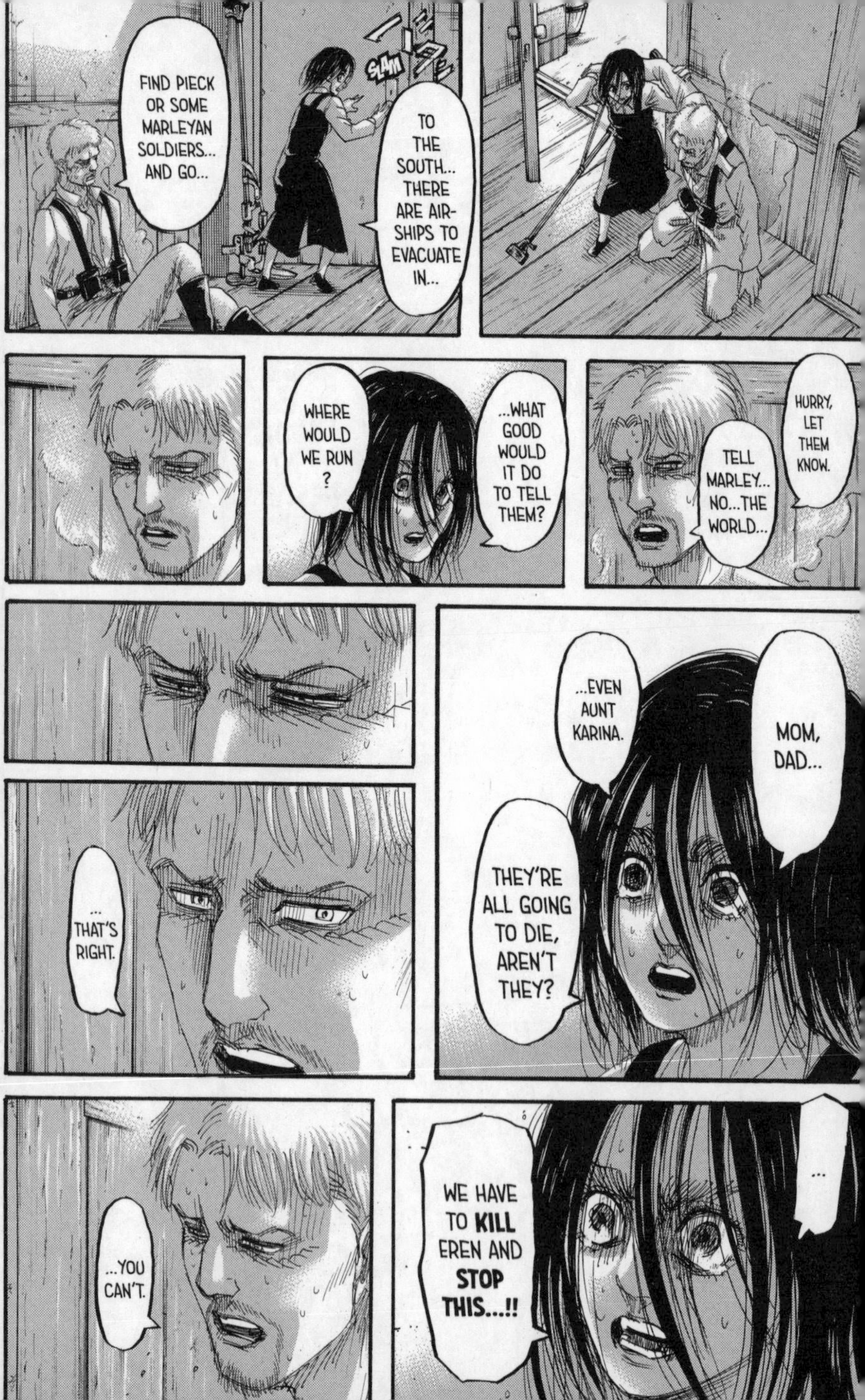
SLAM
FIND PIECK OR SOME MARLEYAN SOLDIERS... AND GO...
TO THE SOUTH... THERE ARE AIRSHIPS TO EVACUATE IN...
HURRY, LET THEM KNOW.
TELL MARLEY... NO...THE WORLD...
...WHAT GOOD WOULD IT DO TO TELL THEM?
WHERE WOULD WE RUN?
MOM, DAD...
...EVEN AUNT KARINA.
THEY'RE ALL GOING TO DIE, AREN'T THEY?
... THAT'S RIGHT.
...
WE HAVE TO **KILL** EREN AND **STOP THIS...!!**
...YOU CAN'T.

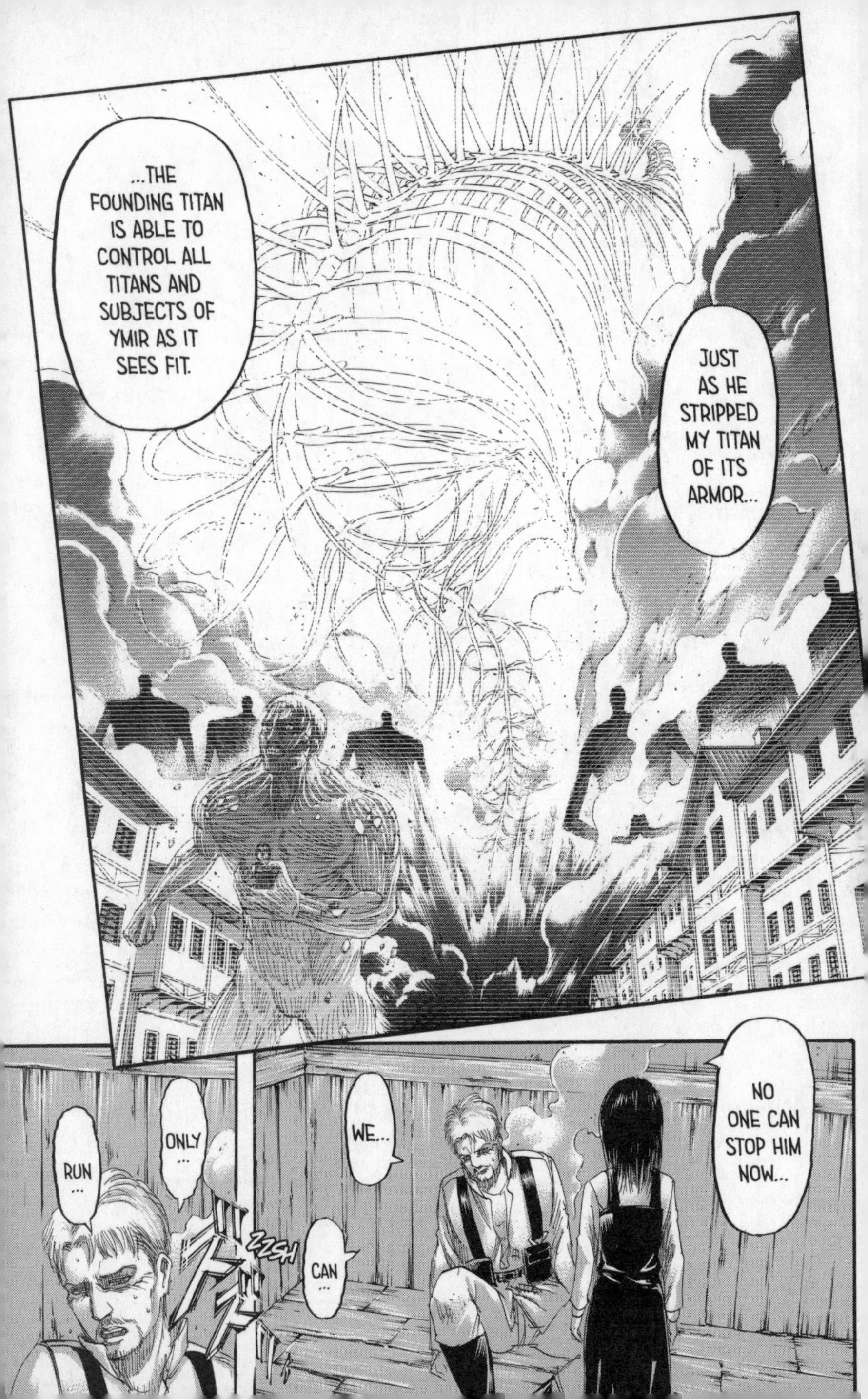
JUST AS HE STRIPPED MY TITAN OF ITS ARMOR...
...THE FOUNDING TITAN IS ABLE TO CONTROL ALL TITANS AND SUBJECTS OF YMIR AS IT SEES FIT.
NO ONE CAN STOP HIM NOW...
WE...
CAN...
ZZSH
ONLY...
RUN...

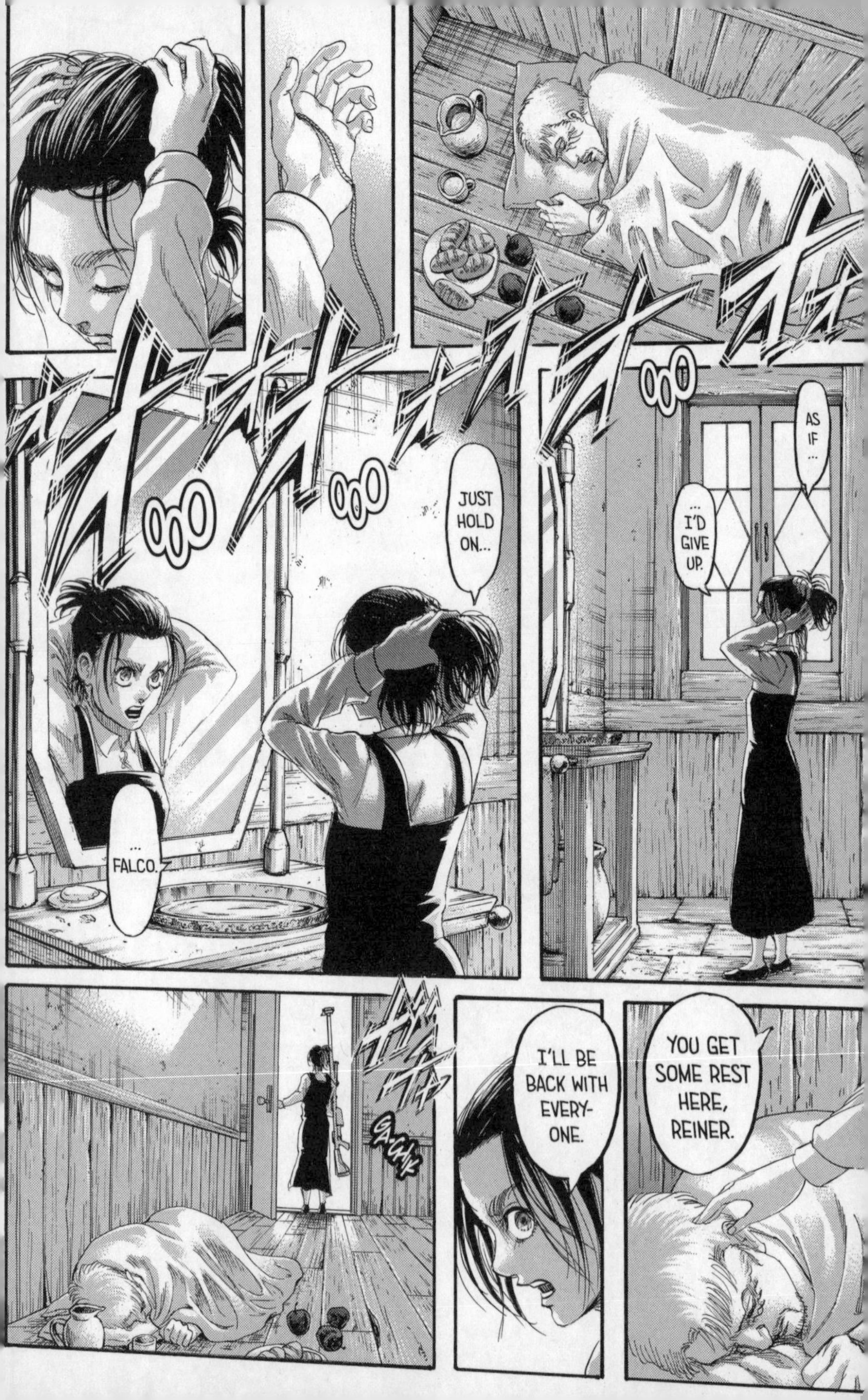
OOO
OOO
AS IF ...
... I'D GIVE UP.
OOO
JUST HOLD ON...
OOO
... FALCO.
YOU GET SOME REST HERE, REINER.
I'LL BE BACK WITH EVERY-ONE.
GA-CHIK

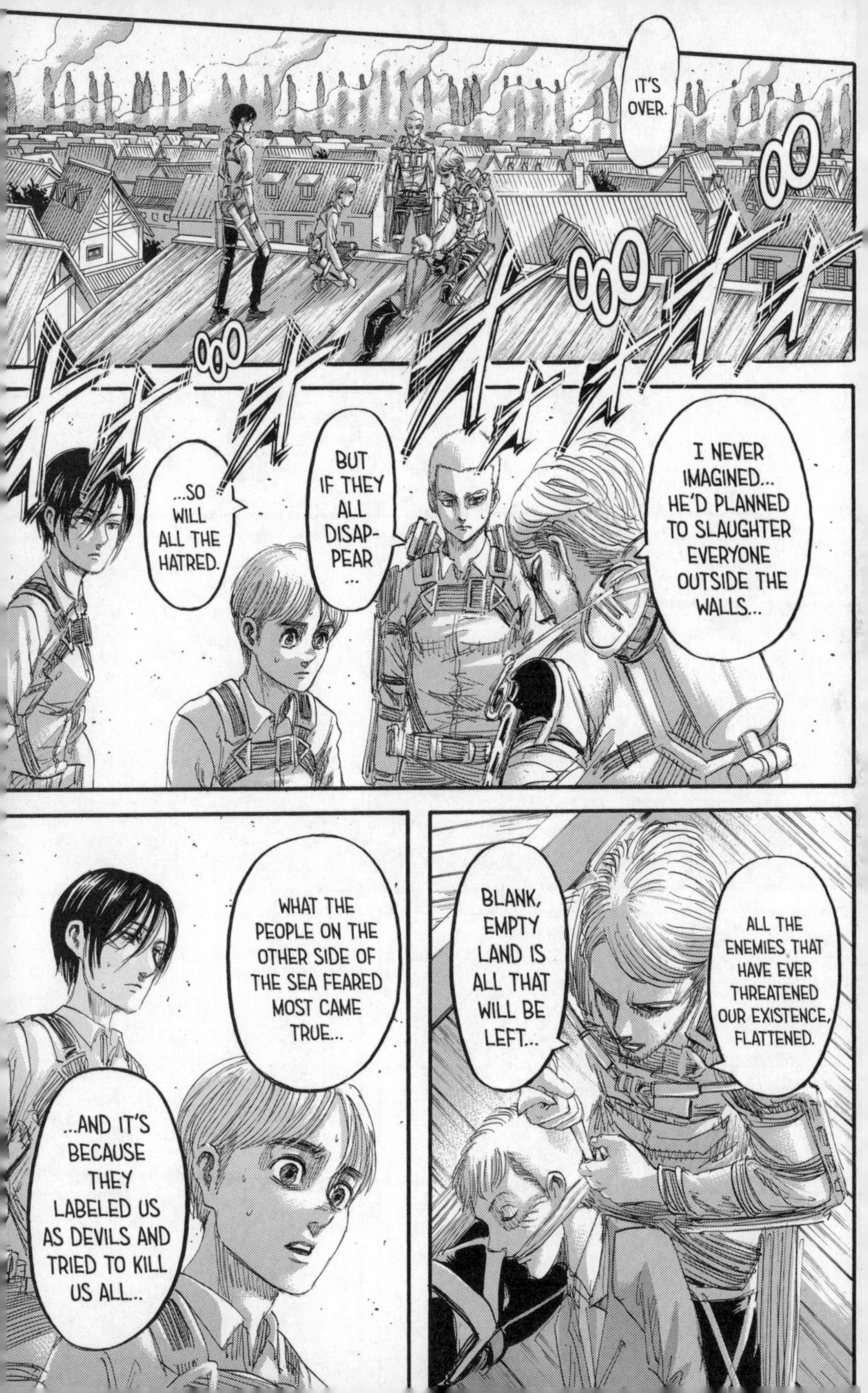
IT'S OVER.
I NEVER IMAGINED... HE'D PLANNED TO SLAUGHTER EVERYONE OUTSIDE THE WALLS...
BUT IF THEY ALL DISAP-PEAR...
...SO WILL ALL THE HATRED.
ALL THE ENEMIES THAT HAVE EVER THREATENED OUR EXISTENCE, FLATTENED.
BLANK, EMPTY LAND IS ALL THAT WILL BE LEFT...
WHAT THE PEOPLE ON THE OTHER SIDE OF THE SEA FEARED MOST CAME TRUE...
...AND IT'S BECAUSE THEY LABELED US AS DEVILS AND TRIED TO KILL US ALL...

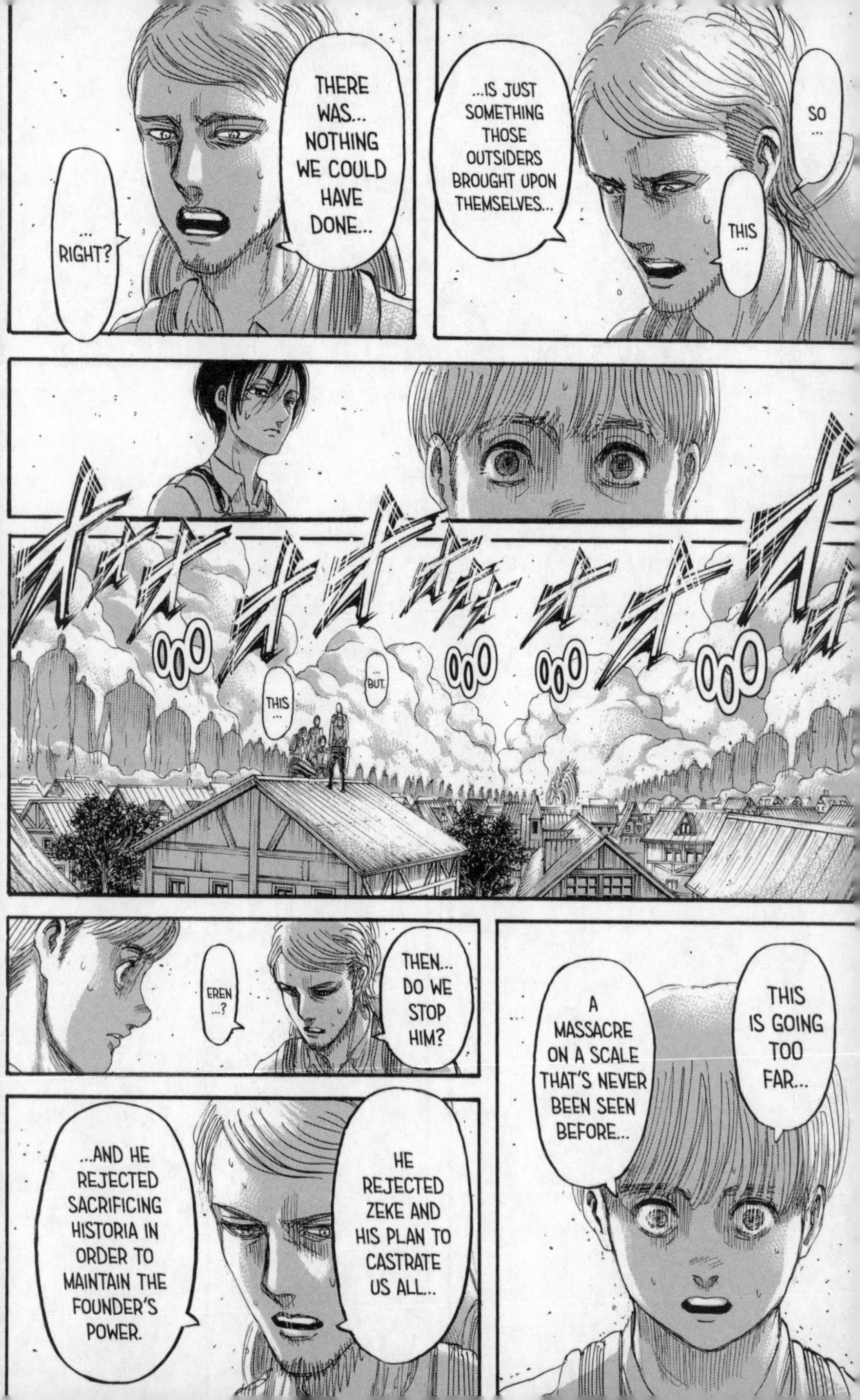
SO...
THIS...
...IS JUST SOMETHING THOSE OUTSIDERS BROUGHT UPON THEMSELVES...
THERE WAS... NOTHING WE COULD HAVE DONE...
...RIGHT?
...BUT.
THIS...
THIS IS GOING TOO FAR...
A MASSACRE ON A SCALE THAT'S NEVER BEEN SEEN BEFORE...
THEN... DO WE STOP HIM?
EREN...?
HE REJECTED ZEKE AND HIS PLAN TO CASTRATE US ALL...
...AND HE REJECTED SACRIFICING HISTORIA IN ORDER TO MAINTAIN THE FOUNDER'S POWER.

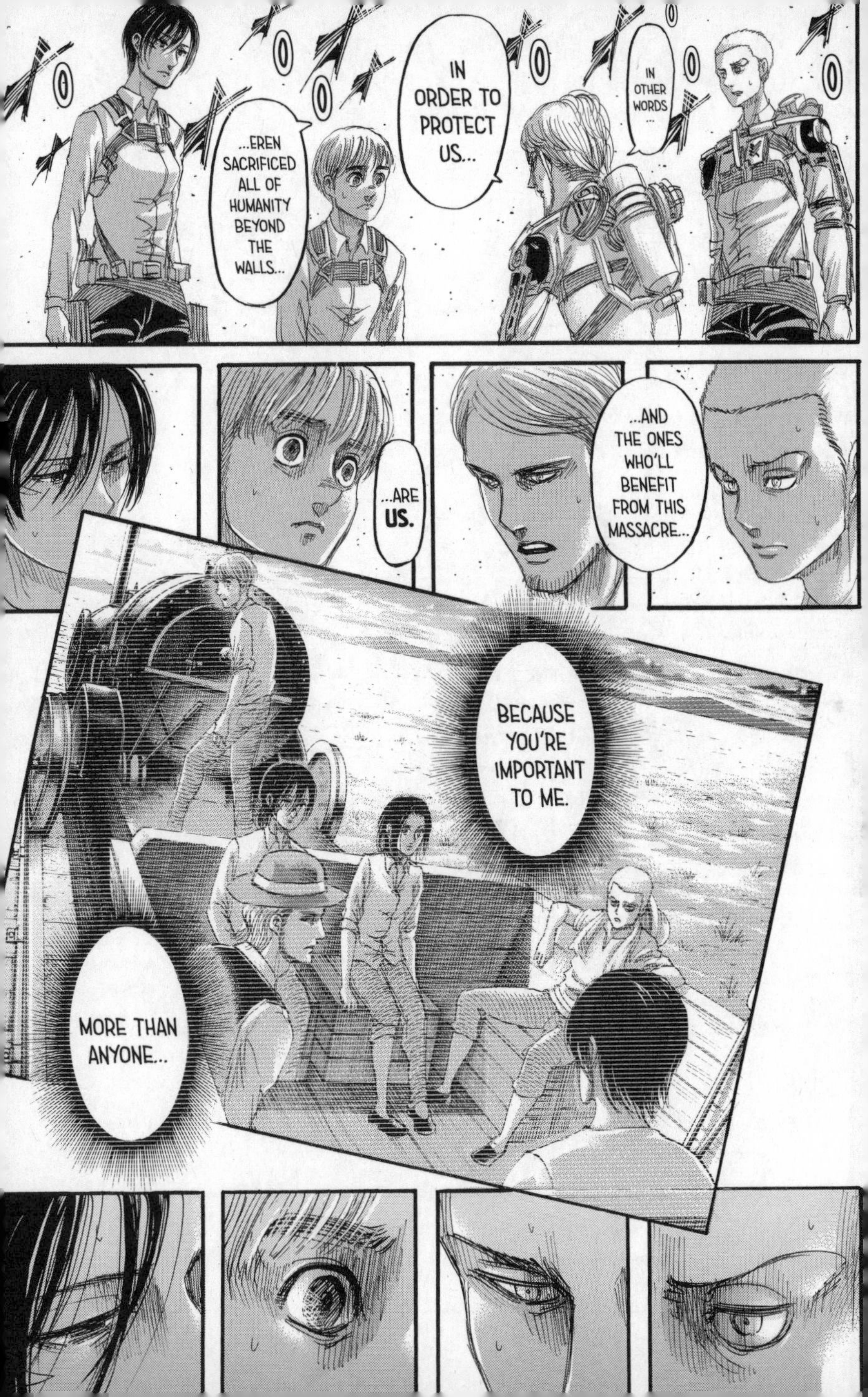
IN OTHER WORDS ...
IN ORDER TO PROTECT US...
...EREN SACRIFICED ALL OF HUMANITY BEYOND THE WALLS...
...AND THE ONES WHO'LL BENEFIT FROM THIS MASSACRE...
...ARE **US.**
BECAUSE YOU'RE IMPORTANT TO ME.
MORE THAN ANYONE...

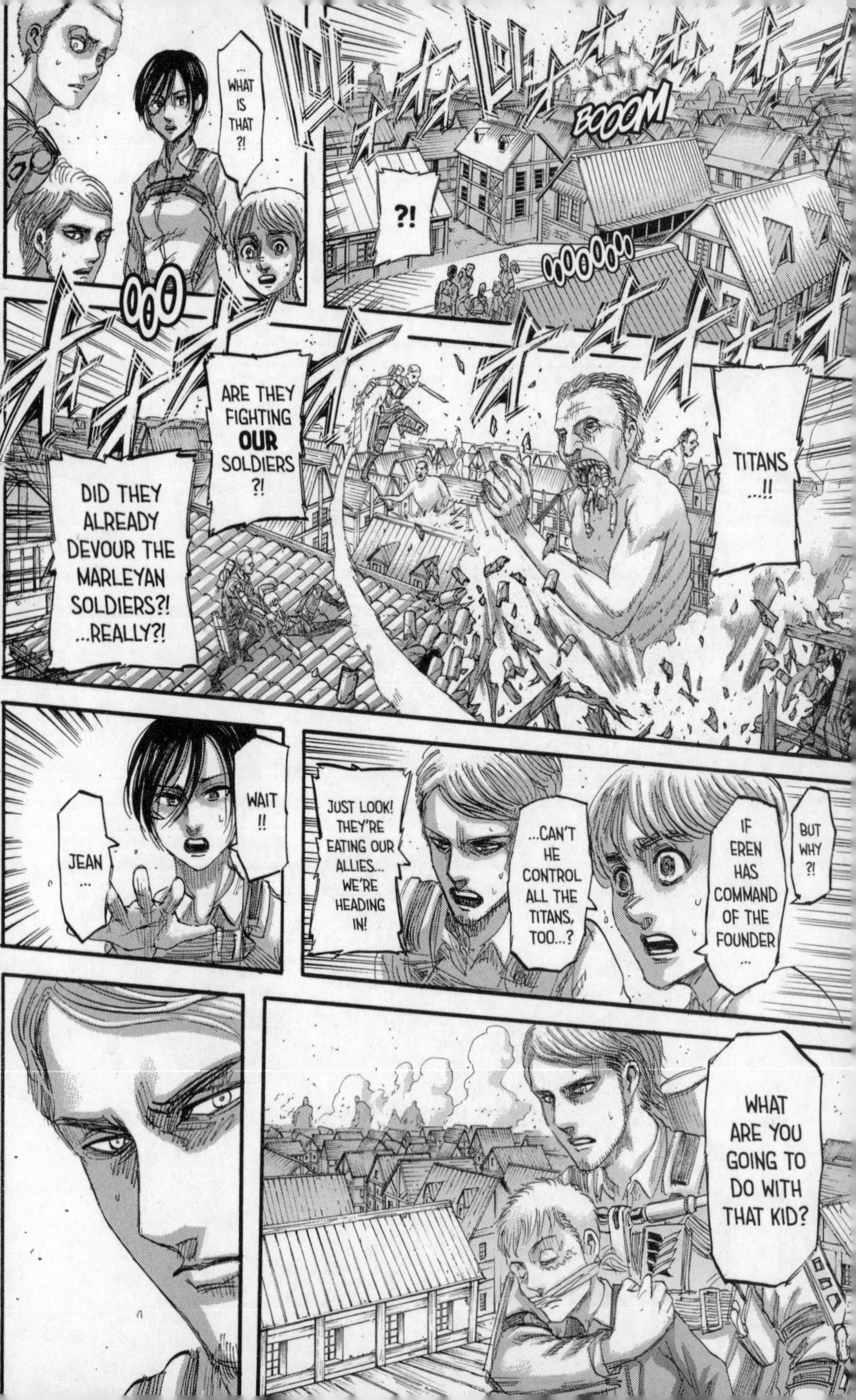
BOOOM
?!
... WHAT IS THAT ?!
TITANS ...!!
ARE THEY FIGHTING **OUR** SOLDIERS ?!
DID THEY ALREADY DEVOUR THE MARLEYAN SOLDIERS?! ...REALLY?!
BUT WHY ?!
IF EREN HAS COMMAND OF THE FOUNDER ...
...CAN'T HE CONTROL ALL THE TITANS, TOO...?
JUST LOOK! THEY'RE EATING OUR ALLIES... WE'RE HEADING IN!
WAIT !!
JEAN ...
WHAT ARE YOU GOING TO DO WITH THAT KID?

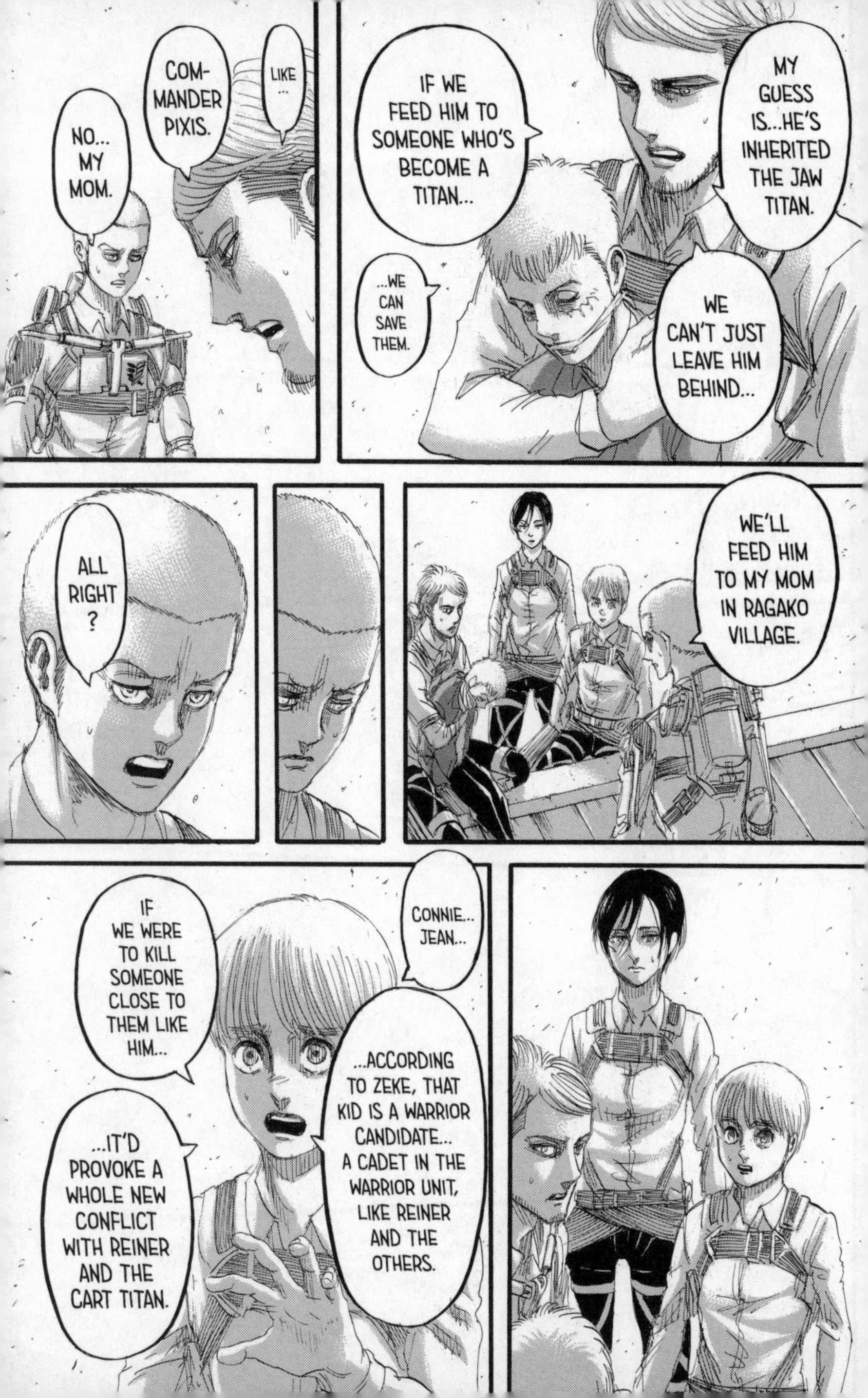
MY GUESS IS...HE'S INHERITED THE JAW TITAN.
IF WE FEED HIM TO SOMEONE WHO'S BECOME A TITAN...
WE CAN'T JUST LEAVE HIM BEHIND...
...WE CAN SAVE THEM.
LIKE ...
COM-MANDER PIXIS.
NO... MY MOM.
WE'LL FEED HIM TO MY MOM IN RAGAKO VILLAGE.
ALL RIGHT ?
CONNIE... JEAN...
...ACCORDING TO ZEKE, THAT KID IS A WARRIOR CANDIDATE... A CADET IN THE WARRIOR UNIT, LIKE REINER AND THE OTHERS.
IF WE WERE TO KILL SOMEONE CLOSE TO THEM LIKE HIM...
...IT'D PROVOKE A WHOLE NEW CONFLICT WITH REINER AND THE CART TITAN.

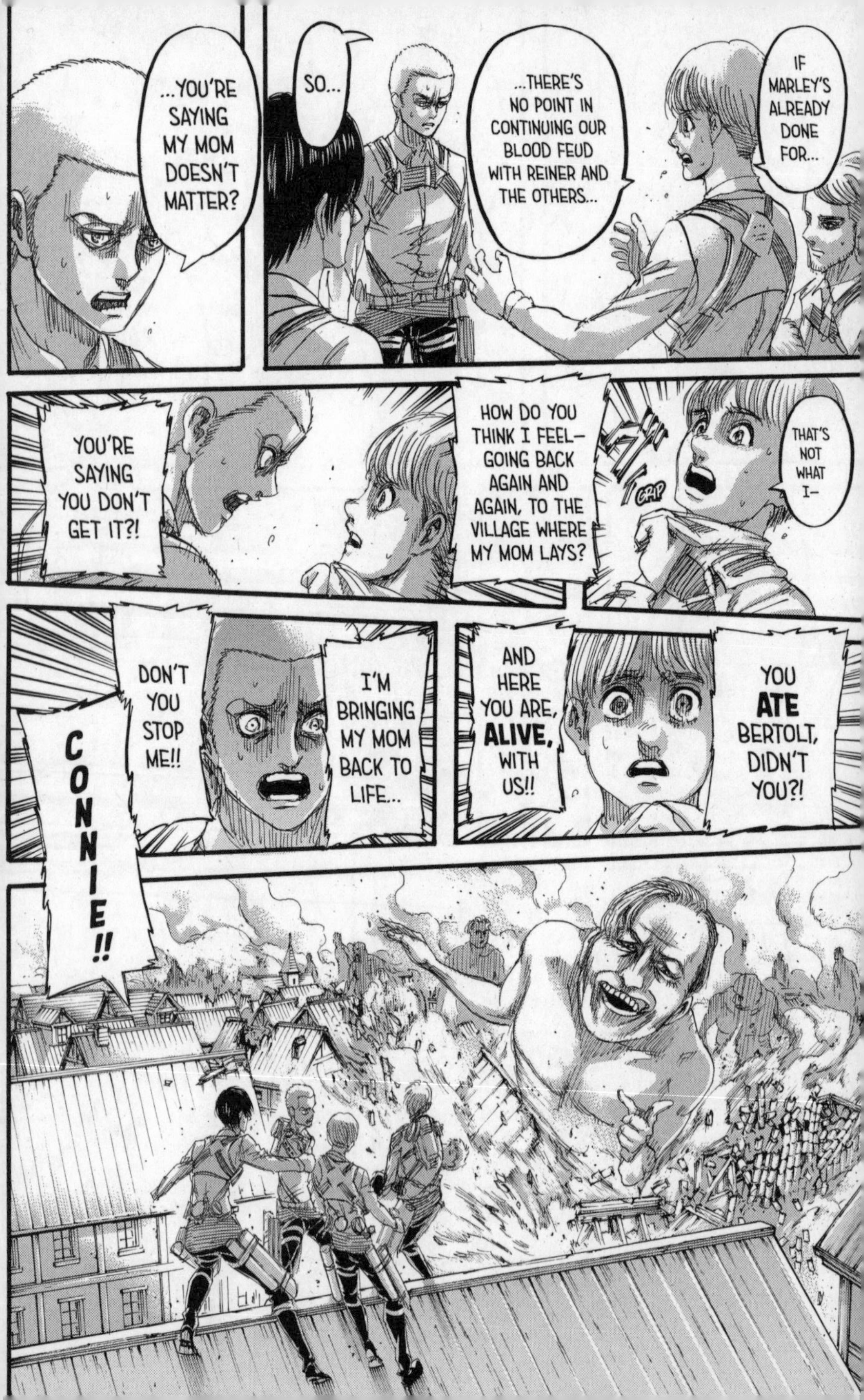
IF MARLEY'S ALREADY DONE FOR...
...THERE'S NO POINT IN CONTINUING OUR BLOOD FEUD WITH REINER AND THE OTHERS...
SO...
...YOU'RE SAYING MY MOM DOESN'T MATTER?
THAT'S NOT WHAT I—
GRIP
HOW DO YOU THINK I FEEL— GOING BACK AGAIN AND AGAIN, TO THE VILLAGE WHERE MY MOM LAYS?
YOU'RE SAYING YOU DON'T GET IT?!
YOU **ATE** BERTOLT, DIDN'T YOU?!
AND HERE YOU ARE, **ALIVE,** WITH US!!
I'M BRINGING MY MOM BACK TO LIFE...
DON'T YOU STOP ME!!
CONNIE!!

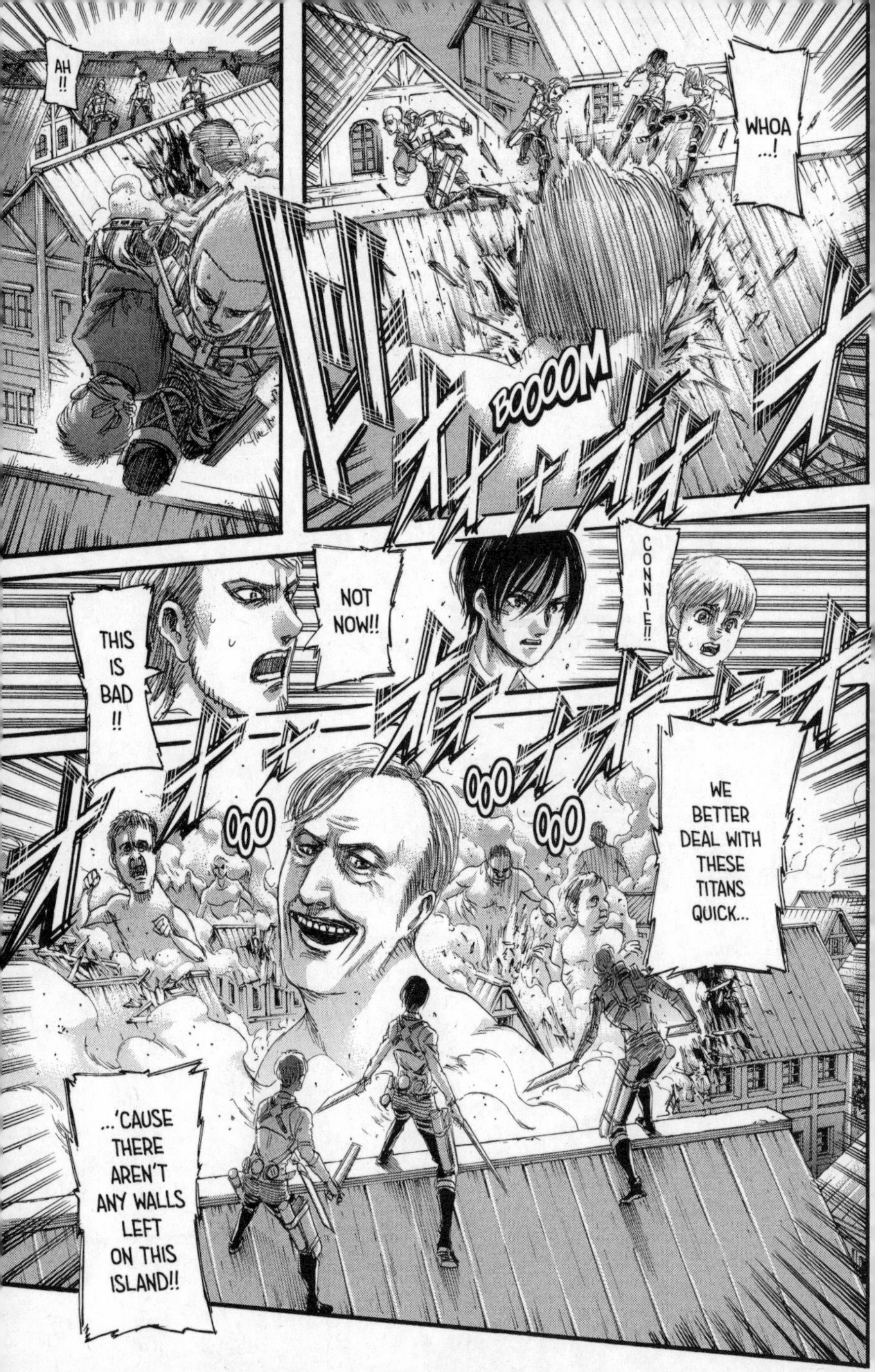
WHOA ...!
BOOOOM
AH !!
CONNIE!!
NOT NOW!!
THIS IS BAD !!
OOO
OOO
OOO
WE BETTER DEAL WITH THESE TITANS QUICK...
...'CAUSE THERE AREN'T ANY WALLS LEFT ON THIS ISLAND!!

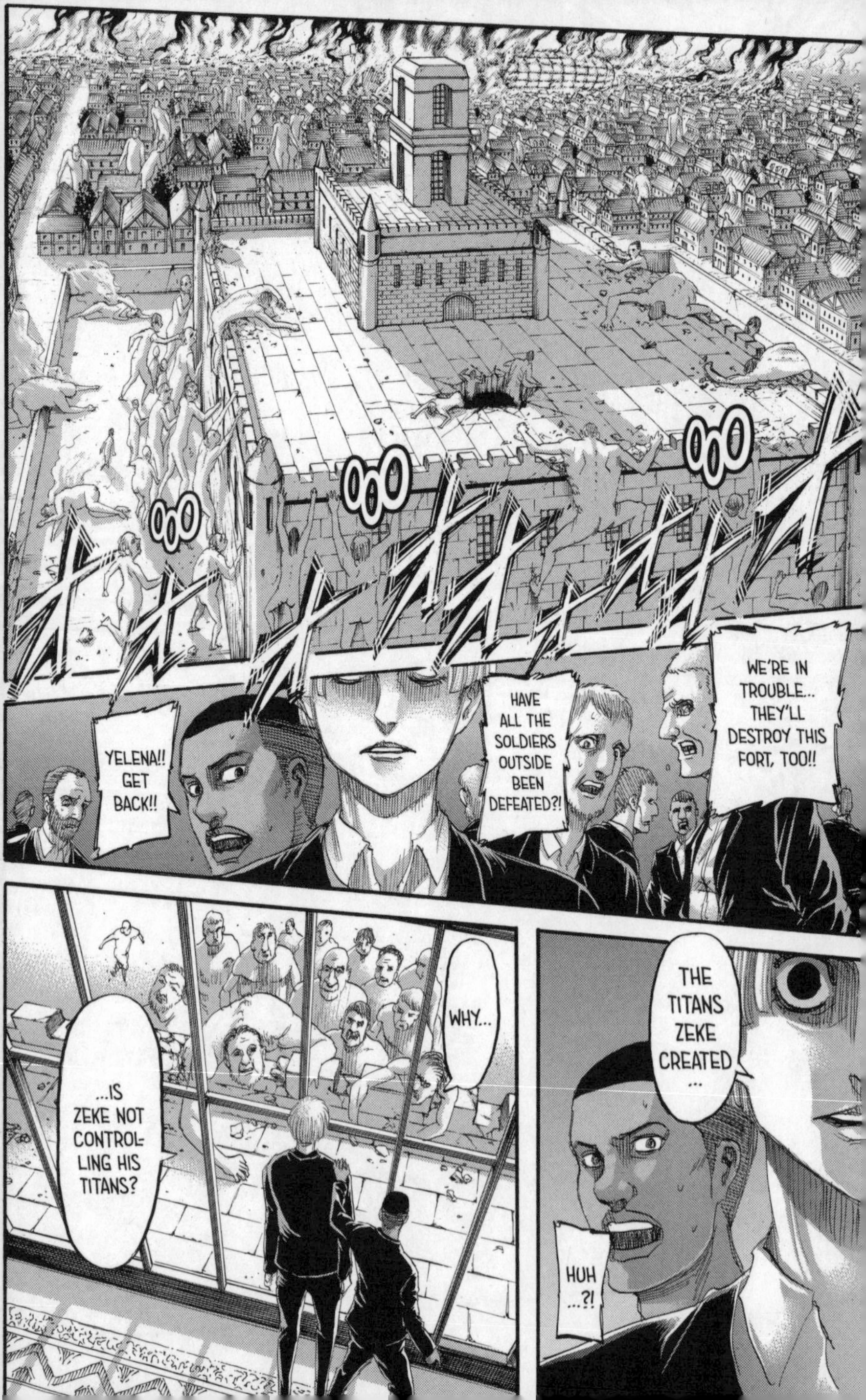
WE'RE IN TROUBLE... THEY'LL DESTROY THIS FORT, TOO!!
HAVE ALL THE SOLDIERS OUTSIDE BEEN DEFEATED?!
YELENA!! GET BACK!!
THE TITANS ZEKE CREATED ...
HUH ...?!
WHY...
...IS ZEKE NOT CONTROL-LING HIS TITANS?

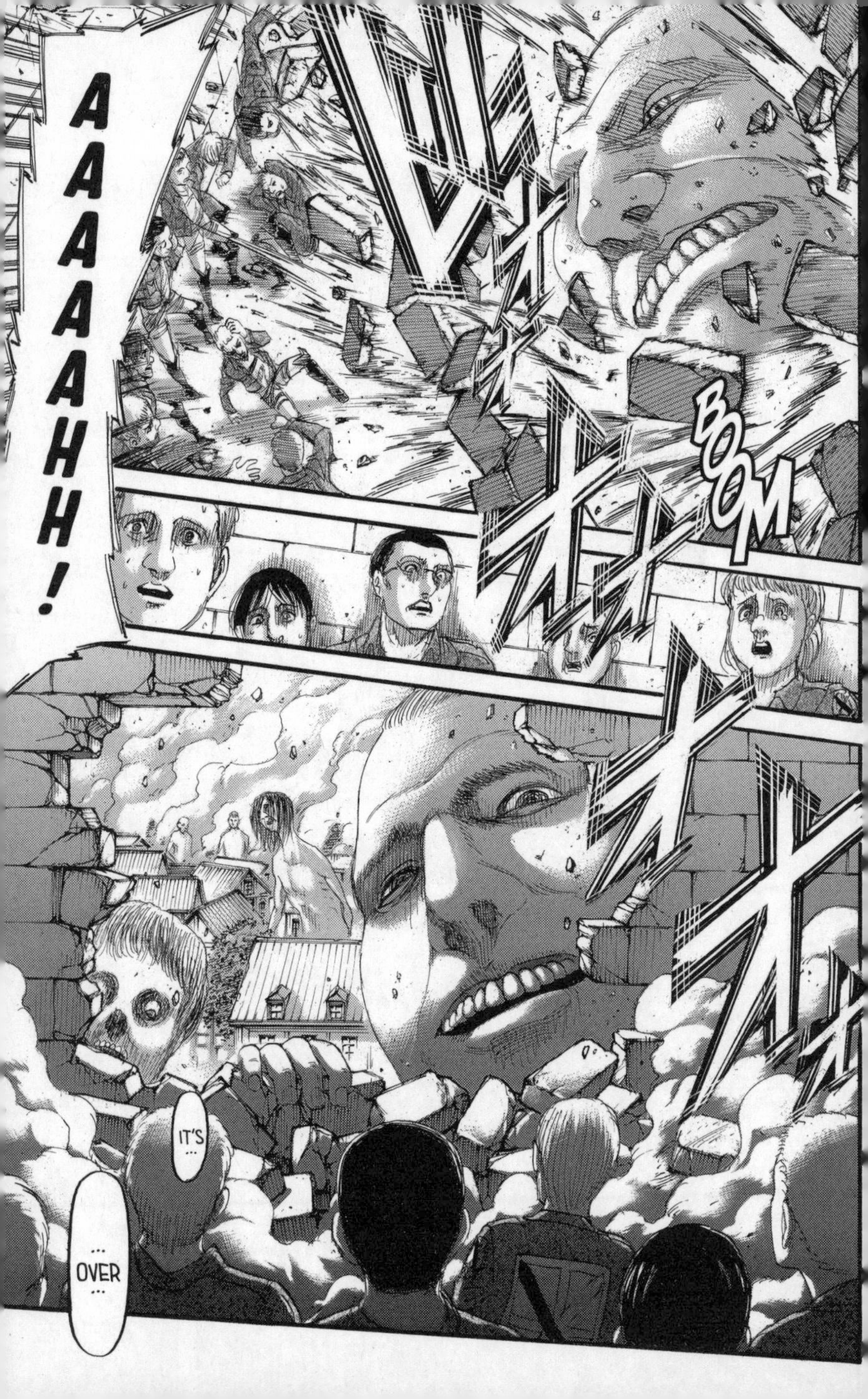

BOOM
AAAAAAHHH!
IT'S ...
... OVER ...

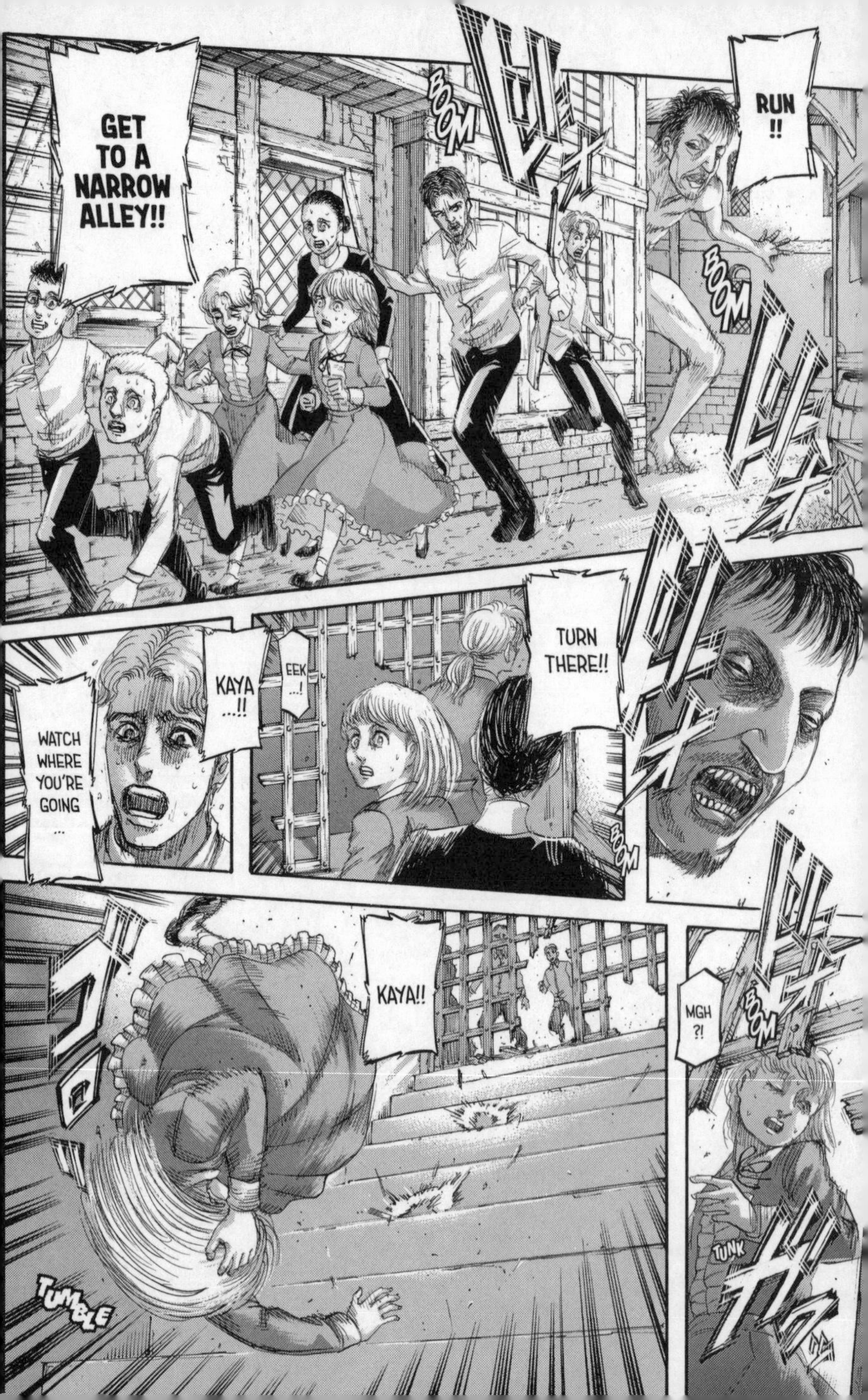
RUN!!
BOOM
BOOM
GET TO A NARROW ALLEY!!
BOOM
TURN THERE!!
EEK ...!
KAYA ...!!
WATCH WHERE YOU'RE GOING ...
BOOM
MGH ?!
TUNK
KAYA!!
TUMBLE

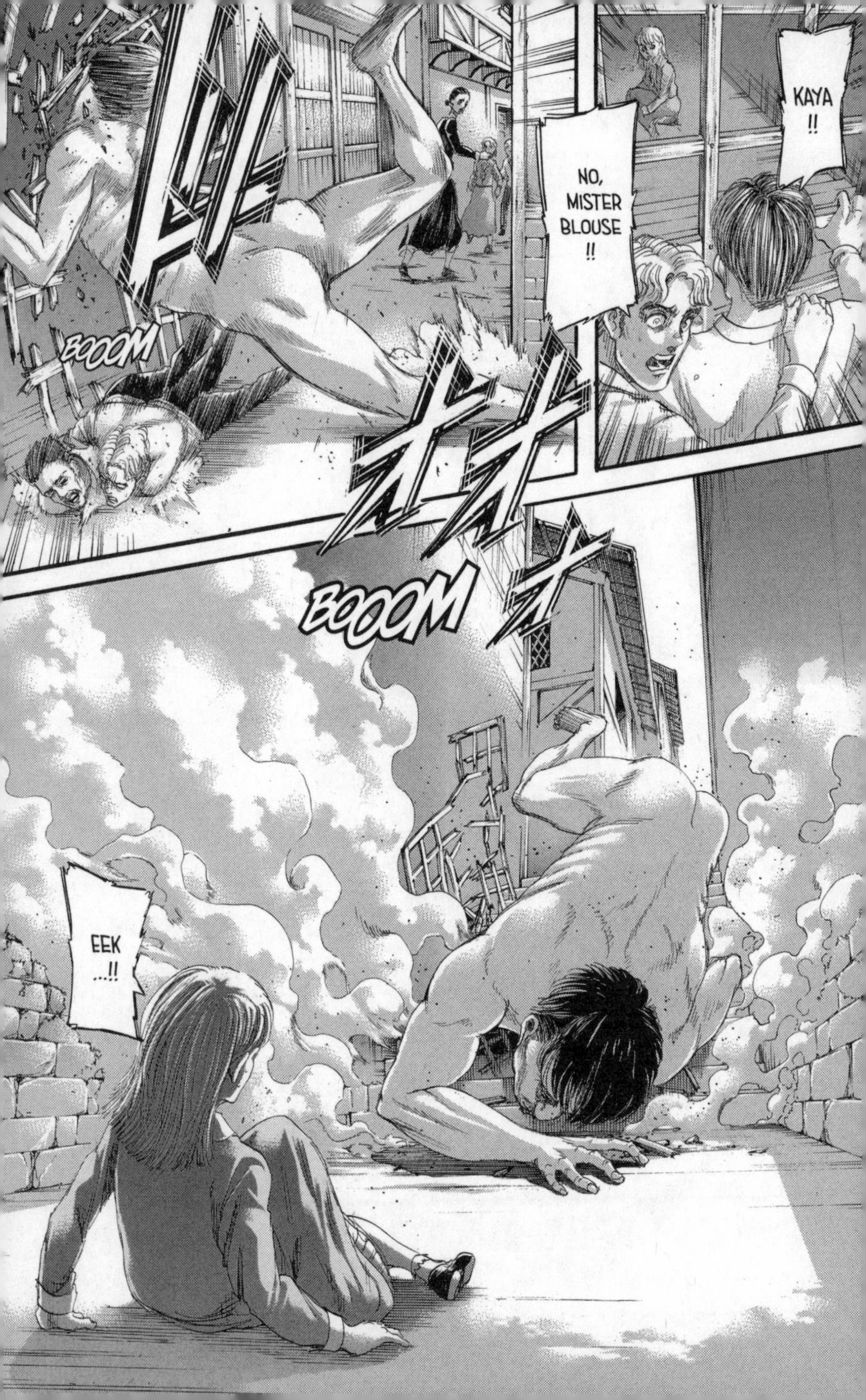
KAYA !!
NO, MISTER BLOUSE !!
BOOOM
BOOOM
EEK ...!!

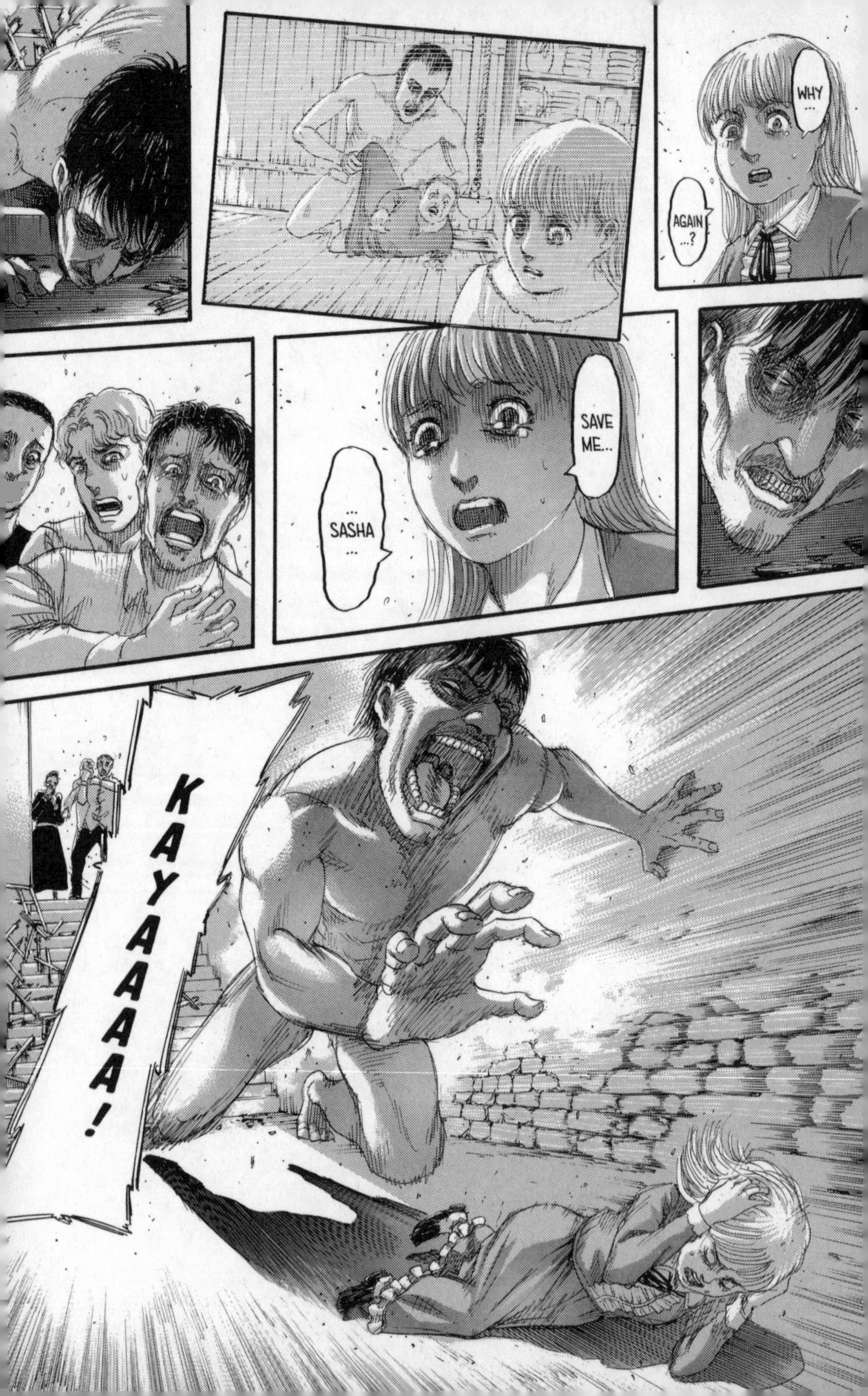

WHY ...
AGAIN ...?
SAVE ME...
... SASHA ...
KAYAAAAAA!

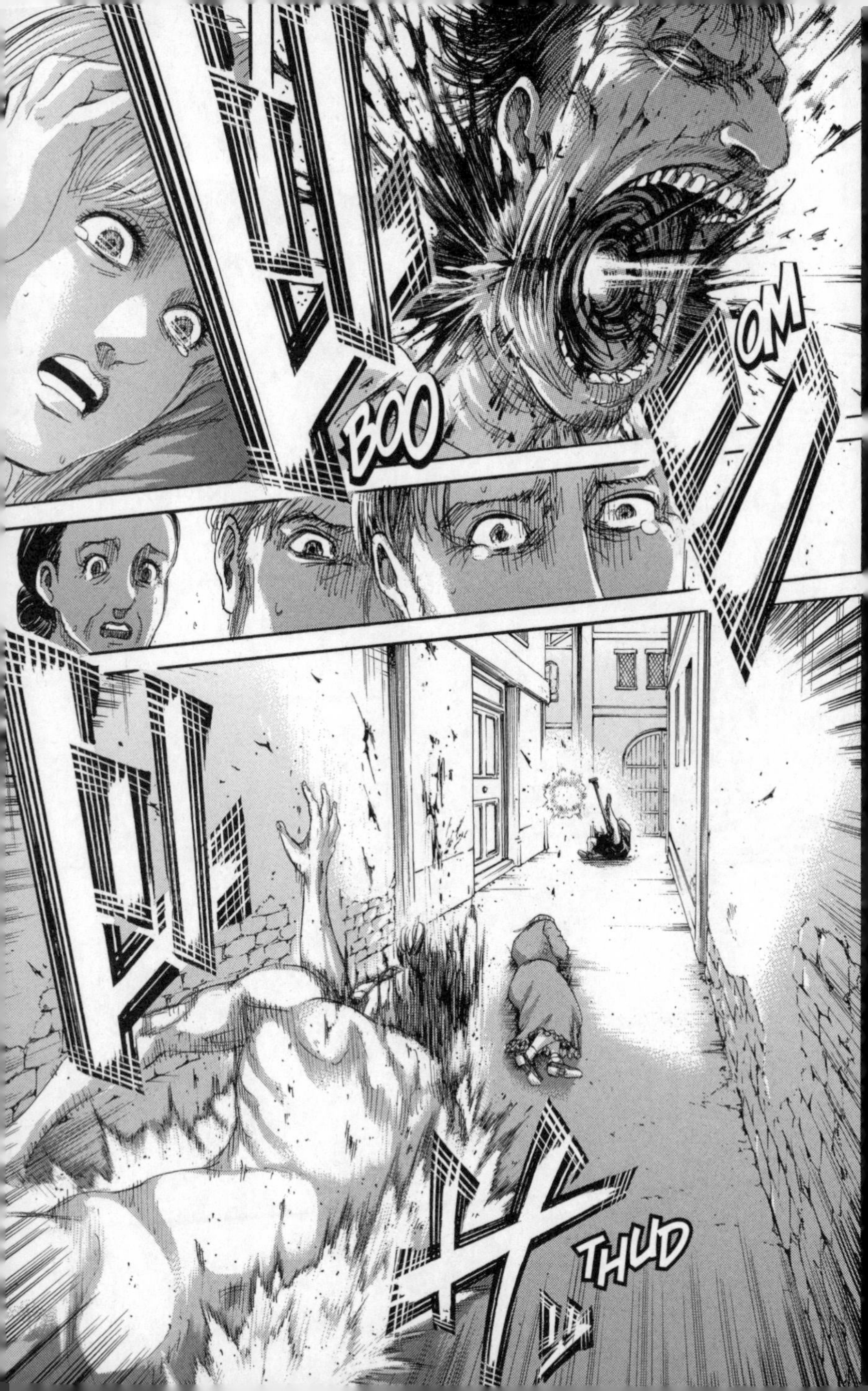
BOO
OM
THUD

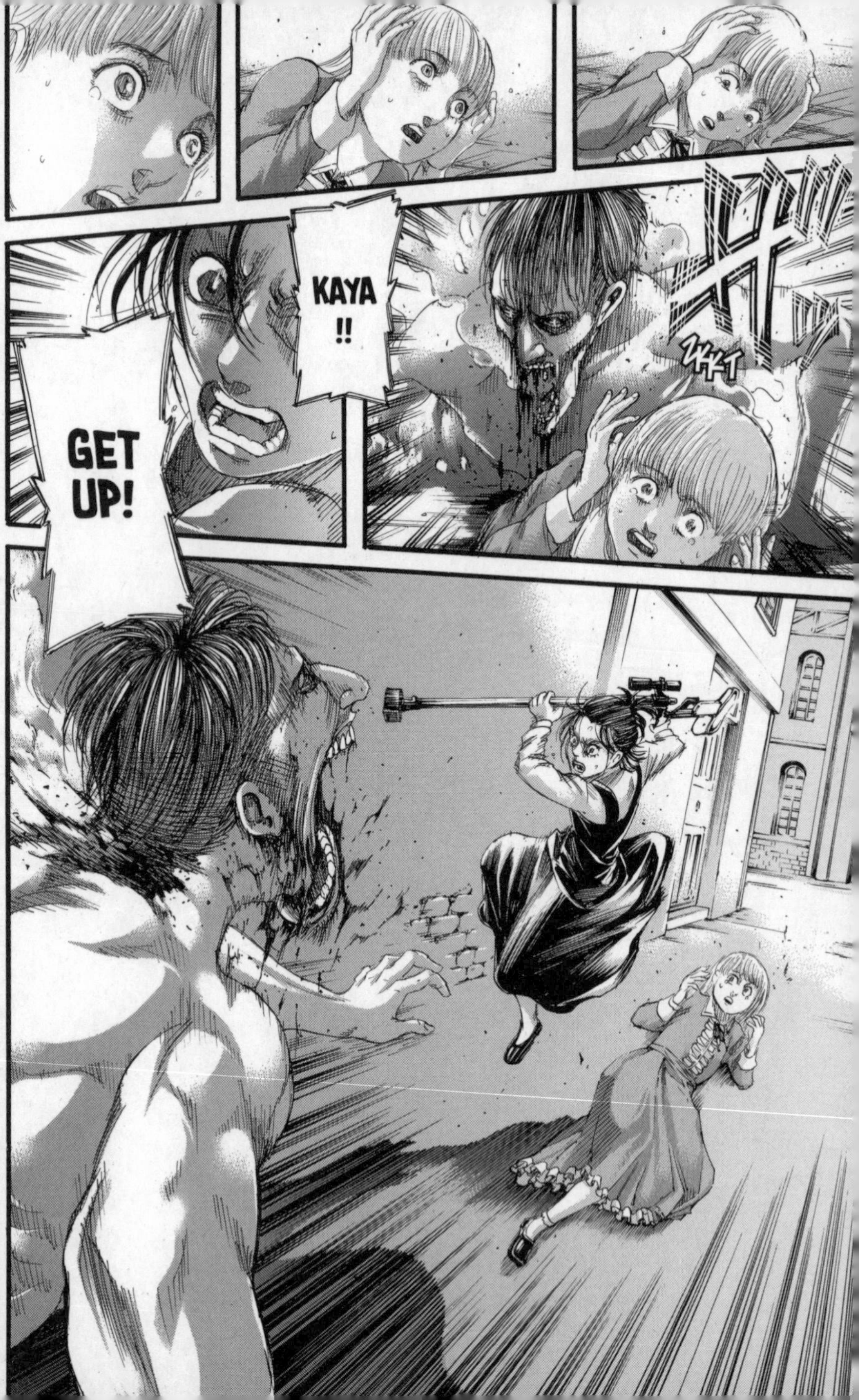
ZUKI
KAYA !!
GET UP!

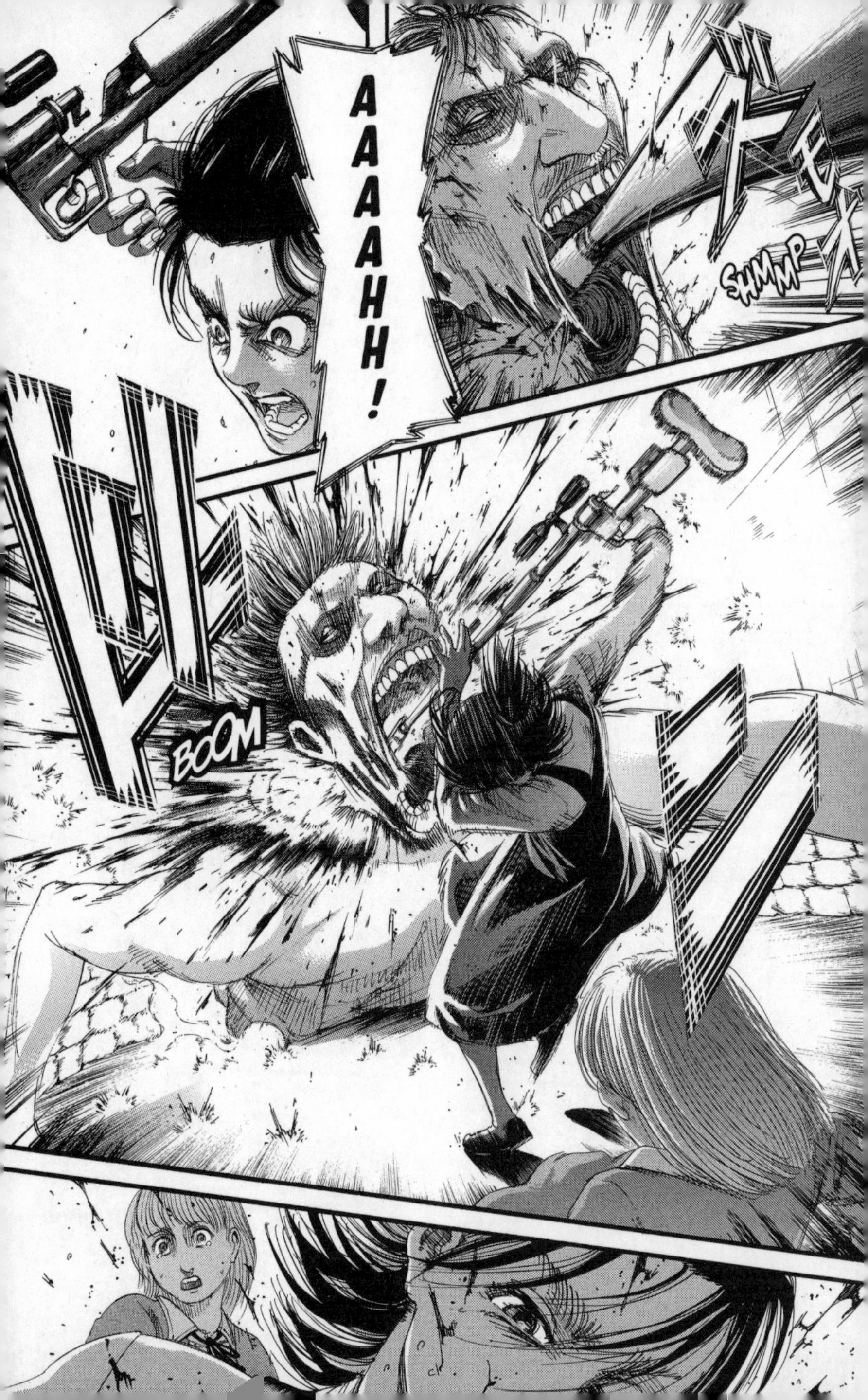
SHMMP
AAAAAHH!
BOOM

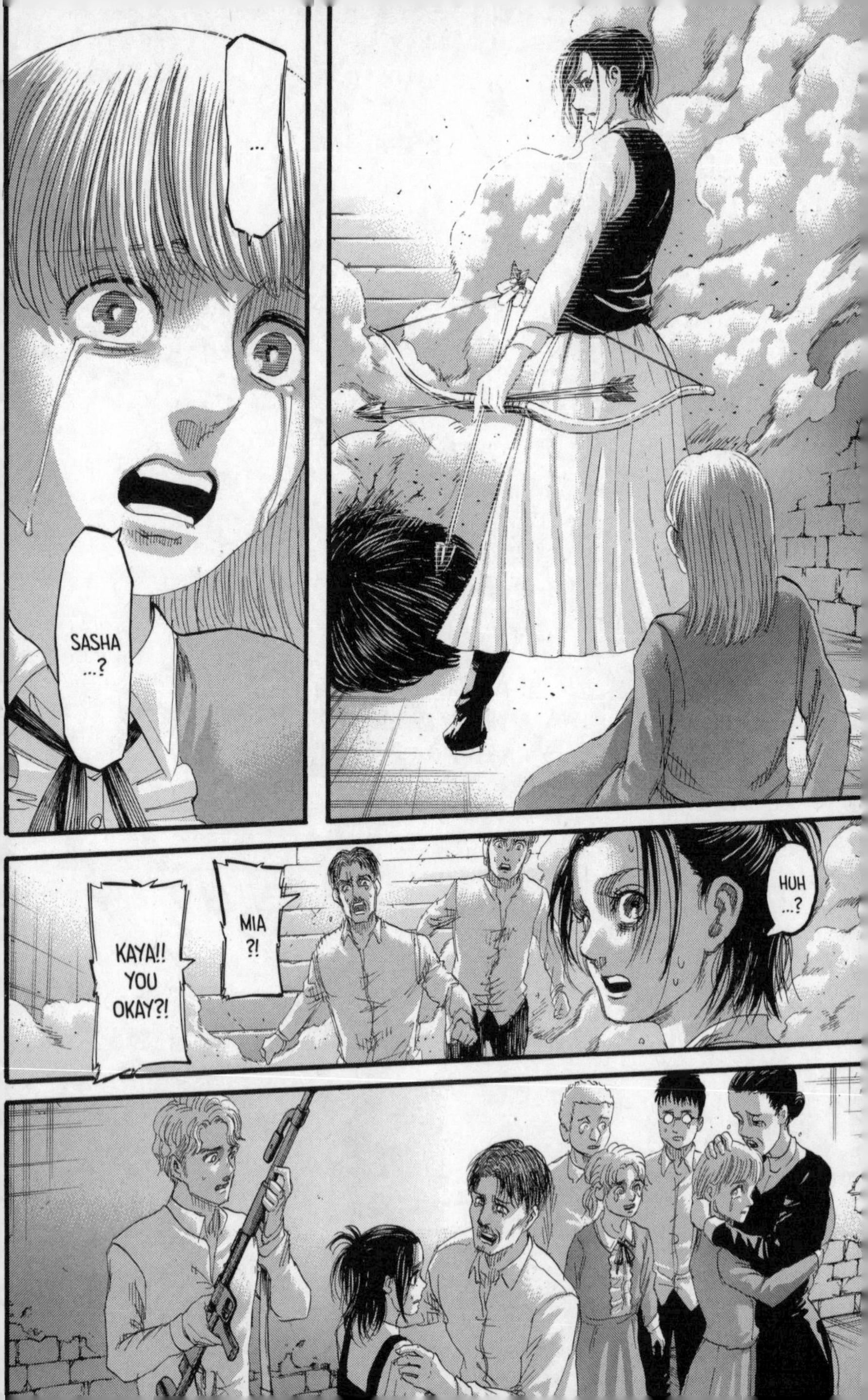
...
SASHA ...?
HUH ...?
MIA ?!
KAYA!! YOU OKAY?!

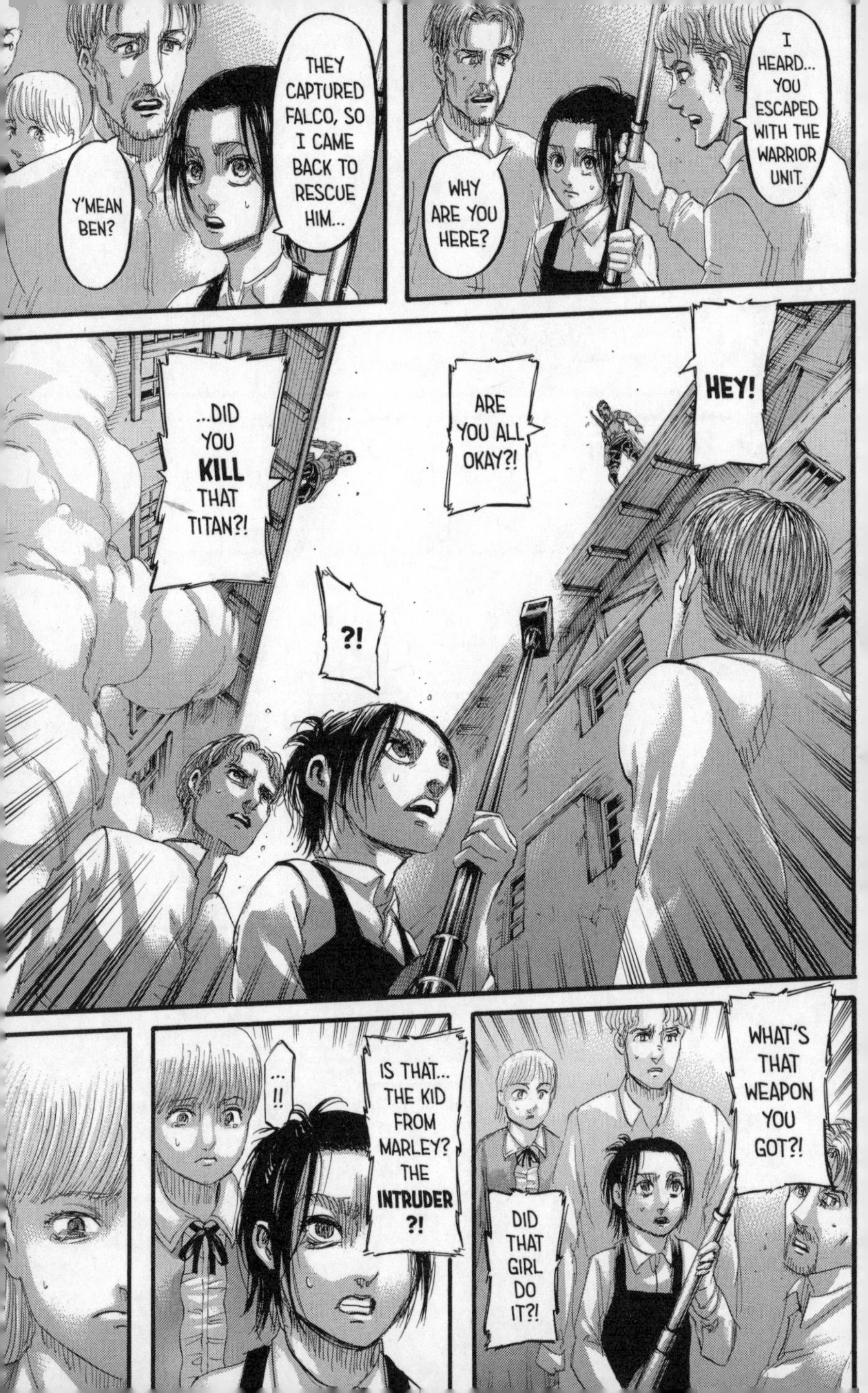
I HEARD... YOU ESCAPED WITH THE WARRIOR UNIT.
WHY ARE YOU HERE?
THEY CAPTURED FALCO, SO I CAME BACK TO RESCUE HIM...
Y'MEAN BEN?
HEY!
ARE YOU ALL OKAY?!
...DID YOU KILL THAT TITAN?!
?!
WHAT'S THAT WEAPON YOU GOT?!
DID THAT GIRL DO IT?!
IS THAT... THE KID FROM MARLEY? THE INTRUDER?!
...!!

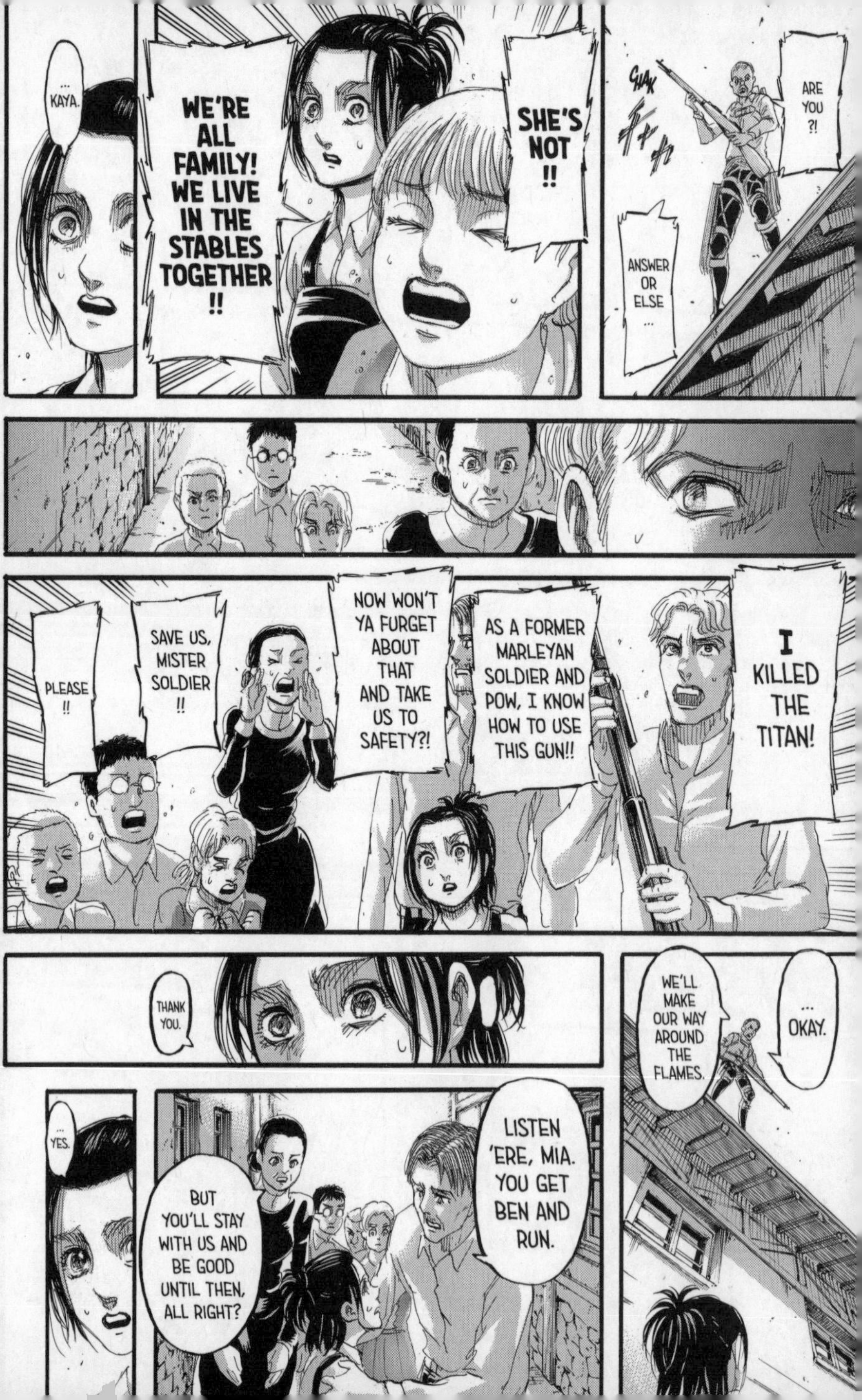
ARE YOU ?!
ANSWER OR ELSE ...
SHE'S NOT !!
WE'RE ALL FAMILY! WE LIVE IN THE STABLES TOGETHER !!
... KAYA.
I KILLED THE TITAN!
AS A FORMER MARLEYAN SOLDIER AND POW, I KNOW HOW TO USE THIS GUN!!
NOW WON'T YA FURGET ABOUT THAT AND TAKE US TO SAFETY?!
SAVE US, MISTER SOLDIER !!
PLEASE !!
... OKAY.
WE'LL MAKE OUR WAY AROUND THE FLAMES.
THANK YOU.
LISTEN 'ERE, MIA. YOU GET BEN AND RUN.
BUT YOU'LL STAY WITH US AND BE GOOD UNTIL THEN, ALL RIGHT?
... YES.

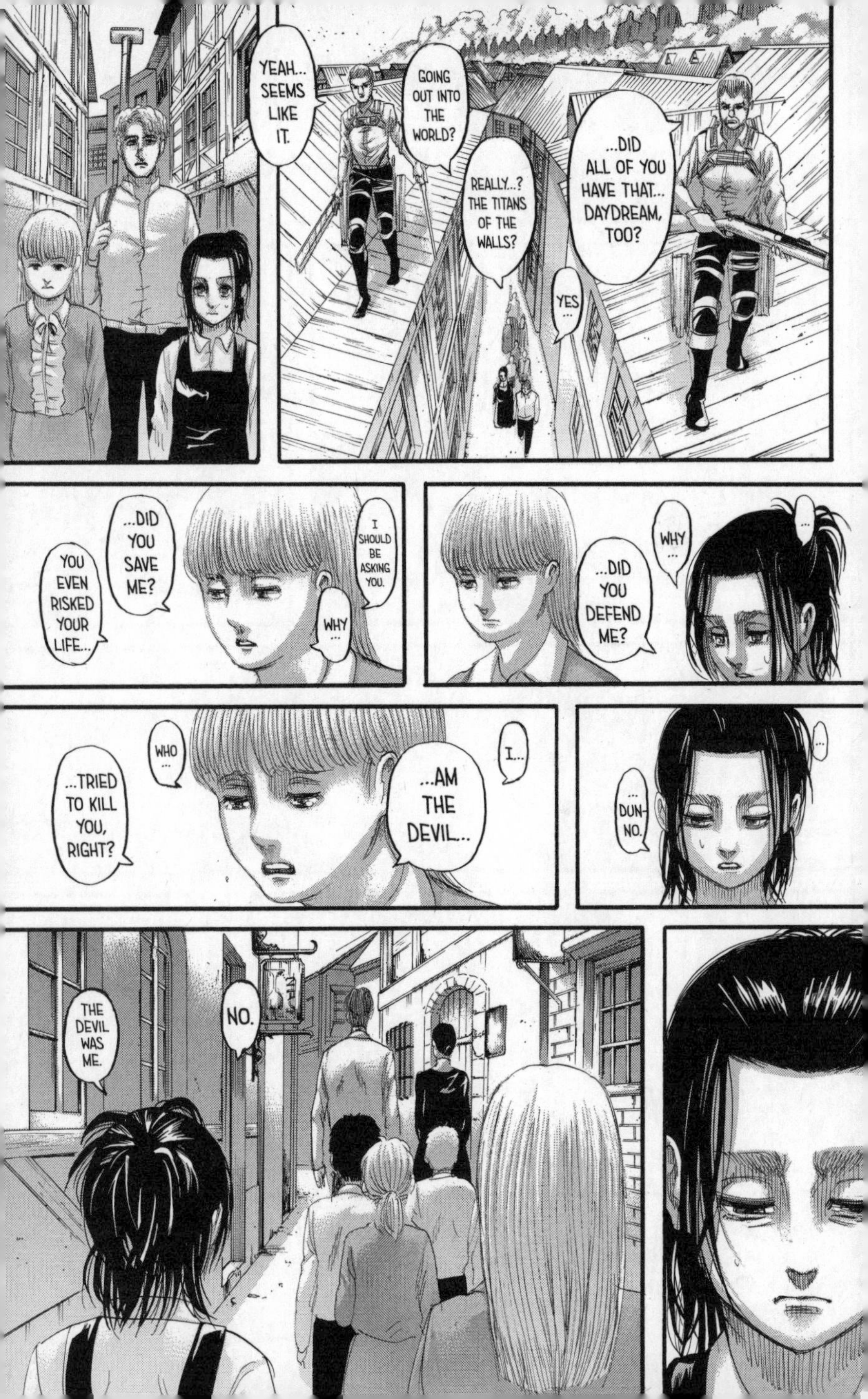
...DID ALL OF YOU HAVE THAT... DAYDREAM, TOO?
YES...
REALLY...? THE TITANS OF THE WALLS?
GOING OUT INTO THE WORLD?
YEAH... SEEMS LIKE IT.
WHY...
...DID YOU DEFEND ME?
I SHOULD BE ASKING YOU.
WHY...
...DID YOU SAVE ME?
YOU EVEN RISKED YOUR LIFE...
...
...DUN-NO.
I...
...AM THE DEVIL...
WHO...
...TRIED TO KILL YOU, RIGHT?
NO.
THE DEVIL WAS ME.

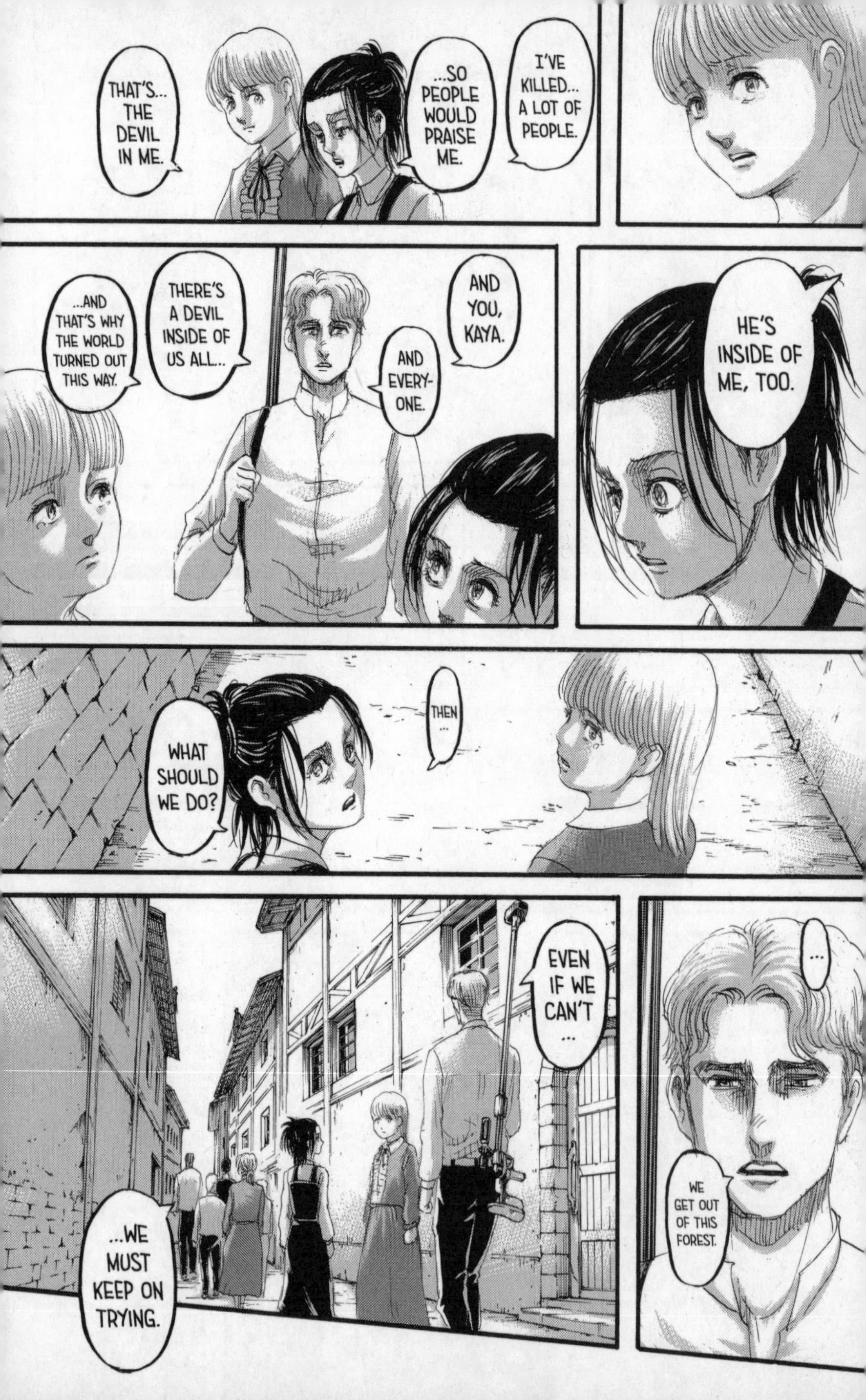
I'VE KILLED... A LOT OF PEOPLE.
...SO PEOPLE WOULD PRAISE ME.
THAT'S... THE DEVIL IN ME.
HE'S INSIDE OF ME, TOO.
AND YOU, KAYA.
AND EVERY-ONE.
THERE'S A DEVIL INSIDE OF US ALL...
...AND THAT'S WHY THE WORLD TURNED OUT THIS WAY.
THEN...
WHAT SHOULD WE DO?
...
WE GET OUT OF THIS FOREST.
EVEN IF WE CAN'T...
...WE MUST KEEP ON TRYING.

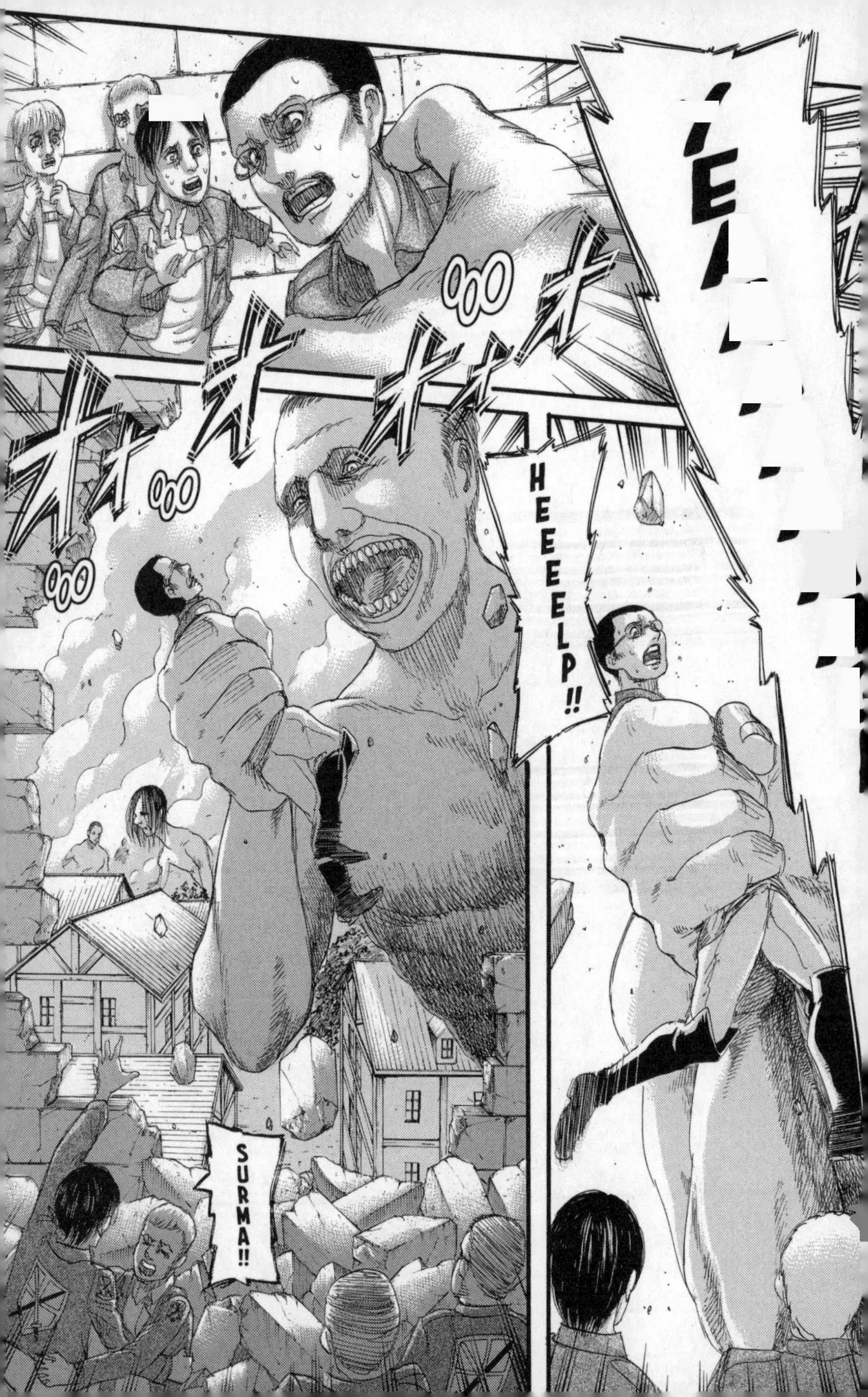
HEEEEELP!!
SURMA!!

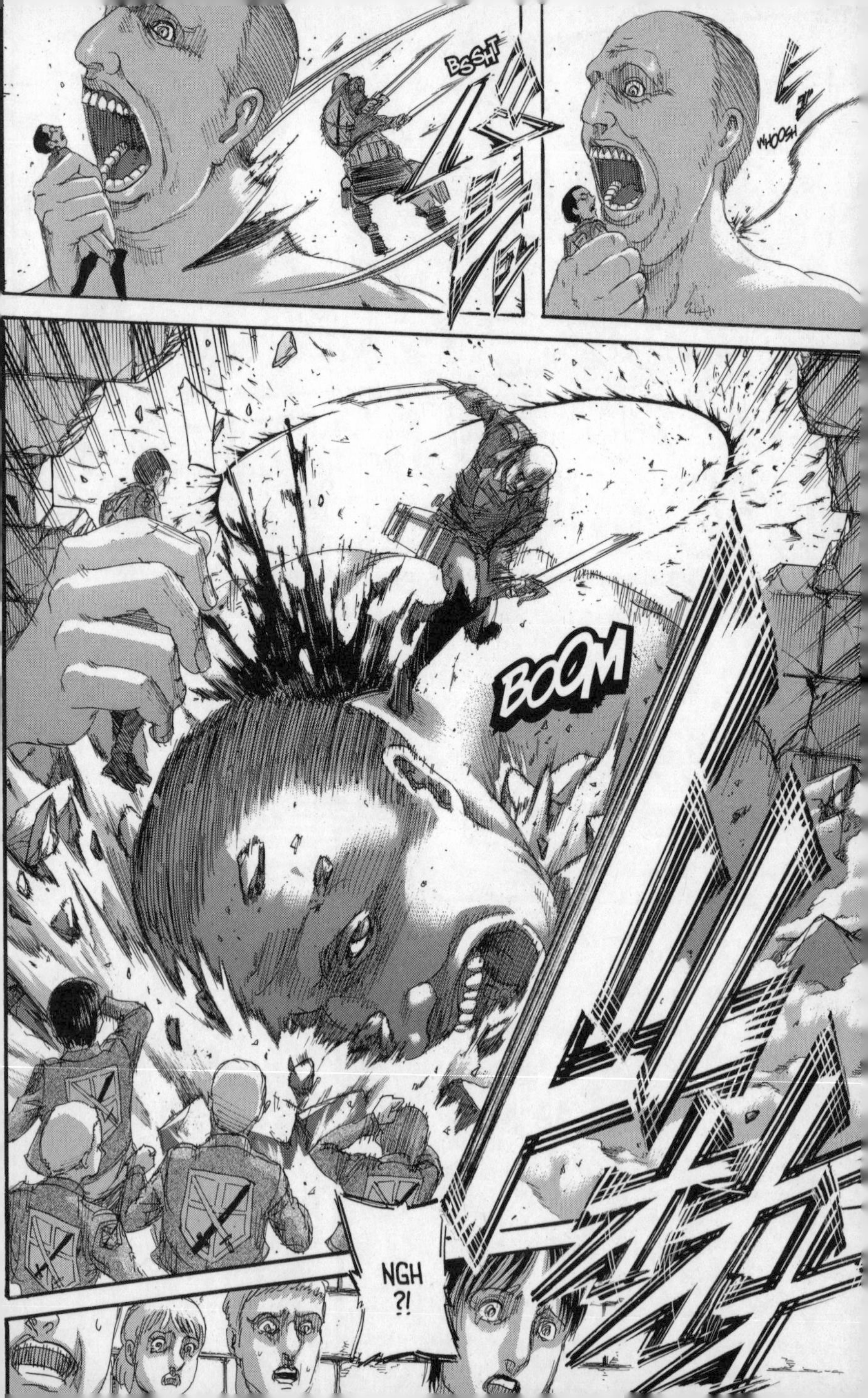
WHOOSH
BSSHT
BOOM
NGH ?!

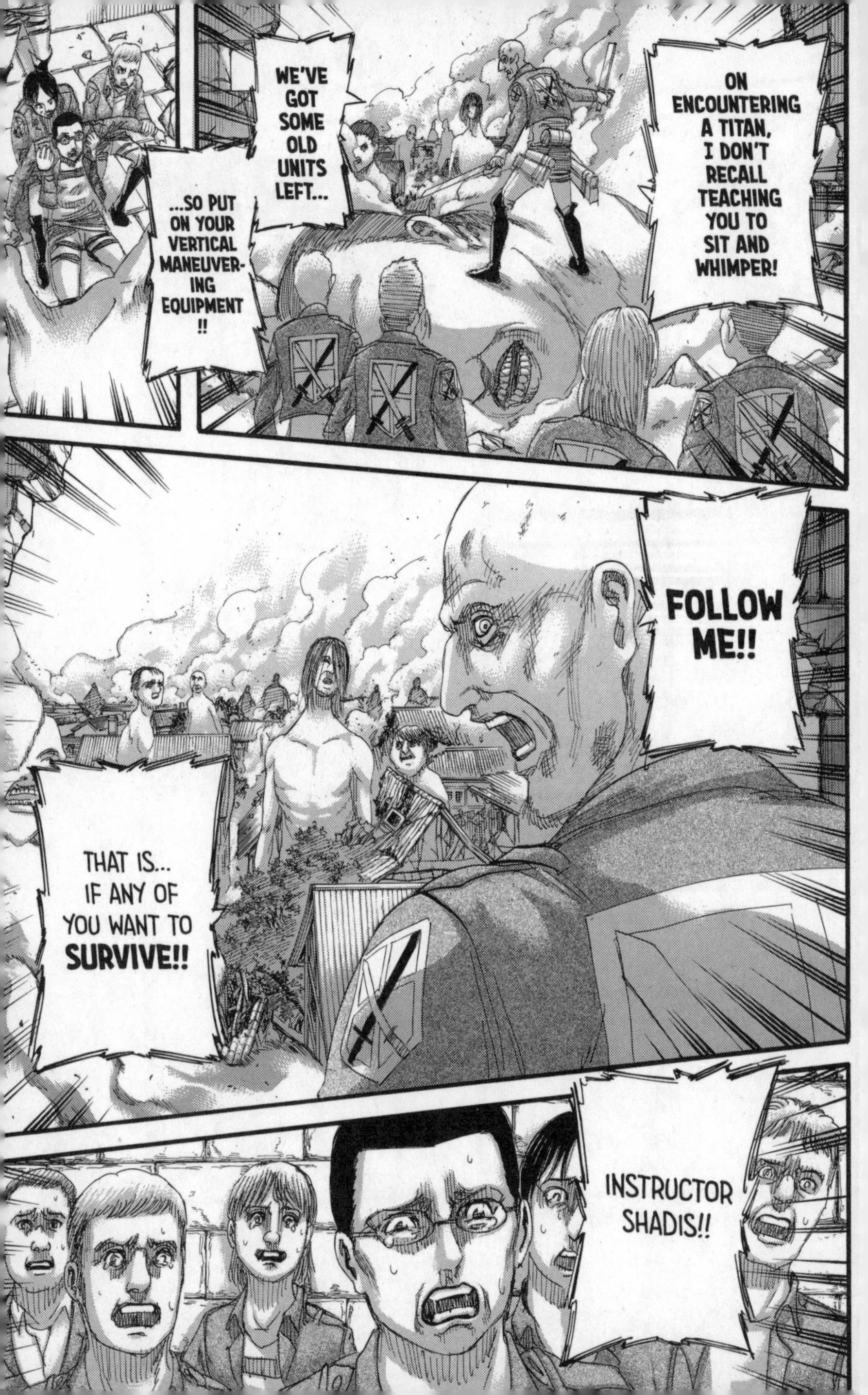
ON ENCOUNTERING A TITAN, I DON'T RECALL TEACHING YOU TO SIT AND WHIMPER!
WE'VE GOT SOME OLD UNITS LEFT...
...SO PUT ON YOUR VERTICAL MANEUVER-ING EQUIPMENT !!
FOLLOW ME!!
THAT IS... IF ANY OF YOU WANT TO **SURVIVE!!**
INSTRUCTOR SHADIS!!

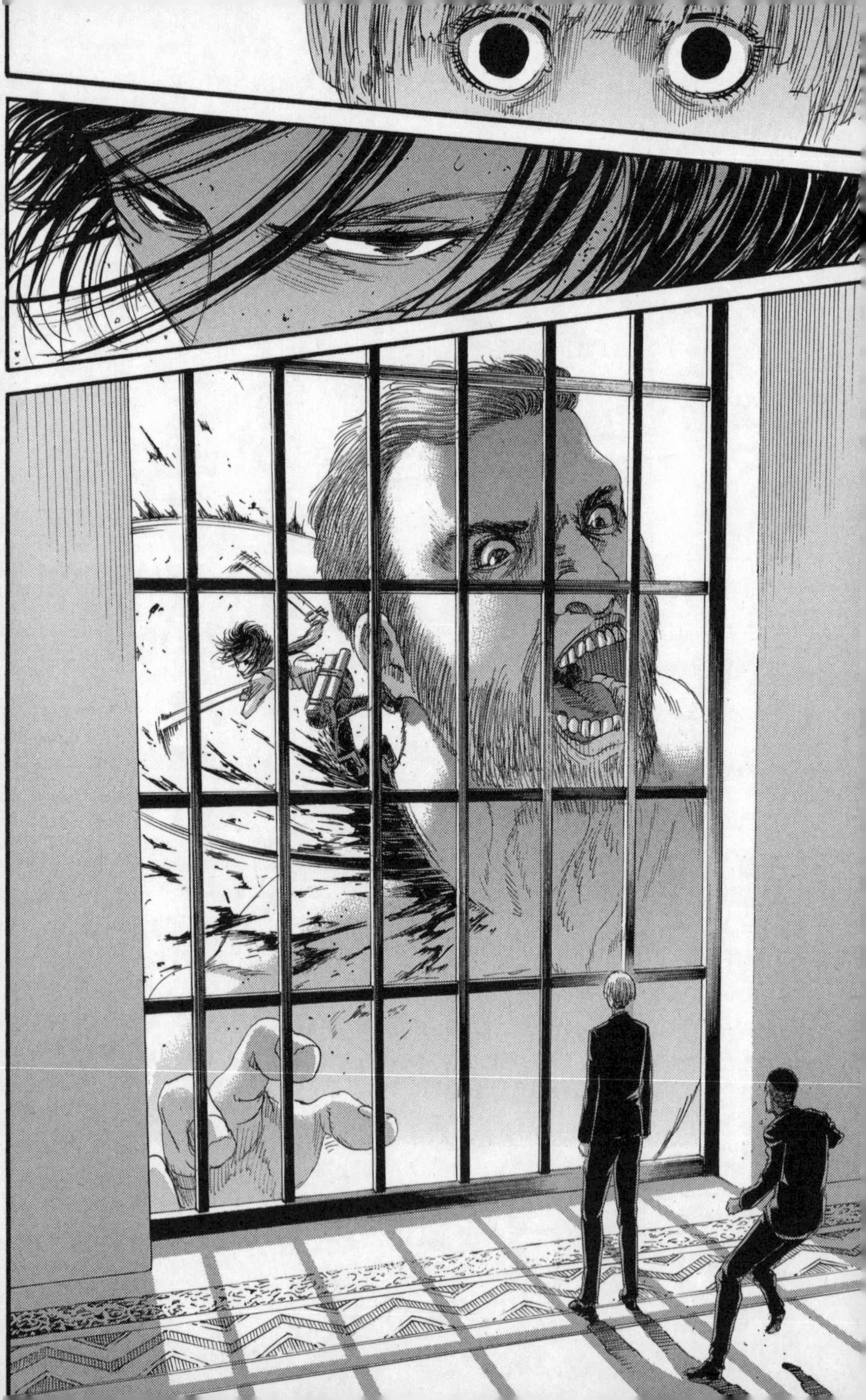

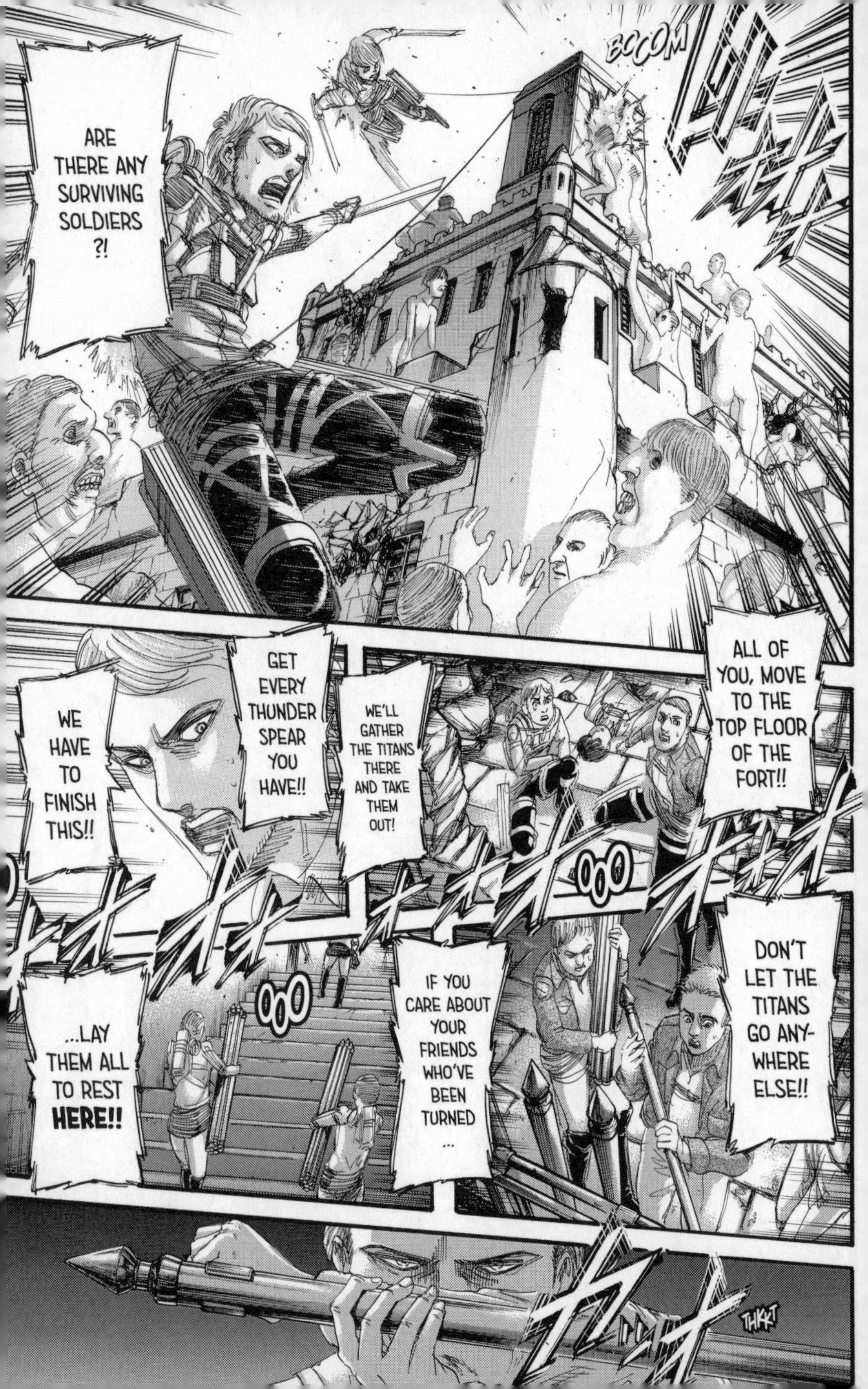

BOOOM
ARE THERE ANY SURVIVING SOLDIERS ?!
ALL OF YOU, MOVE TO THE TOP FLOOR OF THE FORT!!
WE'LL GATHER THE TITANS THERE AND TAKE THEM OUT!
GET EVERY THUNDER SPEAR YOU HAVE!!
WE HAVE TO FINISH THIS!!
DON'T LET THE TITANS GO ANY-WHERE ELSE!!
IF YOU CARE ABOUT YOUR FRIENDS WHO'VE BEEN TURNED ...
...LAY THEM ALL TO REST **HERE!!**
THKKT

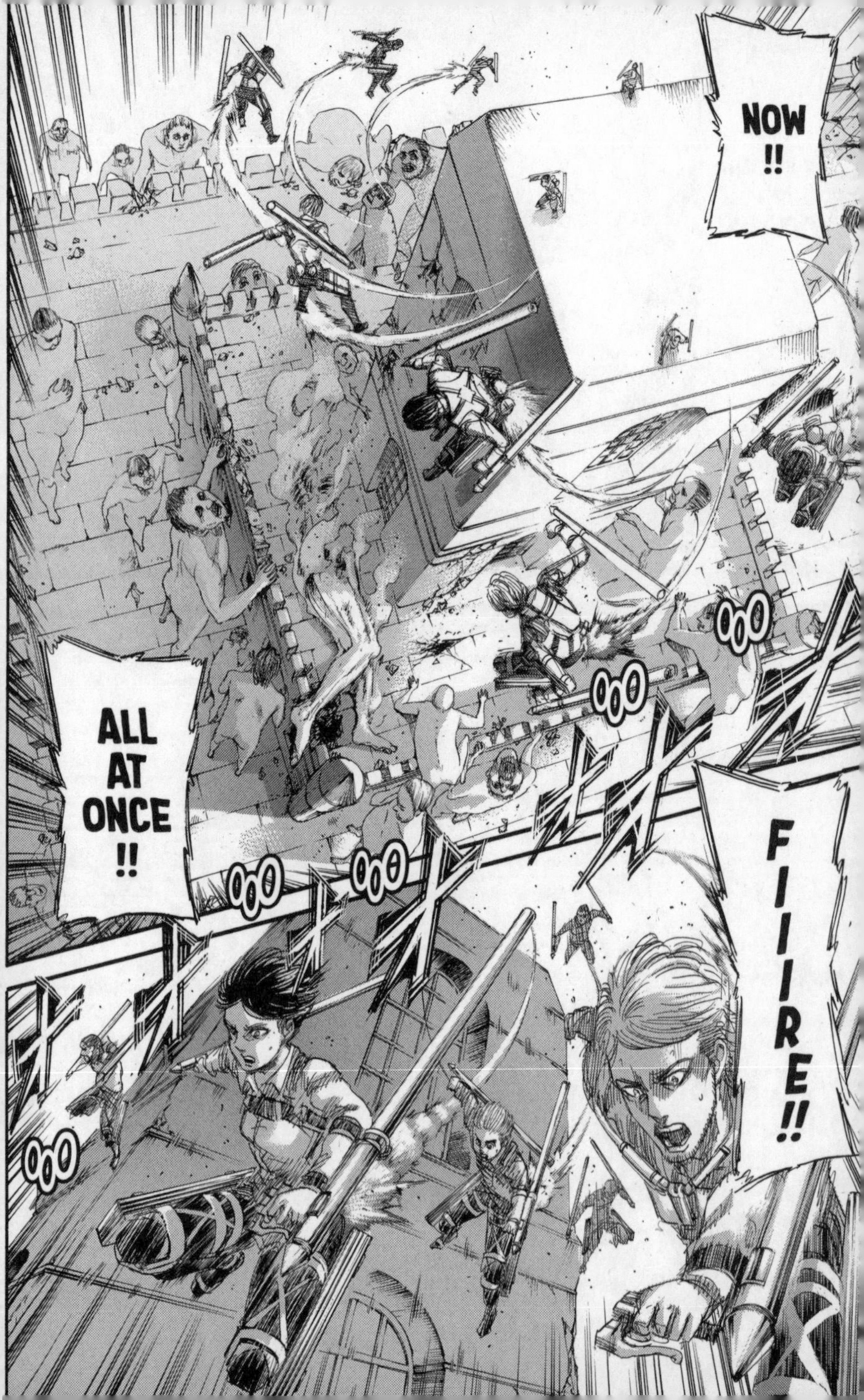
NOW!!
ALL AT ONCE!!
FIIIRE!!

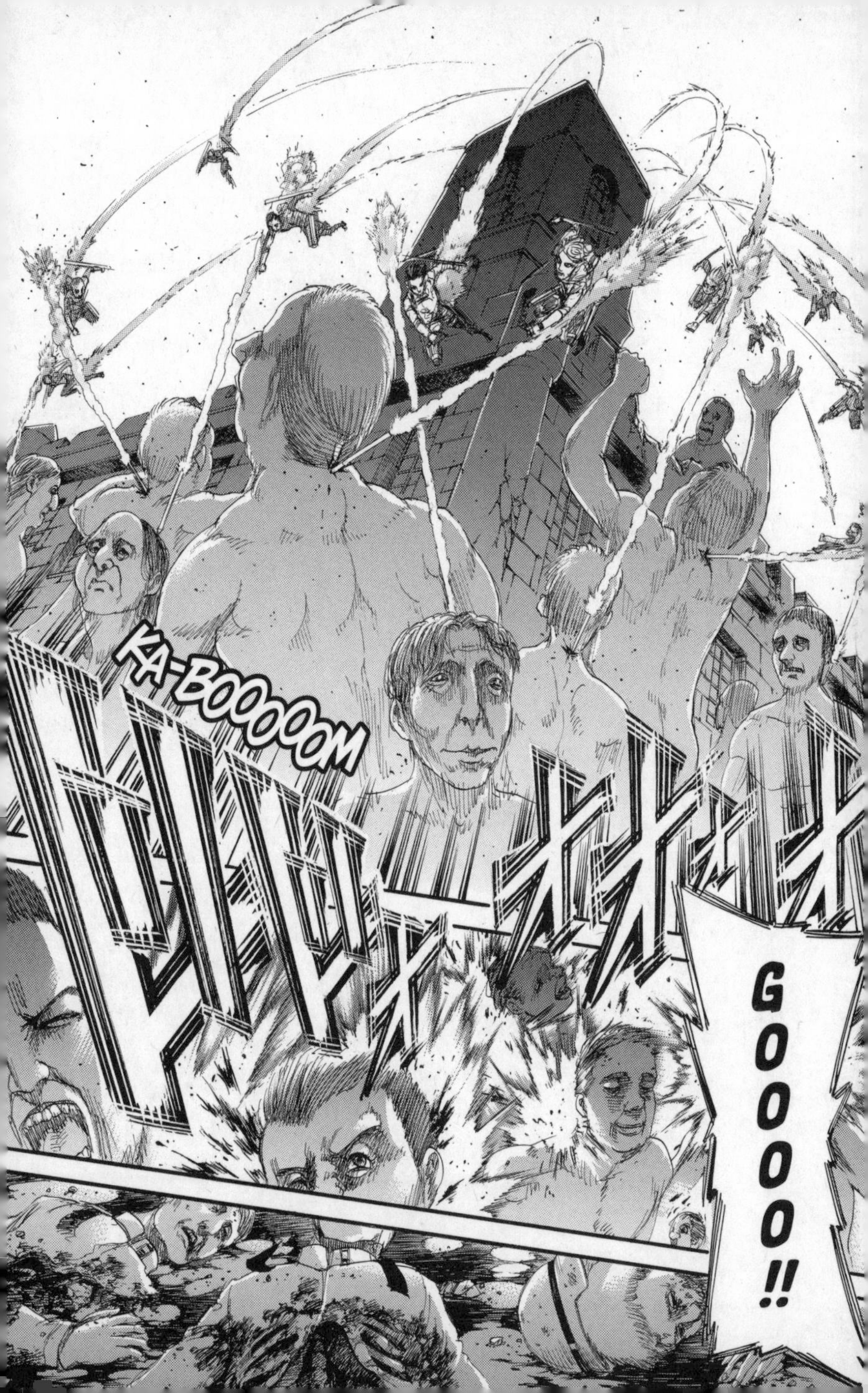
KA-BOOOOOM
GOOOOO!!

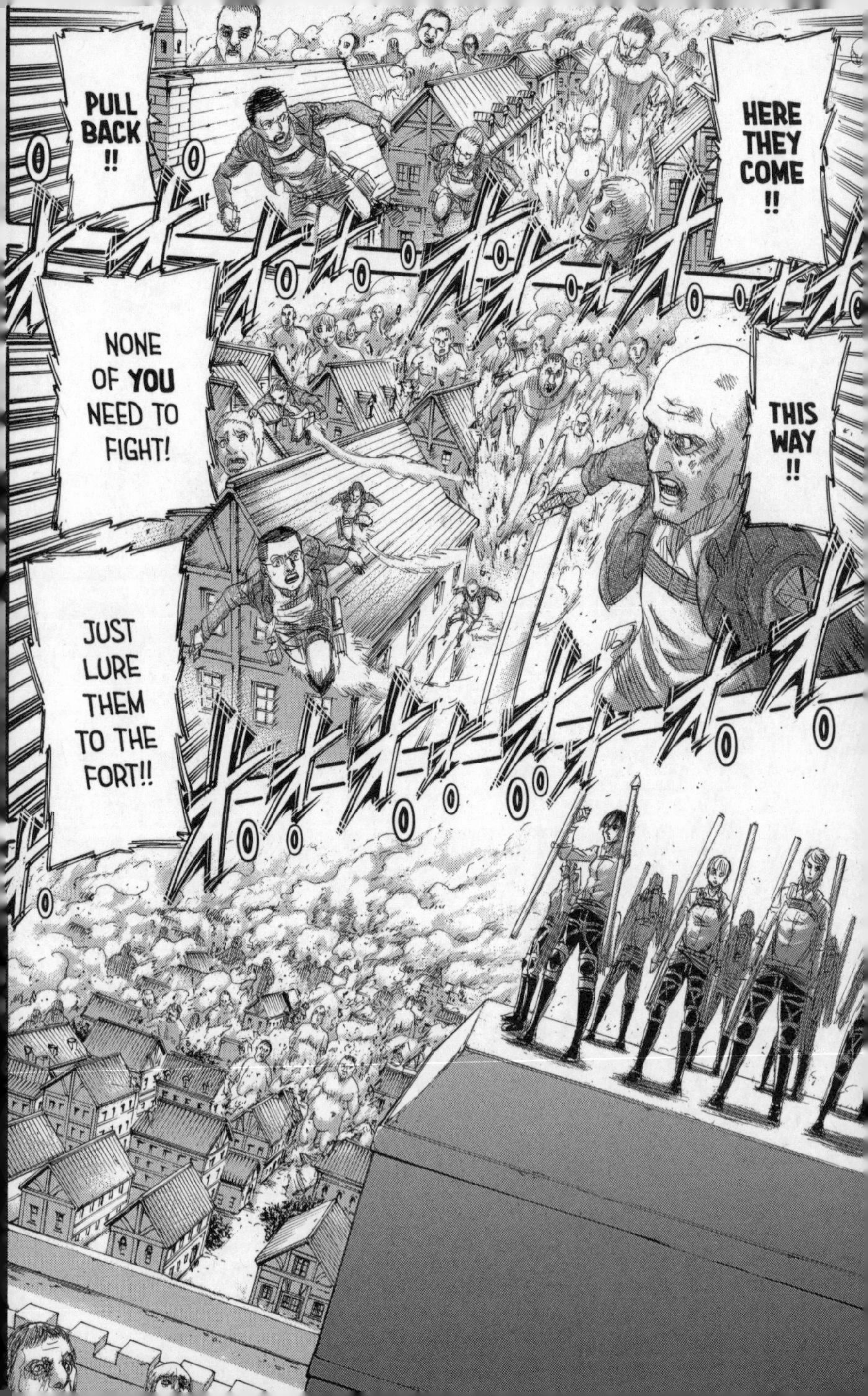
HERE THEY COME!!
PULL BACK!!
THIS WAY!!
NONE OF **YOU** NEED TO FIGHT!
JUST LURE THEM TO THE FORT!!

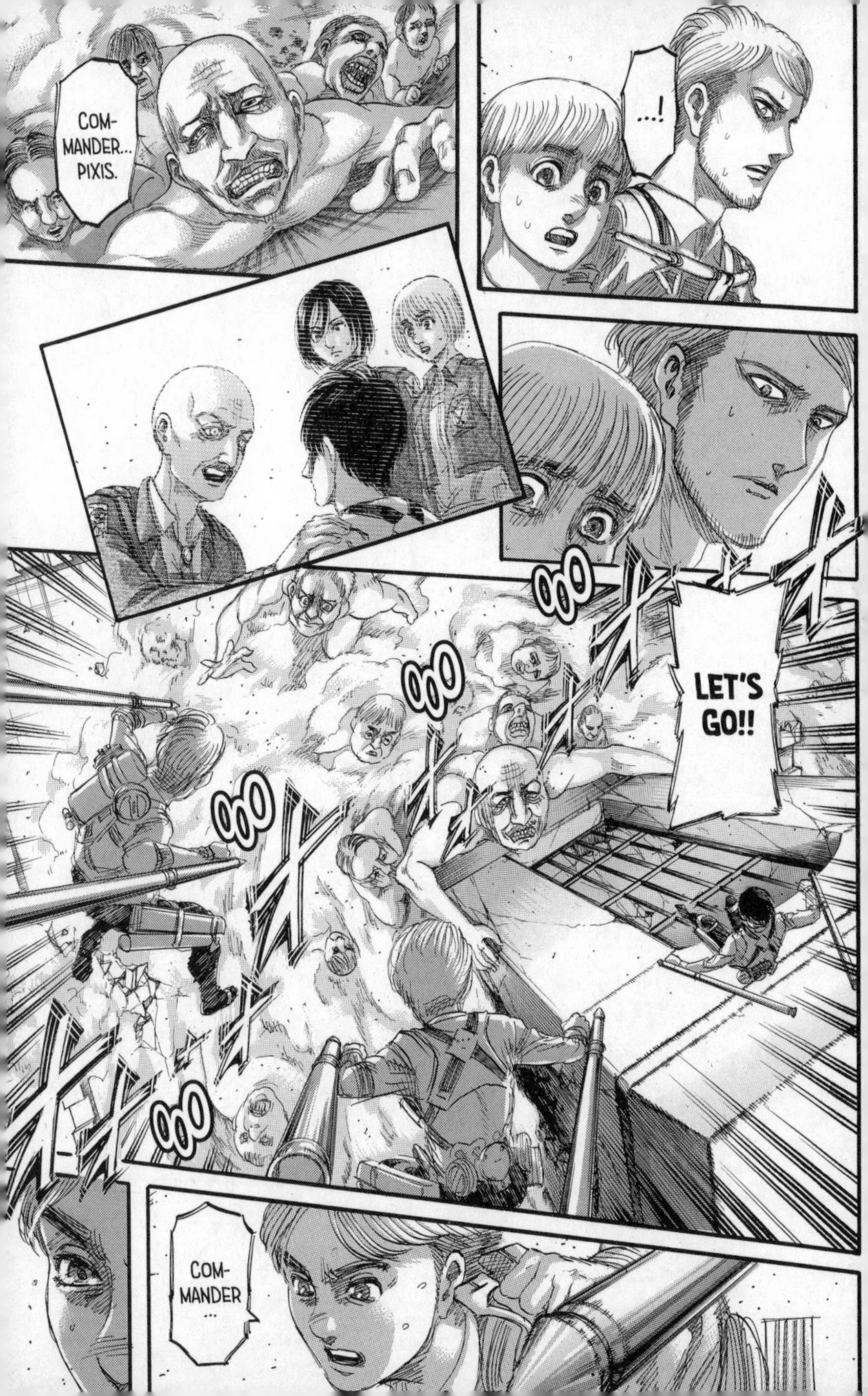

...!
COM-MANDER... PIXIS.
OOO
LET'S GO!!
OOO
OOO
OOO
COM-MANDER ...

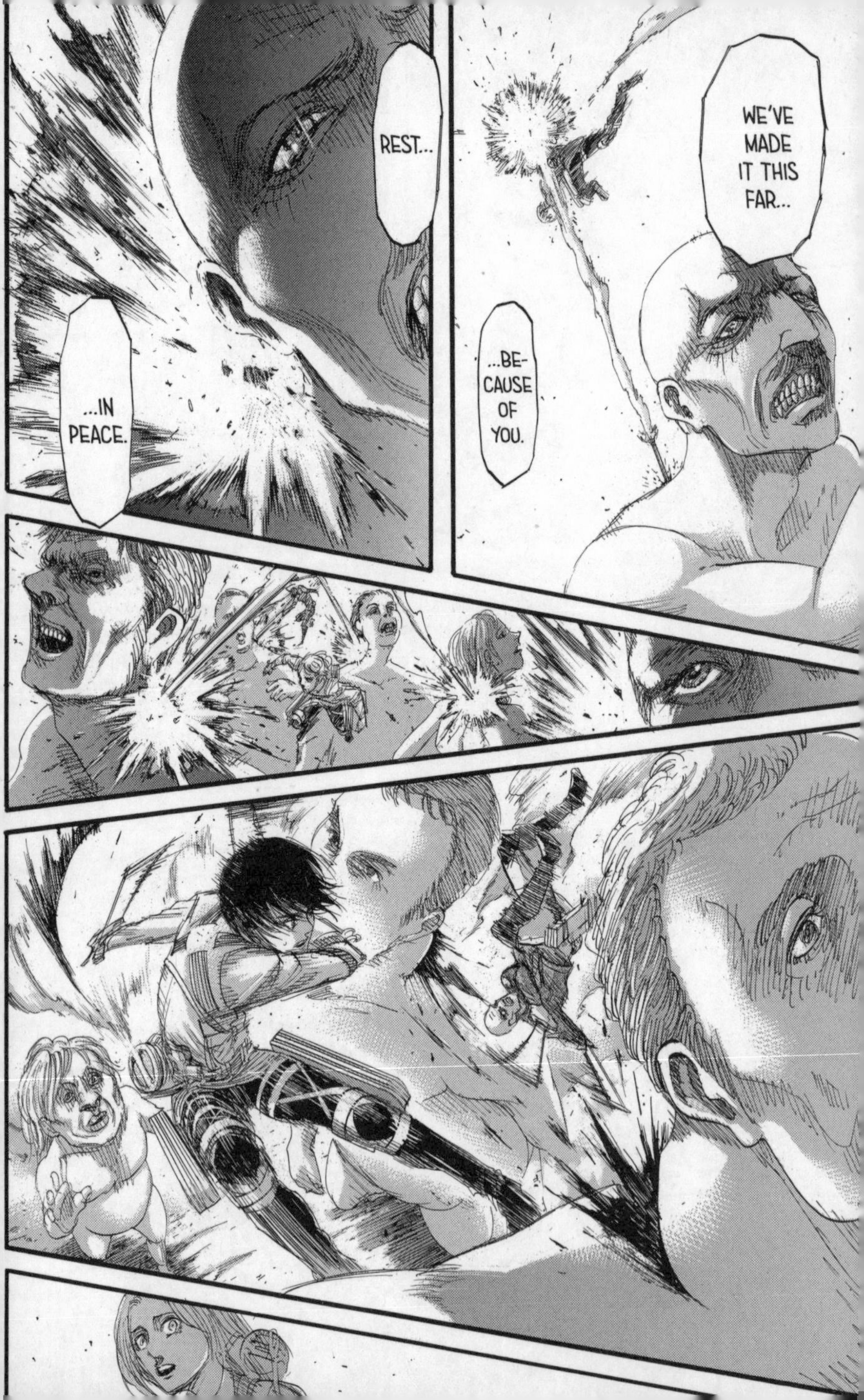
WE'VE MADE IT THIS FAR...
...BE-CAUSE OF YOU.
REST...
...IN PEACE.

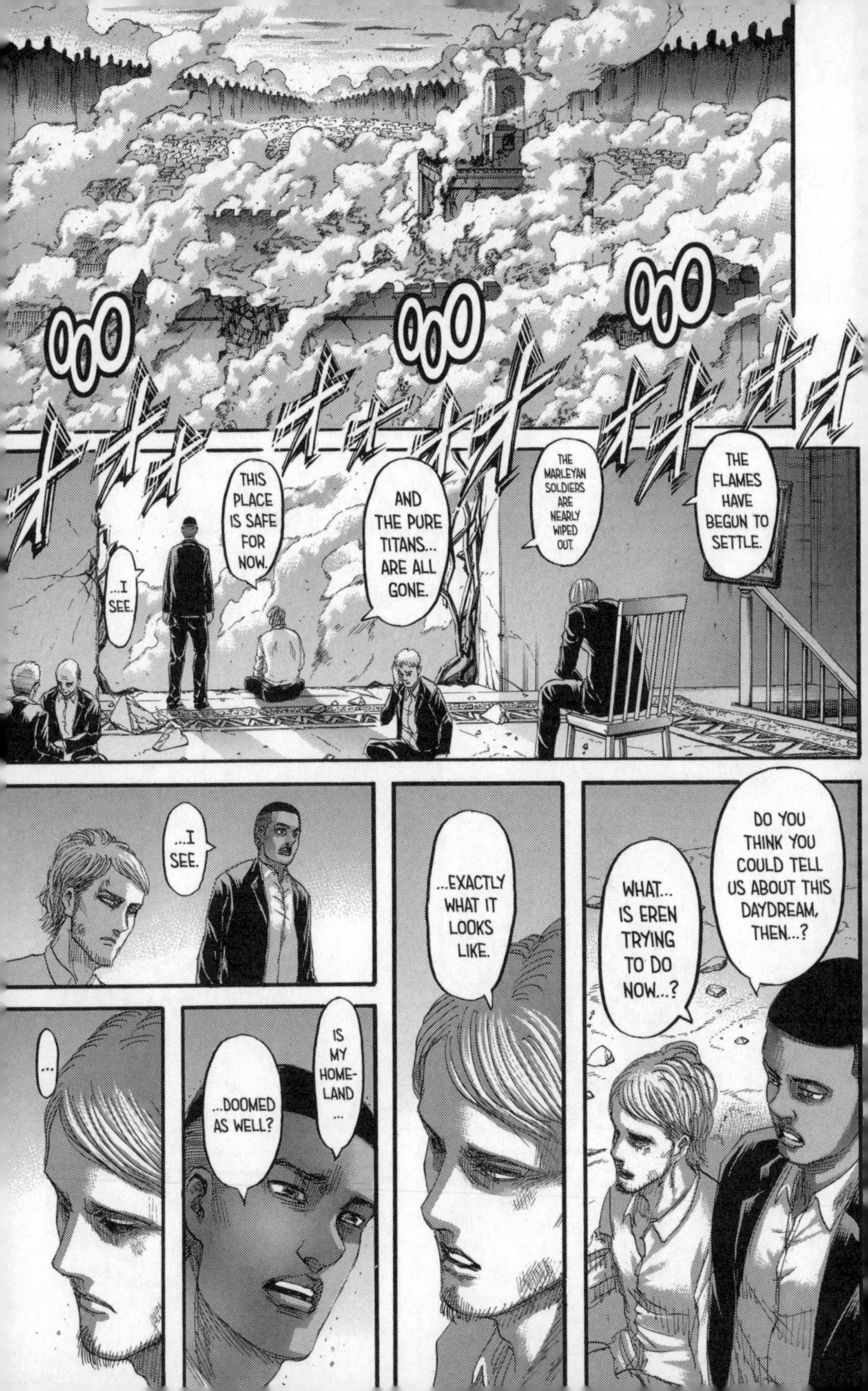
OOO
OOO
OOO
THE FLAMES HAVE BEGUN TO SETTLE.
THE MARLEYAN SOLDIERS ARE NEARLY WIPED OUT.
AND THE PURE TITANS... ARE ALL GONE.
THIS PLACE IS SAFE FOR NOW.
...I SEE.
DO YOU THINK YOU COULD TELL US ABOUT THIS DAYDREAM, THEN...?
WHAT... IS EREN TRYING TO DO NOW...?
...EXACTLY WHAT IT LOOKS LIKE.
...I SEE.
IS MY HOMELAND...
...DOOMED AS WELL?
...

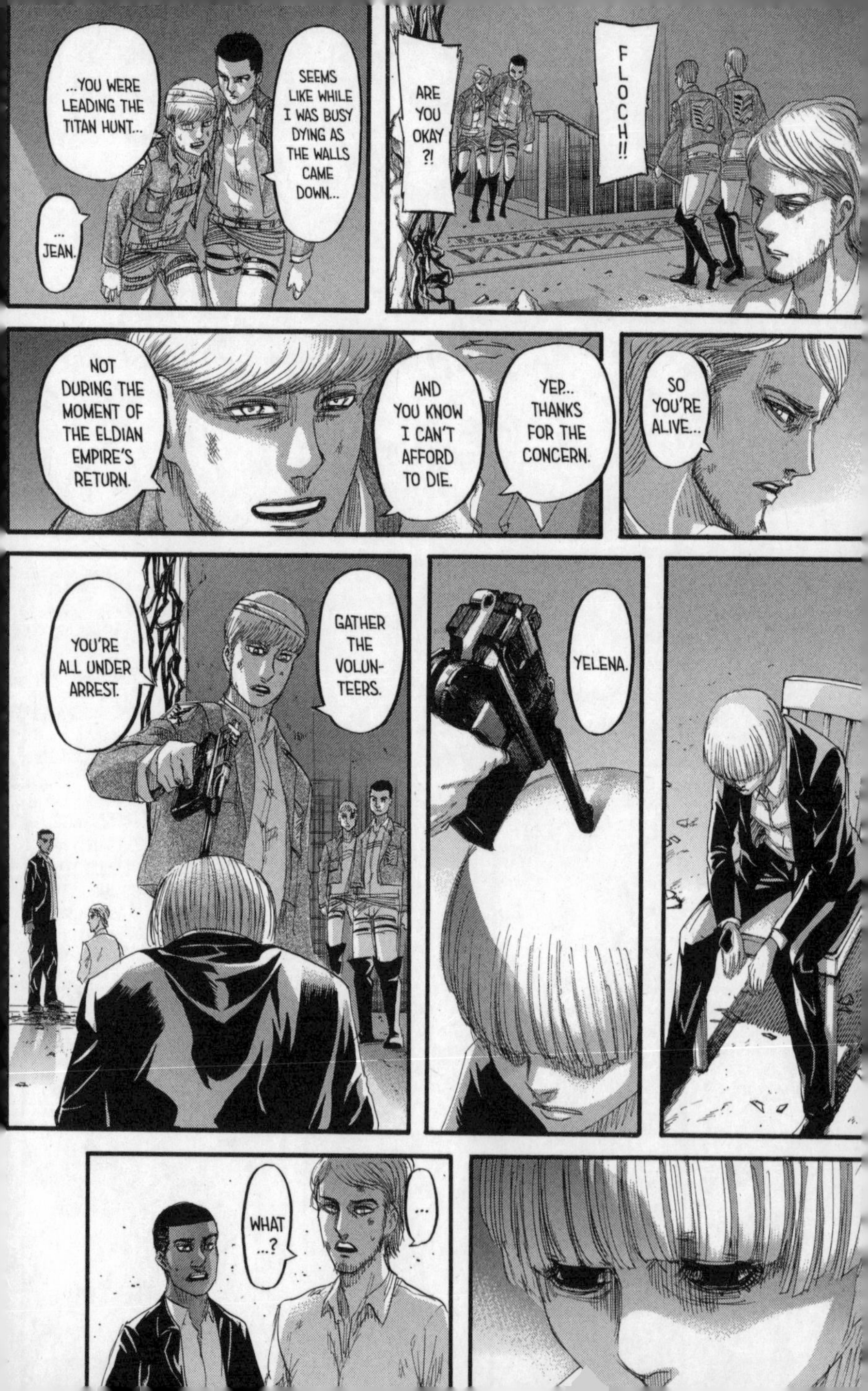
FLOCH!!
ARE YOU OKAY ?!
SEEMS LIKE WHILE I WAS BUSY DYING AS THE WALLS CAME DOWN...
...YOU WERE LEADING THE TITAN HUNT...
... JEAN.
SO YOU'RE ALIVE...
YEP.. THANKS FOR THE CONCERN.
AND YOU KNOW I CAN'T AFFORD TO DIE.
NOT DURING THE MOMENT OF THE ELDIAN EMPIRE'S RETURN.
YELENA.
GATHER THE VOLUN- TEERS.
YOU'RE ALL UNDER ARREST.
...
WHAT ...?

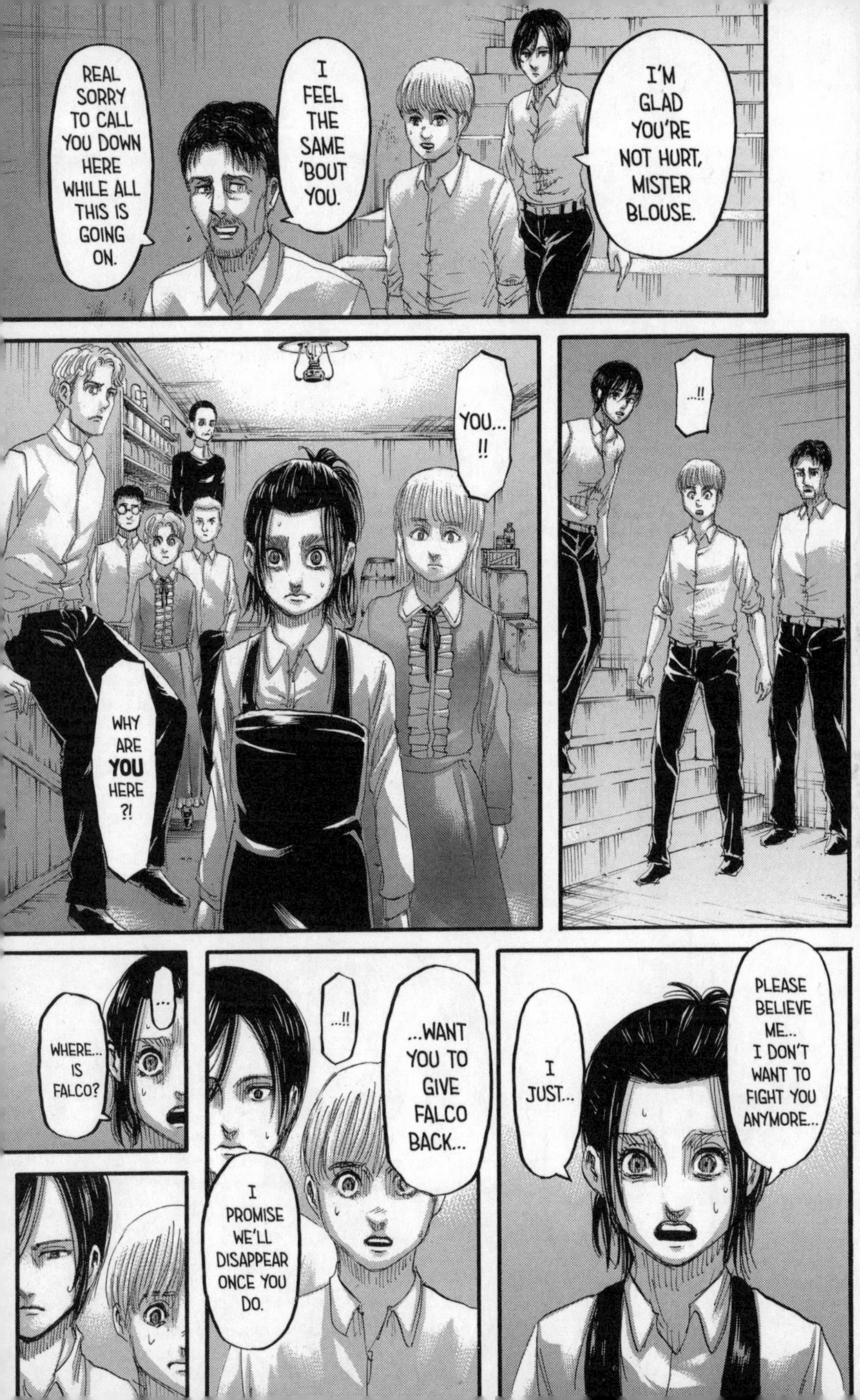
I'M GLAD YOU'RE NOT HURT, MISTER BLOUSE.
I FEEL THE SAME 'BOUT YOU.
REAL SORRY TO CALL YOU DOWN HERE WHILE ALL THIS IS GOING ON.
...!!
YOU... !!
WHY ARE **YOU** HERE?!
PLEASE BELIEVE ME... I DON'T WANT TO FIGHT YOU ANYMORE...
I JUST...
...WANT YOU TO GIVE FALCO BACK...
...!!
I PROMISE WE'LL DISAPPEAR ONCE YOU DO.
...
WHERE... IS FALCO?

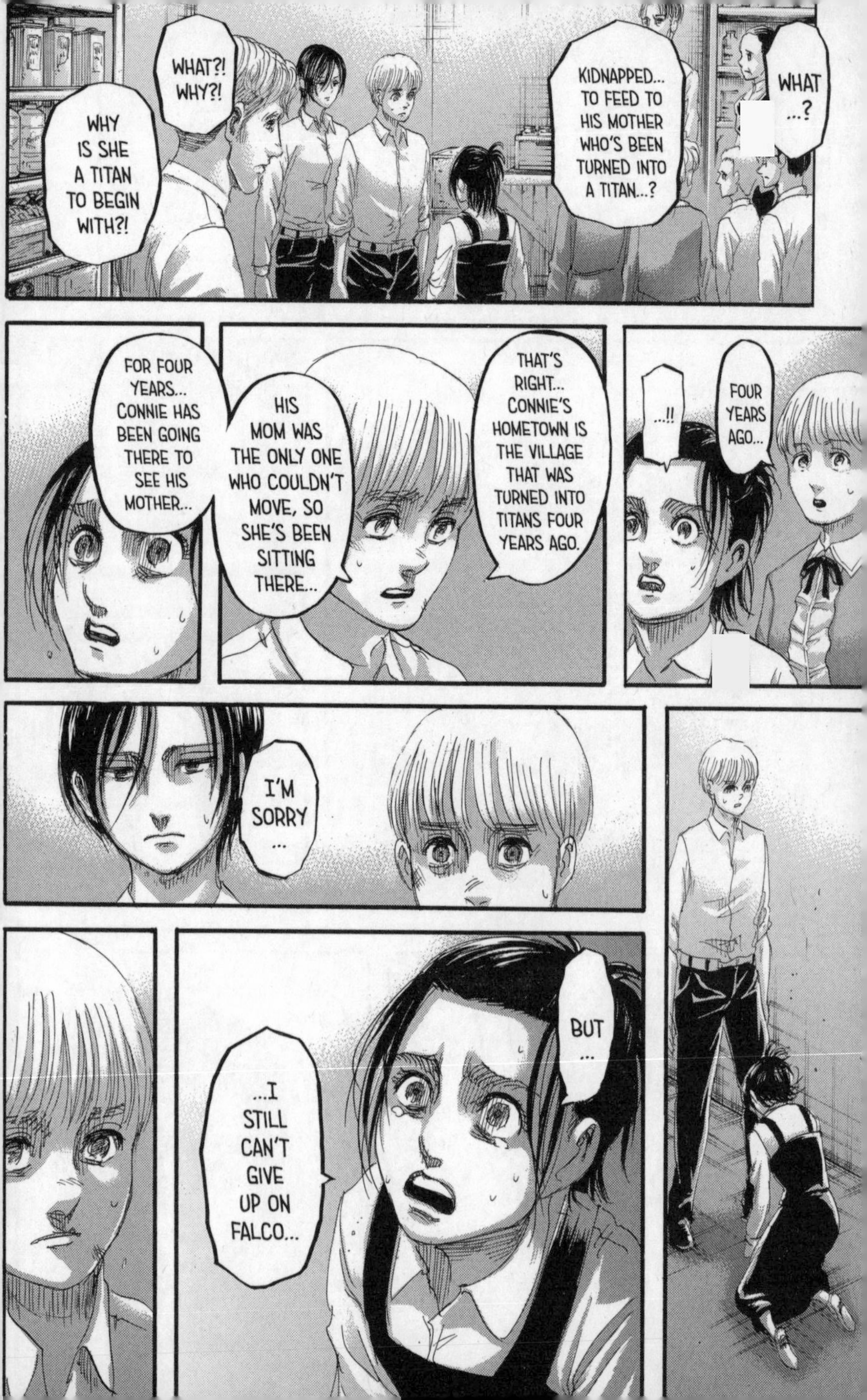
WHAT ...?
KIDNAPPED... TO FEED TO HIS MOTHER WHO'S BEEN TURNED INTO A TITAN...?
WHAT?! WHY?!
WHY IS SHE A TITAN TO BEGIN WITH?!
FOUR YEARS AGO...
...!!
THAT'S RIGHT... CONNIE'S HOMETOWN IS THE VILLAGE THAT WAS TURNED INTO TITANS FOUR YEARS AGO.
HIS MOM WAS THE ONLY ONE WHO COULDN'T MOVE, SO SHE'S BEEN SITTING THERE...
FOR FOUR YEARS... CONNIE HAS BEEN GOING THERE TO SEE HIS MOTHER...
I'M SORRY ...
BUT ...
...I STILL CAN'T GIVE UP ON FALCO...

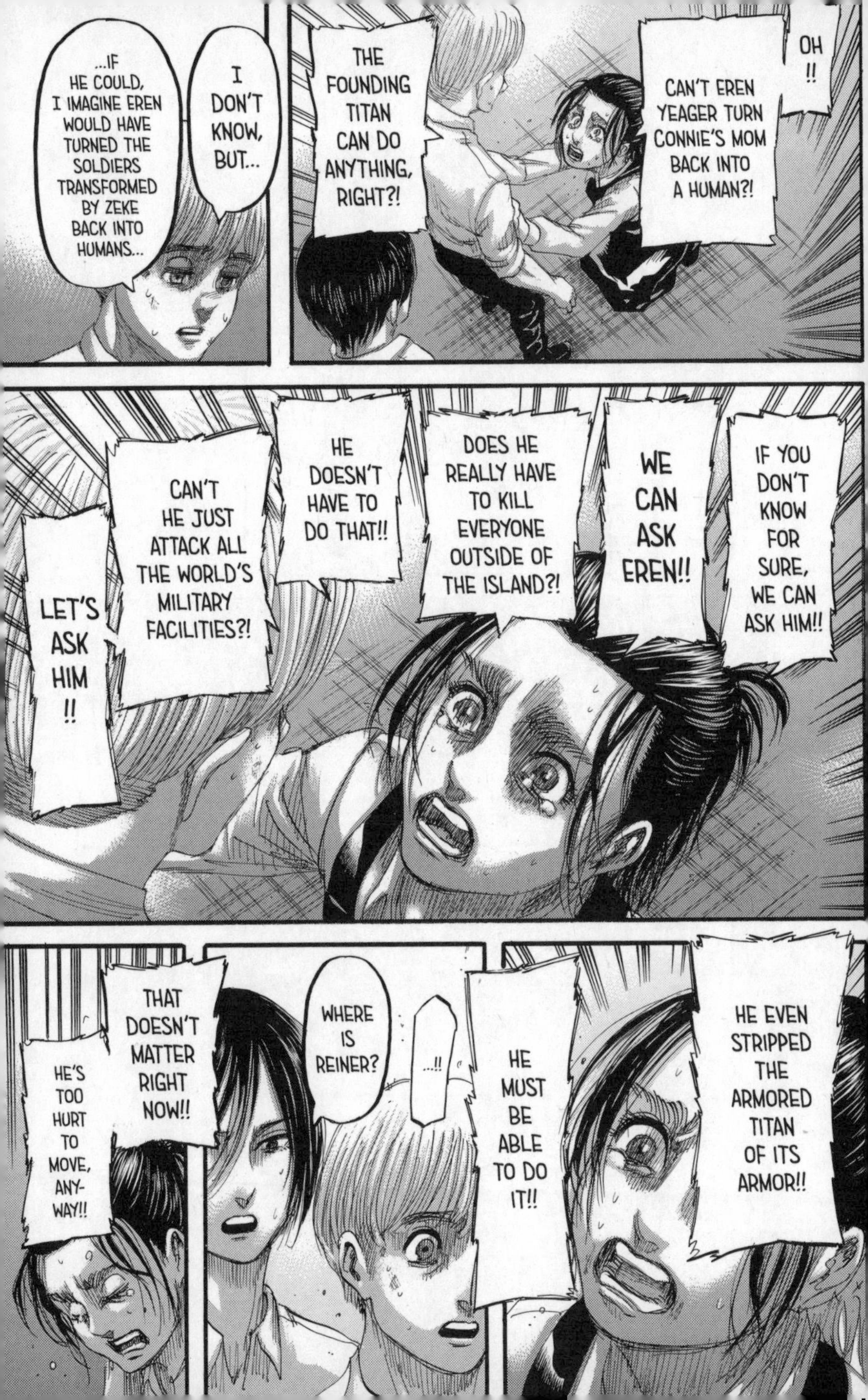
OH !!
CAN'T EREN YEAGER TURN CONNIE'S MOM BACK INTO A HUMAN?!
THE FOUNDING TITAN CAN DO ANYTHING, RIGHT?!
I DON'T KNOW, BUT...
...IF HE COULD, I IMAGINE EREN WOULD HAVE TURNED THE SOLDIERS TRANSFORMED BY ZEKE BACK INTO HUMANS...
IF YOU DON'T KNOW FOR SURE, WE CAN ASK HIM!!
WE CAN ASK EREN!!
DOES HE REALLY HAVE TO KILL EVERYONE OUTSIDE OF THE ISLAND?!
HE DOESN'T HAVE TO DO THAT!!
CAN'T HE JUST ATTACK ALL THE WORLD'S MILITARY FACILITIES?!
LET'S ASK HIM !!
HE EVEN STRIPPED THE ARMORED TITAN OF ITS ARMOR!!
HE MUST BE ABLE TO DO IT!!
...!!
WHERE IS REINER?
THAT DOESN'T MATTER RIGHT NOW!!
HE'S TOO HURT TO MOVE, ANY-WAY!!

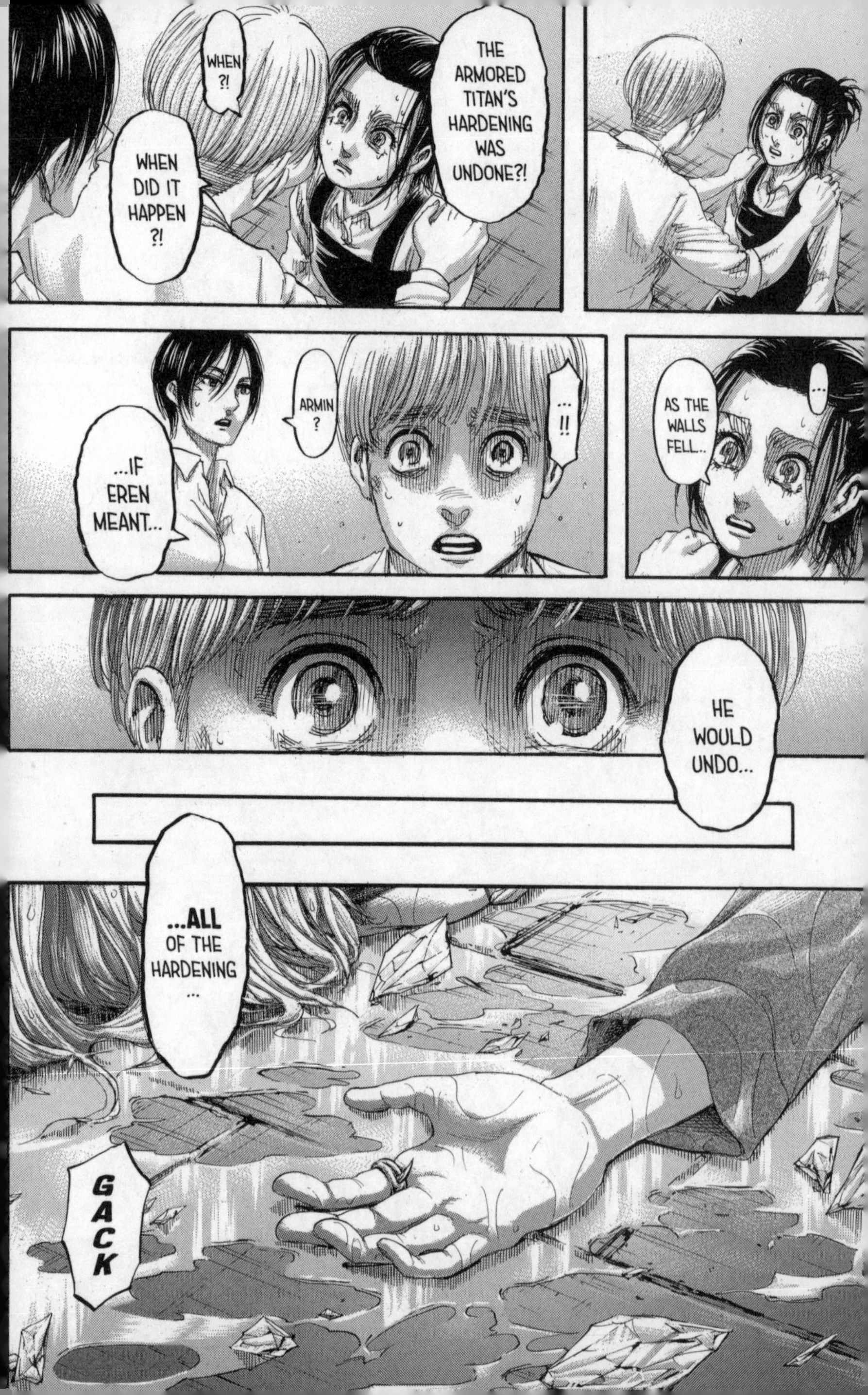
THE ARMORED TITAN'S HARDENING WAS UNDONE?!
WHEN?!
WHEN DID IT HAPPEN?!
...
AS THE WALLS FELL...
...!!
ARMIN?
...IF EREN MEANT...
HE WOULD UNDO...
...ALL OF THE HARDENING...
GACK

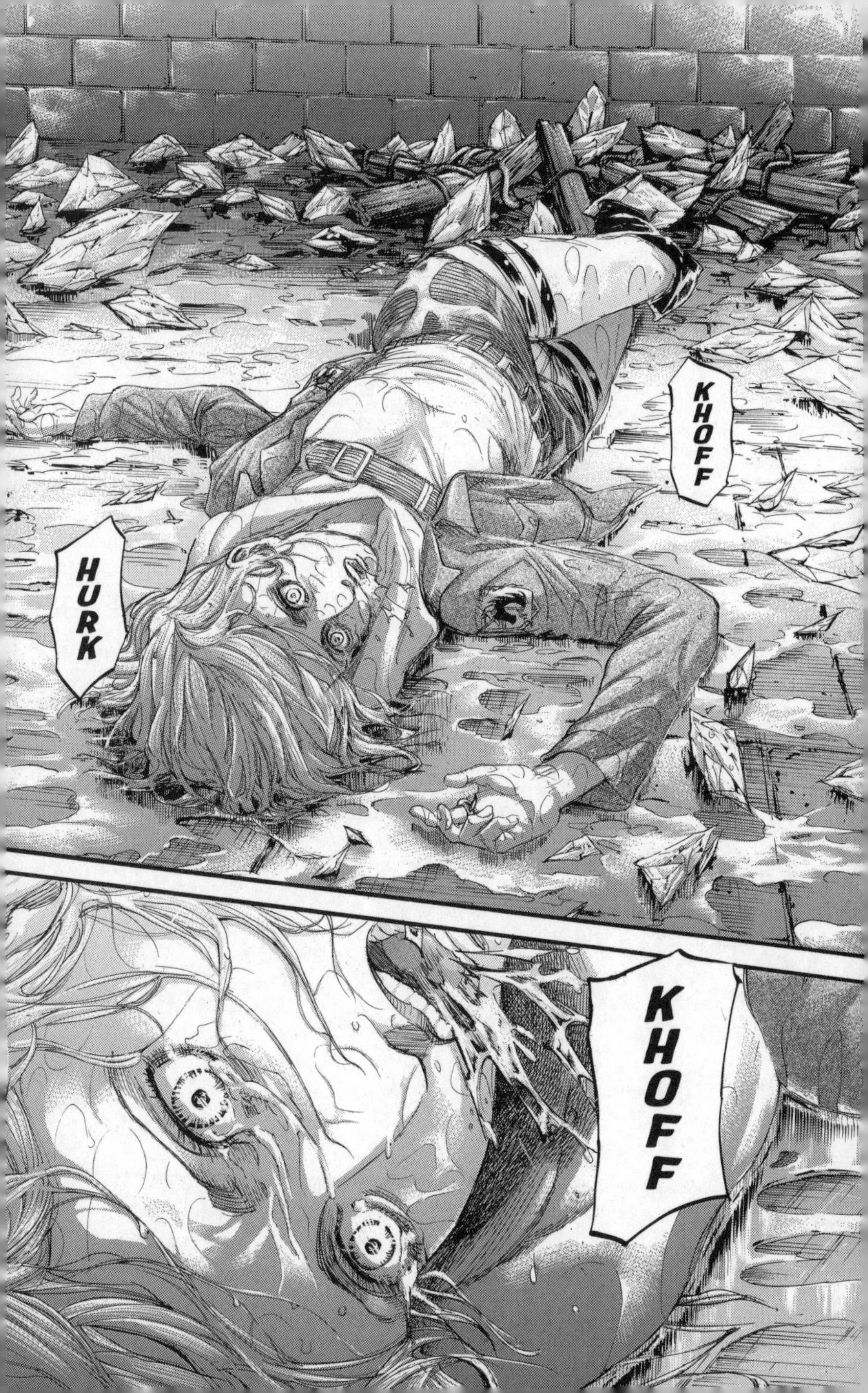
KHOFF
HURK
KHOFF

ATTACK on TITAN

Episode 125: Sunset

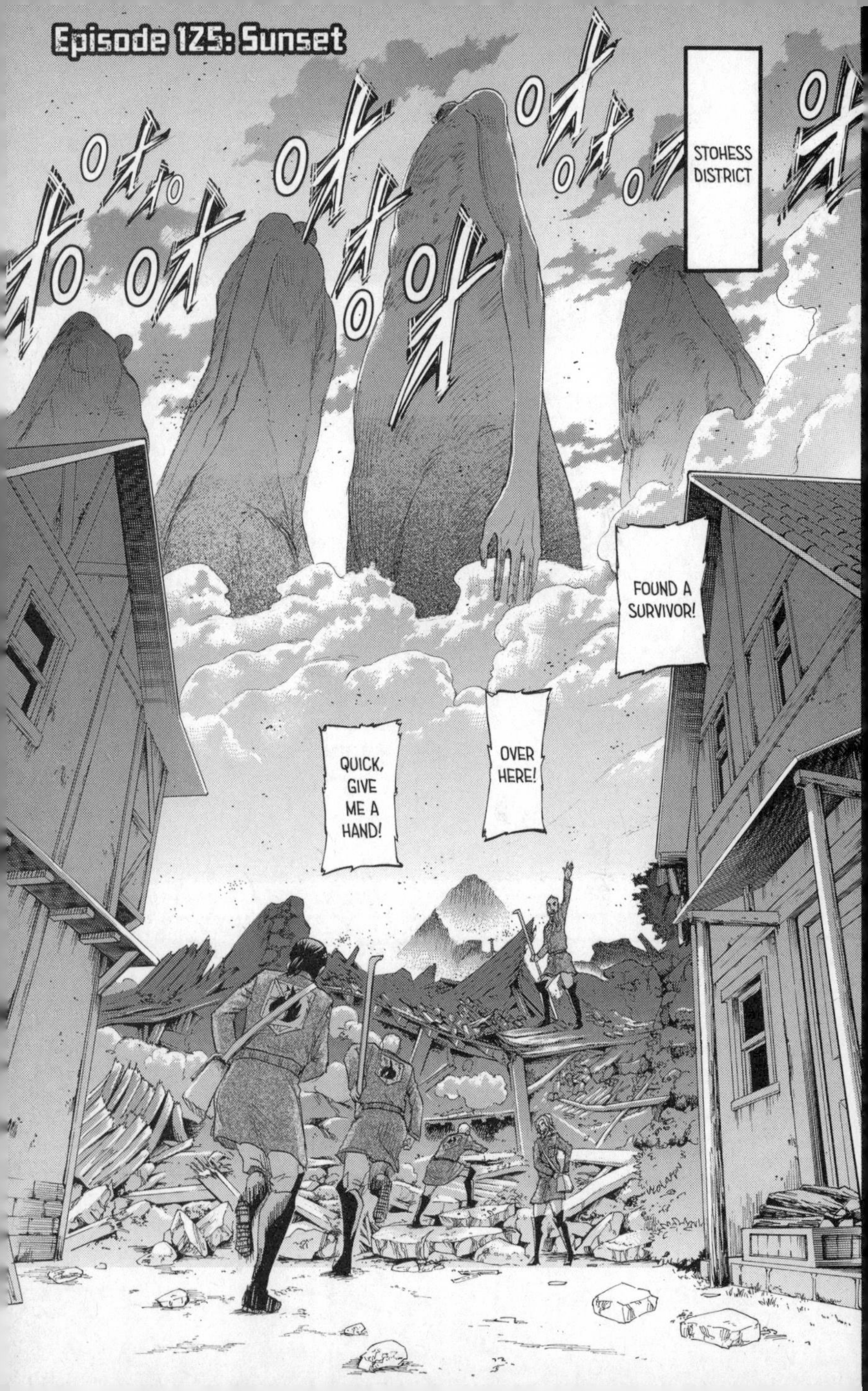
STOHESS DISTRICT
FOUND A SURVIVOR!
OVER HERE!
QUICK, GIVE ME A HAND!

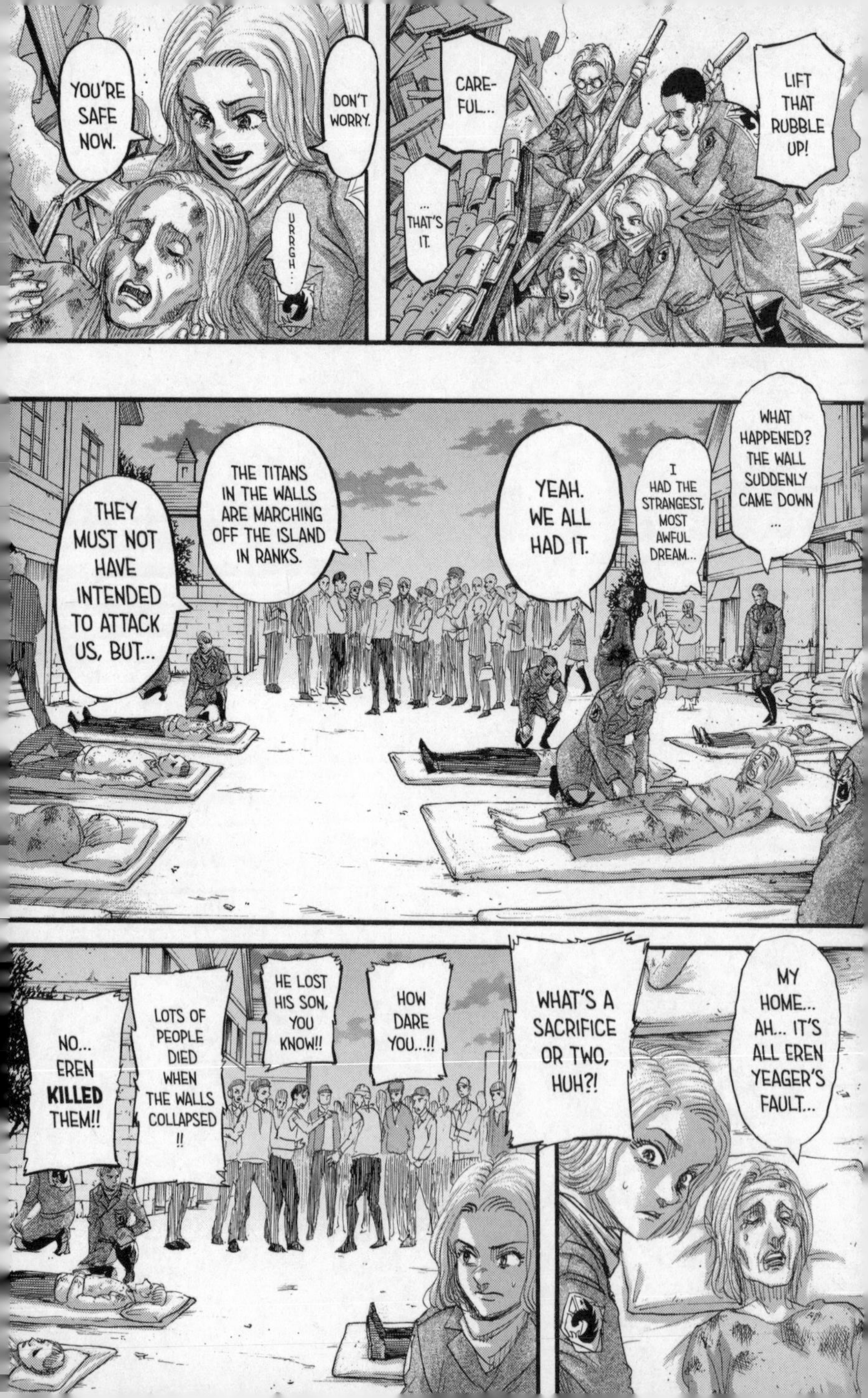
LIFT THAT RUBBLE UP!
CARE-FUL...
... THAT'S IT.
DON'T WORRY.
URRGH...
YOU'RE SAFE NOW.
WHAT HAPPENED? THE WALL SUDDENLY CAME DOWN ...
I HAD THE STRANGEST, MOST AWFUL DREAM...
YEAH. WE ALL HAD IT.
THE TITANS IN THE WALLS ARE MARCHING OFF THE ISLAND IN RANKS.
THEY MUST NOT HAVE INTENDED TO ATTACK US, BUT...
MY HOME... AH... IT'S ALL EREN YEAGER'S FAULT...
WHAT'S A SACRIFICE OR TWO, HUH?!
HOW DARE YOU...!!
HE LOST HIS SON, YOU KNOW!!
LOTS OF PEOPLE DIED WHEN THE WALLS COLLAPSED !!
NO... EREN **KILLED** THEM!!

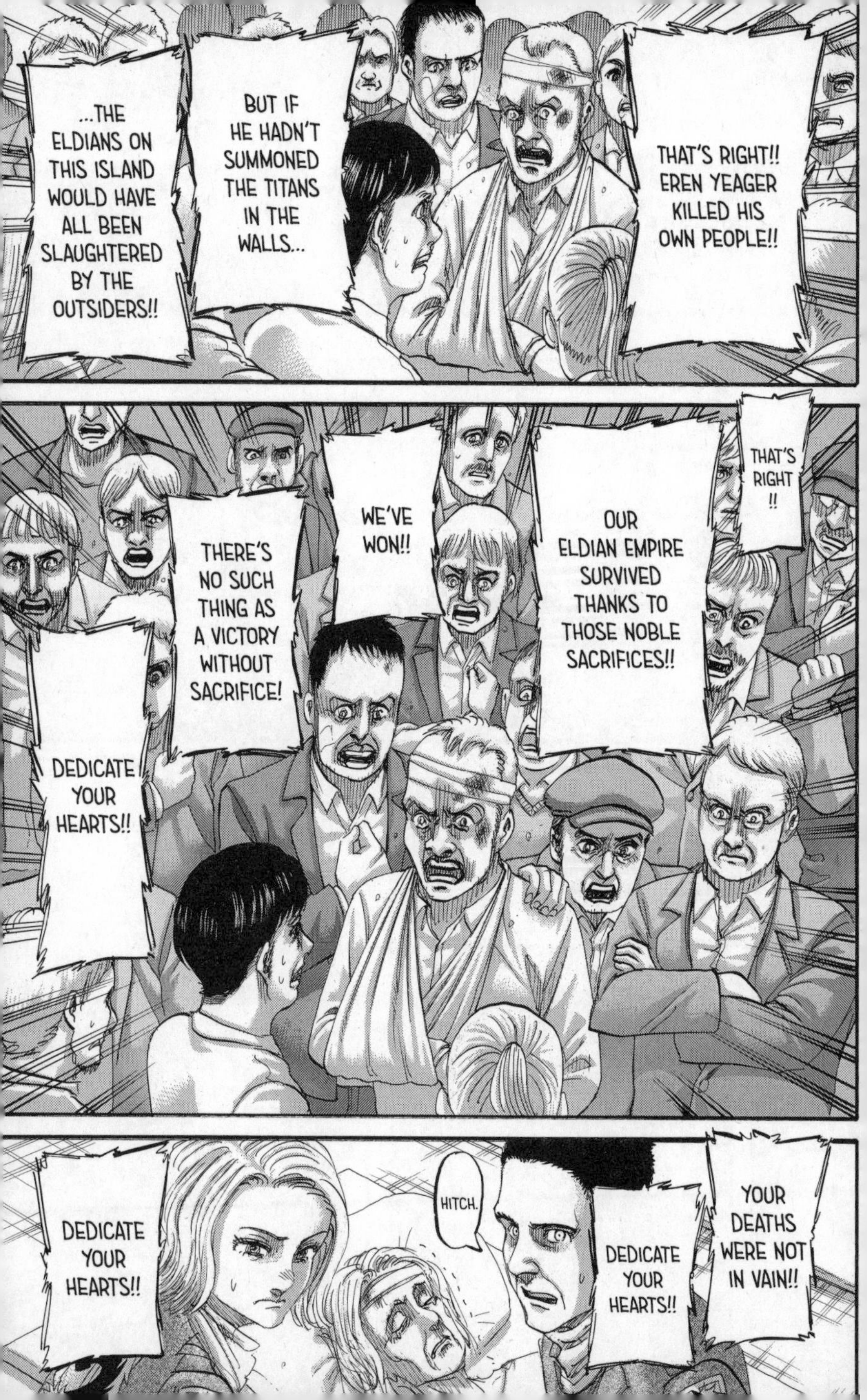
THAT'S RIGHT!! EREN YEAGER KILLED HIS OWN PEOPLE!!
BUT IF HE HADN'T SUMMONED THE TITANS IN THE WALLS...
...THE ELDIANS ON THIS ISLAND WOULD HAVE ALL BEEN SLAUGHTERED BY THE OUTSIDERS!!
THAT'S RIGHT!!
OUR ELDIAN EMPIRE SURVIVED THANKS TO THOSE NOBLE SACRIFICES!!
WE'VE WON!!
THERE'S NO SUCH THING AS A VICTORY WITHOUT SACRIFICE!
DEDICATE YOUR HEARTS!!
YOUR DEATHS WERE NOT IN VAIN!!
DEDICATE YOUR HEARTS!!
HITCH.
DEDICATE YOUR HEARTS!!

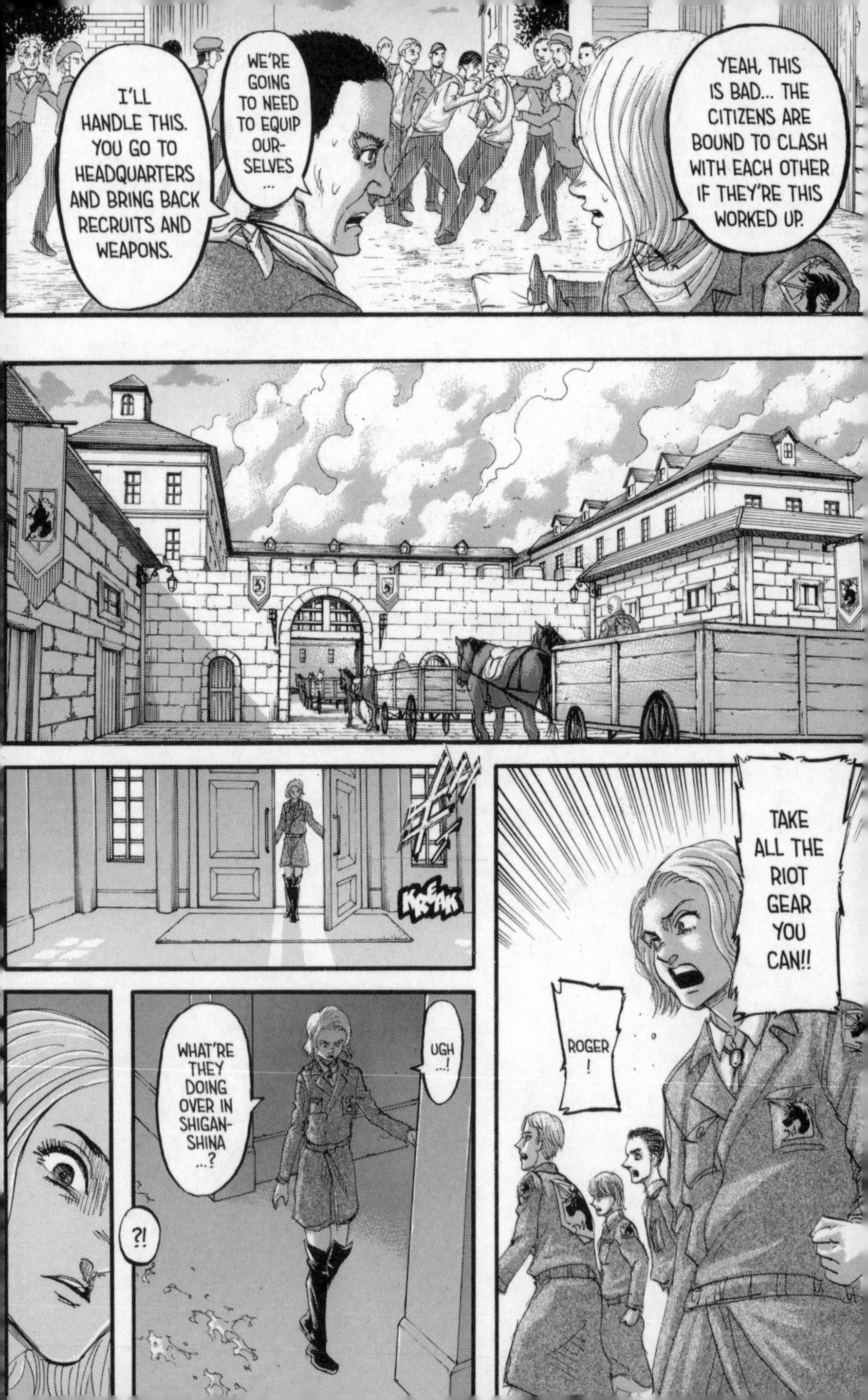
YEAH, THIS IS BAD... THE CITIZENS ARE BOUND TO CLASH WITH EACH OTHER IF THEY'RE THIS WORKED UP.
WE'RE GOING TO NEED TO EQUIP OUR-SELVES ...
I'LL HANDLE THIS. YOU GO TO HEADQUARTERS AND BRING BACK RECRUITS AND WEAPONS.
TAKE ALL THE RIOT GEAR YOU CAN!!
ROGER !
KREAK
UGH ...!
WHAT'RE THEY DOING OVER IN SHIGAN-SHINA ...?
?!

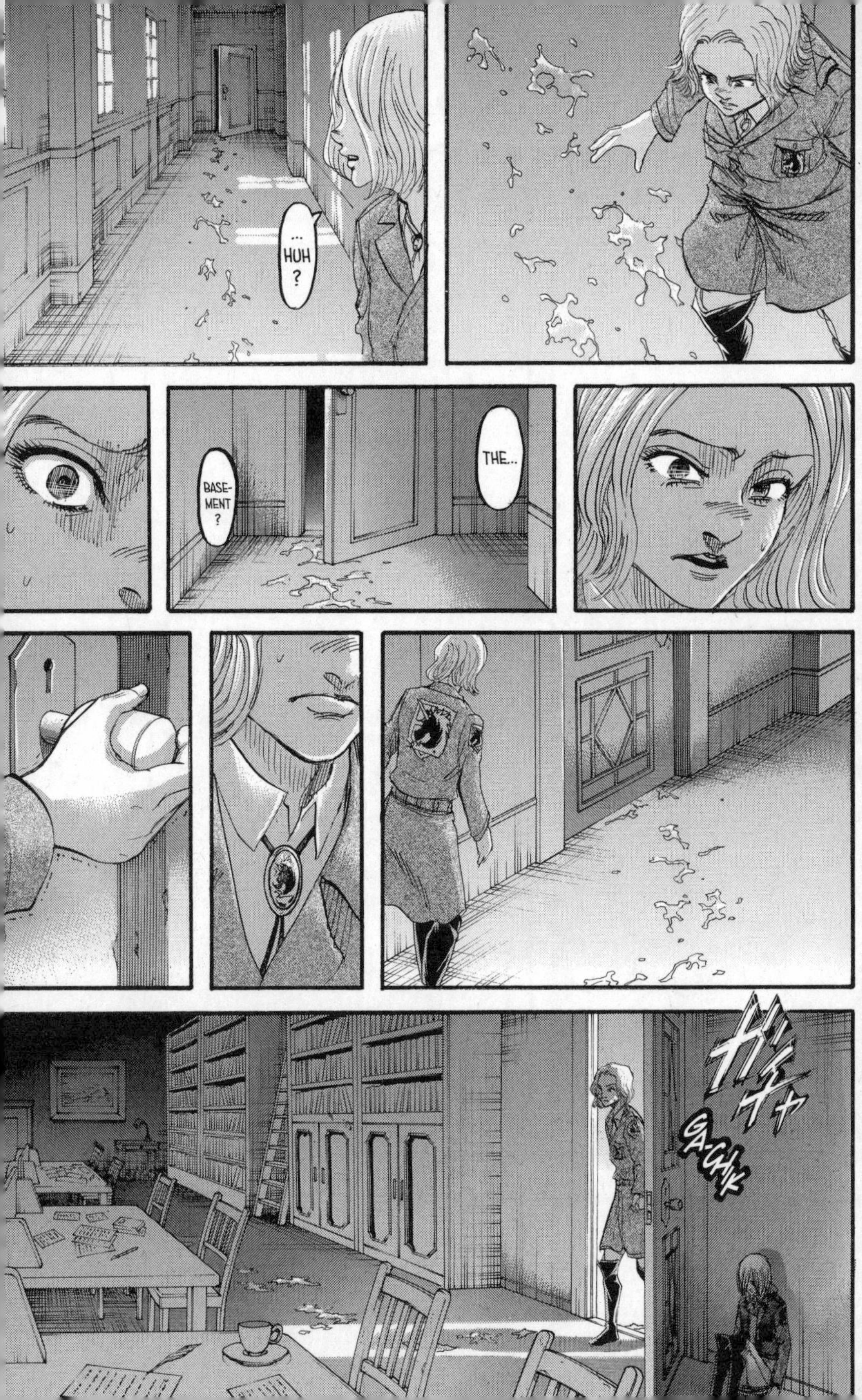
... HUH ?
THE...
BASEMENT ?
ガチャ
GA-CHIK

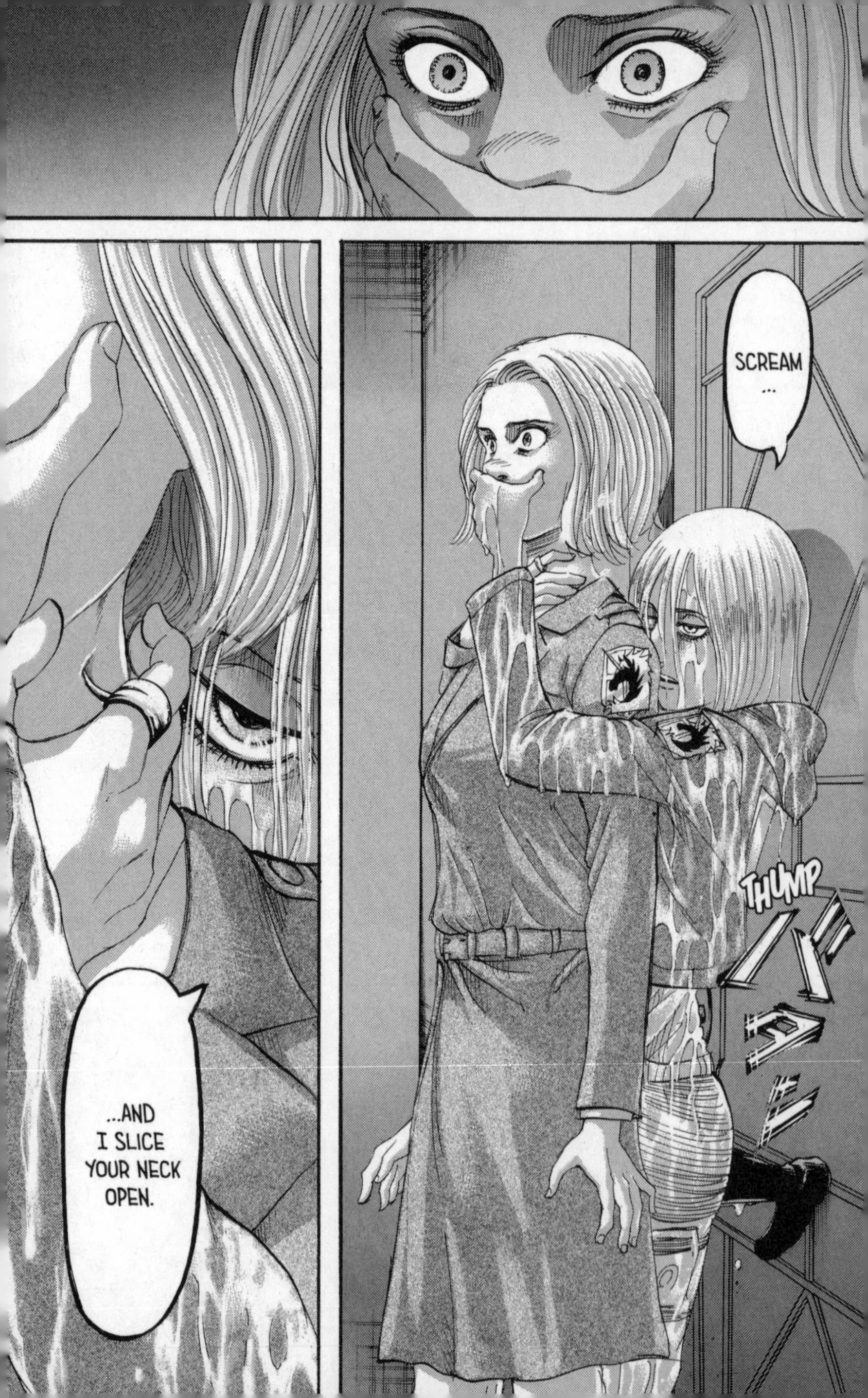
SCREAM ...
THUMP
...AND I SLICE YOUR NECK OPEN.

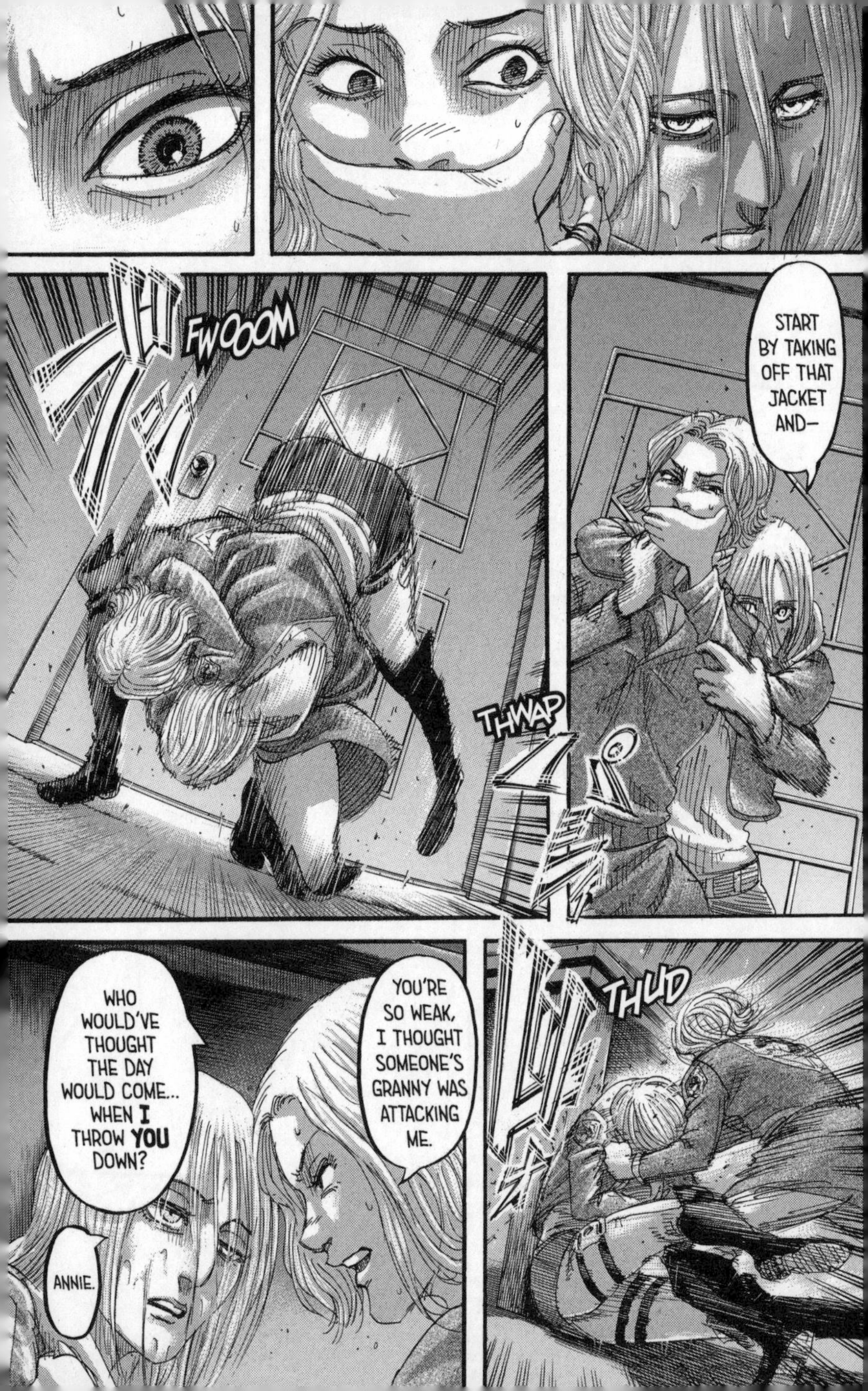
START BY TAKING OFF THAT JACKET AND—
THWAP
FWOOOM
THUD
YOU'RE SO WEAK, I THOUGHT SOMEONE'S GRANNY WAS ATTACKING ME.
WHO WOULD'VE THOUGHT THE DAY WOULD COME... WHEN **I** THROW **YOU** DOWN?
ANNIE.

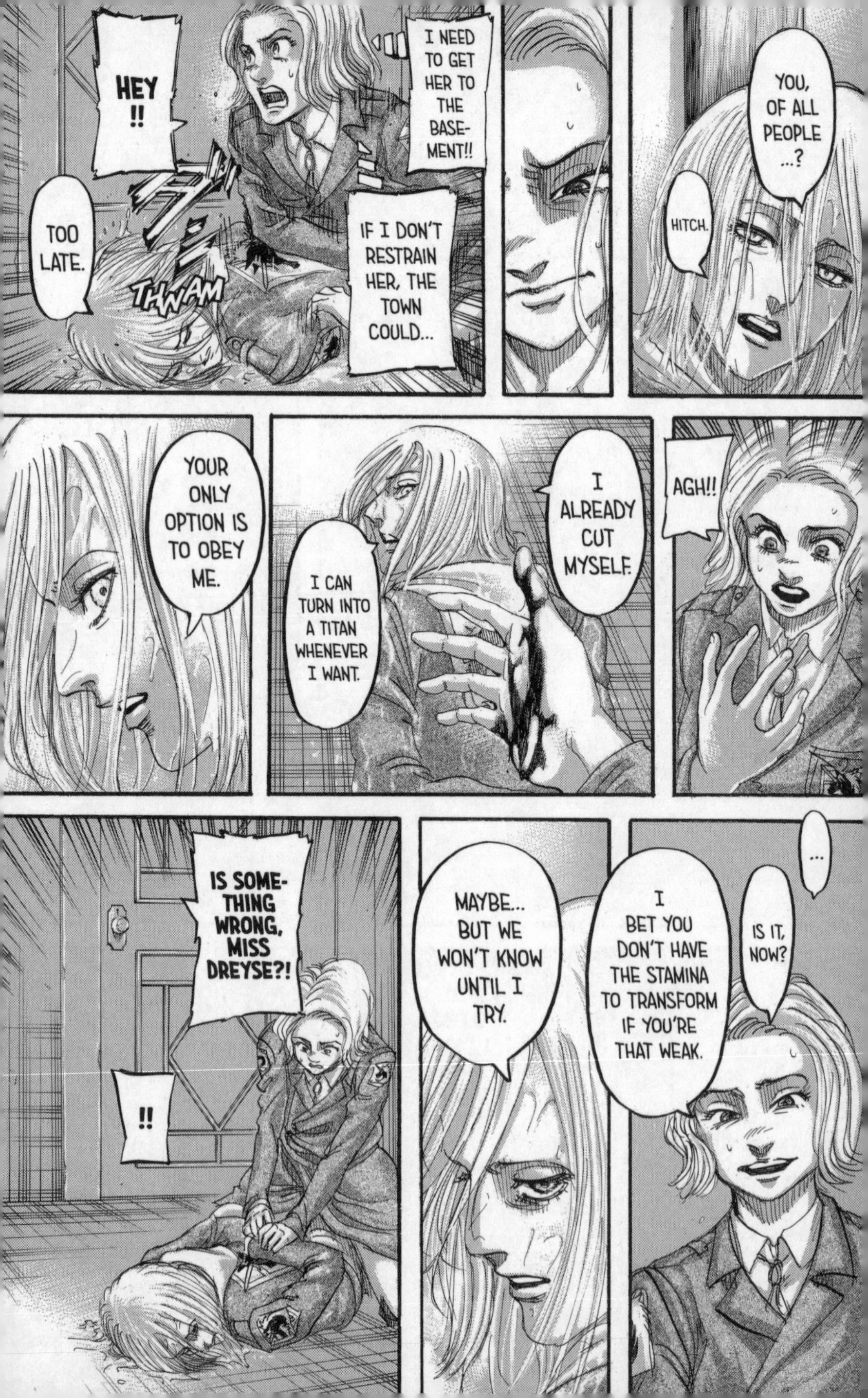
YOU, OF ALL PEOPLE ...?
HITCH.
I NEED TO GET HER TO THE BASEMENT!!
HEY !!
IF I DON'T RESTRAIN HER, THE TOWN COULD...
THWAM
TOO LATE.
AGH!!
I ALREADY CUT MYSELF.
I CAN TURN INTO A TITAN WHENEVER I WANT.
YOUR ONLY OPTION IS TO OBEY ME.
...
IS IT, NOW?
I BET YOU DON'T HAVE THE STAMINA TO TRANSFORM IF YOU'RE THAT WEAK.
MAYBE... BUT WE WON'T KNOW UNTIL I TRY.
IS SOMETHING WRONG, MISS DREYSE?!
!!

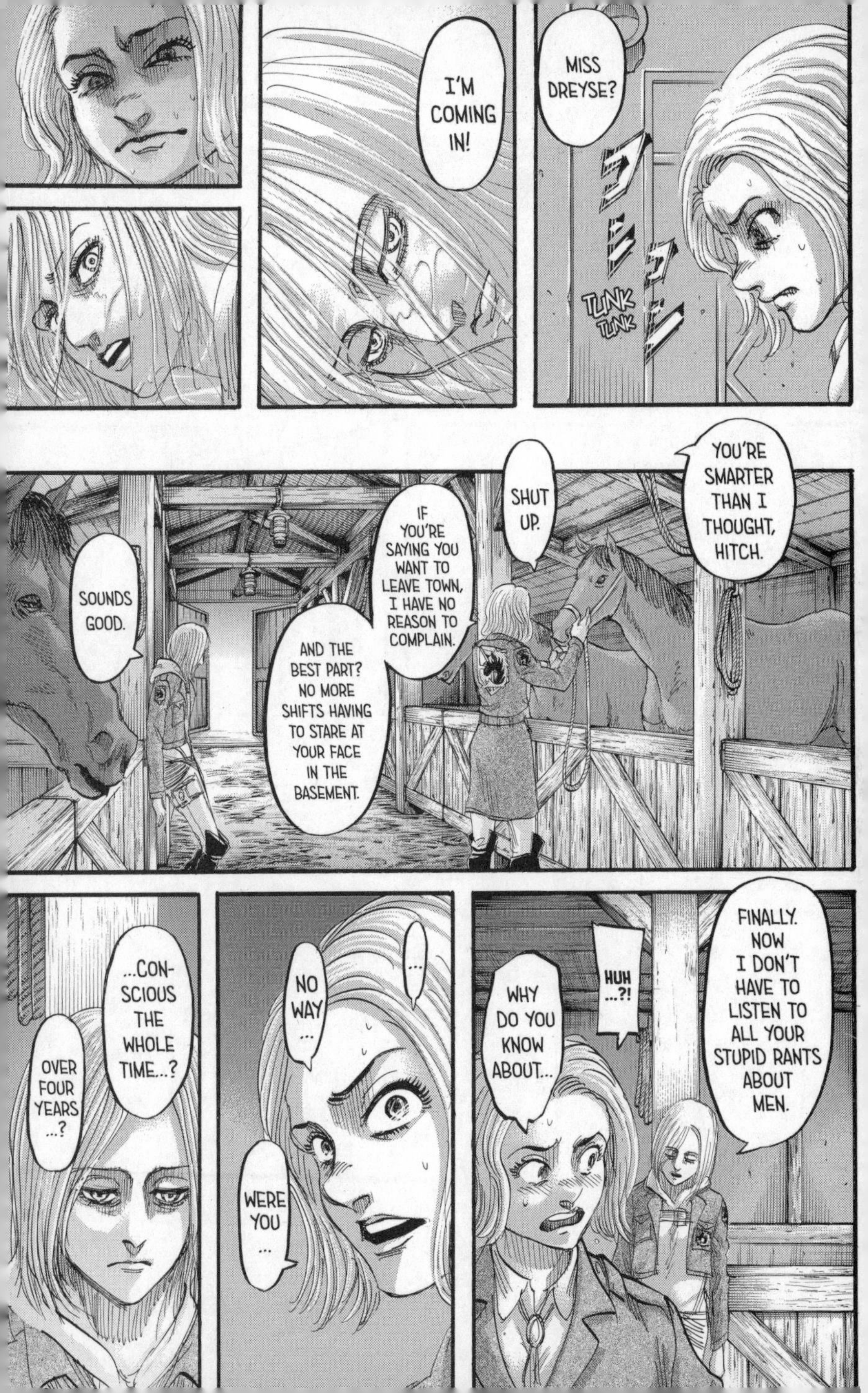
MISS DREYSE?
TUNK TUNK
I'M COMING IN!
YOU'RE SMARTER THAN I THOUGHT, HITCH.
SHUT UP.
IF YOU'RE SAYING YOU WANT TO LEAVE TOWN, I HAVE NO REASON TO COMPLAIN.
AND THE BEST PART? NO MORE SHIFTS HAVING TO STARE AT YOUR FACE IN THE BASEMENT.
SOUNDS GOOD.
FINALLY. NOW I DON'T HAVE TO LISTEN TO ALL YOUR STUPID RANTS ABOUT MEN.
HUH ...?!
WHY DO YOU KNOW ABOUT...
...
NO WAY ...
WERE YOU ...
...CON-SCIOUS THE WHOLE TIME...?
OVER FOUR YEARS ...?

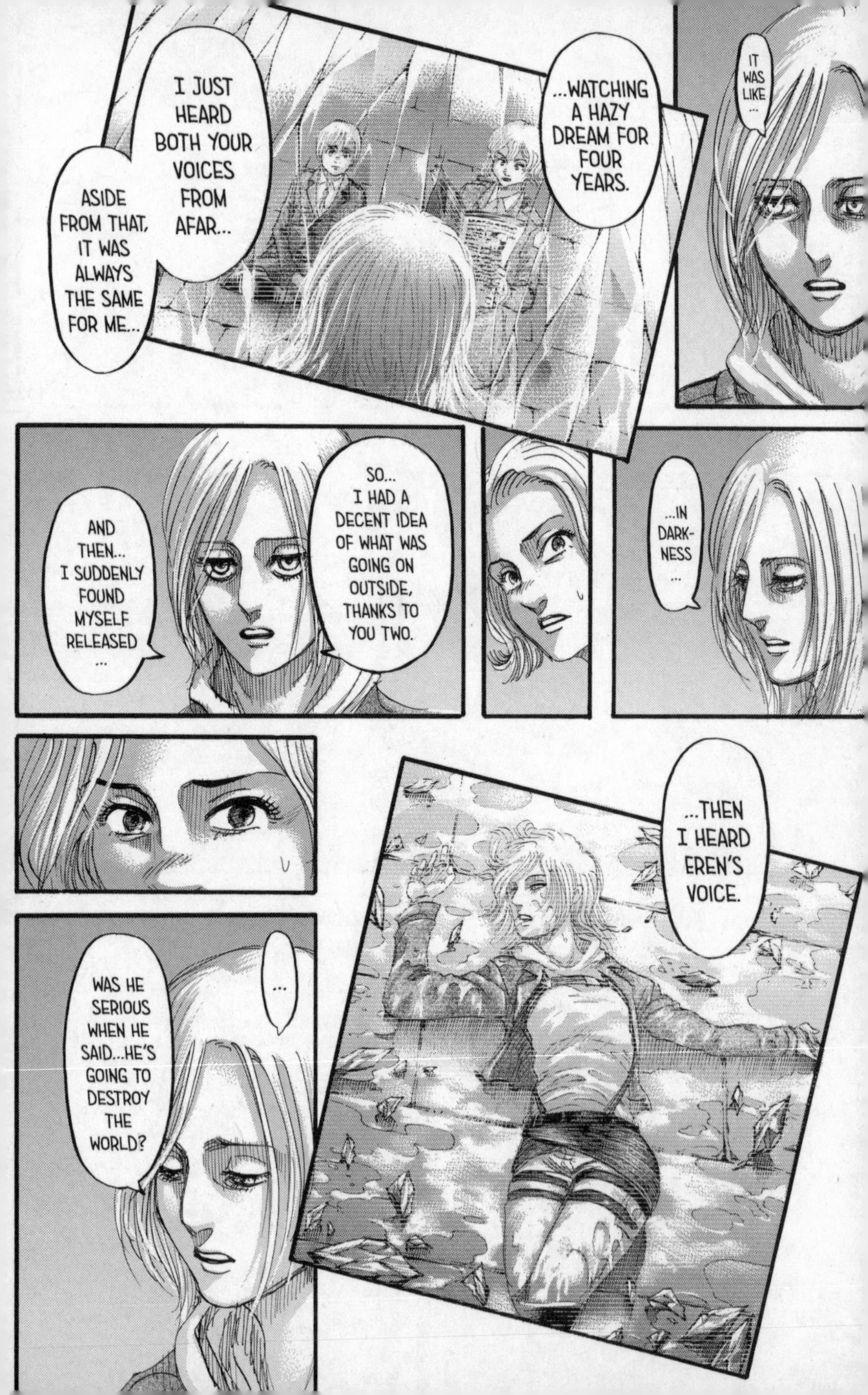
IT WAS LIKE ...
...WATCHING A HAZY DREAM FOR FOUR YEARS.
I JUST HEARD BOTH YOUR VOICES FROM AFAR...
ASIDE FROM THAT, IT WAS ALWAYS THE SAME FOR ME...
...IN DARKNESS ...
SO... I HAD A DECENT IDEA OF WHAT WAS GOING ON OUTSIDE, THANKS TO YOU TWO.
AND THEN... I SUDDENLY FOUND MYSELF RELEASED ...
...THEN I HEARD EREN'S VOICE.
...
WAS HE SERIOUS WHEN HE SAID...HE'S GOING TO DESTROY THE WORLD?

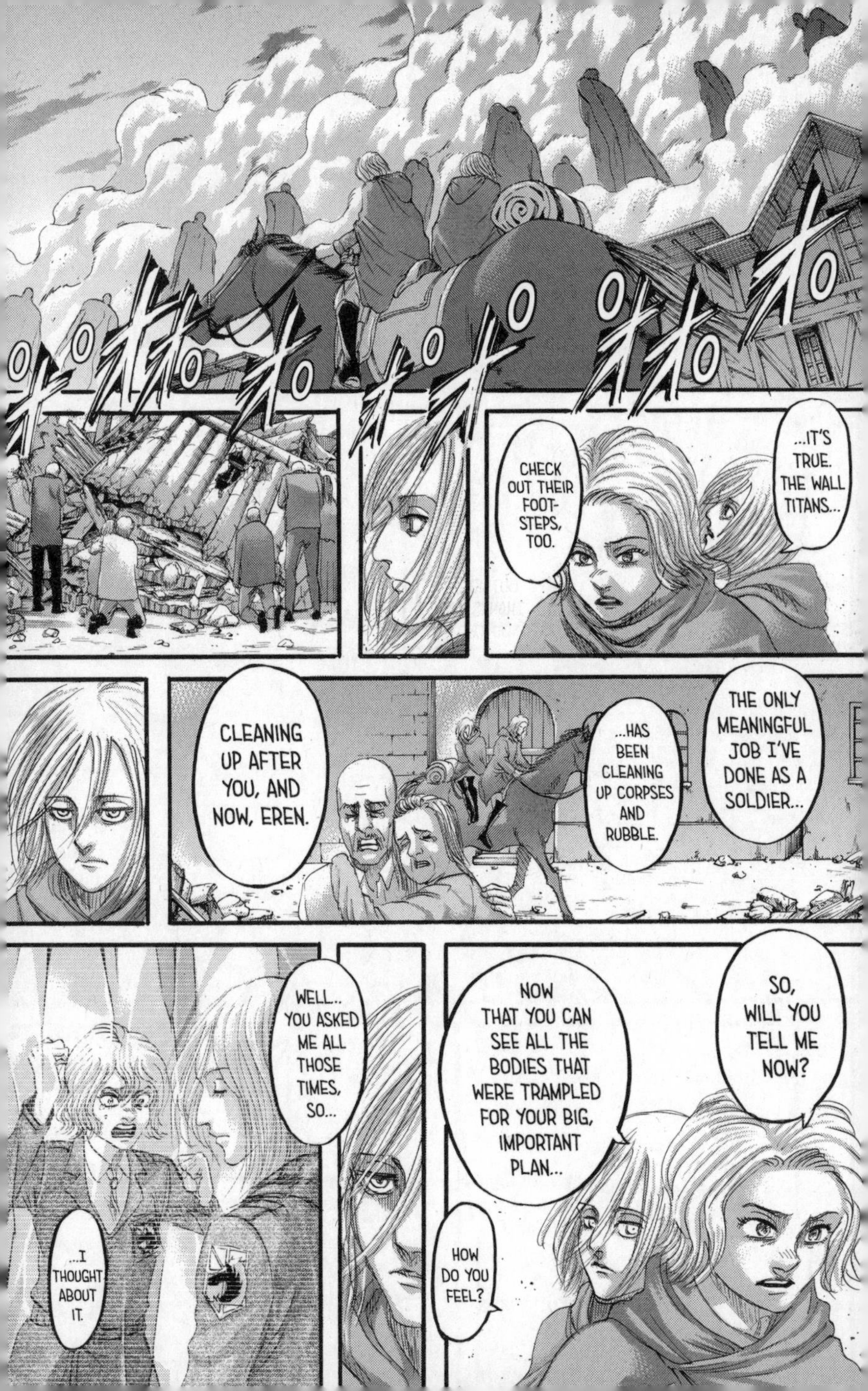
...IT'S TRUE. THE WALL TITANS...
CHECK OUT THEIR FOOT-STEPS, TOO.
THE ONLY MEANINGFUL JOB I'VE DONE AS A SOLDIER...
...HAS BEEN CLEANING UP CORPSES AND RUBBLE.
CLEANING UP AFTER YOU, AND NOW, EREN.
SO, WILL YOU TELL ME NOW?
NOW THAT YOU CAN SEE ALL THE BODIES THAT WERE TRAMPLED FOR YOUR BIG, IMPORTANT PLAN...
HOW DO YOU FEEL?
WELL.. YOU ASKED ME ALL THOSE TIMES, SO...
...I THOUGHT ABOUT IT.

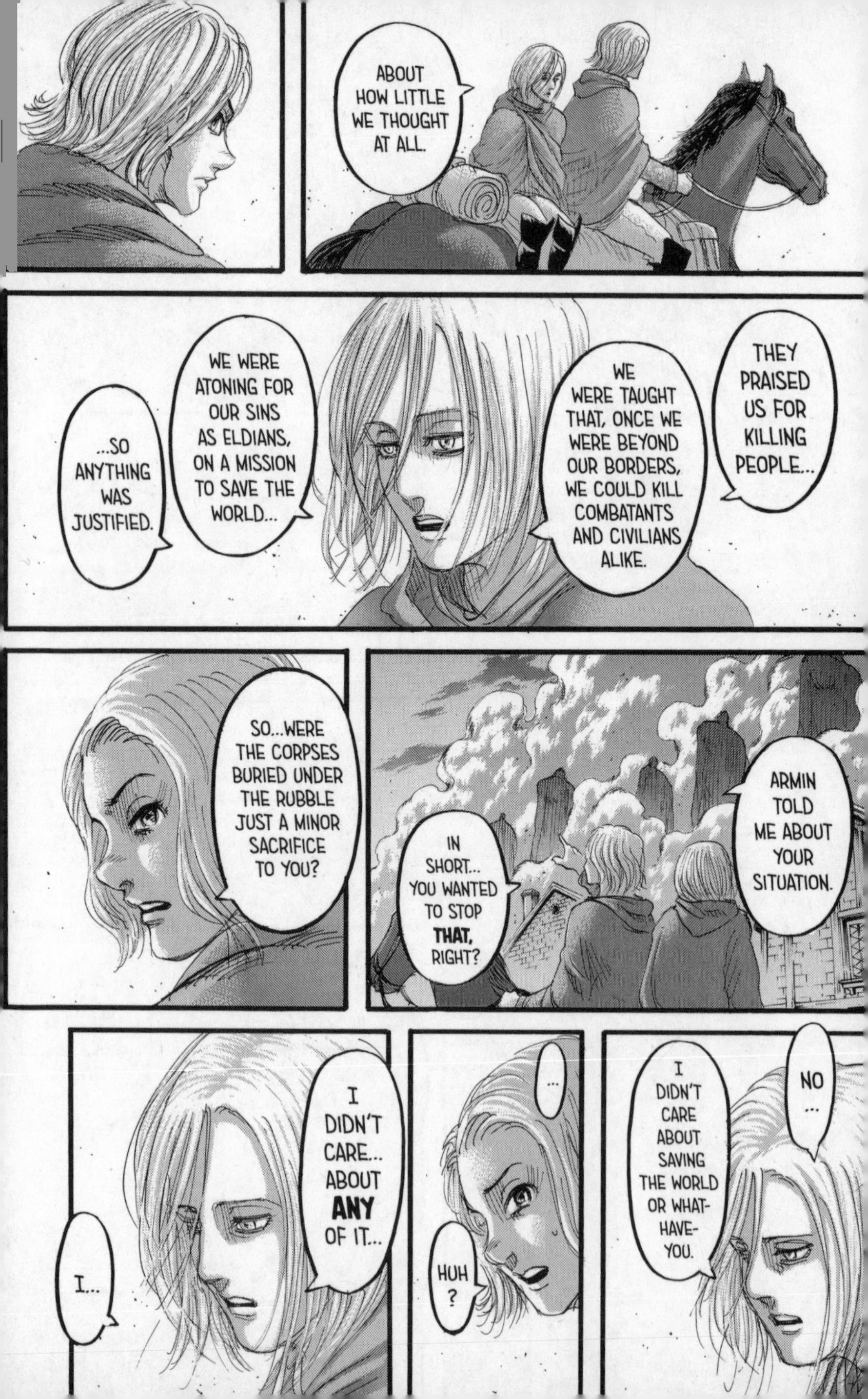
ABOUT HOW LITTLE WE THOUGHT AT ALL.
THEY PRAISED US FOR KILLING PEOPLE...
WE WERE TAUGHT THAT, ONCE WE WERE BEYOND OUR BORDERS, WE COULD KILL COMBATANTS AND CIVILIANS ALIKE.
WE WERE ATONING FOR OUR SINS AS ELDIANS, ON A MISSION TO SAVE THE WORLD...
...SO ANYTHING WAS JUSTIFIED.
ARMIN TOLD ME ABOUT YOUR SITUATION.
IN SHORT... YOU WANTED TO STOP **THAT,** RIGHT?
SO...WERE THE CORPSES BURIED UNDER THE RUBBLE JUST A MINOR SACRIFICE TO YOU?
NO ...
I DIDN'T CARE ABOUT SAVING THE WORLD OR WHAT-HAVE-YOU.
...
HUH ?
I DIDN'T CARE... ABOUT **ANY** OF IT...
I...

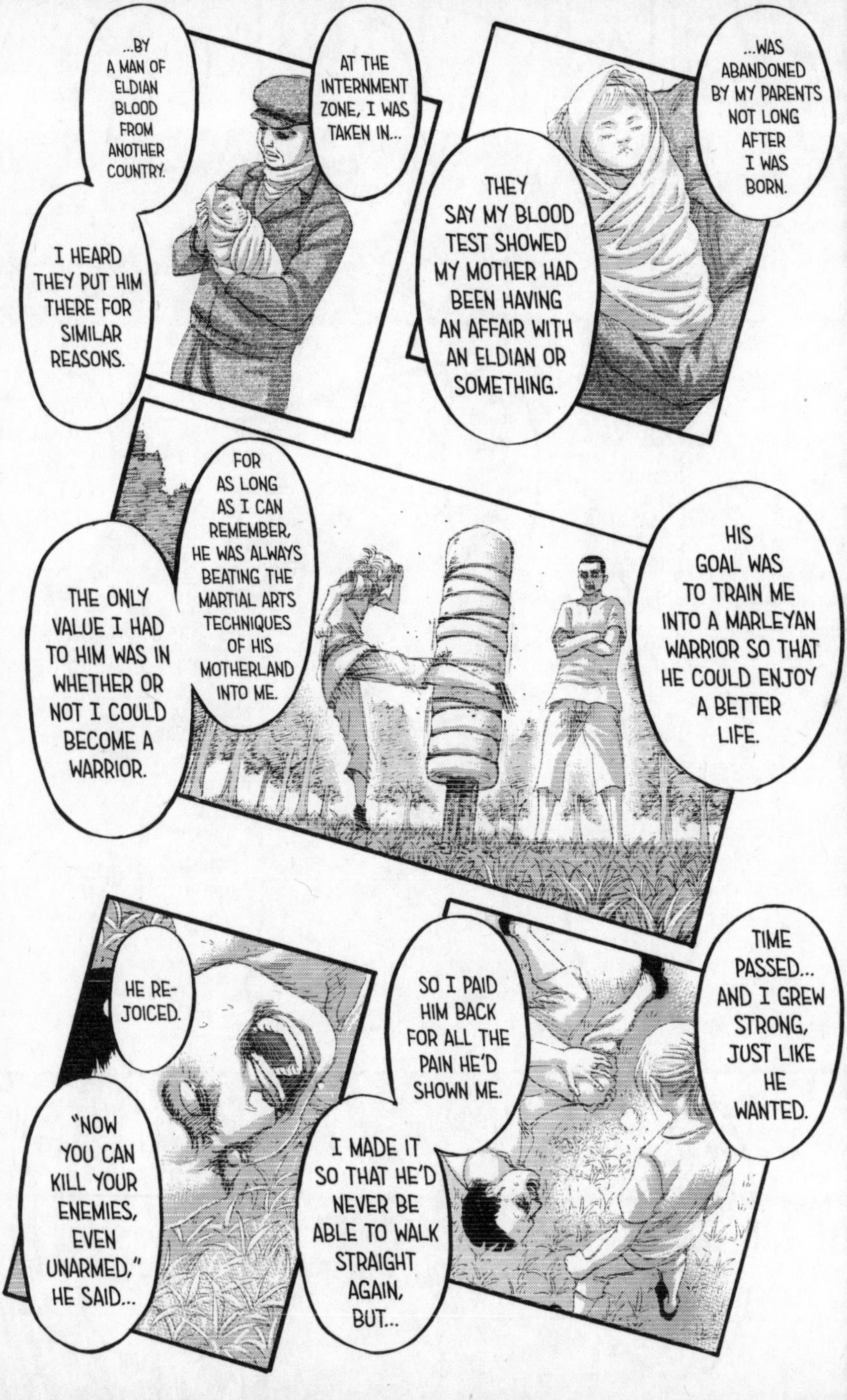
...WAS ABANDONED BY MY PARENTS NOT LONG AFTER I WAS BORN.
THEY SAY MY BLOOD TEST SHOWED MY MOTHER HAD BEEN HAVING AN AFFAIR WITH AN ELDIAN OR SOMETHING.
AT THE INTERNMENT ZONE, I WAS TAKEN IN...
...BY A MAN OF ELDIAN BLOOD FROM ANOTHER COUNTRY.
I HEARD THEY PUT HIM THERE FOR SIMILAR REASONS.
HIS GOAL WAS TO TRAIN ME INTO A MARLEYAN WARRIOR SO THAT HE COULD ENJOY A BETTER LIFE.
FOR AS LONG AS I CAN REMEMBER, HE WAS ALWAYS BEATING THE MARTIAL ARTS TECHNIQUES OF HIS MOTHERLAND INTO ME.
THE ONLY VALUE I HAD TO HIM WAS IN WHETHER OR NOT I COULD BECOME A WARRIOR.
TIME PASSED... AND I GREW STRONG, JUST LIKE HE WANTED.
SO I PAID HIM BACK FOR ALL THE PAIN HE'D SHOWN ME.
I MADE IT SO THAT HE'D NEVER BE ABLE TO WALK STRAIGHT AGAIN, BUT...
HE REJOICED.
"NOW YOU CAN KILL YOUR ENEMIES, EVEN UNARMED," HE SAID...

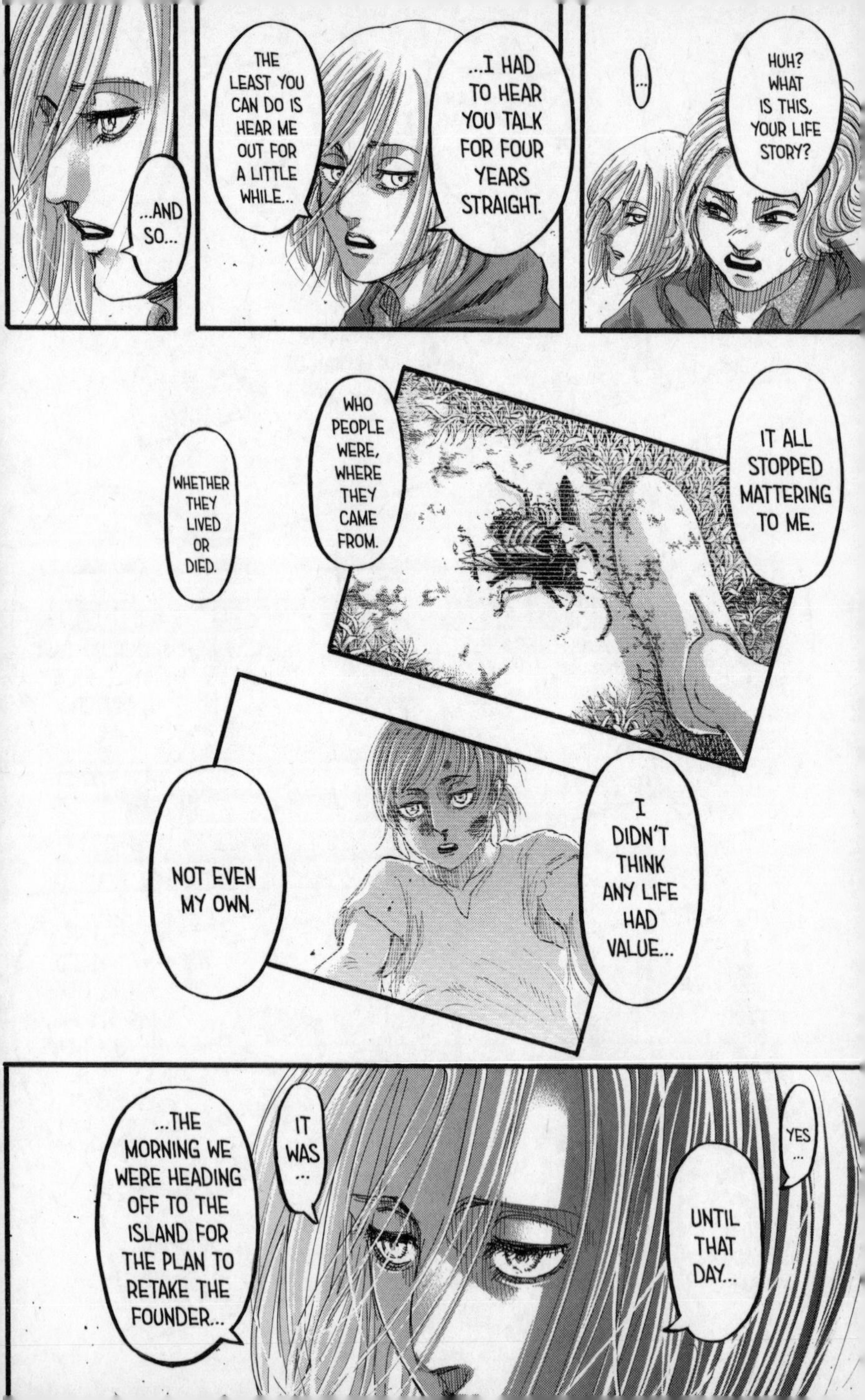
HUH? WHAT IS THIS, YOUR LIFE STORY?
...
...I HAD TO HEAR YOU TALK FOR FOUR YEARS STRAIGHT.
THE LEAST YOU CAN DO IS HEAR ME OUT FOR A LITTLE WHILE...
...AND SO...
IT ALL STOPPED MATTERING TO ME.
WHO PEOPLE WERE, WHERE THEY CAME FROM.
WHETHER THEY LIVED OR DIED.
I DIDN'T THINK ANY LIFE HAD VALUE...
NOT EVEN MY OWN.
YES...
UNTIL THAT DAY...
IT WAS...
...THE MORNING WE WERE HEADING OFF TO THE ISLAND FOR THE PLAN TO RETAKE THE FOUNDER...

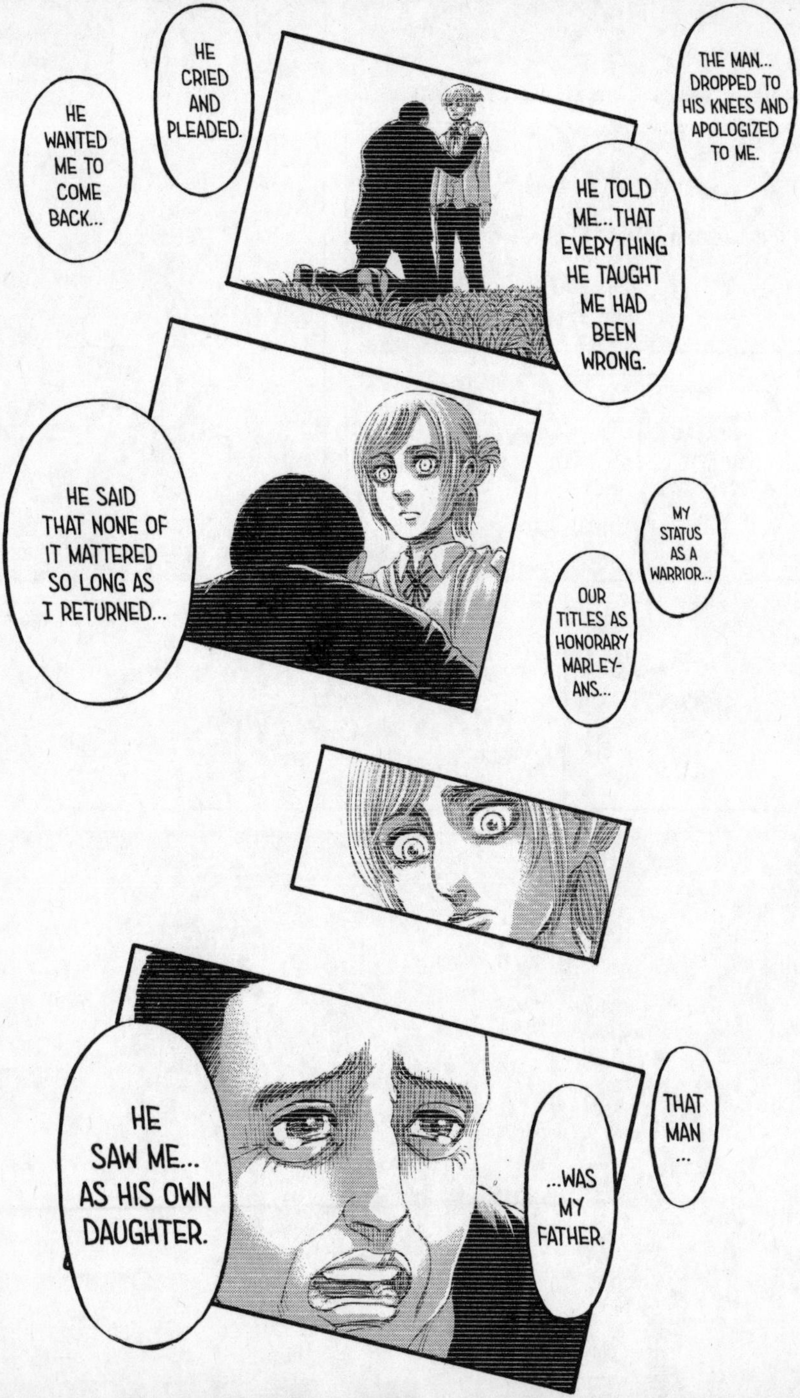
THE MAN... DROPPED TO HIS KNEES AND APOLOGIZED TO ME.
HE TOLD ME...THAT EVERYTHING HE TAUGHT ME HAD BEEN WRONG.
HE CRIED AND PLEADED.
HE WANTED ME TO COME BACK...
MY STATUS AS A WARRIOR...
OUR TITLES AS HONORARY MARLEY-ANS...
HE SAID THAT NONE OF IT MATTERED SO LONG AS I RETURNED...
THAT MAN ...
...WAS MY FATHER.
HE SAW ME... AS HIS OWN DAUGHTER.

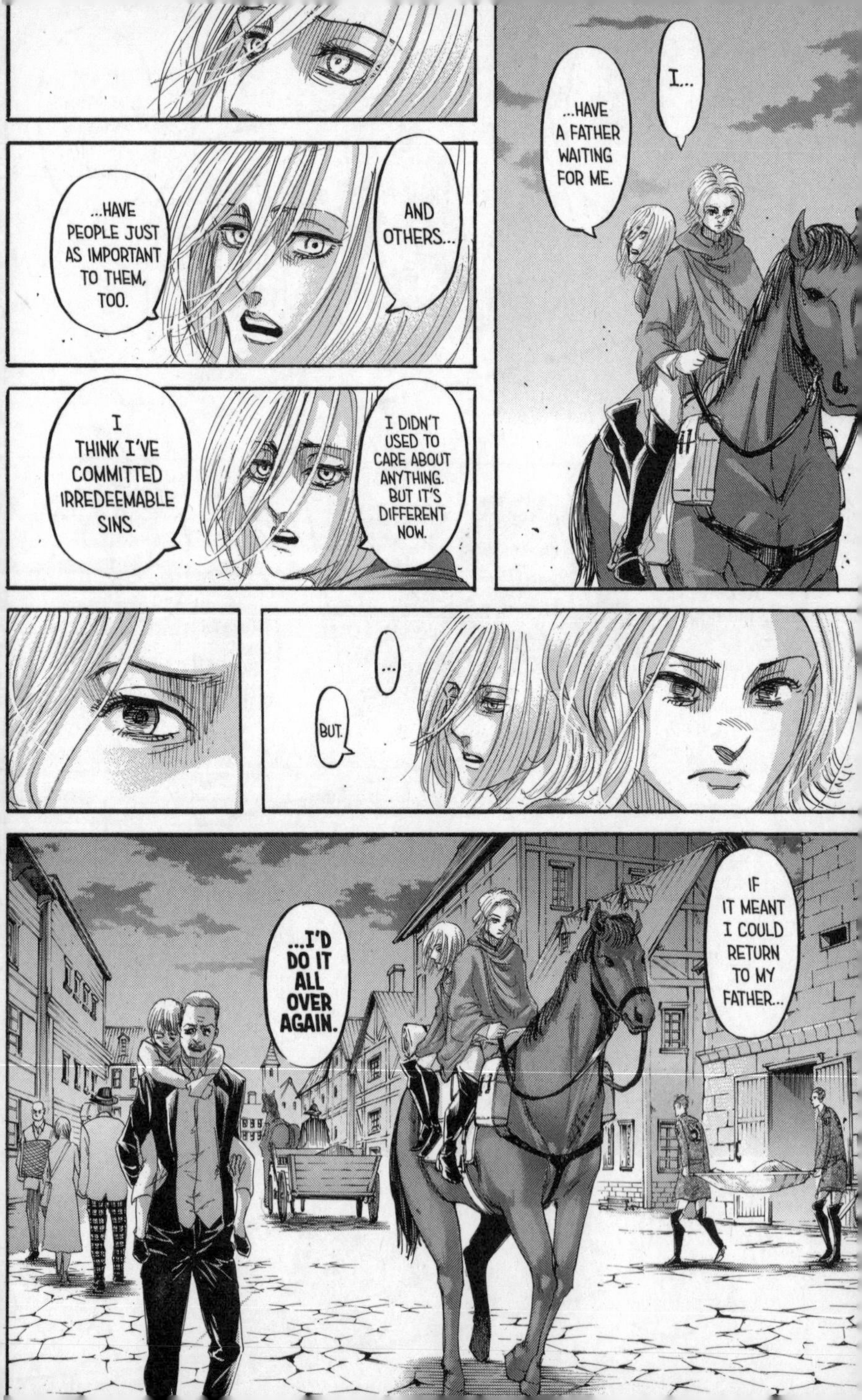

I...
...HAVE A FATHER WAITING FOR ME.
AND OTHERS...
...HAVE PEOPLE JUST AS IMPORTANT TO THEM, TOO.
I DIDN'T USED TO CARE ABOUT ANYTHING. BUT IT'S DIFFERENT NOW.
I THINK I'VE COMMITTED IRREDEEMABLE SINS.
...
BUT.
IF IT MEANT I COULD RETURN TO MY FATHER...
...I'D DO IT ALL OVER AGAIN.

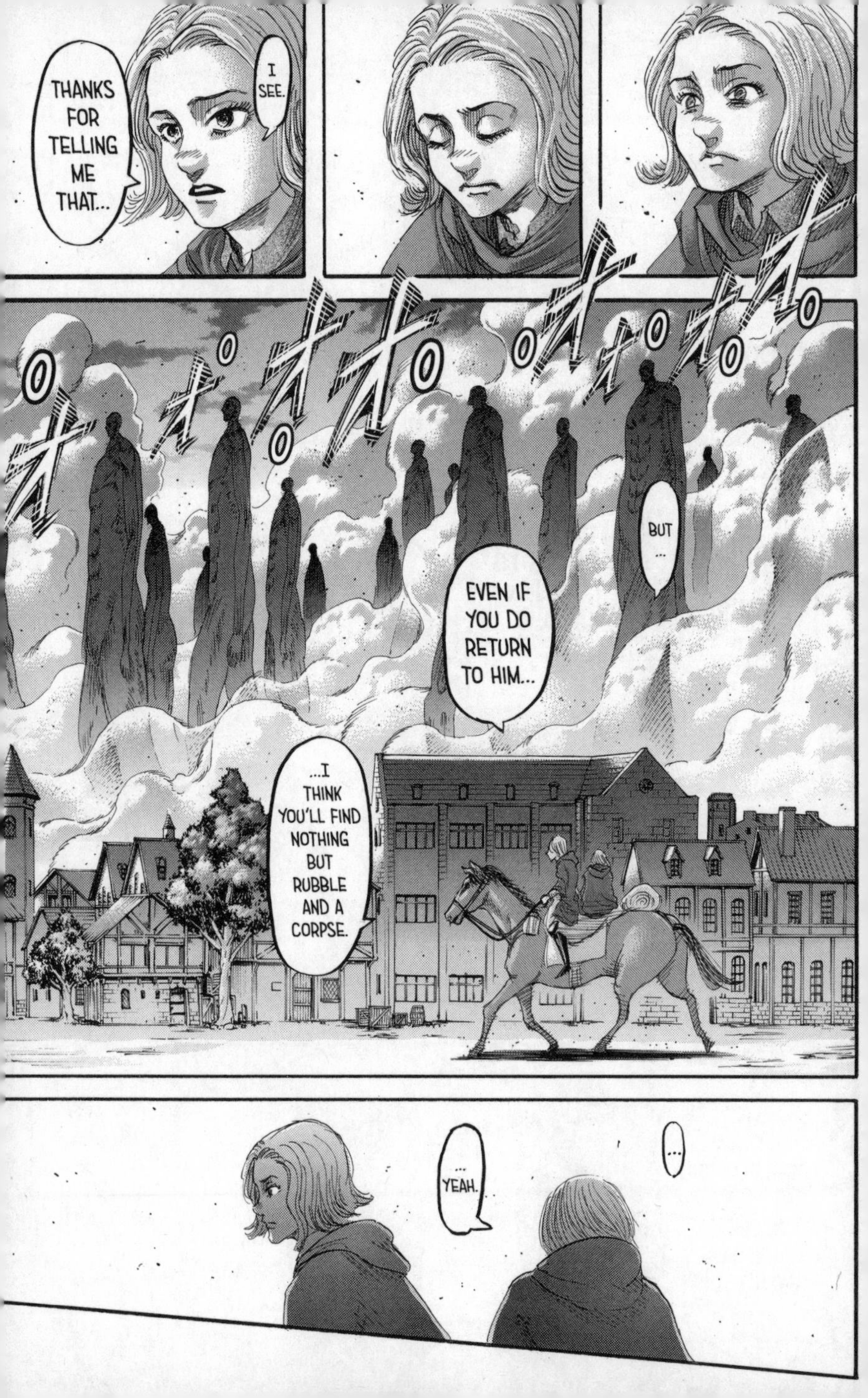
I SEE.
THANKS FOR TELLING ME THAT...
BUT ...
EVEN IF YOU DO RETURN TO HIM...
...I THINK YOU'LL FIND NOTHING BUT RUBBLE AND A CORPSE.
...
... YEAH.

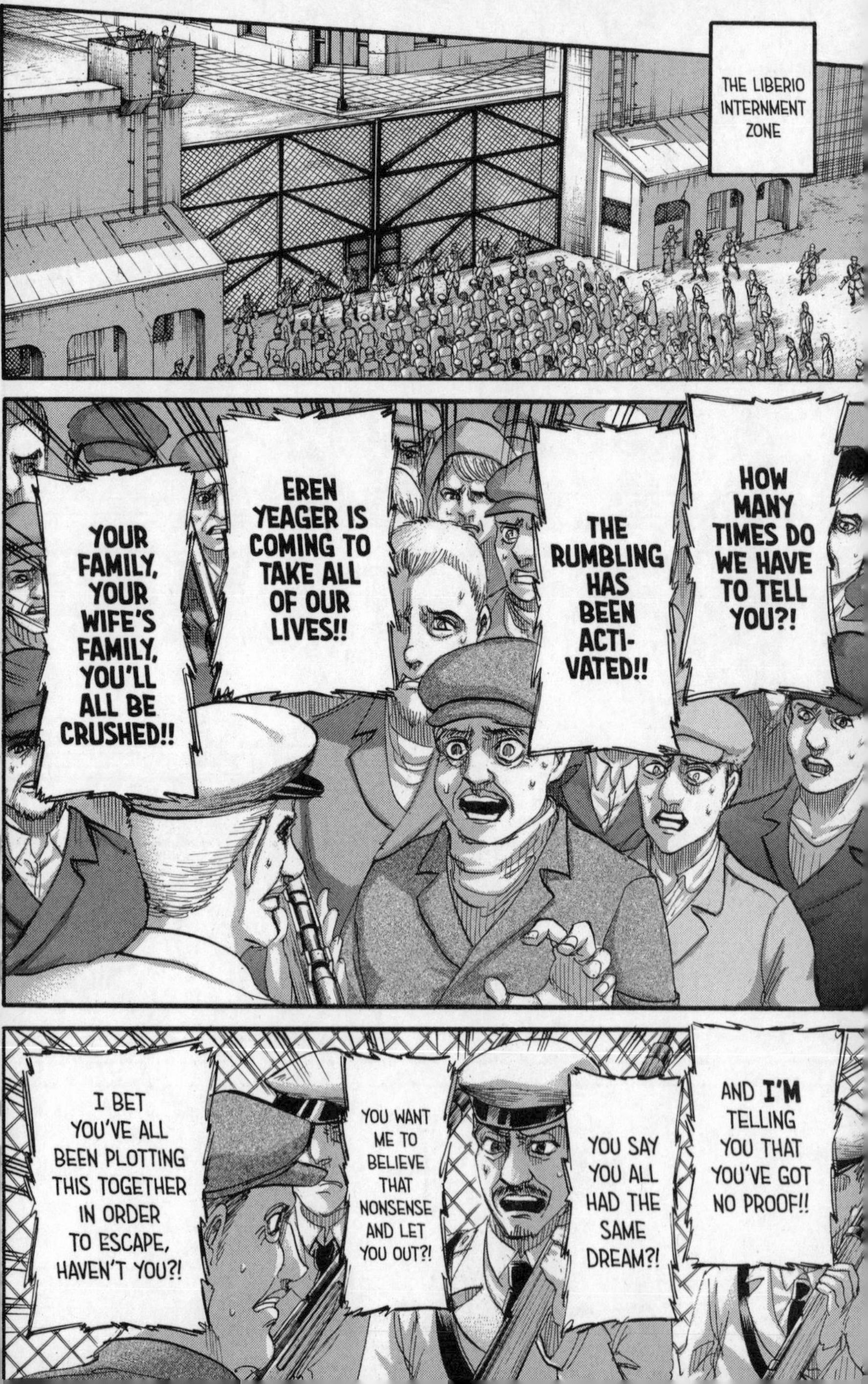
THE LIBERIO INTERNMENT ZONE
HOW MANY TIMES DO WE HAVE TO TELL YOU?!
THE RUMBLING HAS BEEN ACTI-VATED!!
EREN YEAGER IS COMING TO TAKE ALL OF OUR LIVES!!
YOUR FAMILY, YOUR WIFE'S FAMILY, YOU'LL ALL BE CRUSHED!!
AND **I'M** TELLING YOU THAT YOU'VE GOT NO PROOF!!
YOU SAY YOU ALL HAD THE SAME DREAM?!
YOU WANT ME TO BELIEVE THAT NONSENSE AND LET YOU OUT?!
I BET YOU'VE ALL BEEN PLOTTING THIS TOGETHER IN ORDER TO ESCAPE, HAVEN'T YOU?!

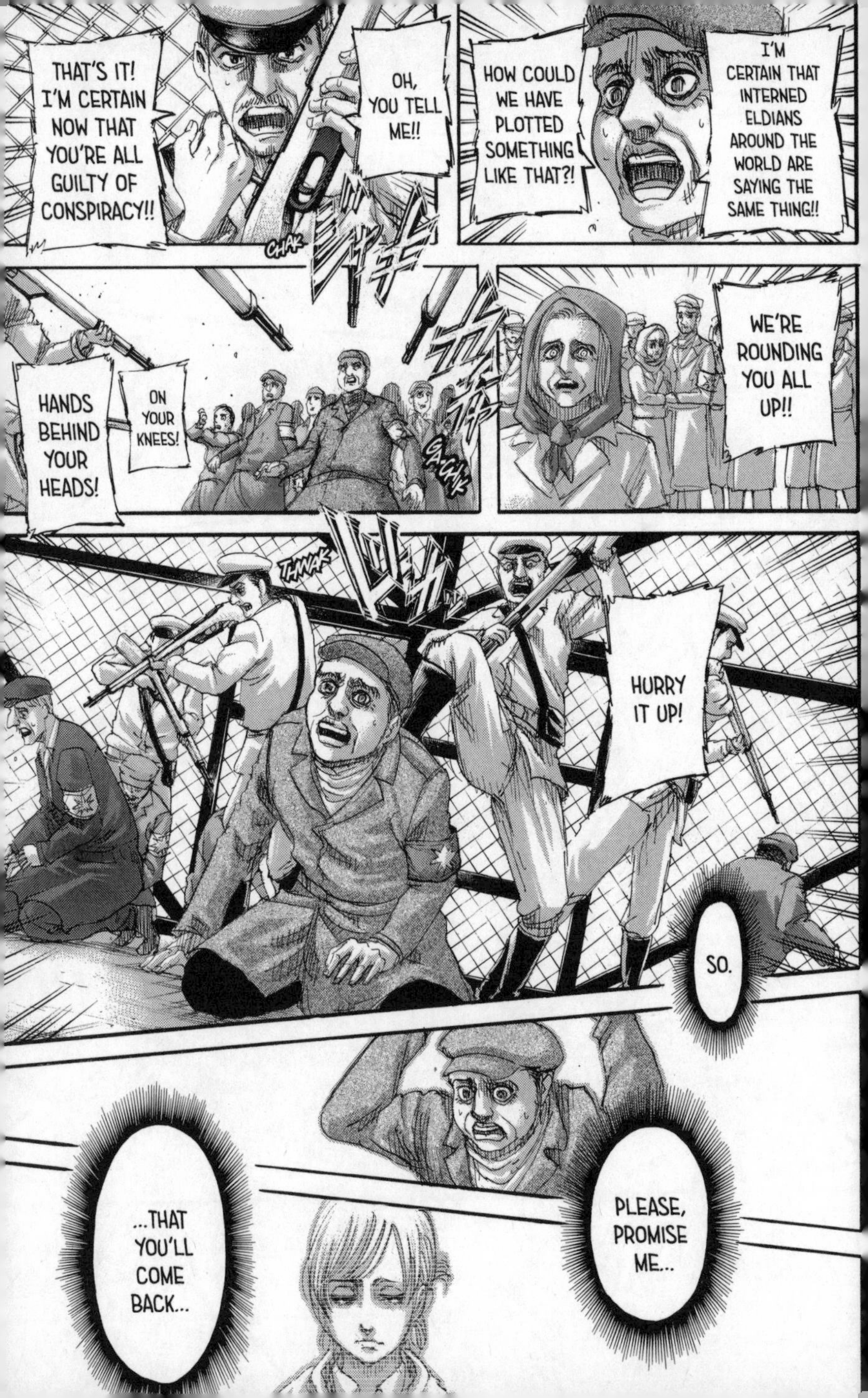
I'M CERTAIN THAT INTERNED ELDIANS AROUND THE WORLD ARE SAYING THE SAME THING!!
HOW COULD WE HAVE PLOTTED SOMETHING LIKE THAT?!
OH, YOU TELL ME!!
THAT'S IT! I'M CERTAIN NOW THAT YOU'RE ALL GUILTY OF CONSPIRACY!!
CHAK
WE'RE ROUNDING YOU ALL UP!!
GACHAK
ON YOUR KNEES!
HANDS BEHIND YOUR HEADS!
HURRY IT UP!
THWAK
SO.
PLEASE, PROMISE ME...
...THAT YOU'LL COME BACK...

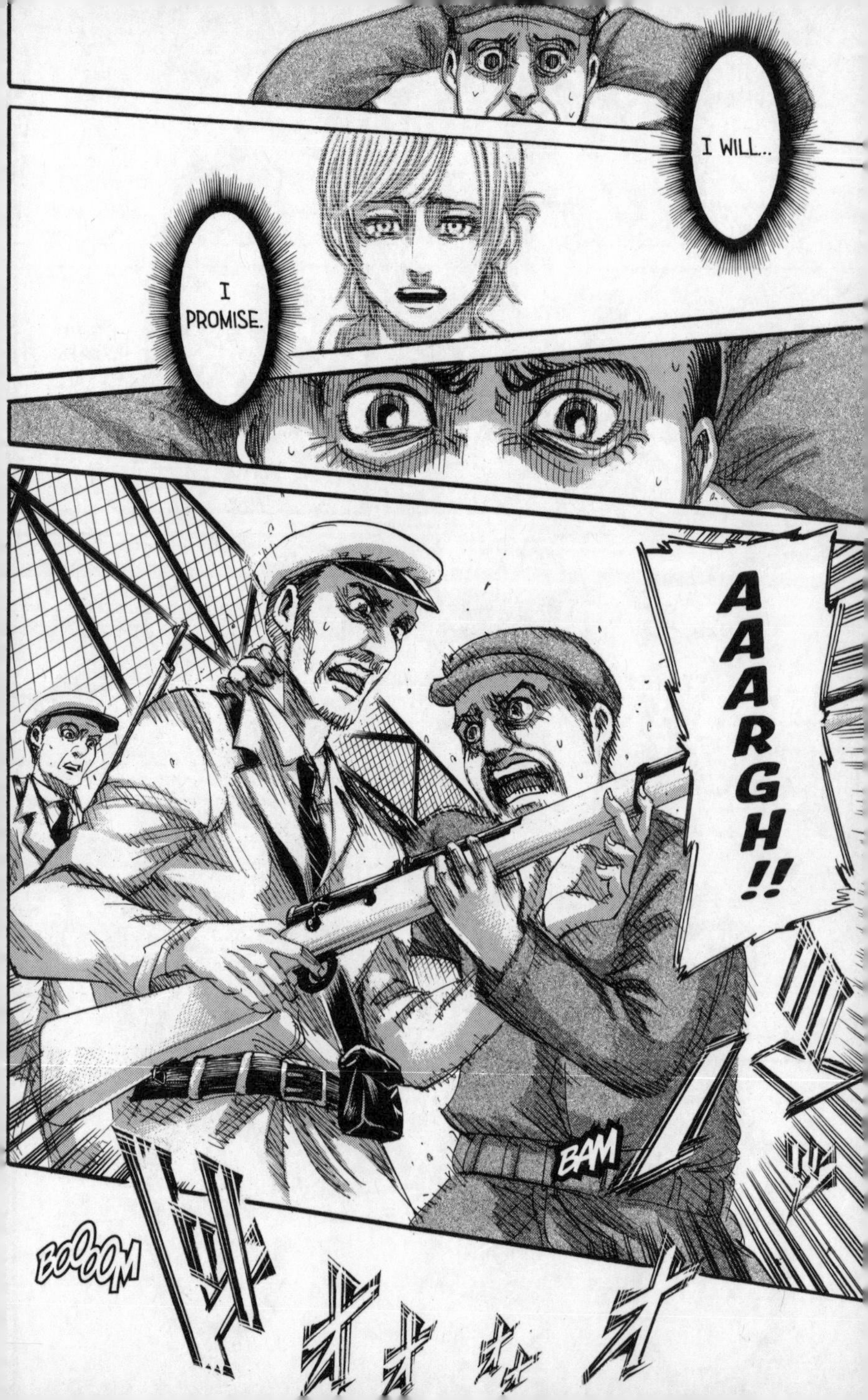
I WILL...
I PROMISE.
AAARGH!!
BAM
BOOOOM

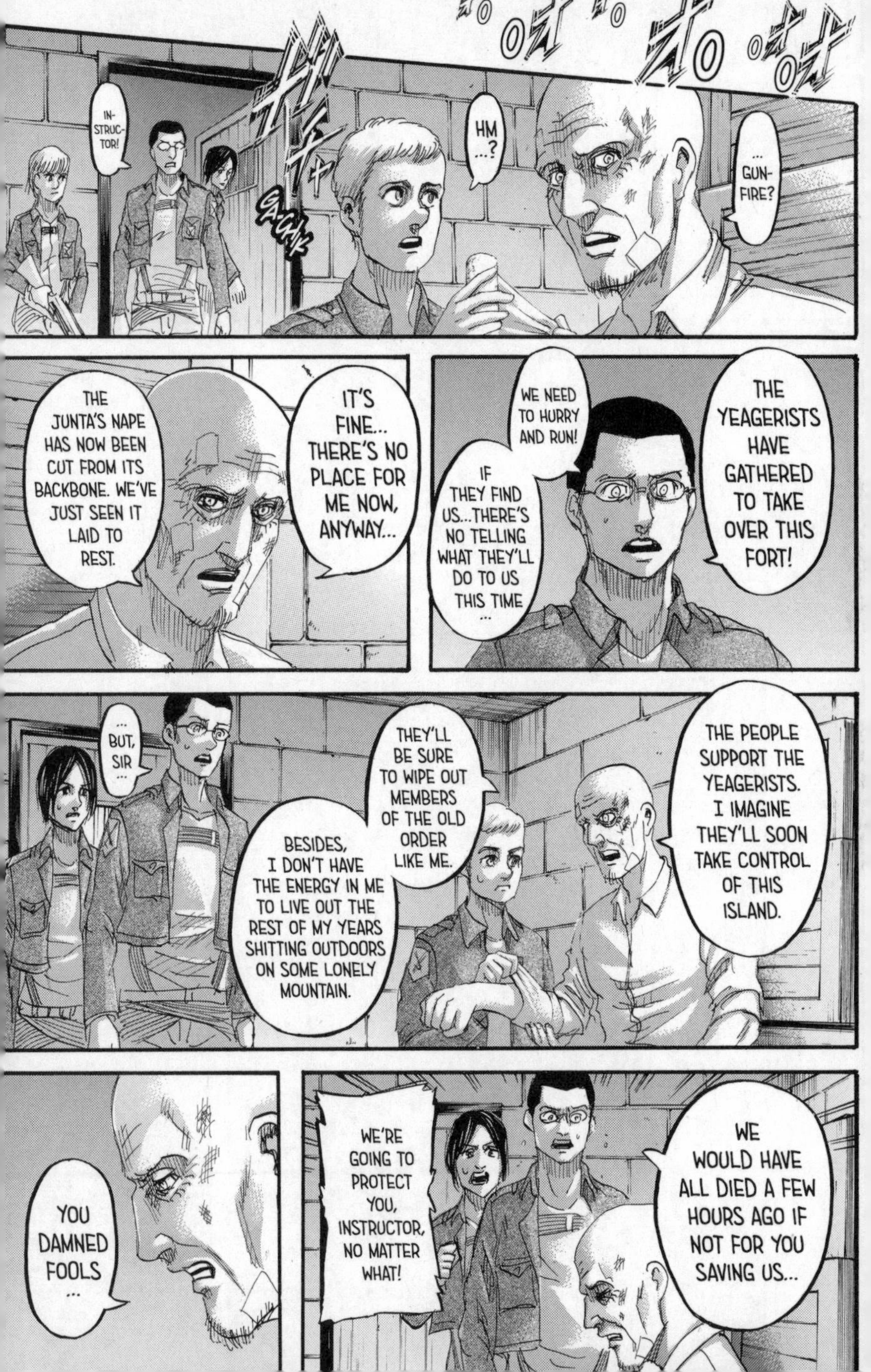
...GUNFIRE?
HM ...?
GA-CHAK
INSTRUCTOR!
THE YEAGERISTS HAVE GATHERED TO TAKE OVER THIS FORT!
WE NEED TO HURRY AND RUN!
IF THEY FIND US...THERE'S NO TELLING WHAT THEY'LL DO TO US THIS TIME ...
IT'S FINE... THERE'S NO PLACE FOR ME NOW, ANYWAY...
THE JUNTA'S NAPE HAS NOW BEEN CUT FROM ITS BACKBONE. WE'VE JUST SEEN IT LAID TO REST.
THE PEOPLE SUPPORT THE YEAGERISTS. I IMAGINE THEY'LL SOON TAKE CONTROL OF THIS ISLAND.
THEY'LL BE SURE TO WIPE OUT MEMBERS OF THE OLD ORDER LIKE ME.
BESIDES, I DON'T HAVE THE ENERGY IN ME TO LIVE OUT THE REST OF MY YEARS SHITTING OUTDOORS ON SOME LONELY MOUNTAIN.
... BUT, SIR ...
WE WOULD HAVE ALL DIED A FEW HOURS AGO IF NOT FOR YOU SAVING US...
WE'RE GOING TO PROTECT YOU, INSTRUCTOR, NO MATTER WHAT!
YOU DAMNED FOOLS ...

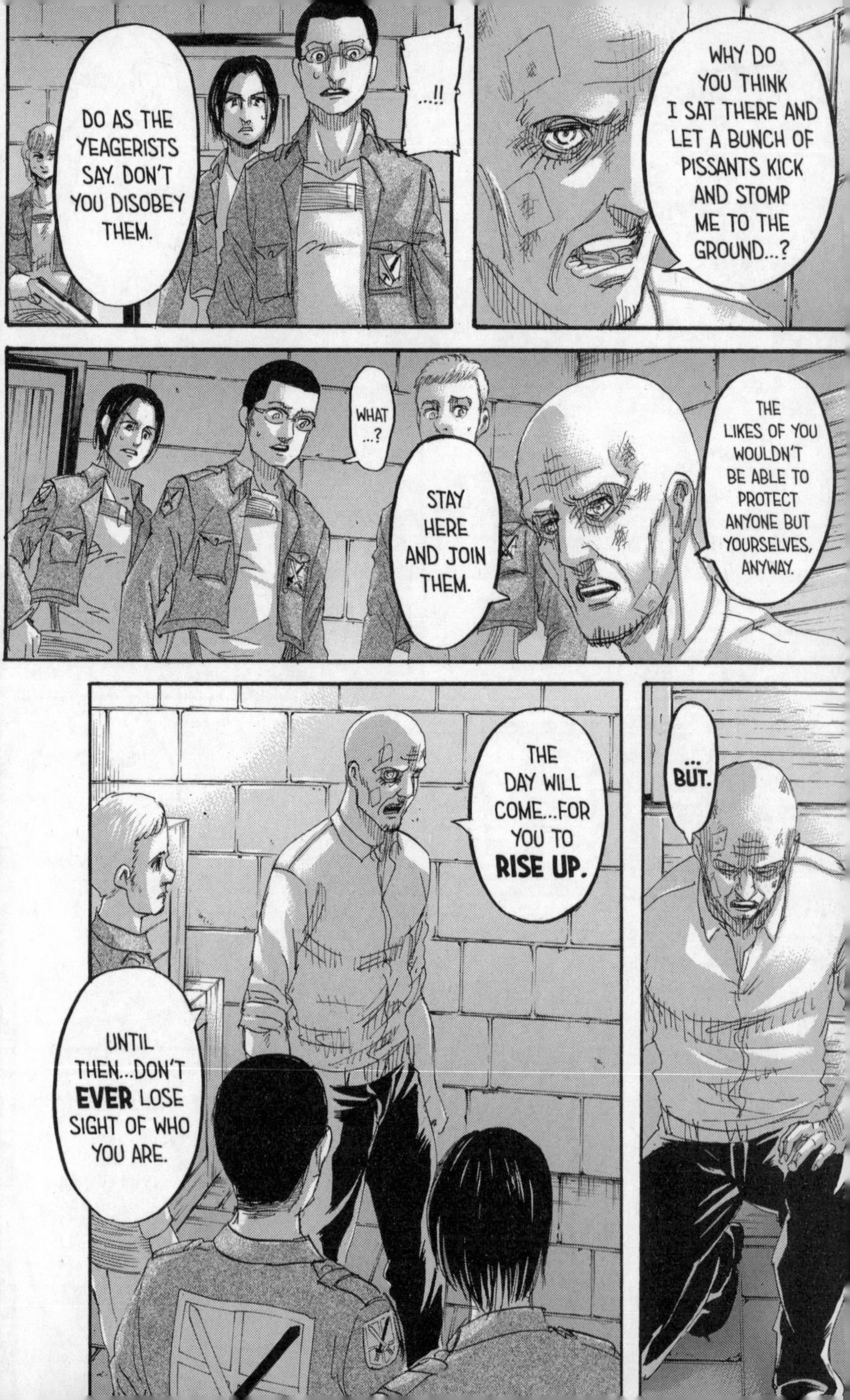
WHY DO YOU THINK I SAT THERE AND LET A BUNCH OF PISSANTS KICK AND STOMP ME TO THE GROUND...?
...!!
DO AS THE YEAGERISTS SAY. DON'T YOU DISOBEY THEM.
THE LIKES OF YOU WOULDN'T BE ABLE TO PROTECT ANYONE BUT YOURSELVES, ANYWAY.
WHAT...?
STAY HERE AND JOIN THEM.
...BÜT.
THE DAY WILL COME...FOR YOU TO **RISE UP.**
UNTIL THEN...DON'T **EVER** LOSE SIGHT OF WHO YOU ARE.

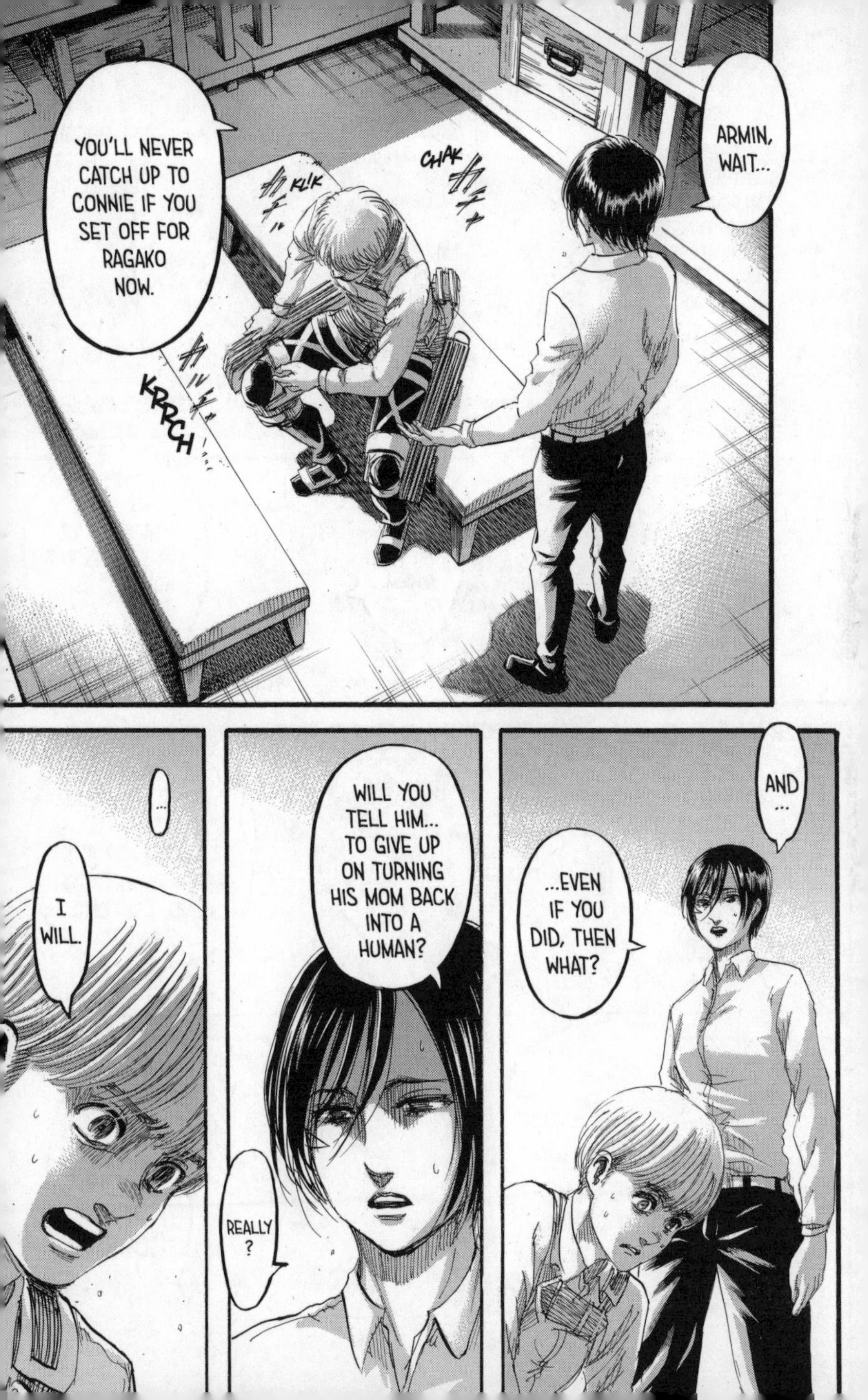
ARMIN, WAIT...
CHAK
KLIK
YOU'LL NEVER CATCH UP TO CONNIE IF YOU SET OFF FOR RAGAKO NOW.
KRRCH
AND...
...EVEN IF YOU DID, THEN WHAT?
WILL YOU TELL HIM... TO GIVE UP ON TURNING HIS MOM BACK INTO A HUMAN?
REALLY?
...
I WILL.

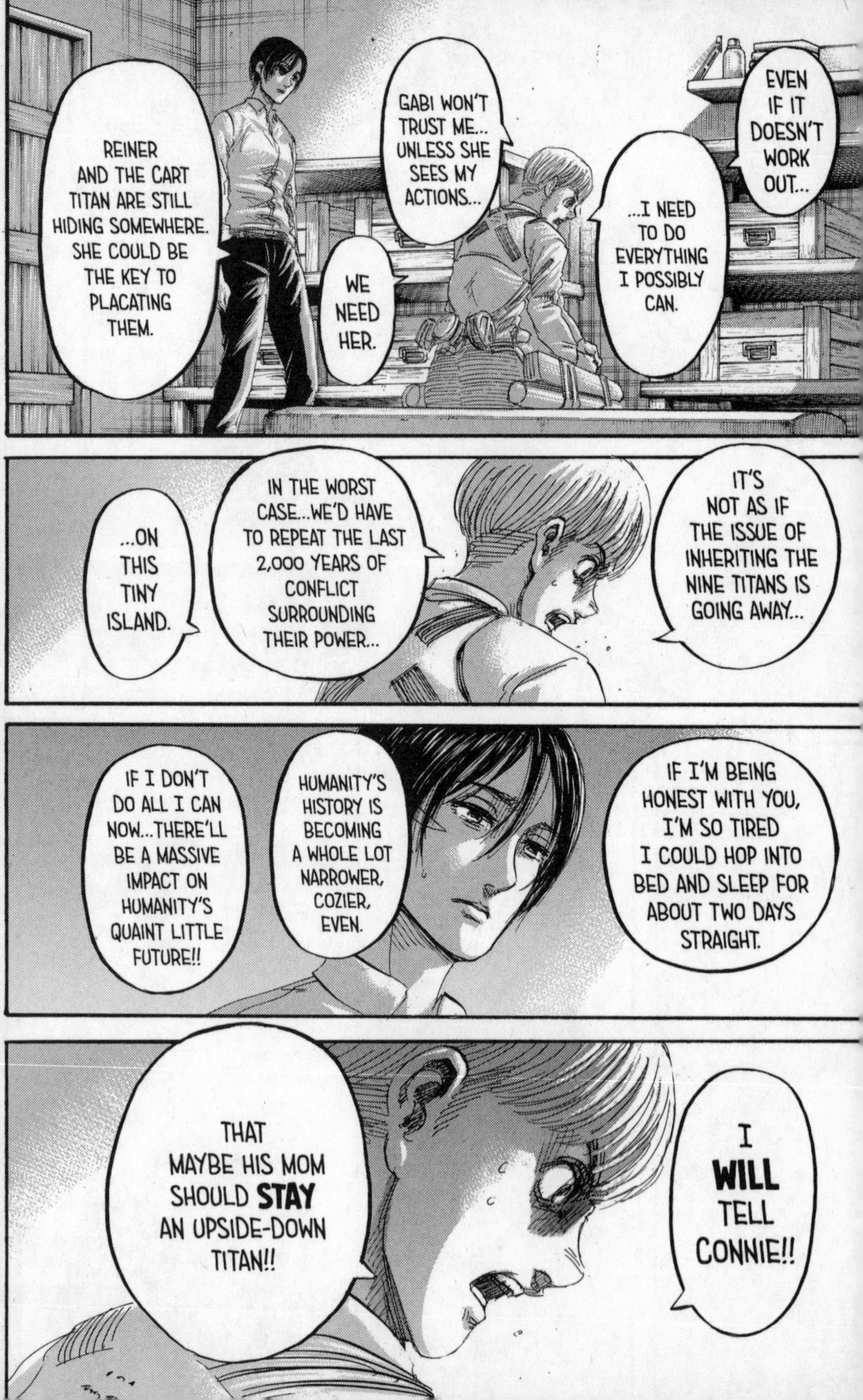
EVEN IF IT DOESN'T WORK OUT...
...I NEED TO DO EVERYTHING I POSSIBLY CAN.
GABI WON'T TRUST ME... UNLESS SHE SEES MY ACTIONS...
WE NEED HER.
REINER AND THE CART TITAN ARE STILL HIDING SOMEWHERE. SHE COULD BE THE KEY TO PLACATING THEM.
IT'S NOT AS IF THE ISSUE OF INHERITING THE NINE TITANS IS GOING AWAY...
IN THE WORST CASE...WE'D HAVE TO REPEAT THE LAST 2,000 YEARS OF CONFLICT SURROUNDING THEIR POWER...
...ON THIS TINY ISLAND.
IF I'M BEING HONEST WITH YOU, I'M SO TIRED I COULD HOP INTO BED AND SLEEP FOR ABOUT TWO DAYS STRAIGHT.
HUMANITY'S HISTORY IS BECOMING A WHOLE LOT NARROWER, COZIER, EVEN.
IF I DON'T DO ALL I CAN NOW...THERE'LL BE A MASSIVE IMPACT ON HUMANITY'S QUAINT LITTLE FUTURE!!
I **WILL** TELL CONNIE!!
THAT MAYBE HIS MOM SHOULD **STAY** AN UPSIDE-DOWN TITAN!!

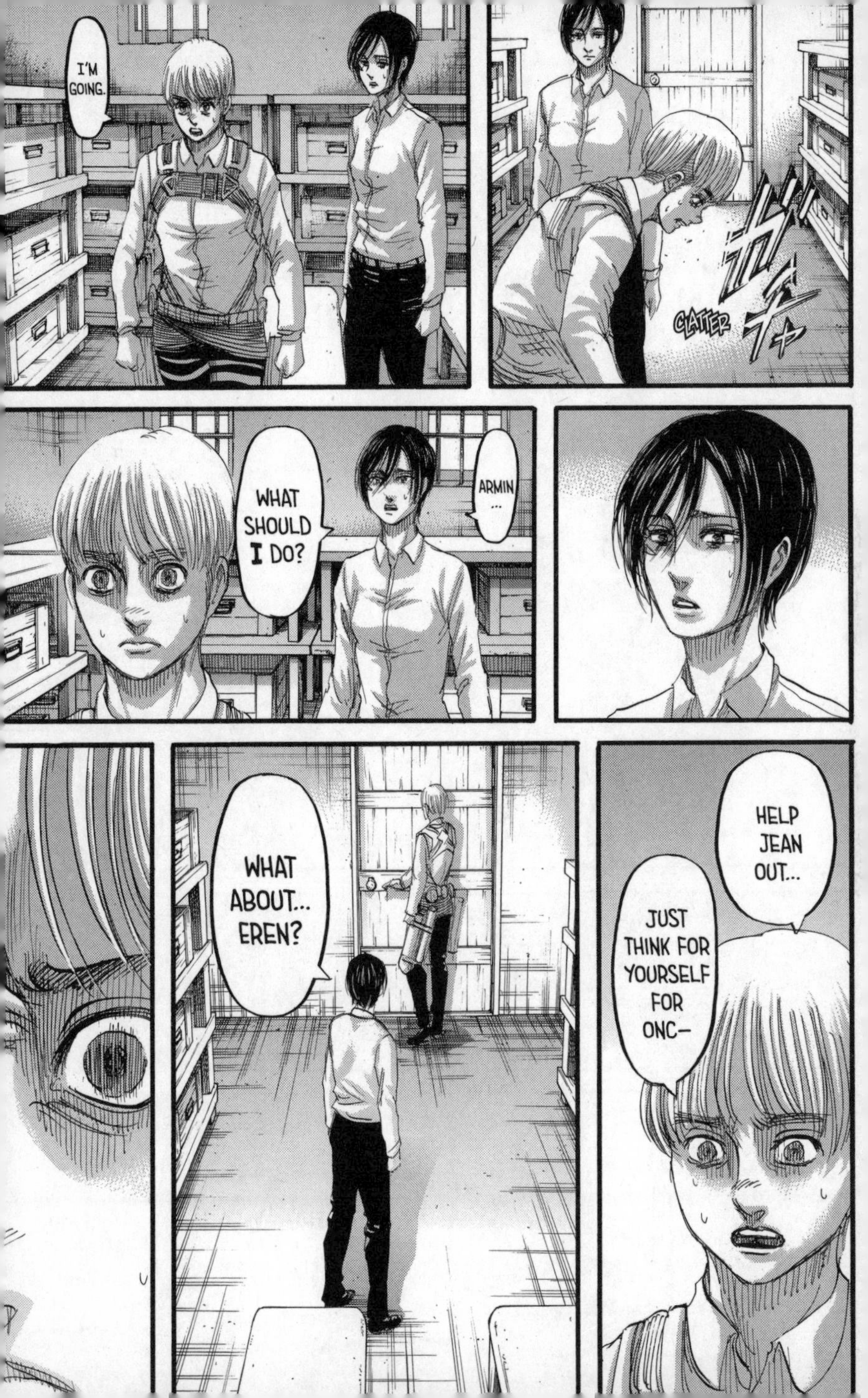
ガチャ
CLATTER
I'M GOING.
ARMIN...
WHAT SHOULD I DO?
HELP JEAN OUT...
JUST THINK FOR YOURSELF FOR ONC—
WHAT ABOUT... EREN?

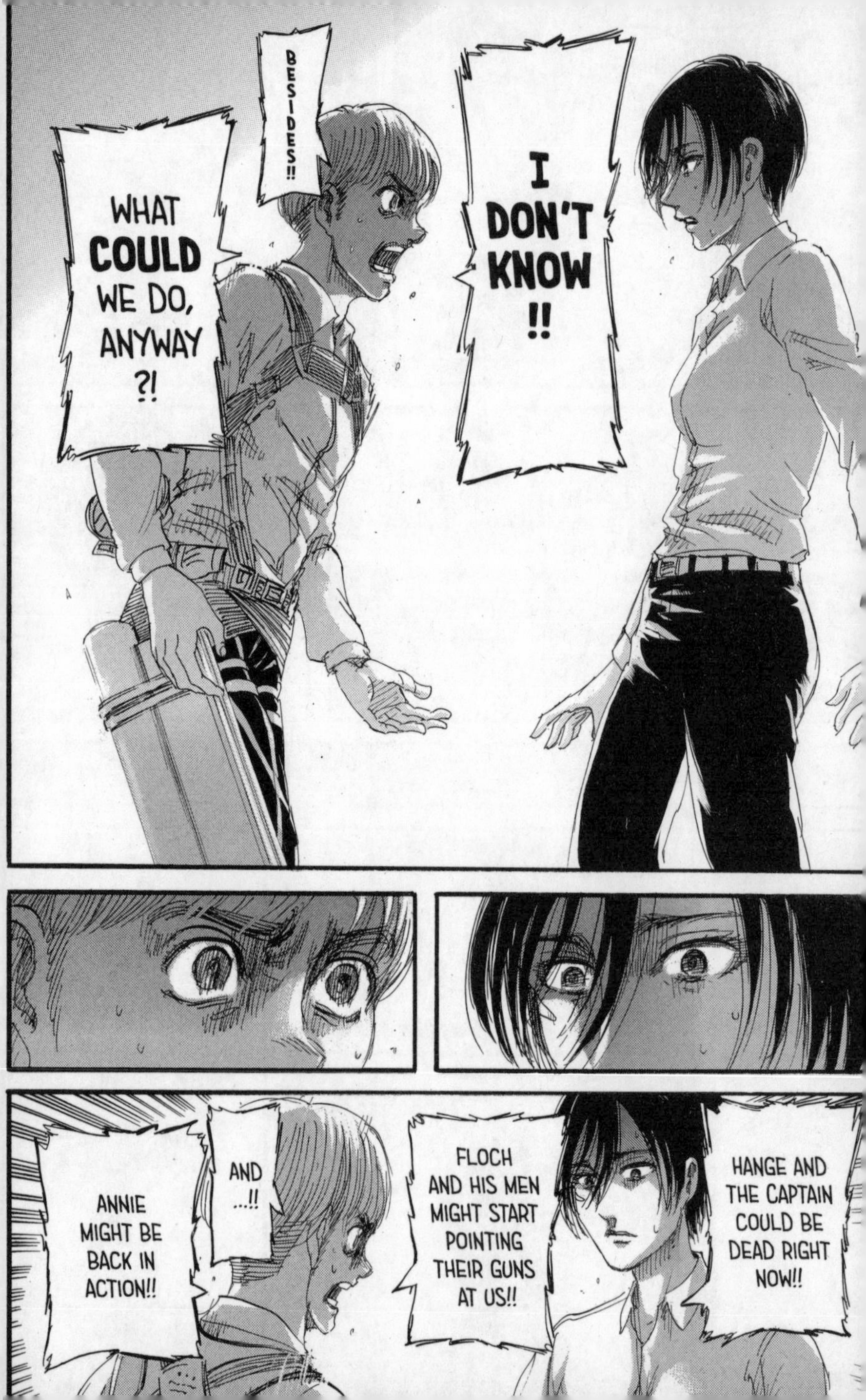
I DON'T KNOW!!
BESIDES!!
WHAT COULD WE DO, ANYWAY?!
HANGE AND THE CAPTAIN COULD BE DEAD RIGHT NOW!!
FLOCH AND HIS MEN MIGHT START POINTING THEIR GUNS AT US!!
AND ...!!
ANNIE MIGHT BE BACK IN ACTION!!

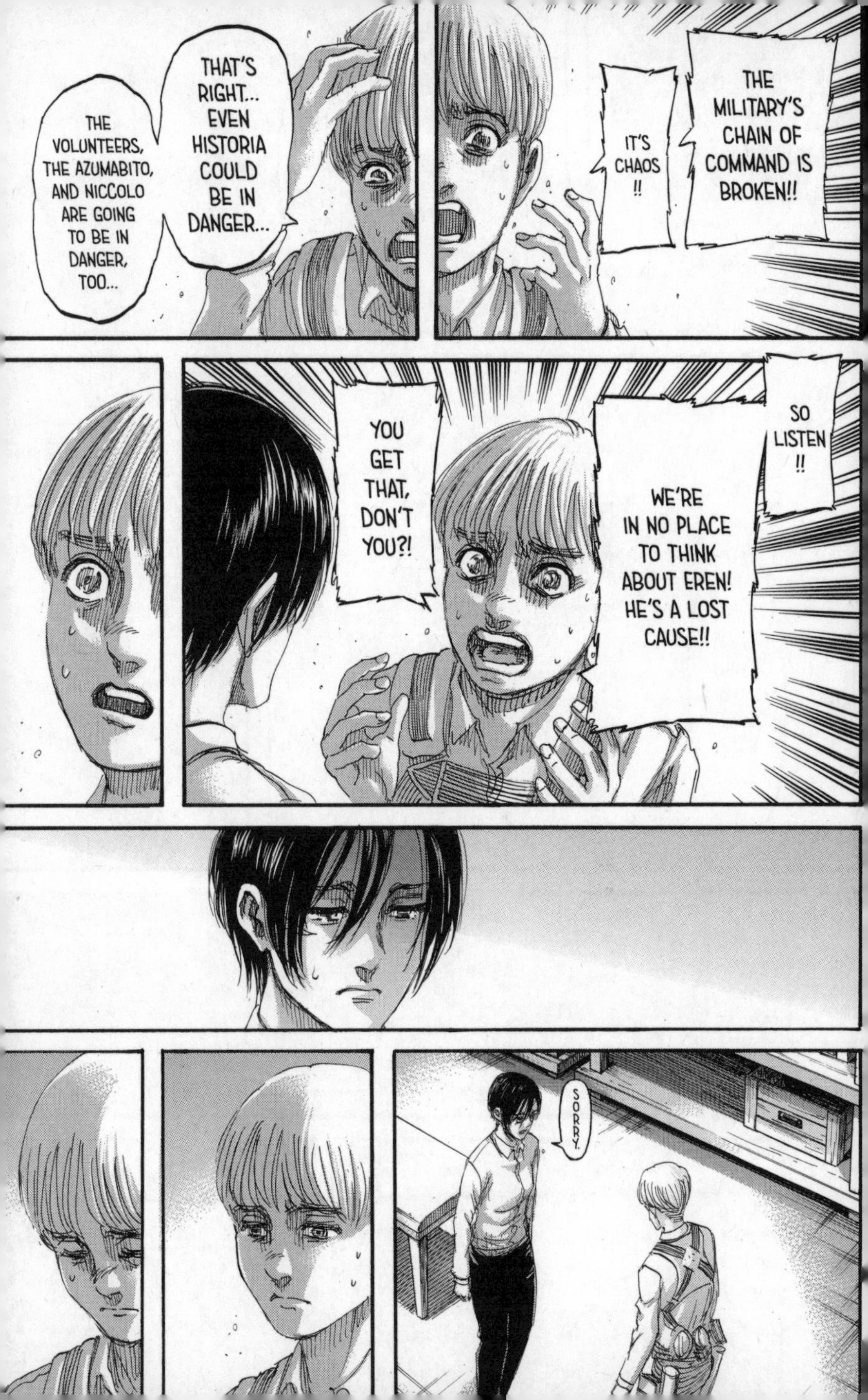
THE MILITARY'S CHAIN OF COMMAND IS BROKEN!!
IT'S CHAOS !!
THAT'S RIGHT... EVEN HISTORIA COULD BE IN DANGER...
THE VOLUNTEERS, THE AZUMABITO, AND NICCOLO ARE GOING TO BE IN DANGER, TOO...
SO LISTEN !!
WE'RE IN NO PLACE TO THINK ABOUT EREN! HE'S A LOST CAUSE!!
YOU GET THAT, DON'T YOU?!
SORRY.

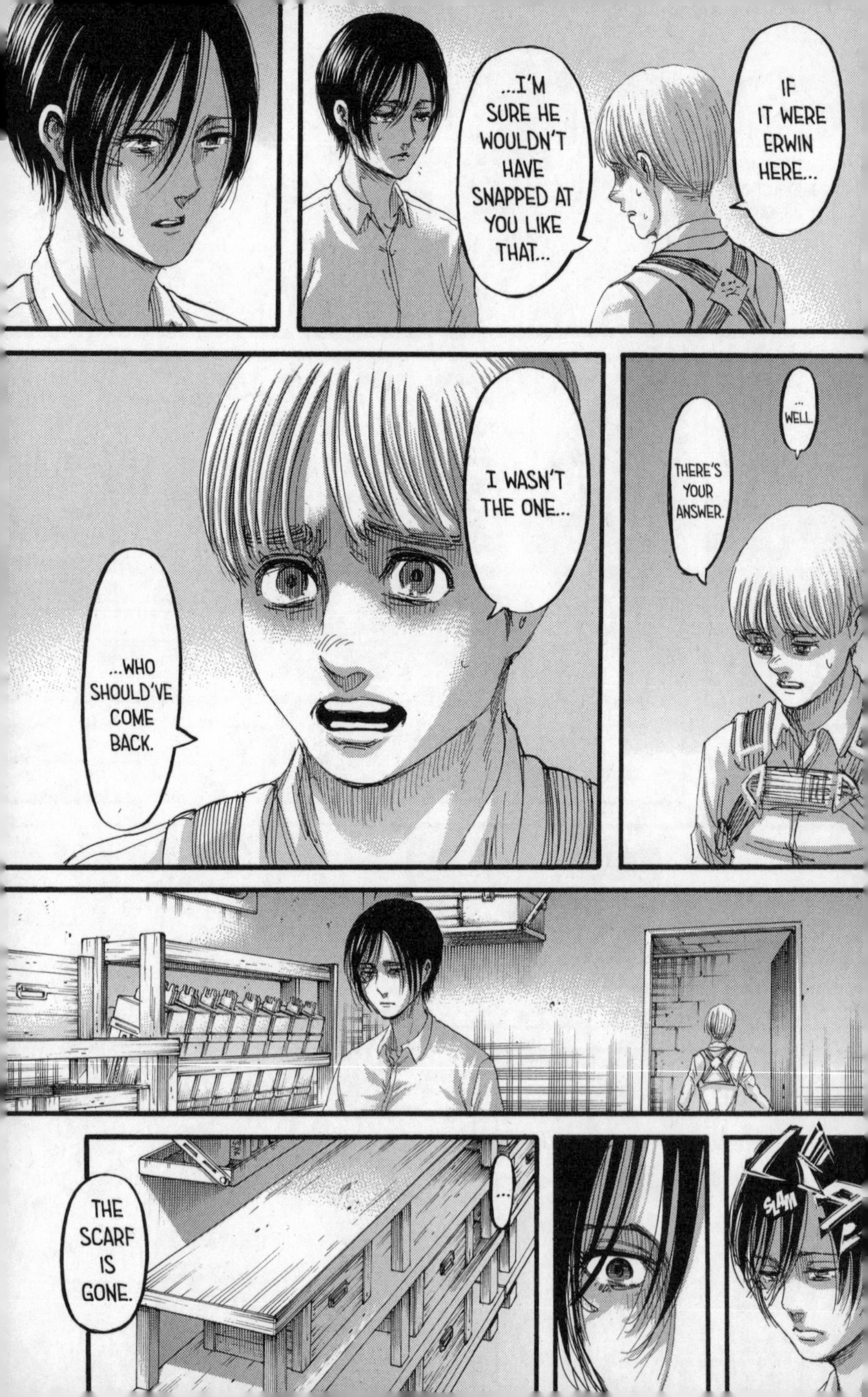
IF IT WERE ERWIN HERE...
...I'M SURE HE WOULDN'T HAVE SNAPPED AT YOU LIKE THAT...
...WELL.
THERE'S YOUR ANSWER.
I WASN'T THE ONE...
...WHO SHOULD'VE COME BACK.
SLAM
...
THE SCARF IS GONE.

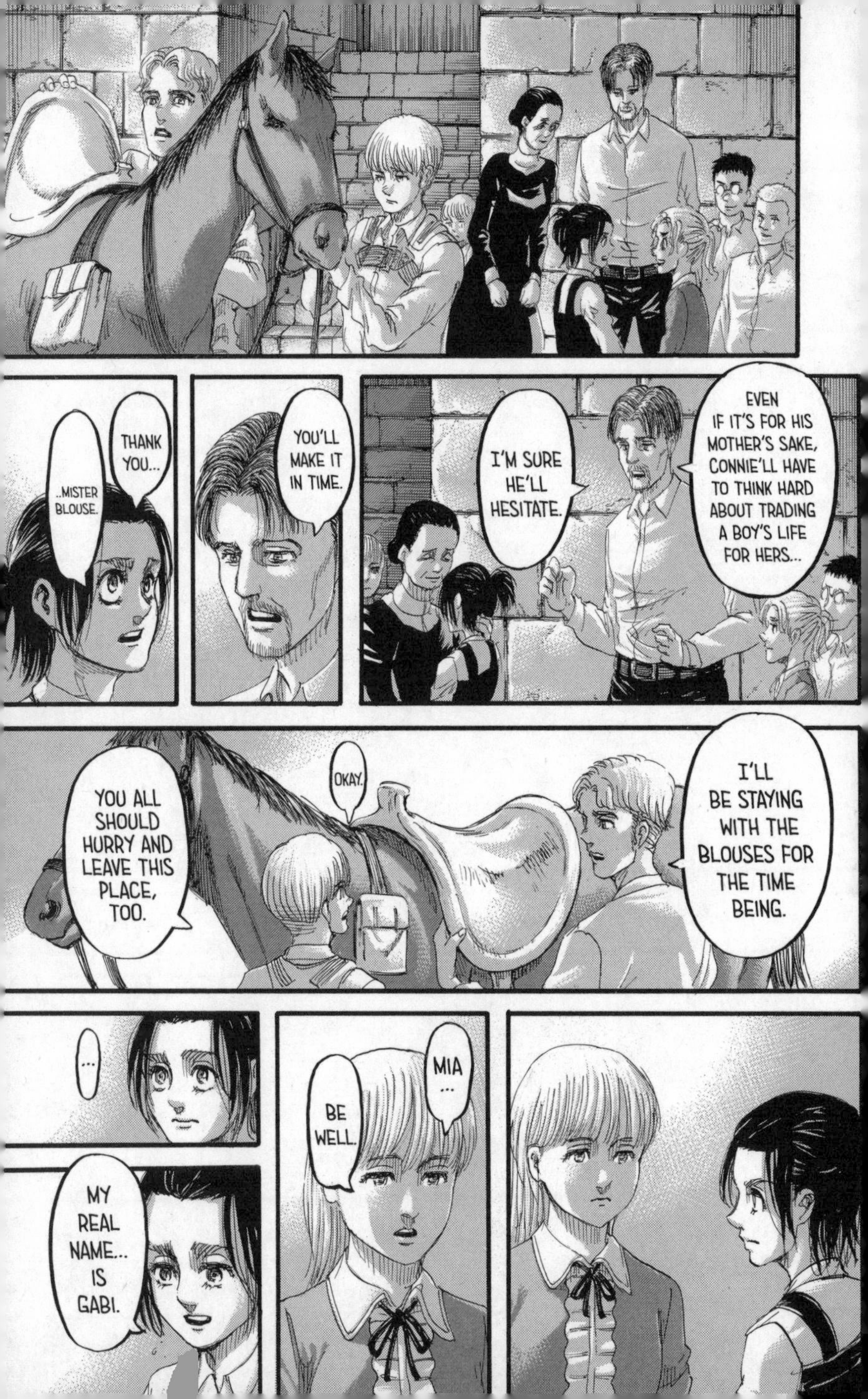
EVEN IF IT'S FOR HIS MOTHER'S SAKE, CONNIE'LL HAVE TO THINK HARD ABOUT TRADING A BOY'S LIFE FOR HERS...
I'M SURE HE'LL HESITATE.
YOU'LL MAKE IT IN TIME.
THANK YOU...
..MISTER BLOUSE.
I'LL BE STAYING WITH THE BLOUSES FOR THE TIME BEING.
OKAY.
YOU ALL SHOULD HURRY AND LEAVE THIS PLACE, TOO.
MIA...
BE WELL.
...
MY REAL NAME... IS GABI.

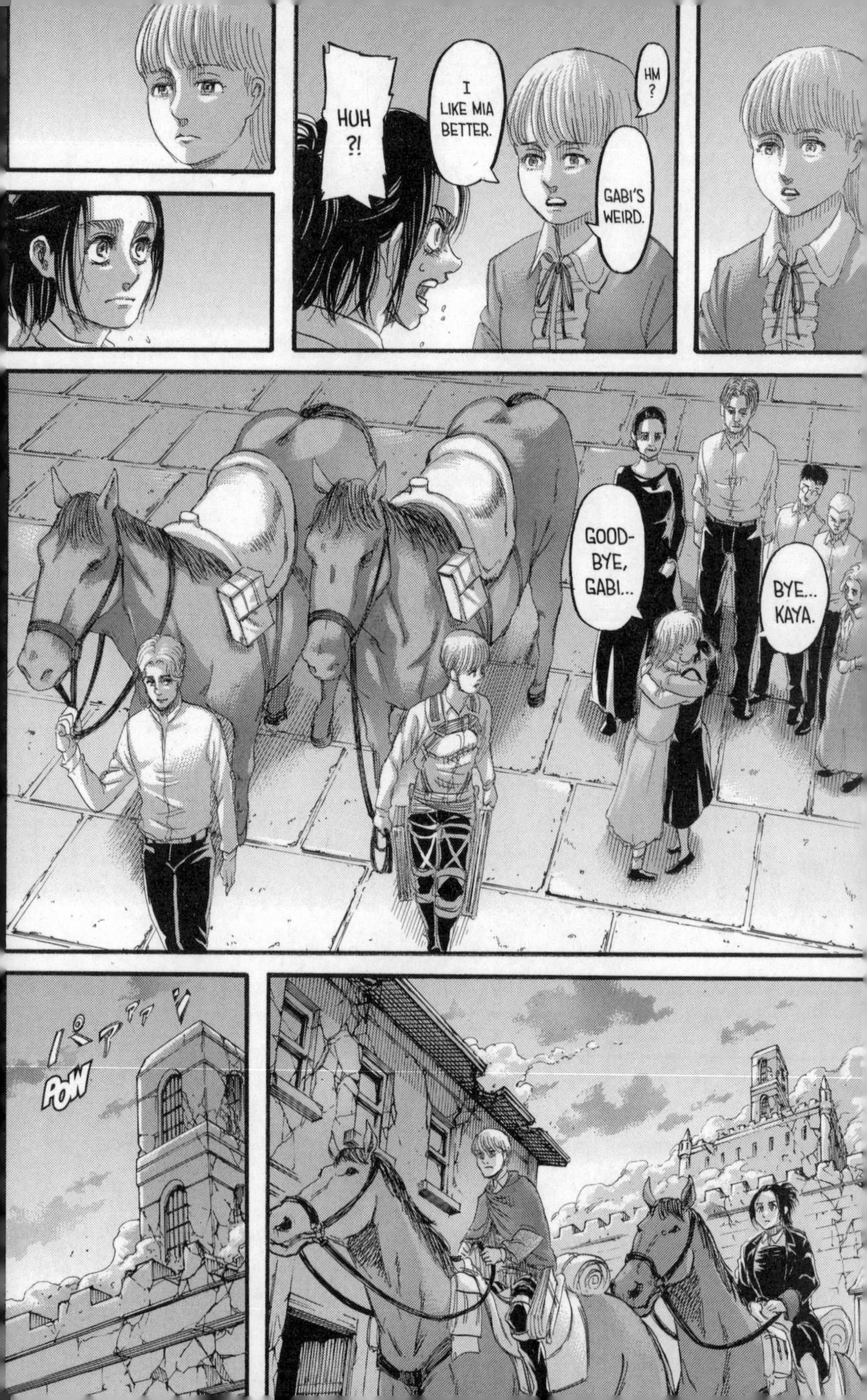
HM?
GABI'S WEIRD.
I LIKE MIA BETTER.
HUH?!
BYE... KAYA.
GOOD-BYE, GABI...
パァァァン
POW

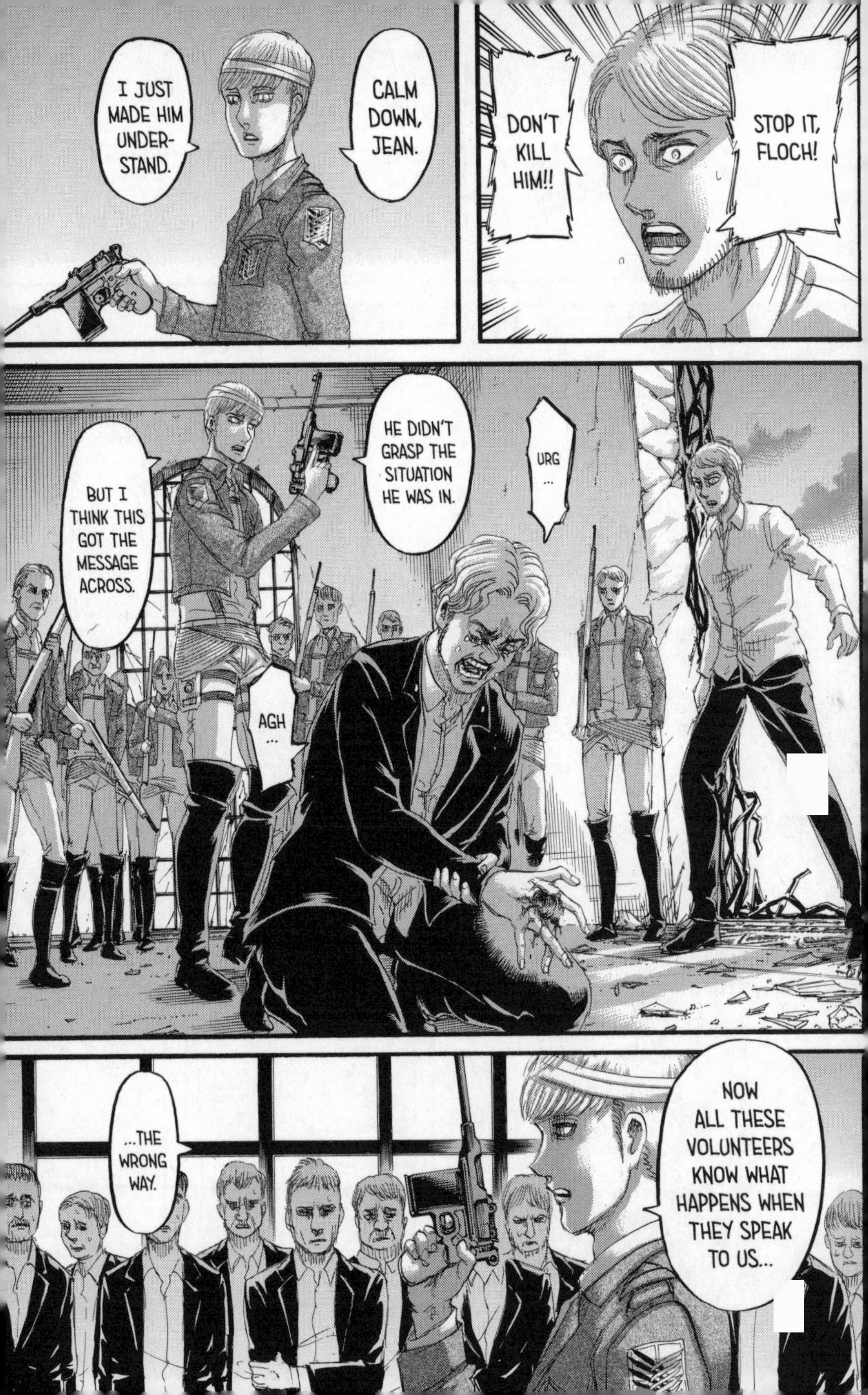
STOP IT, FLOCH!
DON'T KILL HIM!!
CALM DOWN, JEAN.
I JUST MADE HIM UNDER-STAND.
URG ...
HE DIDN'T GRASP THE SITUATION HE WAS IN.
BUT I THINK THIS GOT THE MESSAGE ACROSS.
AGH ...
NOW ALL THESE VOLUNTEERS KNOW WHAT HAPPENS WHEN THEY SPEAK TO US...
...THE WRONG WAY.

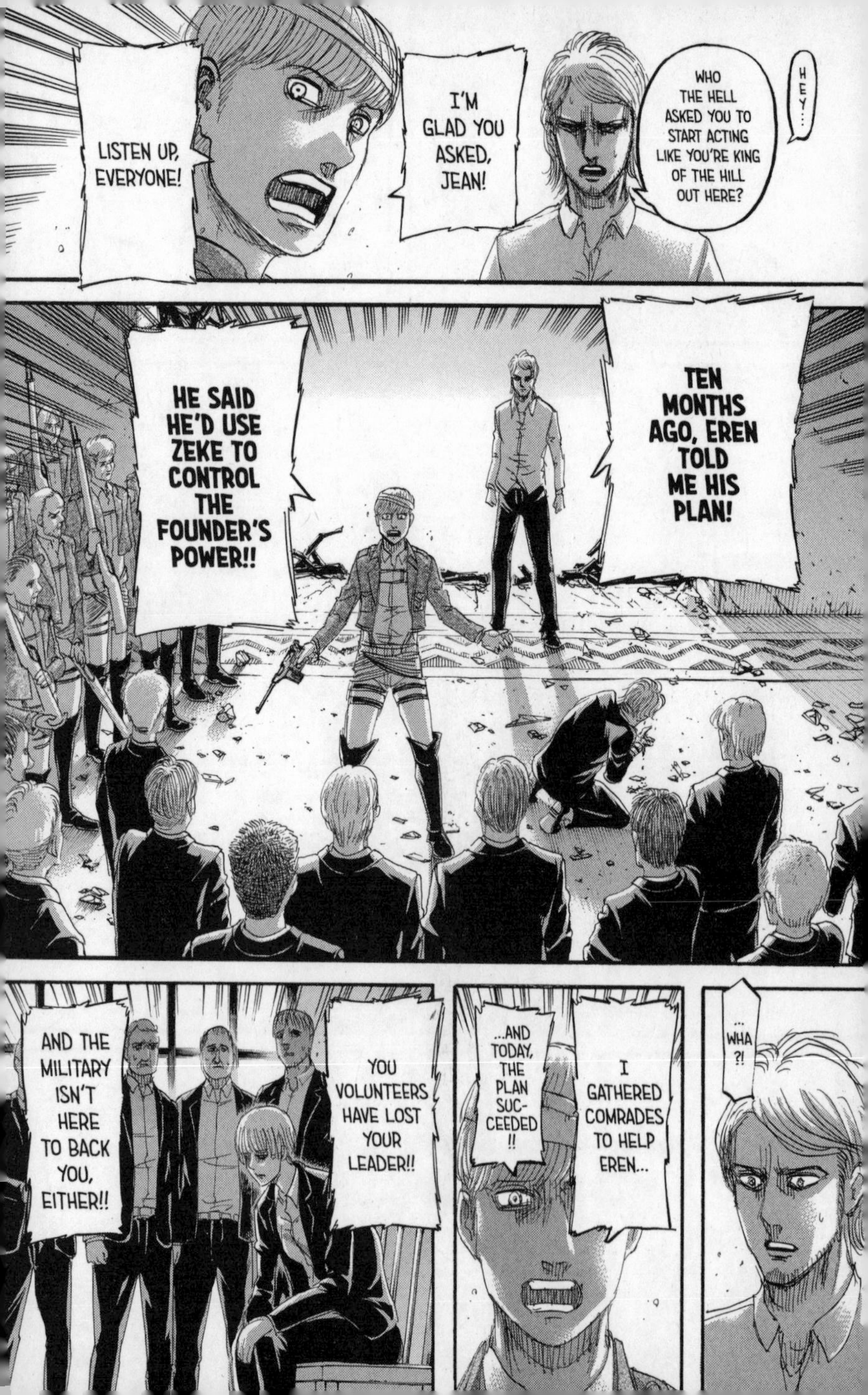

HEY...
WHO THE HELL ASKED YOU TO START ACTING LIKE YOU'RE KING OF THE HILL OUT HERE?
I'M GLAD YOU ASKED, JEAN!
LISTEN UP, EVERYONE!
TEN MONTHS AGO, EREN TOLD ME HIS PLAN!
HE SAID HE'D USE ZEKE TO CONTROL THE FOUNDER'S POWER!!
...WHA?!
I GATHERED COMRADES TO HELP EREN...
...AND TODAY, THE PLAN SUC-CEEDED!!
YOU VOLUNTEERS HAVE LOST YOUR LEADER!!
AND THE MILITARY ISN'T HERE TO BACK YOU, EITHER!!

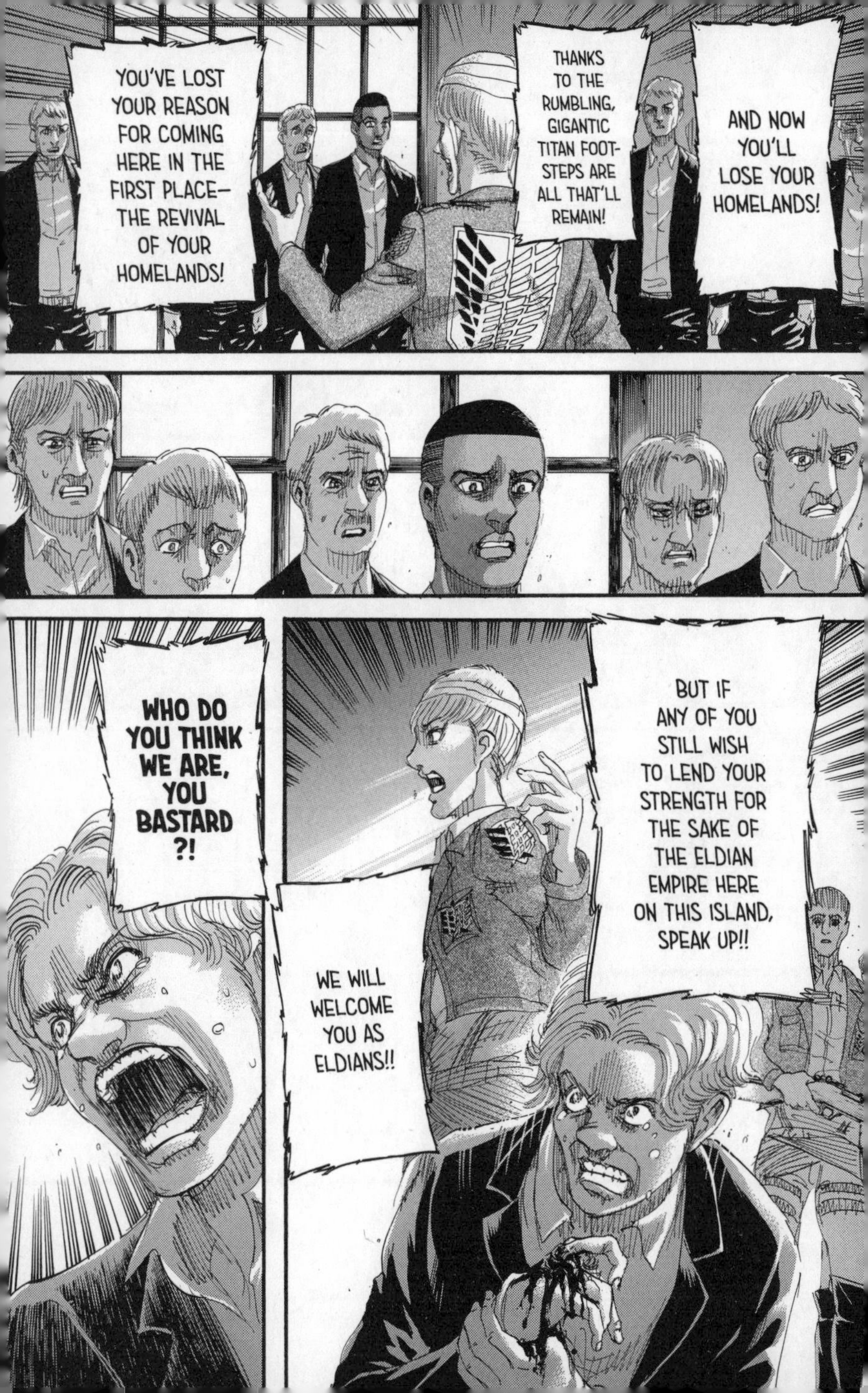
AND NOW YOU'LL LOSE YOUR HOMELANDS!
THANKS TO THE RUMBLING, GIGANTIC TITAN FOOT-STEPS ARE ALL THAT'LL REMAIN!
YOU'VE LOST YOUR REASON FOR COMING HERE IN THE FIRST PLACE—THE REVIVAL OF YOUR HOMELANDS!
BUT IF ANY OF YOU STILL WISH TO LEND YOUR STRENGTH FOR THE SAKE OF THE ELDIAN EMPIRE HERE ON THIS ISLAND, SPEAK UP!!
WE WILL WELCOME YOU AS ELDIANS!!
WHO DO YOU THINK WE ARE, YOU BASTARD?!

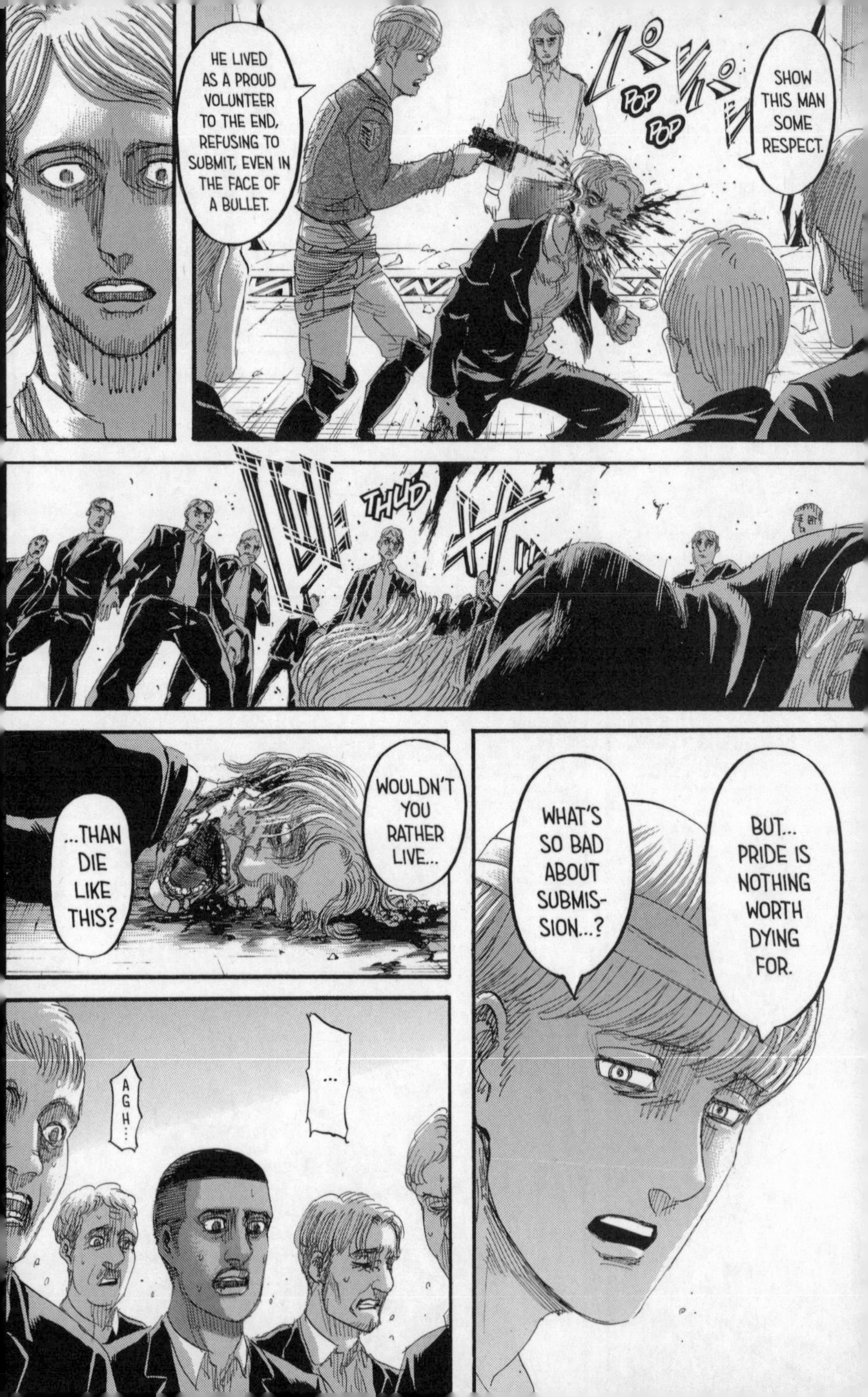
SHOW THIS MAN SOME RESPECT.
POP
POP
POP
HE LIVED AS A PROUD VOLUNTEER TO THE END, REFUSING TO SUBMIT, EVEN IN THE FACE OF A BULLET.
THUD
BUT... PRIDE IS NOTHING WORTH DYING FOR.
WHAT'S SO BAD ABOUT SUBMISSION...?
WOULDN'T YOU RATHER LIVE...
...THAN DIE LIKE THIS?
...
AGH...

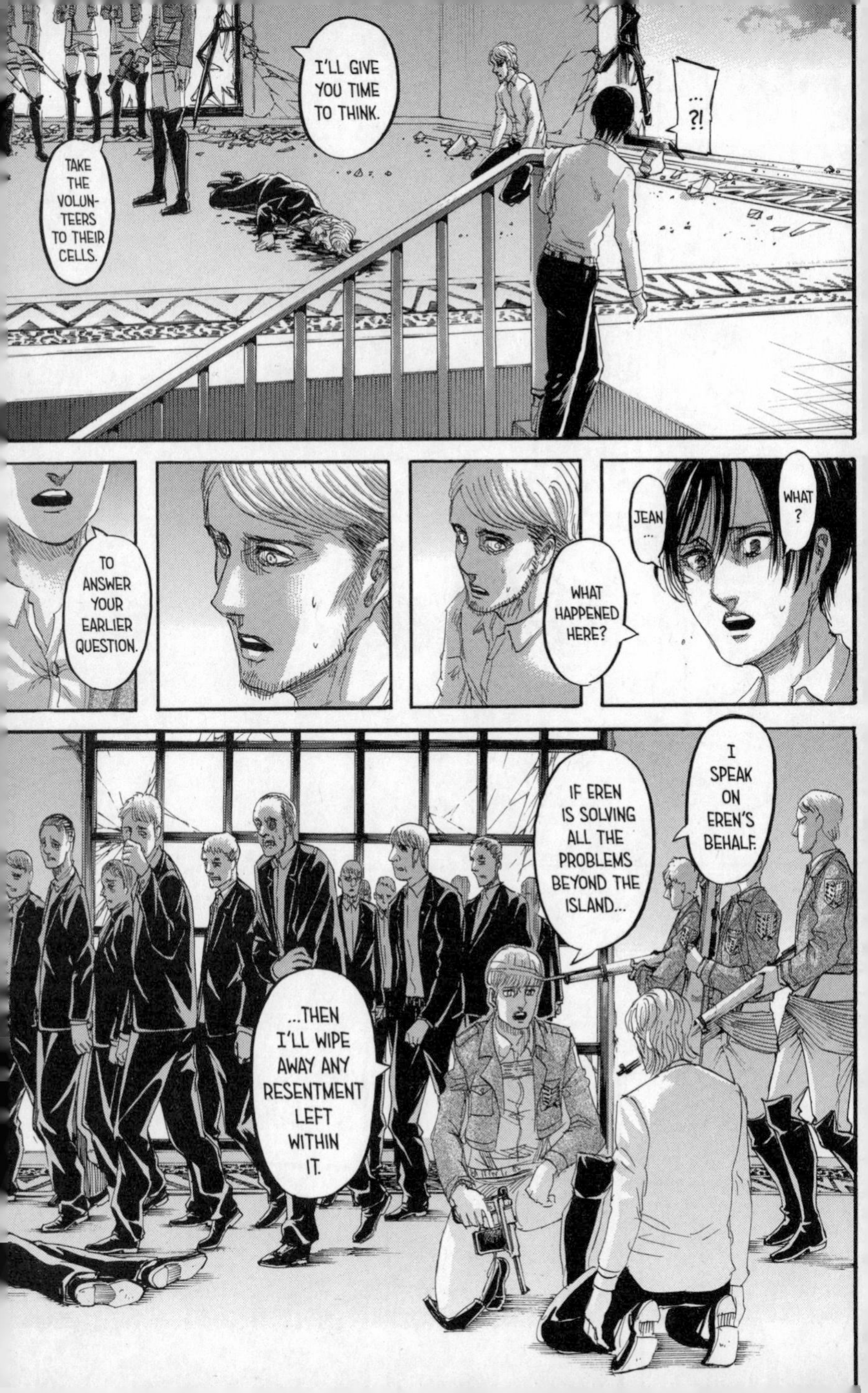
...
?!
I'LL GIVE YOU TIME TO THINK.
TAKE THE VOLUNTEERS TO THEIR CELLS.
WHAT ?
JEAN ...
WHAT HAPPENED HERE?
TO ANSWER YOUR EARLIER QUESTION.
I SPEAK ON EREN'S BEHALF.
IF EREN IS SOLVING ALL THE PROBLEMS BEYOND THE ISLAND...
...THEN I'LL WIPE AWAY ANY RESENTMENT LEFT WITHIN IT.

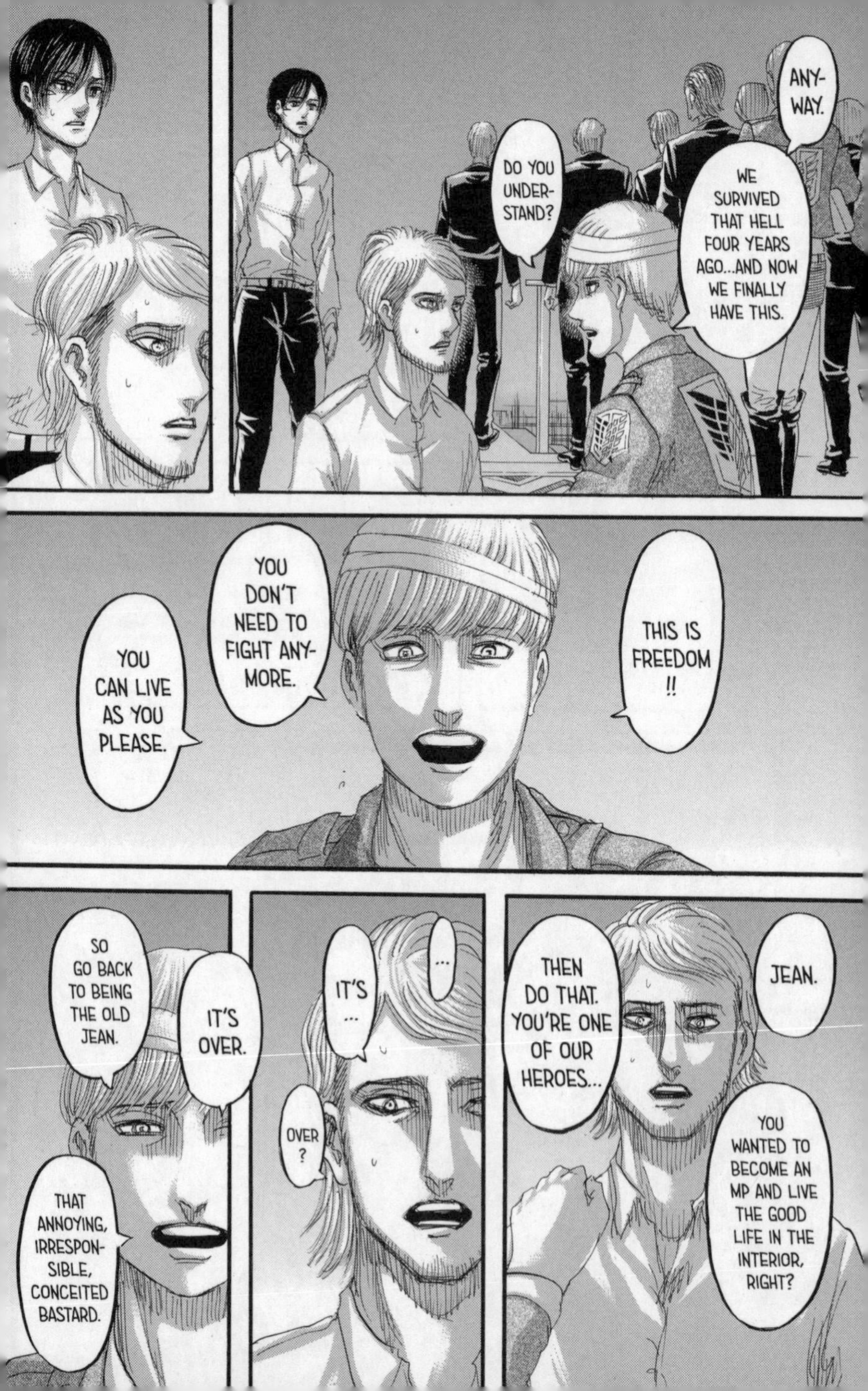
ANY-WAY.
WE SURVIVED THAT HELL FOUR YEARS AGO...AND NOW WE FINALLY HAVE THIS.
DO YOU UNDER-STAND?
THIS IS FREEDOM!!
YOU DON'T NEED TO FIGHT ANY-MORE.
YOU CAN LIVE AS YOU PLEASE.
JEAN.
YOU WANTED TO BECOME AN MP AND LIVE THE GOOD LIFE IN THE INTERIOR, RIGHT?
THEN DO THAT. YOU'RE ONE OF OUR HEROES...
...
IT'S ...
OVER?
IT'S OVER.
SO GO BACK TO BEING THE OLD JEAN.
THAT ANNOYING, IRRESPON-SIBLE, CONCEITED BASTARD.

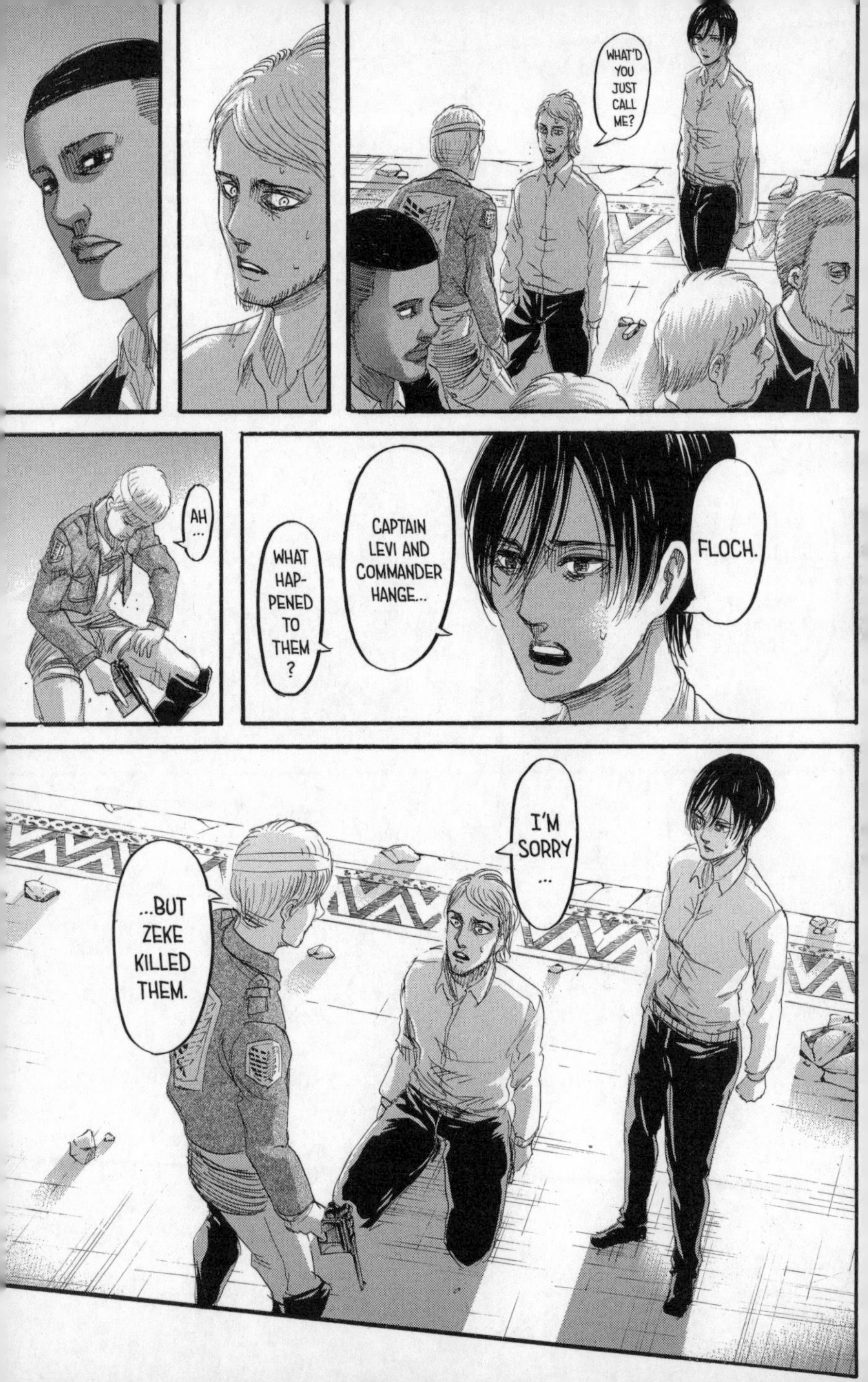
WHAT'D YOU JUST CALL ME?
FLOCH.
CAPTAIN LEVI AND COMMANDER HANGE...
WHAT HAPPENED TO THEM?
AH...
I'M SORRY...
...BUT ZEKE KILLED THEM.

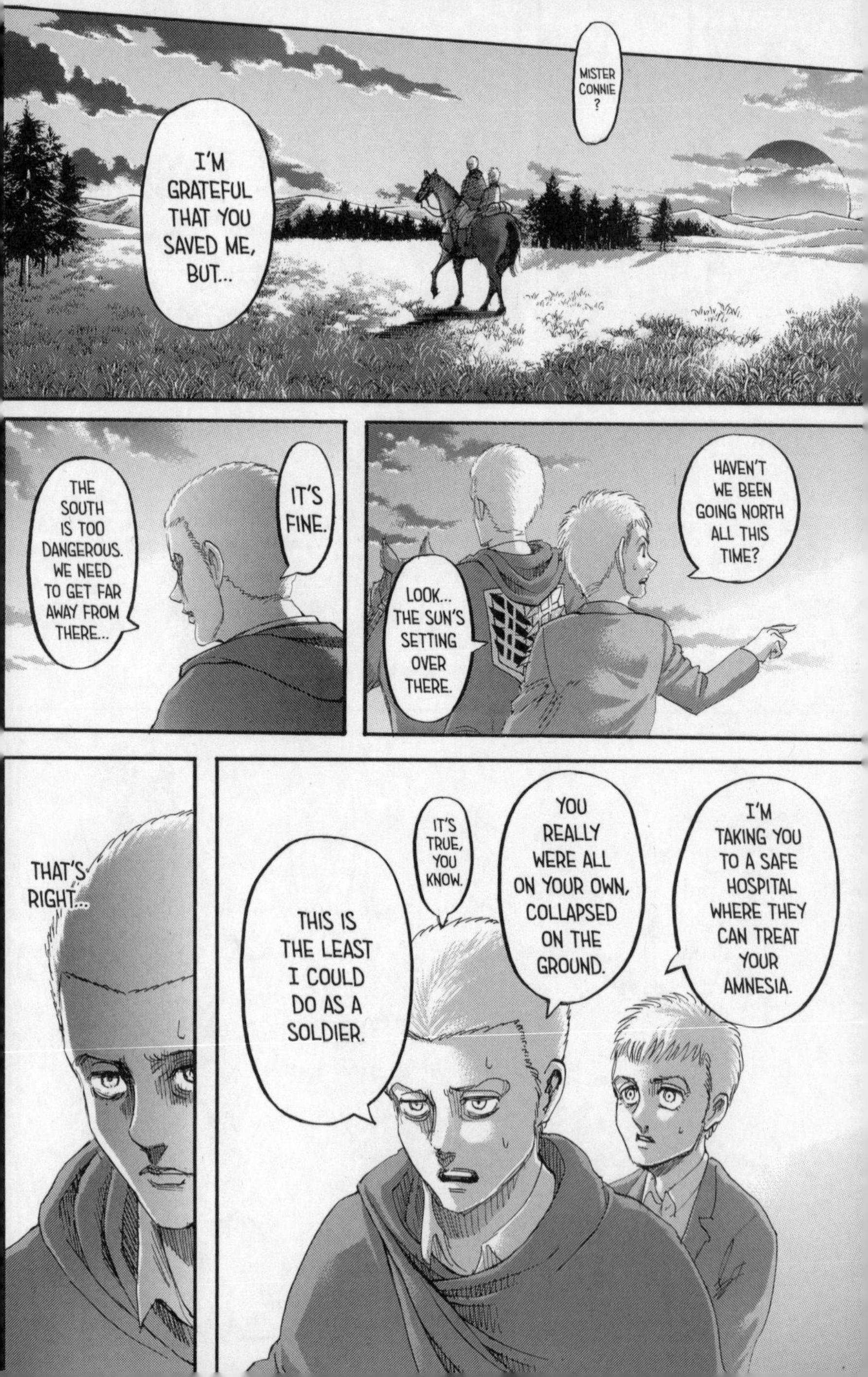
MISTER CONNIE?
I'M GRATEFUL THAT YOU SAVED ME, BUT...
HAVEN'T WE BEEN GOING NORTH ALL THIS TIME?
LOOK... THE SUN'S SETTING OVER THERE.
IT'S FINE.
THE SOUTH IS TOO DANGEROUS. WE NEED TO GET FAR AWAY FROM THERE...
I'M TAKING YOU TO A SAFE HOSPITAL WHERE THEY CAN TREAT YOUR AMNESIA.
YOU REALLY WERE ALL ON YOUR OWN, COLLAPSED ON THE GROUND.
IT'S TRUE, YOU KNOW.
THIS IS THE LEAST I COULD DO AS A SOLDIER.
THAT'S RIGHT...

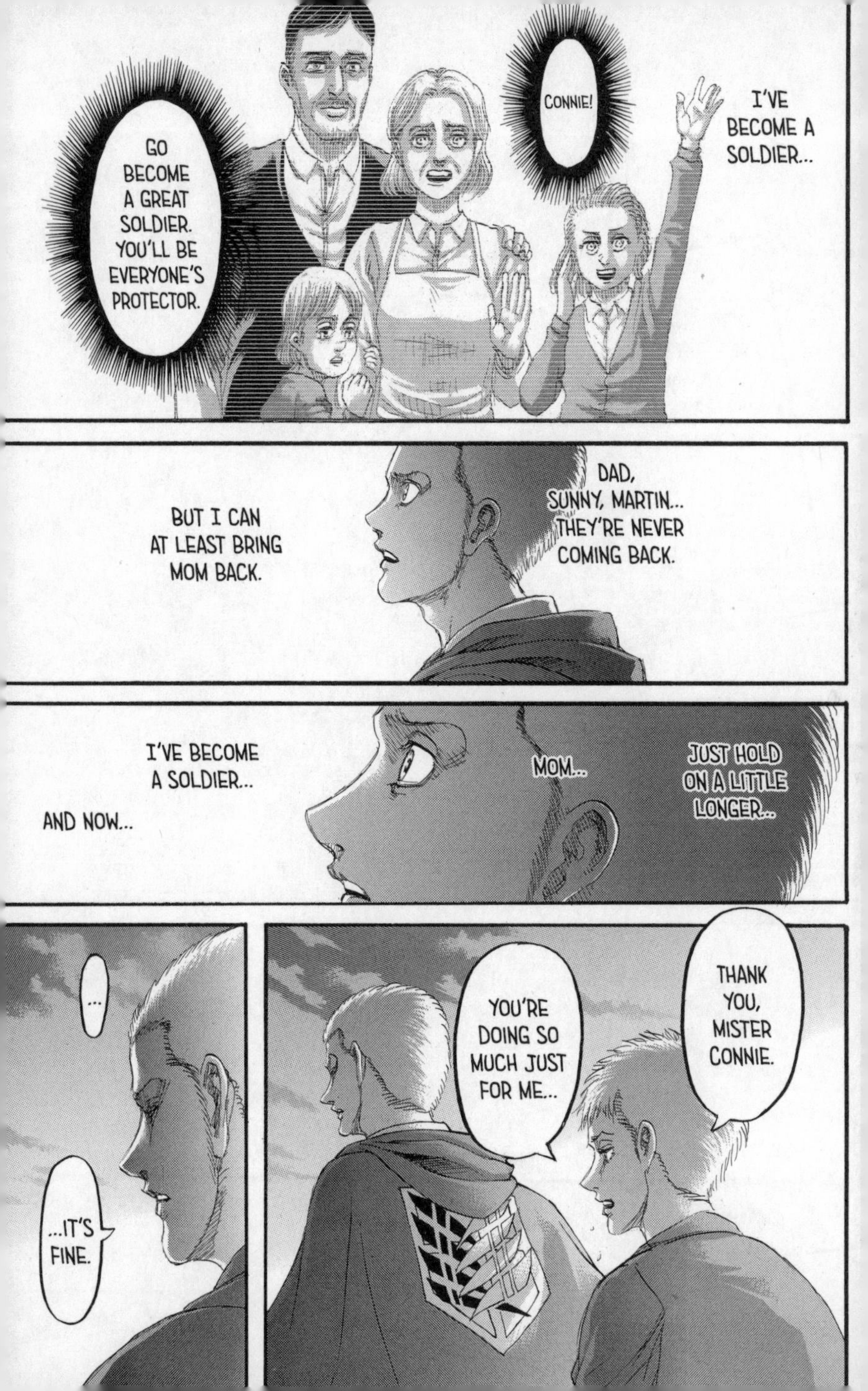
I'VE BECOME A SOLDIER...
CONNIE!
GO BECOME A GREAT SOLDIER. YOU'LL BE EVERYONE'S PROTECTOR.
DAD, SUNNY, MARTIN... THEY'RE NEVER COMING BACK.
BUT I CAN AT LEAST BRING MOM BACK.
JUST HOLD ON A LITTLE LONGER...
MOM...
I'VE BECOME A SOLDIER...
AND NOW...
THANK YOU, MISTER CONNIE.
YOU'RE DOING SO MUCH JUST FOR ME...
...
...IT'S FINE.

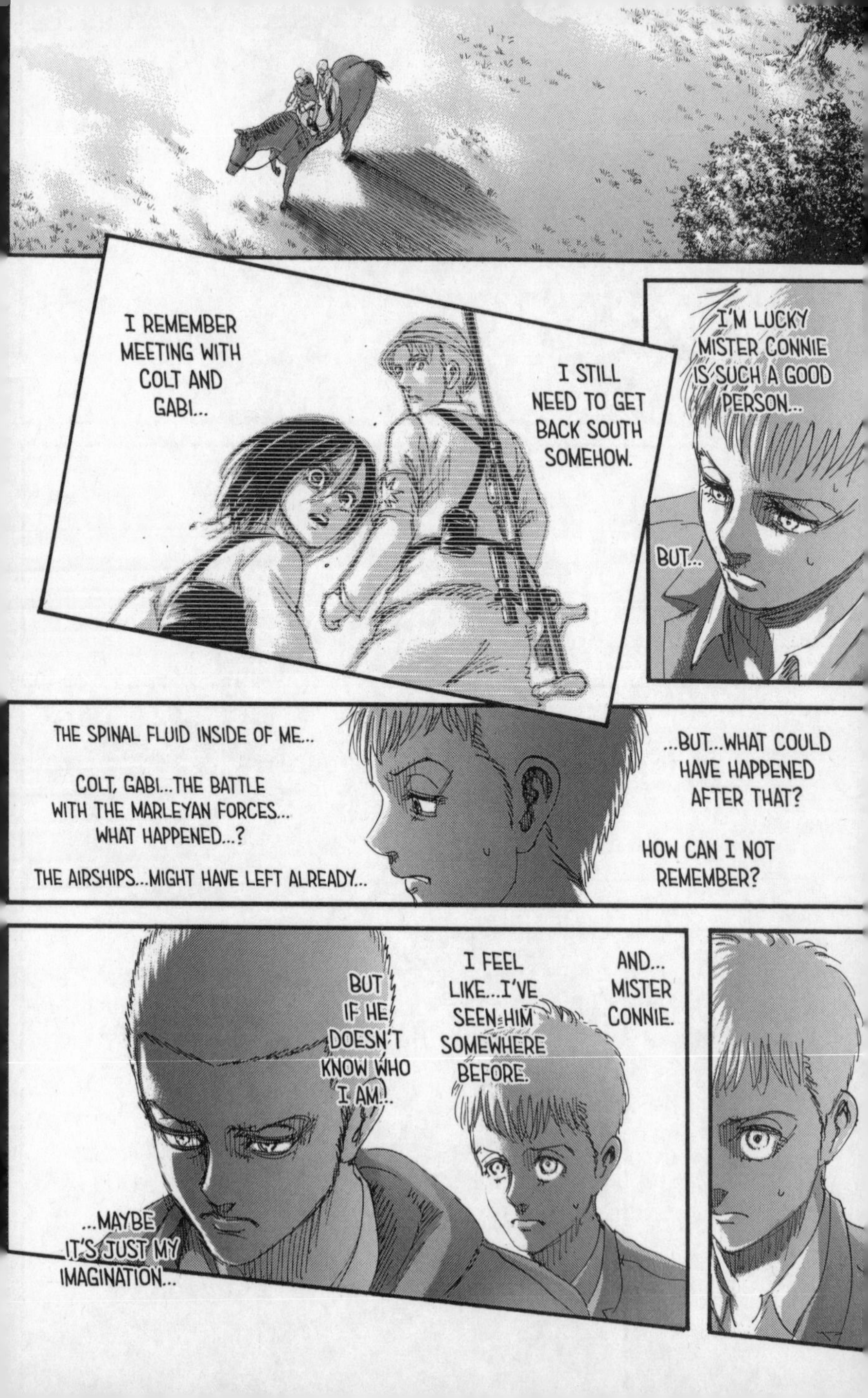
I'M LUCKY MISTER CONNIE IS SUCH A GOOD PERSON...
BUT...
I STILL NEED TO GET BACK SOUTH SOMEHOW.
I REMEMBER MEETING WITH COLT AND GABI...
...BUT...WHAT COULD HAVE HAPPENED AFTER THAT?
HOW CAN I NOT REMEMBER?
THE SPINAL FLUID INSIDE OF ME...
COLT, GABI...THE BATTLE WITH THE MARLEYAN FORCES... WHAT HAPPENED...?
THE AIRSHIPS...MIGHT HAVE LEFT ALREADY...
AND... MISTER CONNIE.
I FEEL LIKE...I'VE SEEN HIM SOMEWHERE BEFORE.
BUT IF HE DOESN'T KNOW WHO I AM...
...MAYBE IT'S JUST MY IMAGINATION...

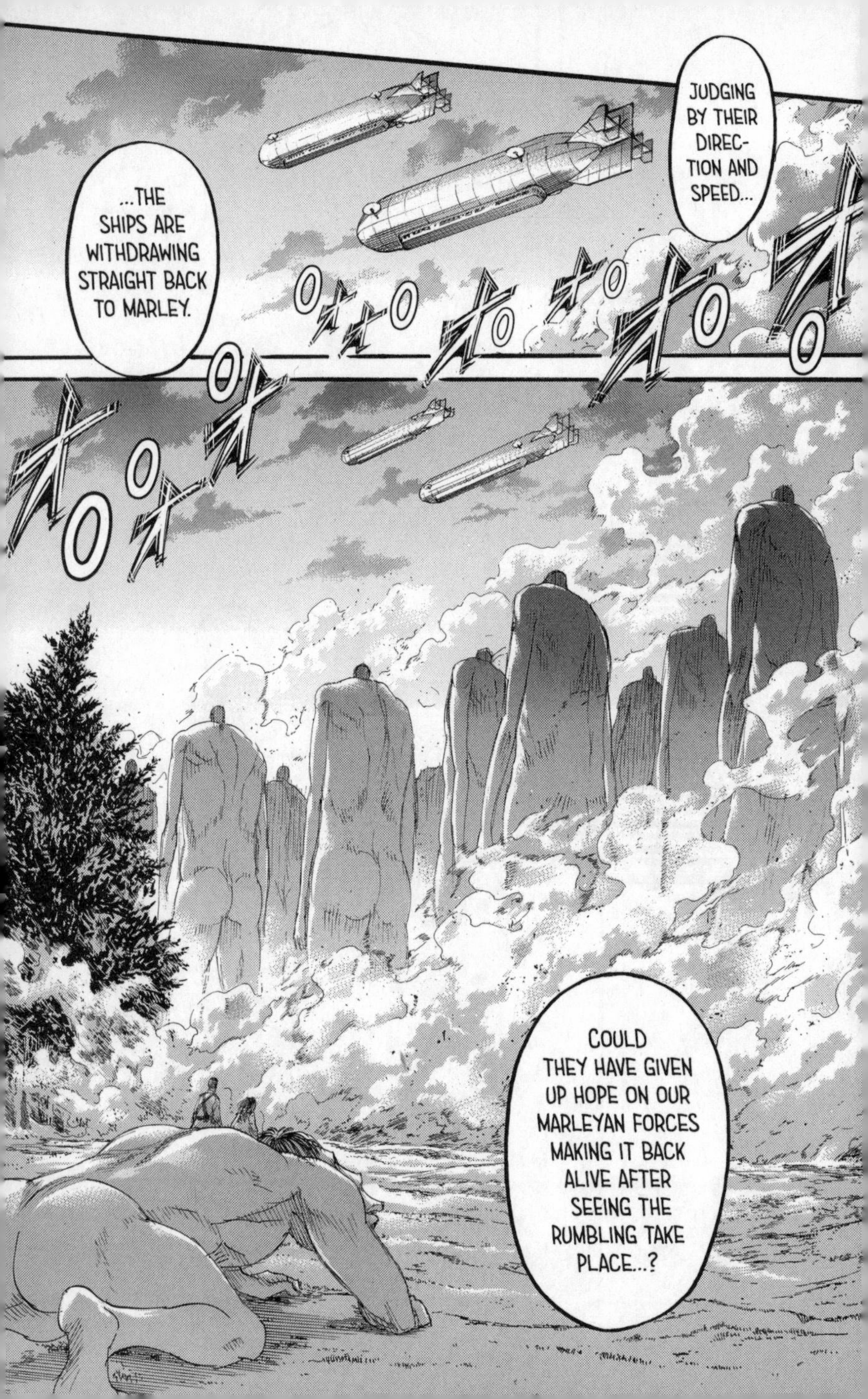
JUDGING BY THEIR DIRECTION AND SPEED...
...THE SHIPS ARE WITHDRAWING STRAIGHT BACK TO MARLEY.
COULD THEY HAVE GIVEN UP HOPE ON OUR MARLEYAN FORCES MAKING IT BACK ALIVE AFTER SEEING THE RUMBLING TAKE PLACE...?

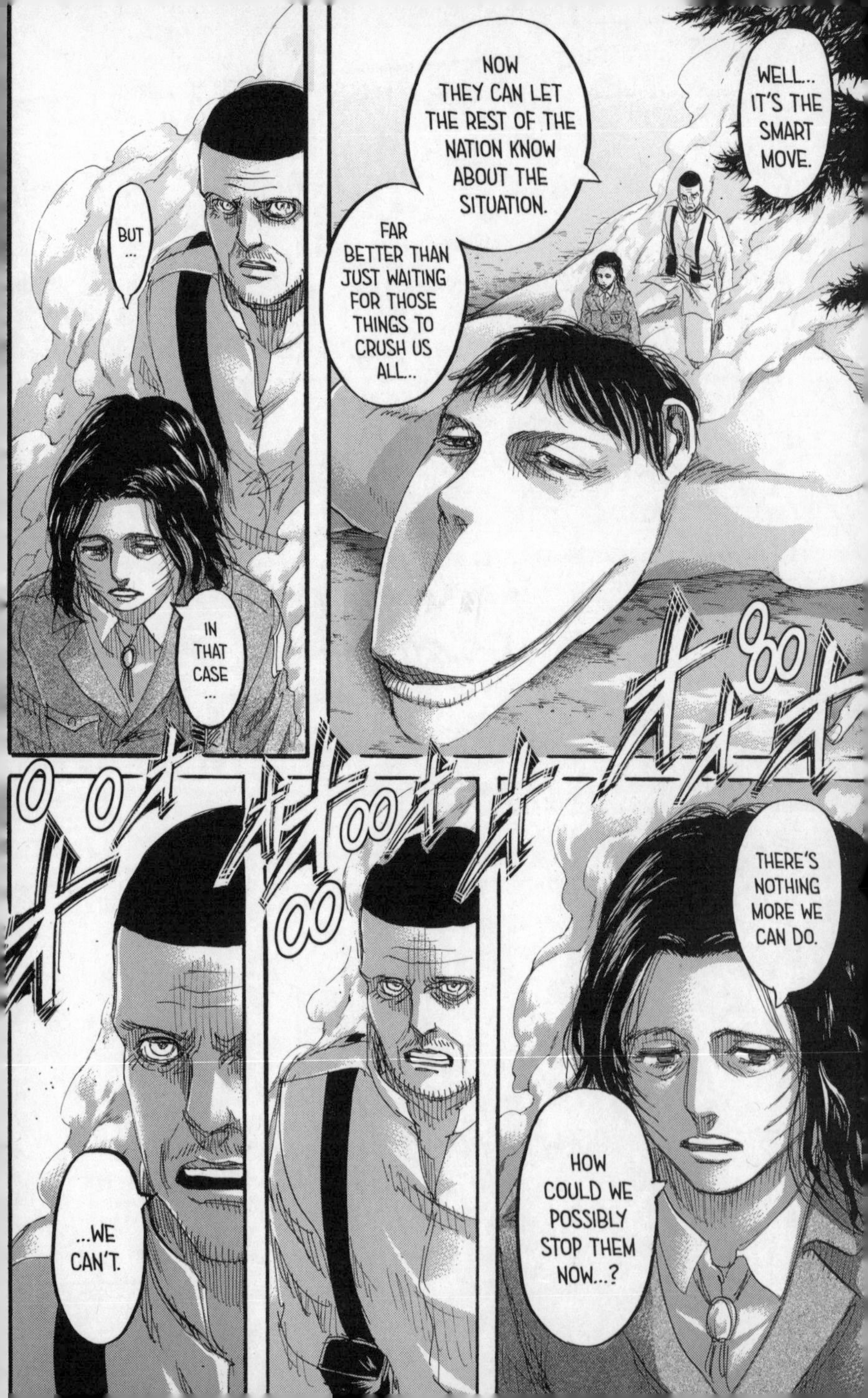
WELL... IT'S THE SMART MOVE.
NOW THEY CAN LET THE REST OF THE NATION KNOW ABOUT THE SITUATION.
FAR BETTER THAN JUST WAITING FOR THOSE THINGS TO CRUSH US ALL...
OO
BUT ...
IN THAT CASE ...
OO
OO
O O
THERE'S NOTHING MORE WE CAN DO.
HOW COULD WE POSSIBLY STOP THEM NOW...?
...WE CAN'T.

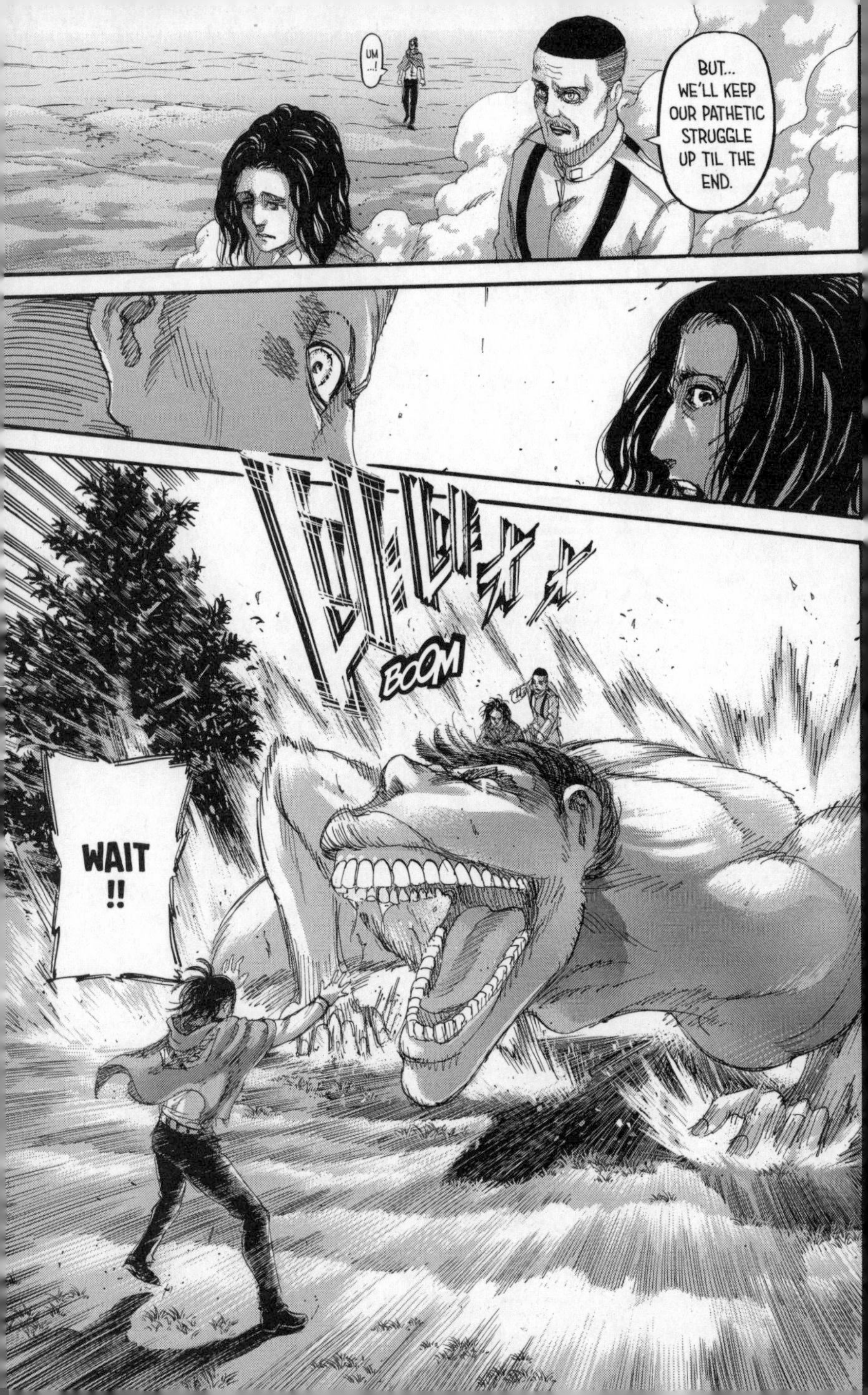
BUT... WE'LL KEEP OUR PATHETIC STRUGGLE UP TIL THE END.
UM ...!
BOOM
WAIT !!

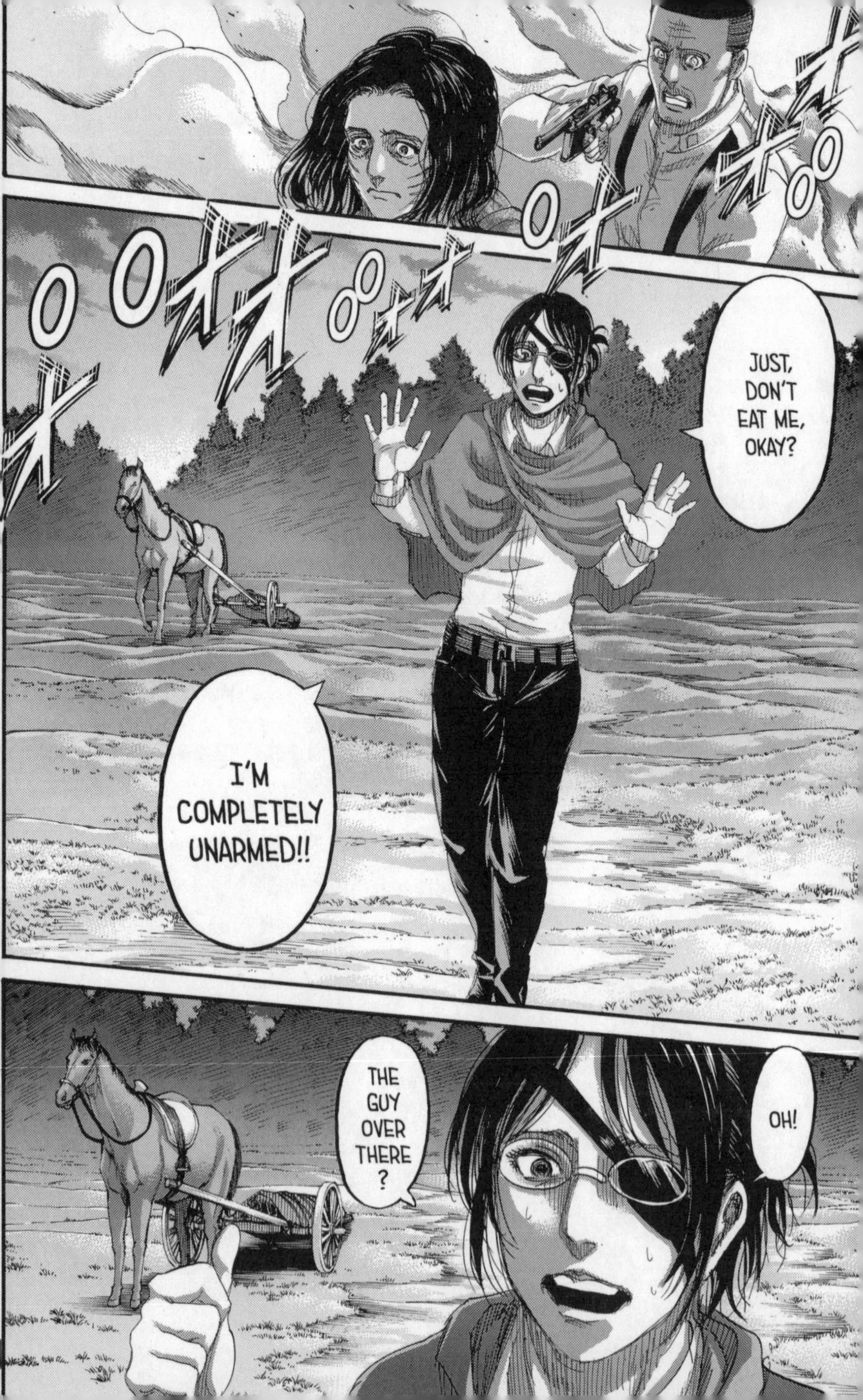
JUST, DON'T EAT ME, OKAY?
I'M COMPLETELY UNARMED!!
OH!
THE GUY OVER THERE ?

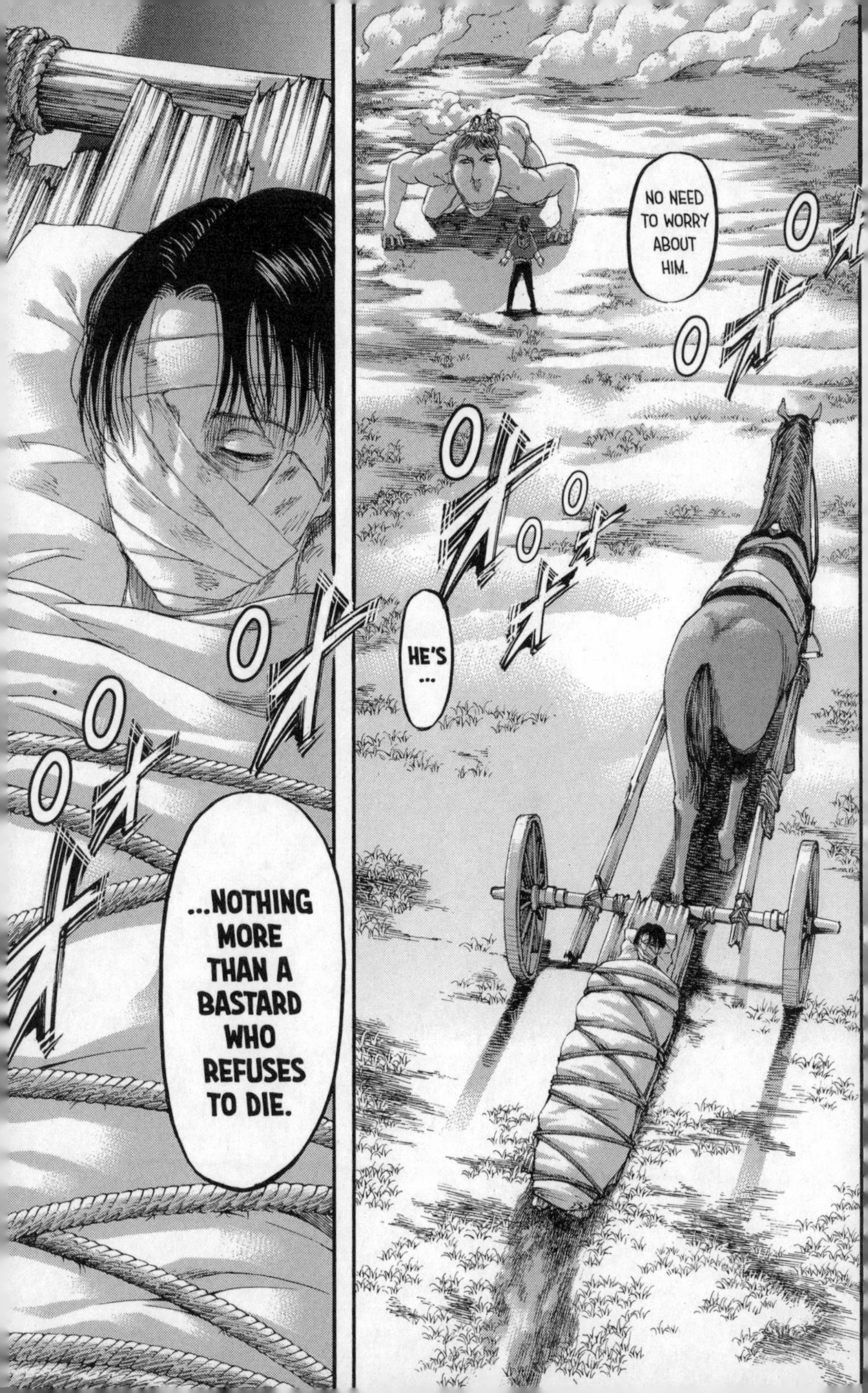
NO NEED TO WORRY ABOUT HIM.
HE'S ...
...NOTHING MORE THAN A BASTARD WHO REFUSES TO DIE.

ATTACK on TITAN

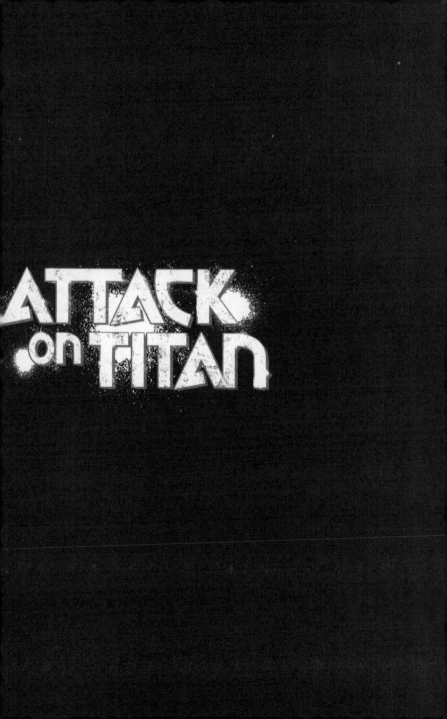

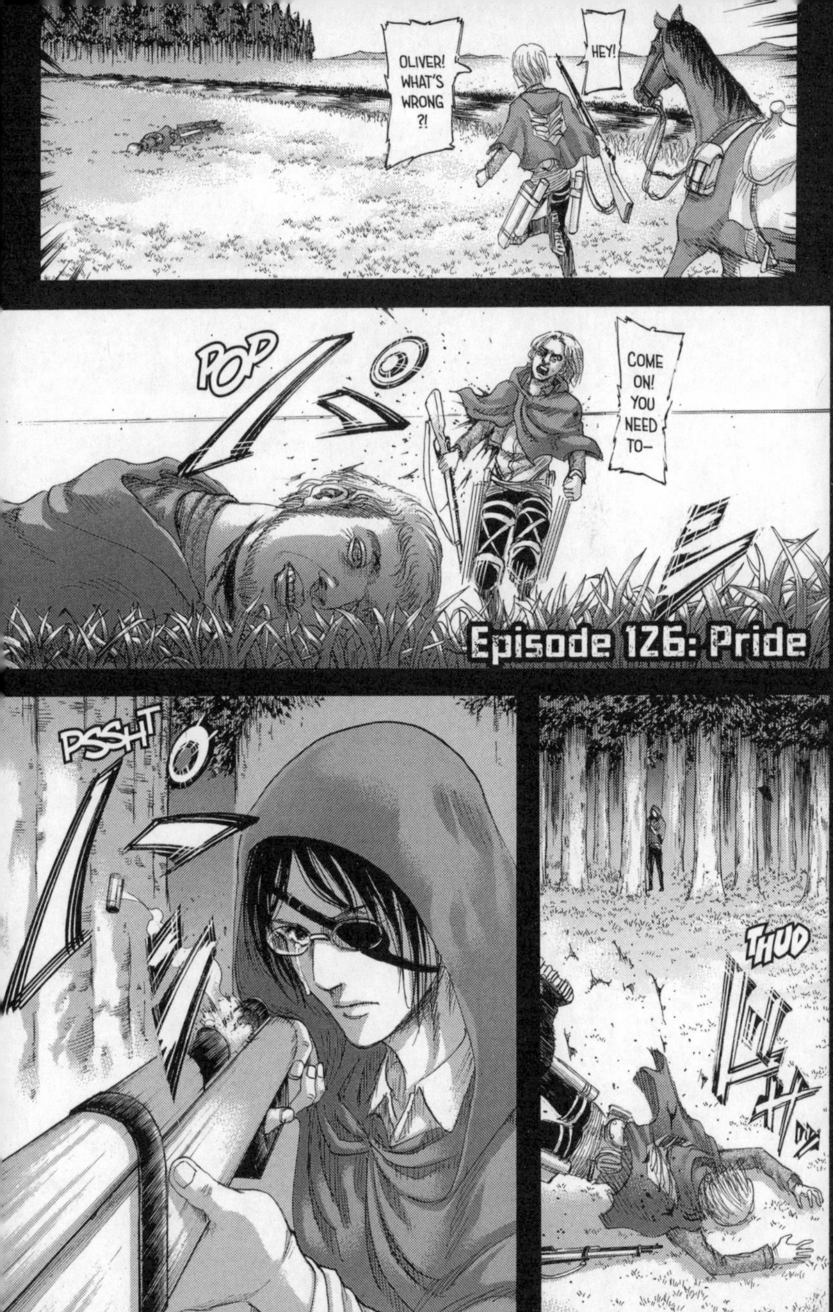
HEY!
OLIVER! WHAT'S WRONG?!
COME ON! YOU NEED TO—
POP
Episode 126: Pride
THUD
PSSHT

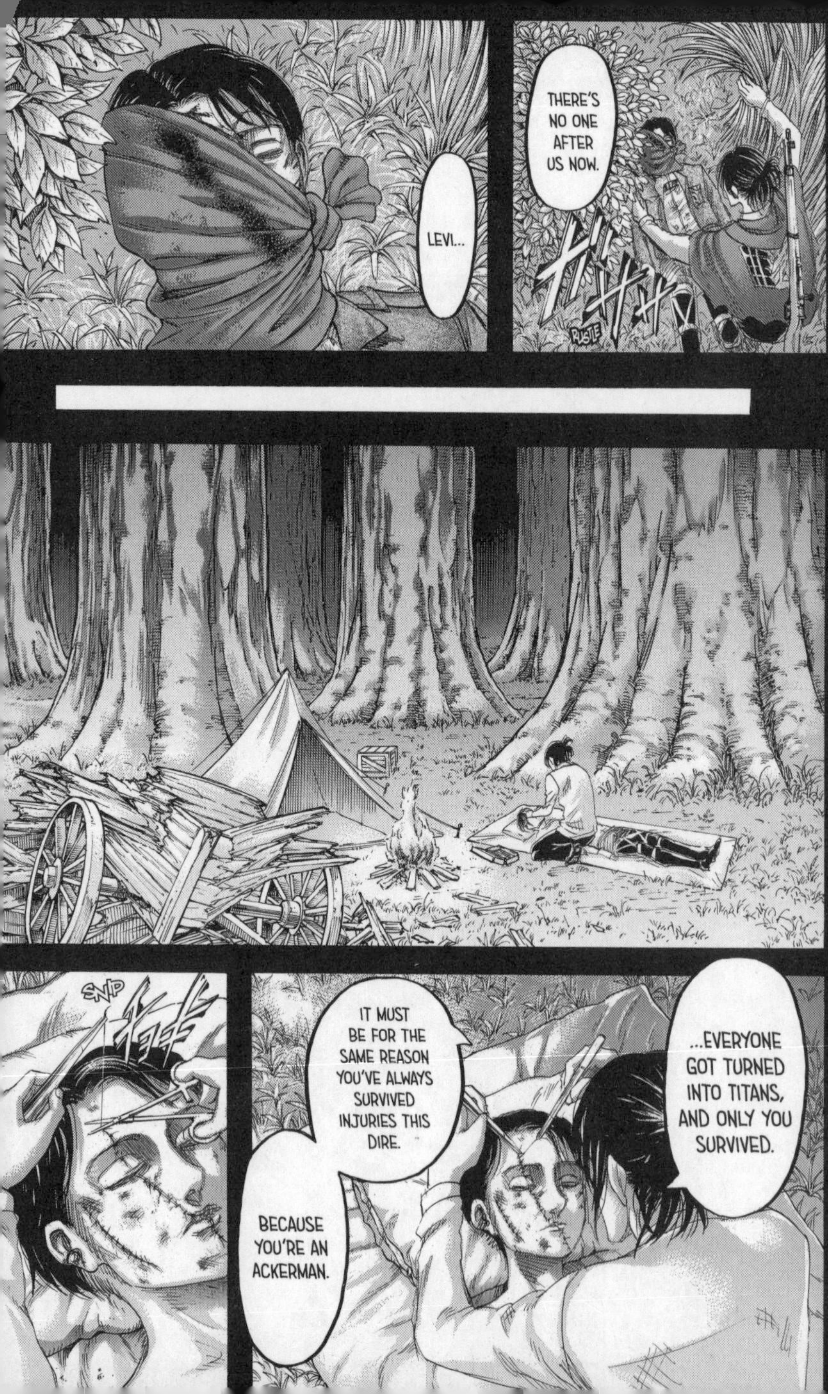
THERE'S NO ONE AFTER US NOW.
RUSTLE
LEVI...
...EVERYONE GOT TURNED INTO TITANS, AND ONLY YOU SURVIVED.
IT MUST BE FOR THE SAME REASON YOU'VE ALWAYS SURVIVED INJURIES THIS DIRE.
BECAUSE YOU'RE AN ACKERMAN.
SNIP

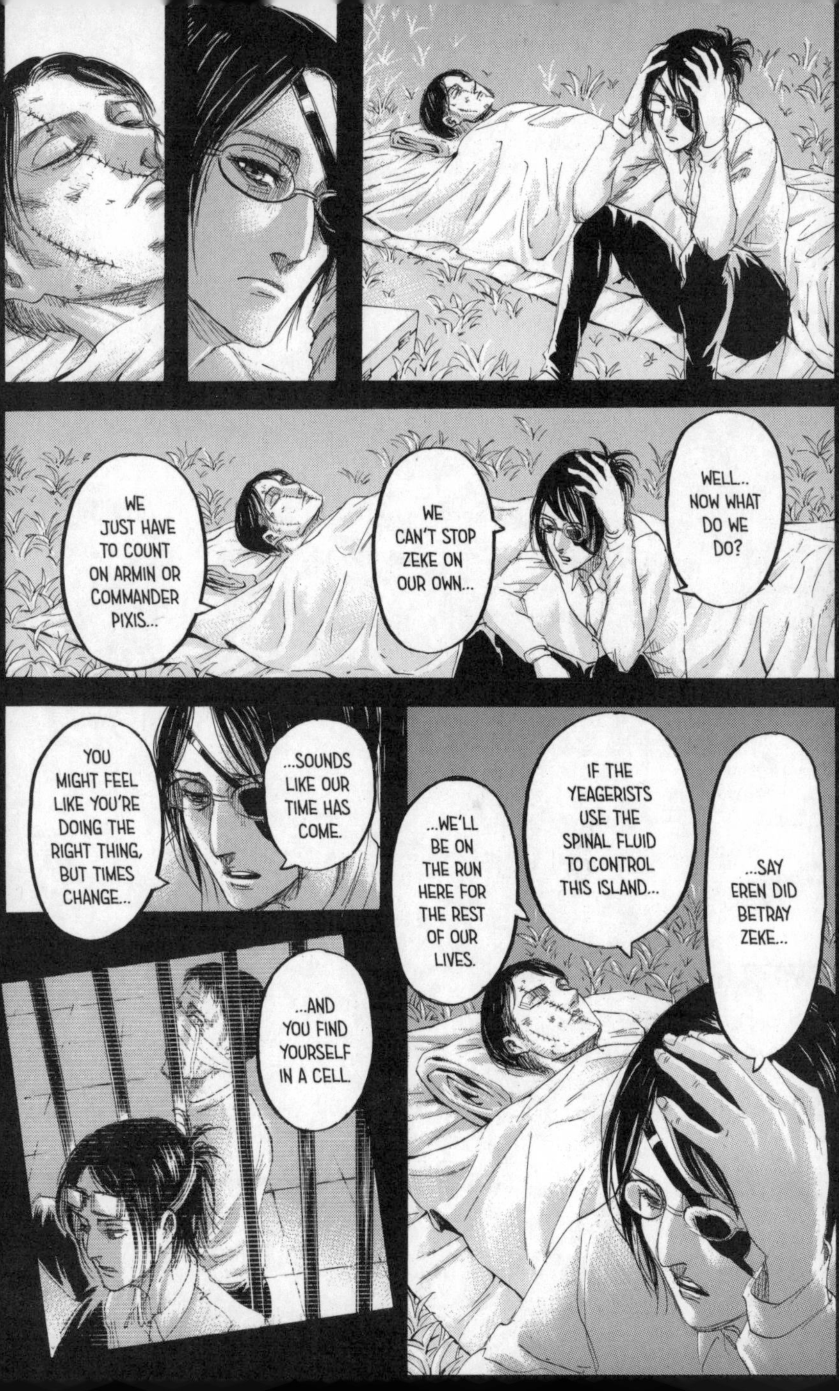
WELL.. NOW WHAT DO WE DO?
WE CAN'T STOP ZEKE ON OUR OWN...
WE JUST HAVE TO COUNT ON ARMIN OR COMMANDER PIXIS...
...SAY EREN DID BETRAY ZEKE...
IF THE YEAGERISTS USE THE SPINAL FLUID TO CONTROL THIS ISLAND...
...WE'LL BE ON THE RUN HERE FOR THE REST OF OUR LIVES.
...SOUNDS LIKE OUR TIME HAS COME.
YOU MIGHT FEEL LIKE YOU'RE DOING THE RIGHT THING, BUT TIMES CHANGE...
...AND YOU FIND YOURSELF IN A CELL.

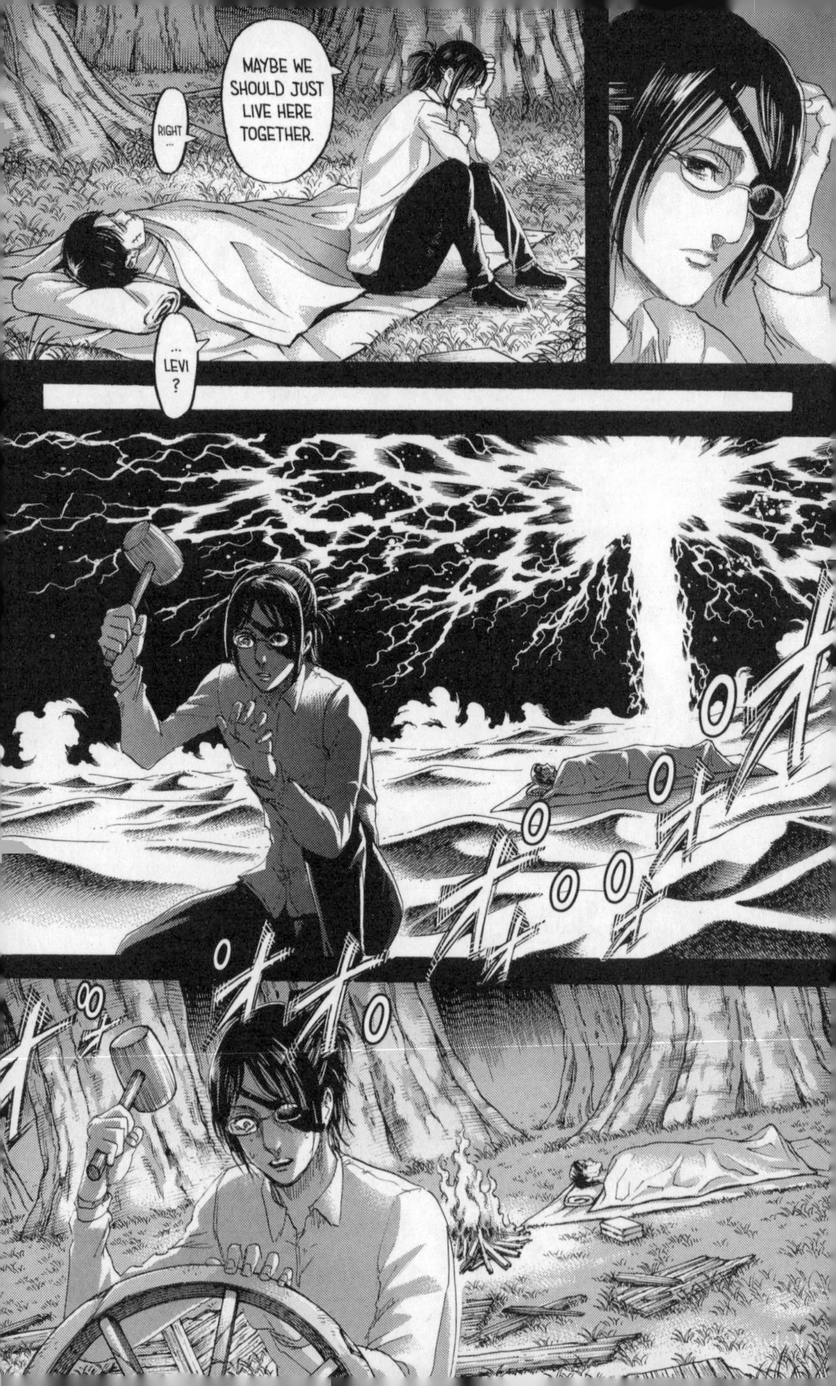
MAYBE WE SHOULD JUST LIVE HERE TOGETHER.
RIGHT ...
... LEVI ?

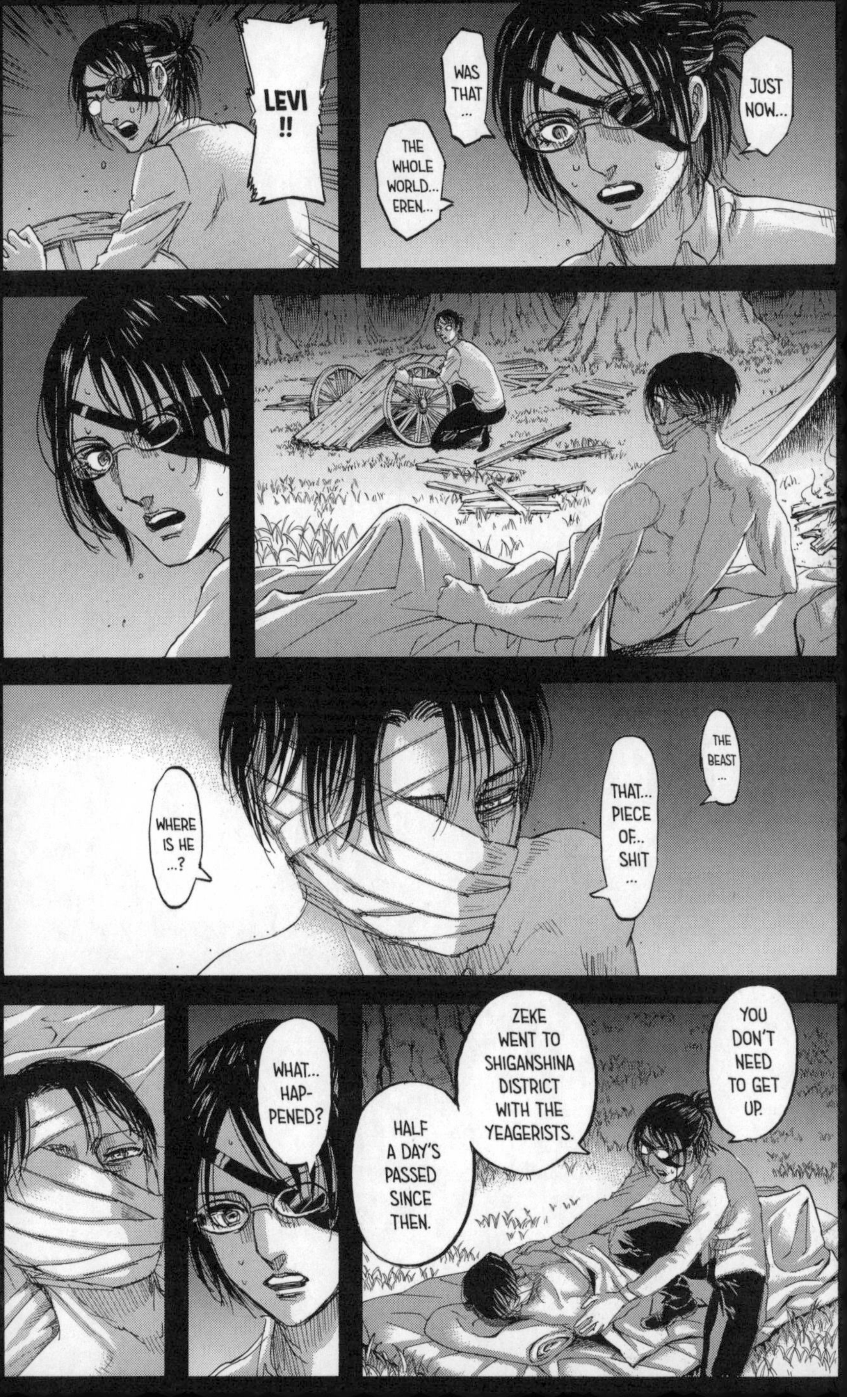
JUST NOW...
WAS THAT ...
THE WHOLE WORLD... EREN...
LEVI !!
THE BEAST ...
THAT... PIECE OF.. SHIT ...
WHERE IS HE ...?
YOU DON'T NEED TO GET UP.
ZEKE WENT TO SHIGANSHINA DISTRICT WITH THE YEAGERISTS.
HALF A DAY'S PASSED SINCE THEN.
WHAT... HAP-PENED?

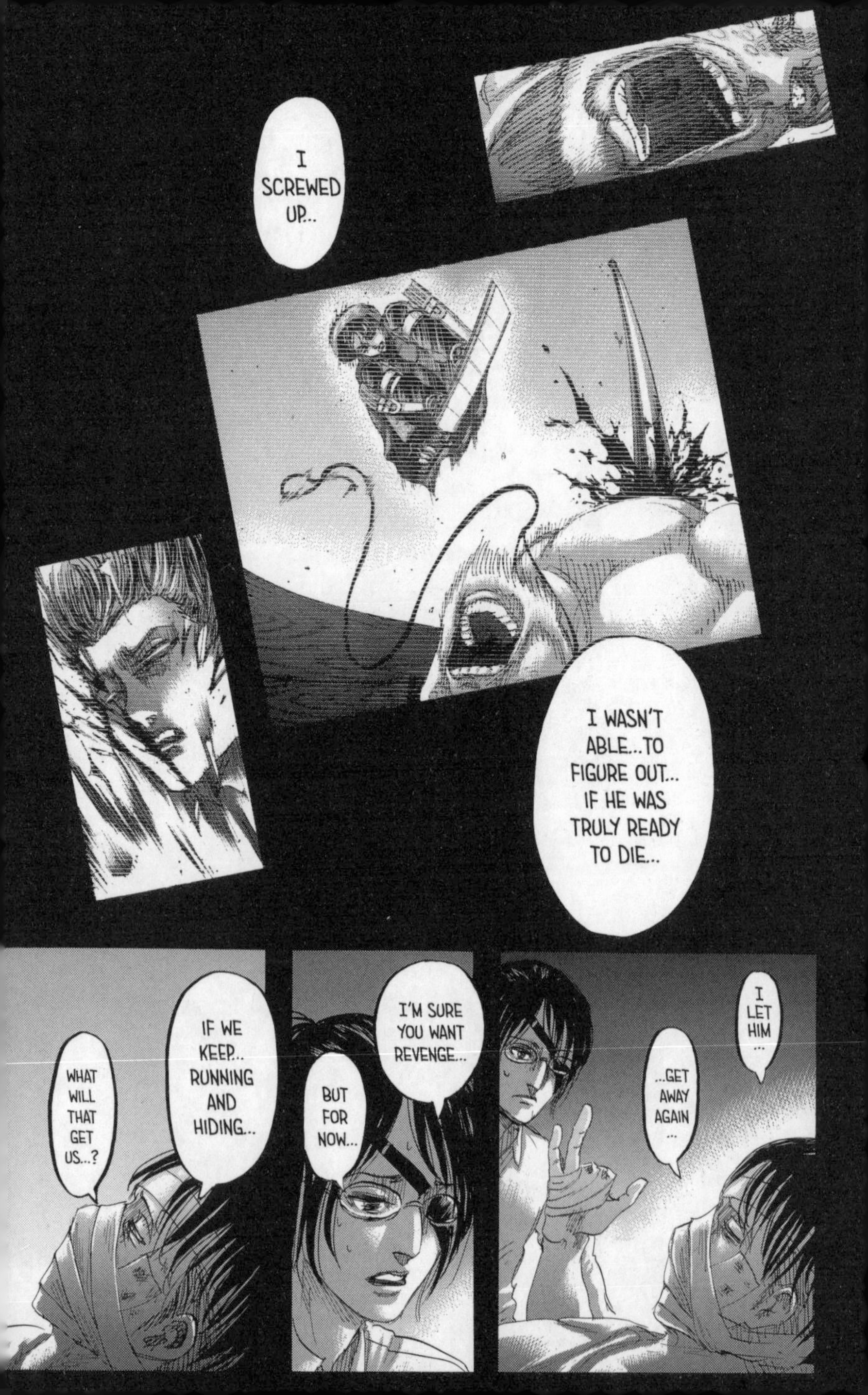
I SCREWED UP...
I WASN'T ABLE...TO FIGURE OUT... IF HE WAS TRULY READY TO DIE...
I LET HIM...
...GET AWAY AGAIN...
I'M SURE YOU WANT REVENGE...
BUT FOR NOW...
IF WE KEEP... RUNNING AND HIDING...
WHAT WILL THAT GET US...?

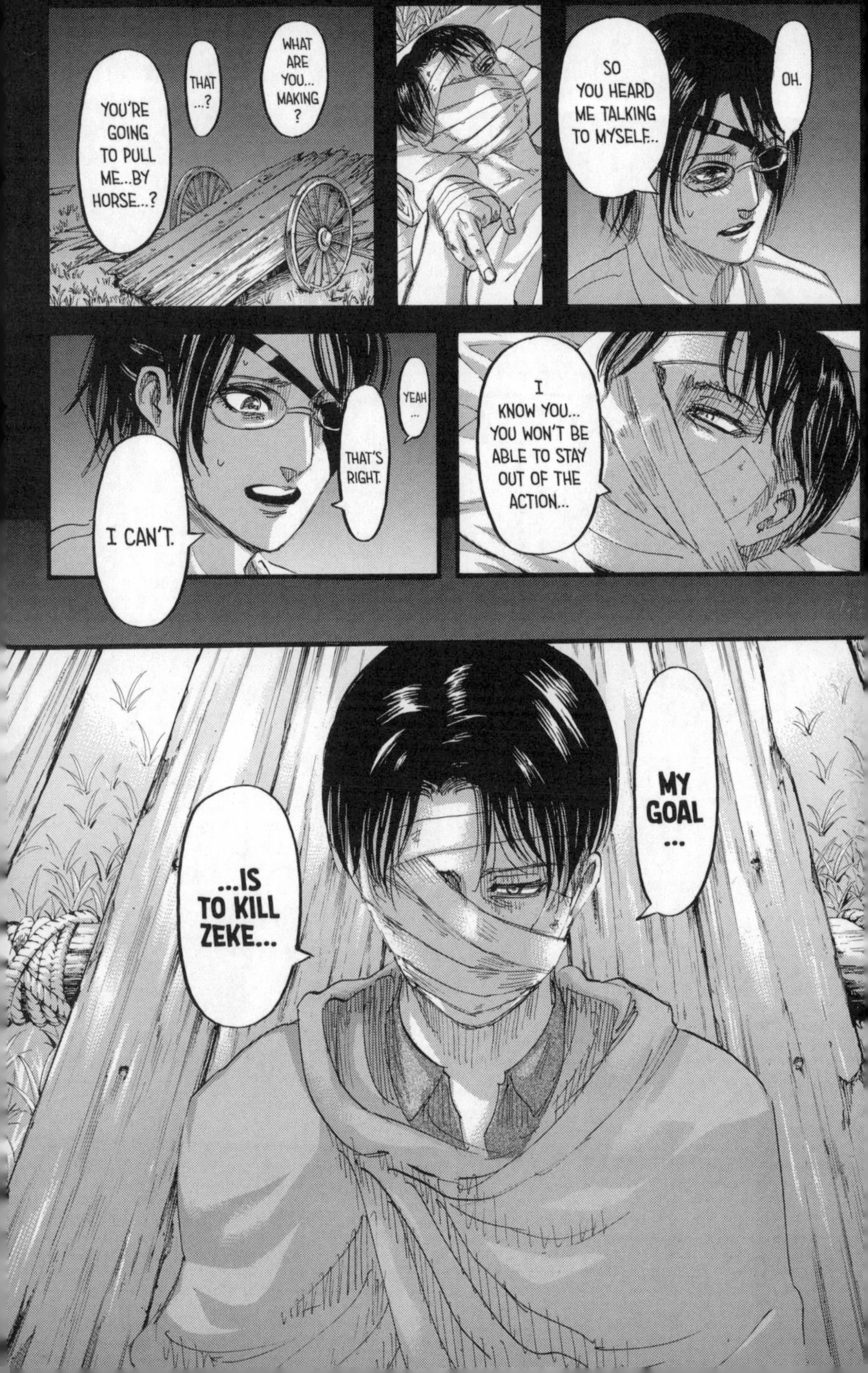
OH.
SO YOU HEARD ME TALKING TO MYSELF..
WHAT ARE YOU... MAKING ?
THAT ...?
YOU'RE GOING TO PULL ME...BY HORSE...?
I KNOW YOU... YOU WON'T BE ABLE TO STAY OUT OF THE ACTION...
YEAH ...
THAT'S RIGHT.
I CAN'T.
MY GOAL ...
...IS TO KILL ZEKE...

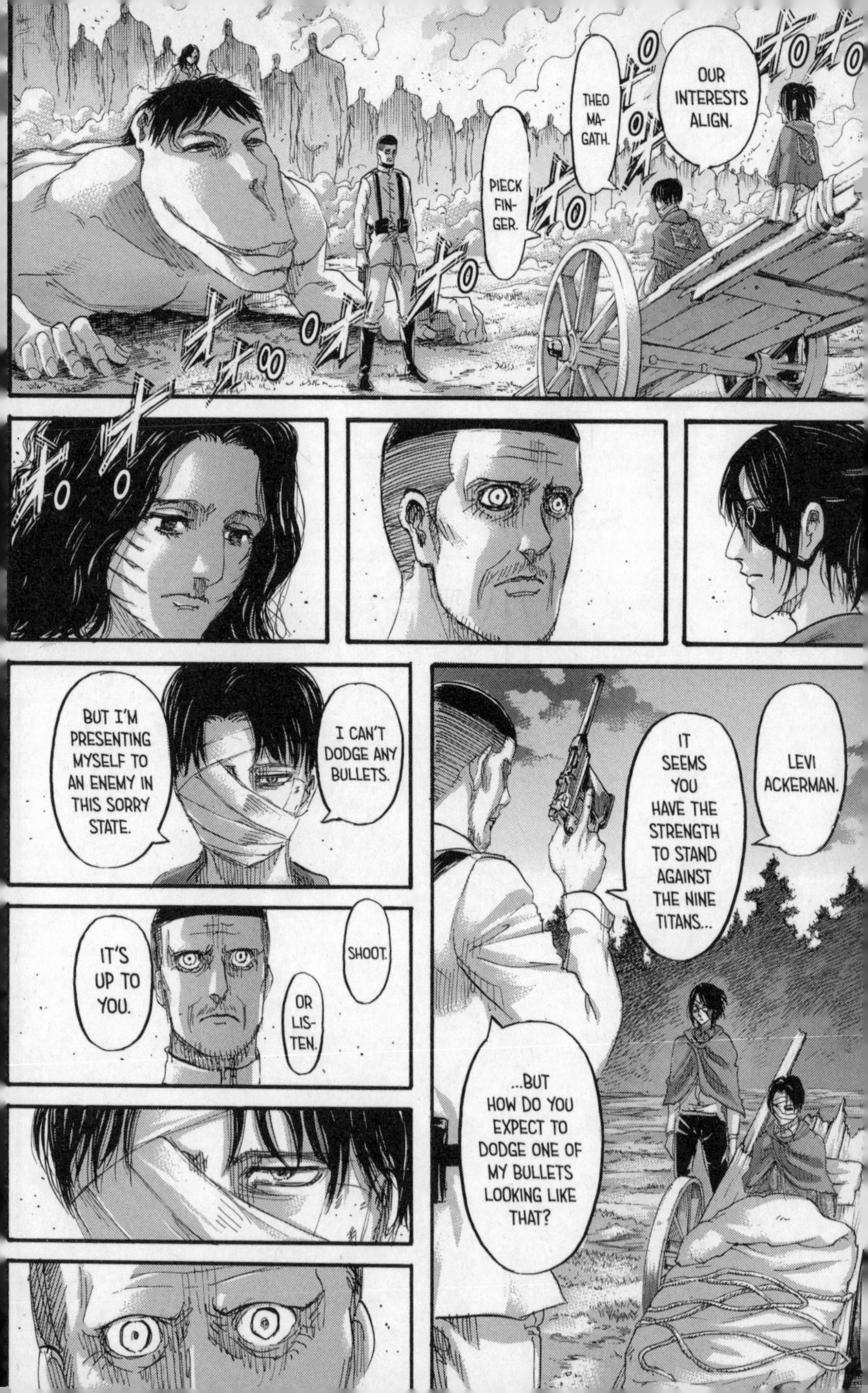
OUR INTERESTS ALIGN.
THEO MA-GATH.
PIECK FIN-GER.
LEVI ACKERMAN.
IT SEEMS YOU HAVE THE STRENGTH TO STAND AGAINST THE NINE TITANS...
...BUT HOW DO YOU EXPECT TO DODGE ONE OF MY BULLETS LOOKING LIKE THAT?
I CAN'T DODGE ANY BULLETS.
BUT I'M PRESENTING MYSELF TO AN ENEMY IN THIS SORRY STATE.
SHOOT.
OR LIS-TEN.
IT'S UP TO YOU.

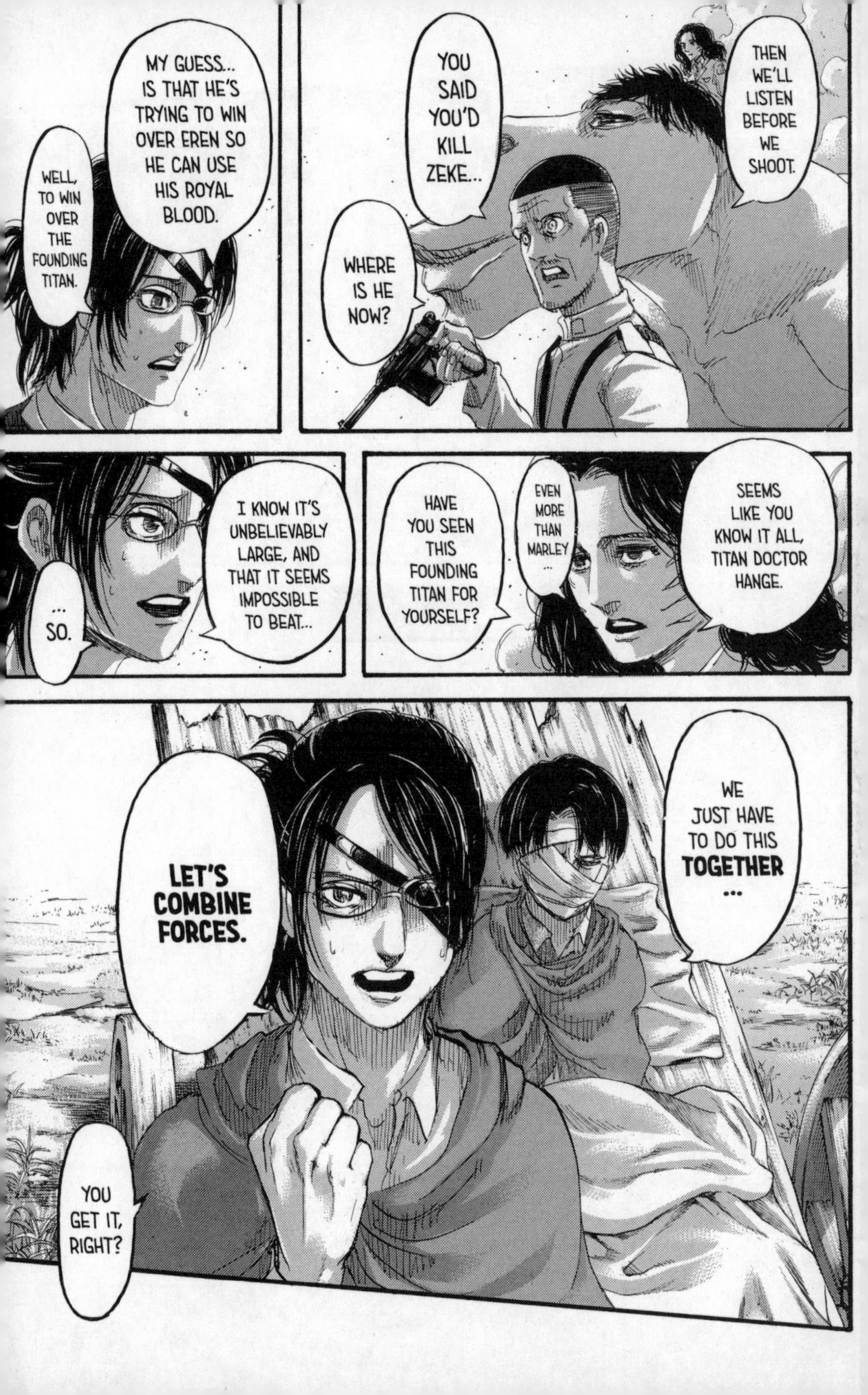
THEN WE'LL LISTEN BEFORE WE SHOOT.
YOU SAID YOU'D KILL ZEKE...
WHERE IS HE NOW?
MY GUESS... IS THAT HE'S TRYING TO WIN OVER EREN SO HE CAN USE HIS ROYAL BLOOD.
WELL, TO WIN OVER THE FOUNDING TITAN.
SEEMS LIKE YOU KNOW IT ALL, TITAN DOCTOR HANGE.
EVEN MORE THAN MARLEY...
HAVE YOU SEEN THIS FOUNDING TITAN FOR YOURSELF?
I KNOW IT'S UNBELIEVABLY LARGE, AND THAT IT SEEMS IMPOSSIBLE TO BEAT...
... SO.
WE JUST HAVE TO DO THIS TOGETHER ...
LET'S COMBINE FORCES.
YOU GET IT, RIGHT?

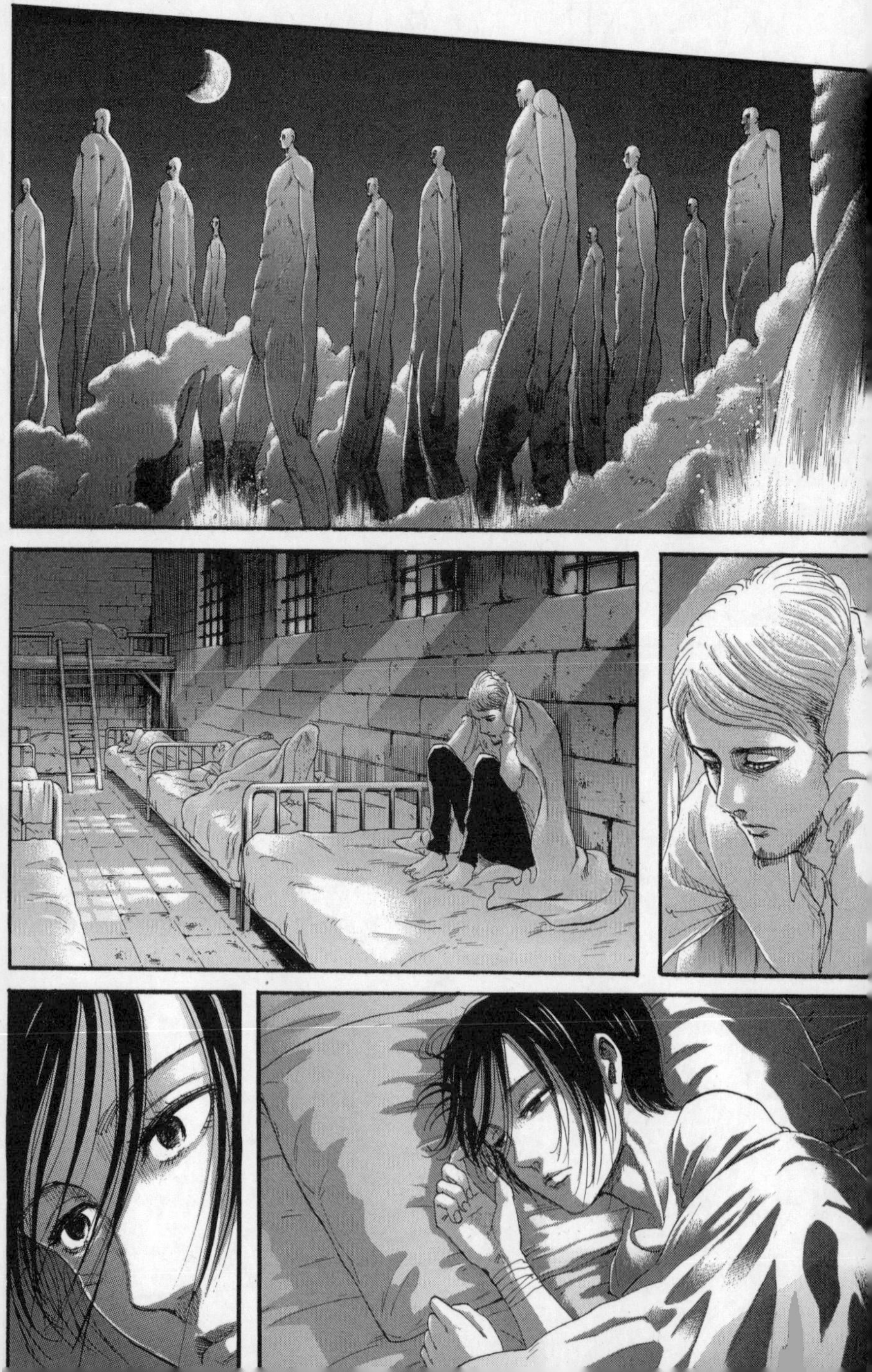

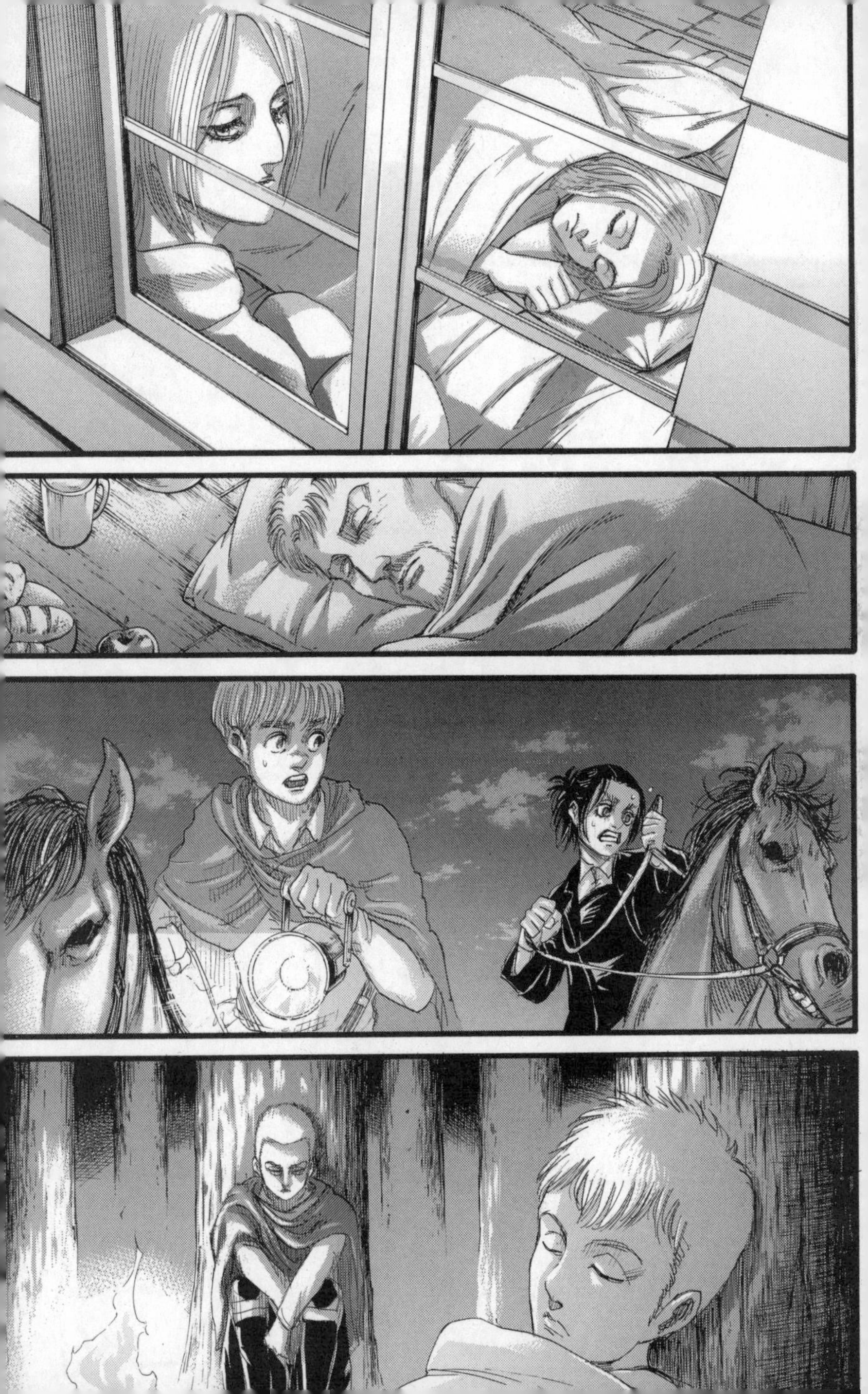

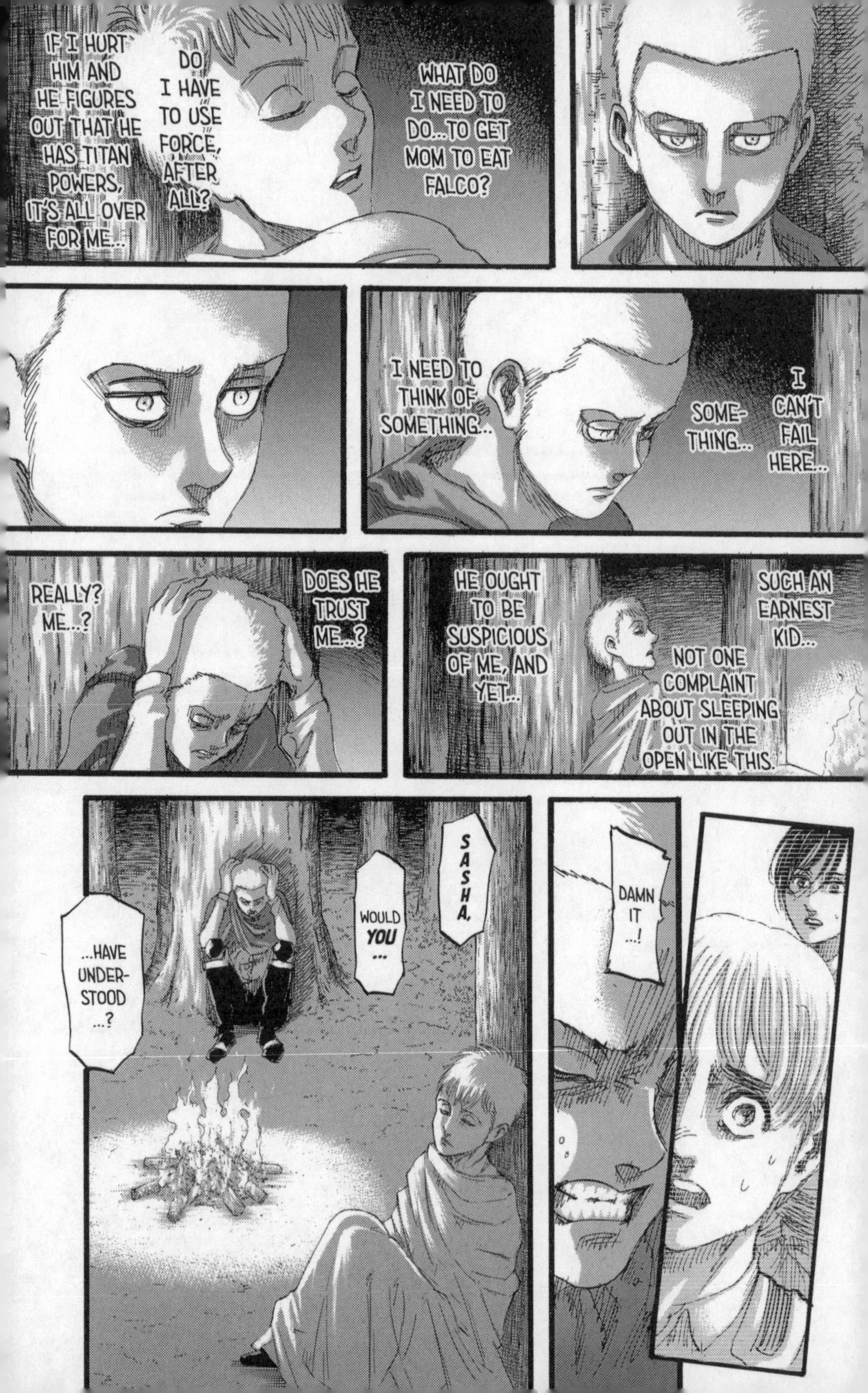
WHAT DO I NEED TO DO...TO GET MOM TO EAT FALCO?
DO I HAVE TO USE FORCE, AFTER ALL?
IF I HURT HIM AND HE FIGURES OUT THAT HE HAS TITAN POWERS, IT'S ALL OVER FOR ME...
I CAN'T FAIL HERE...
SOME-THING...
I NEED TO THINK OF SOMETHING...
SUCH AN EARNEST KID...
NOT ONE COMPLAINT ABOUT SLEEPING OUT IN THE OPEN LIKE THIS.
HE OUGHT TO BE SUSPICIOUS OF ME, AND YET...
DOES HE TRUST ME...?
REALLY? ME...?
DAMN IT...!
SASHA,
WOULD YOU...
...HAVE UNDERSTOOD...?

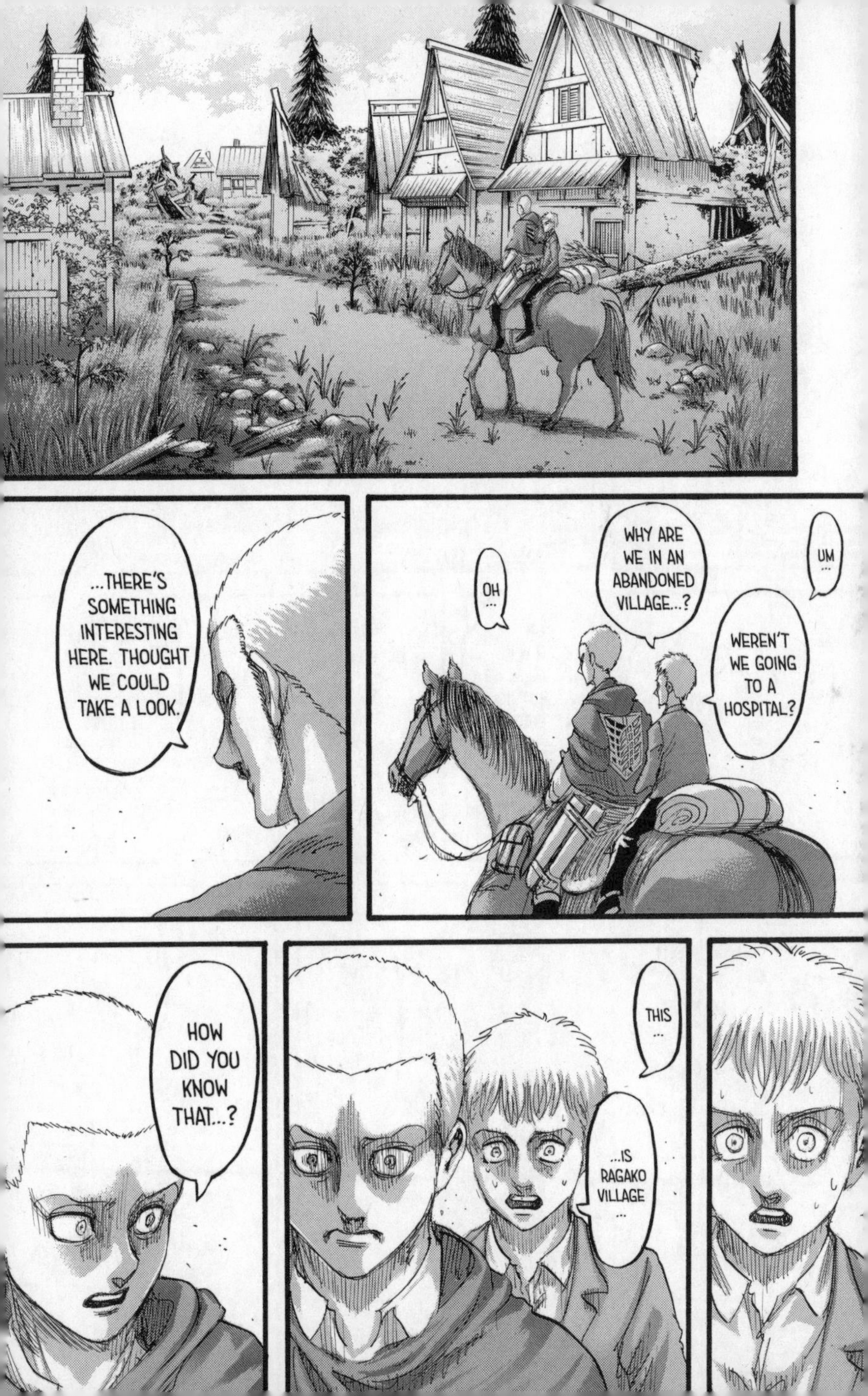
UM...
WEREN'T WE GOING TO A HOSPITAL?
WHY ARE WE IN AN ABANDONED VILLAGE...?
OH...
...THERE'S SOMETHING INTERESTING HERE. THOUGHT WE COULD TAKE A LOOK.
THIS...
...IS RAGAKO VILLAGE...
HOW DID YOU KNOW THAT...?

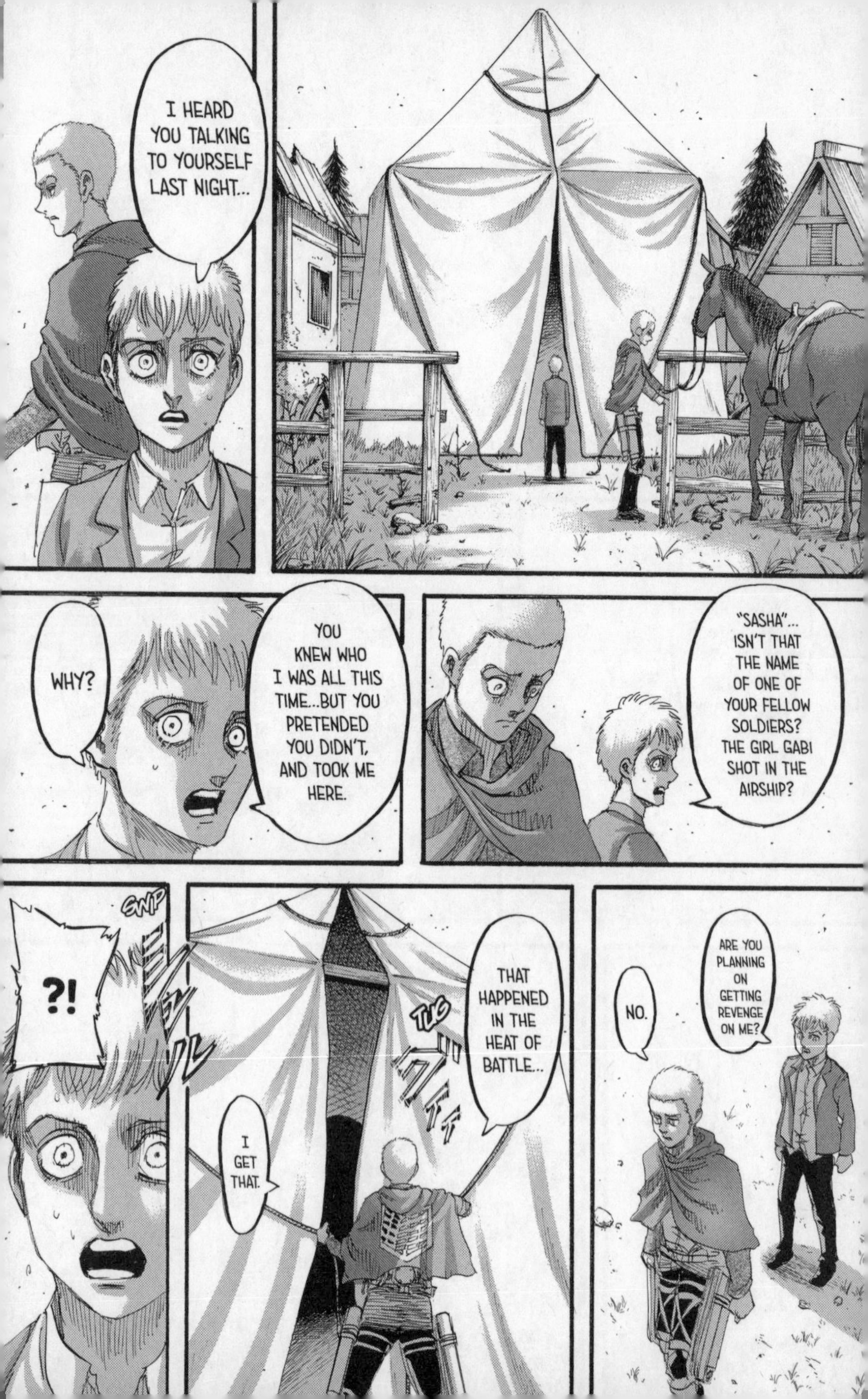
I HEARD YOU TALKING TO YOURSELF LAST NIGHT...
"SASHA"... ISN'T THAT THE NAME OF ONE OF YOUR FELLOW SOLDIERS? THE GIRL GABI SHOT IN THE AIRSHIP?
YOU KNEW WHO I WAS ALL THIS TIME...BUT YOU PRETENDED YOU DIDN'T, AND TOOK ME HERE.
WHY?
ARE YOU PLANNING ON GETTING REVENGE ON ME?
NO.
THAT HAPPENED IN THE HEAT OF BATTLE...
TUG
I GET THAT.
SWIP
?!

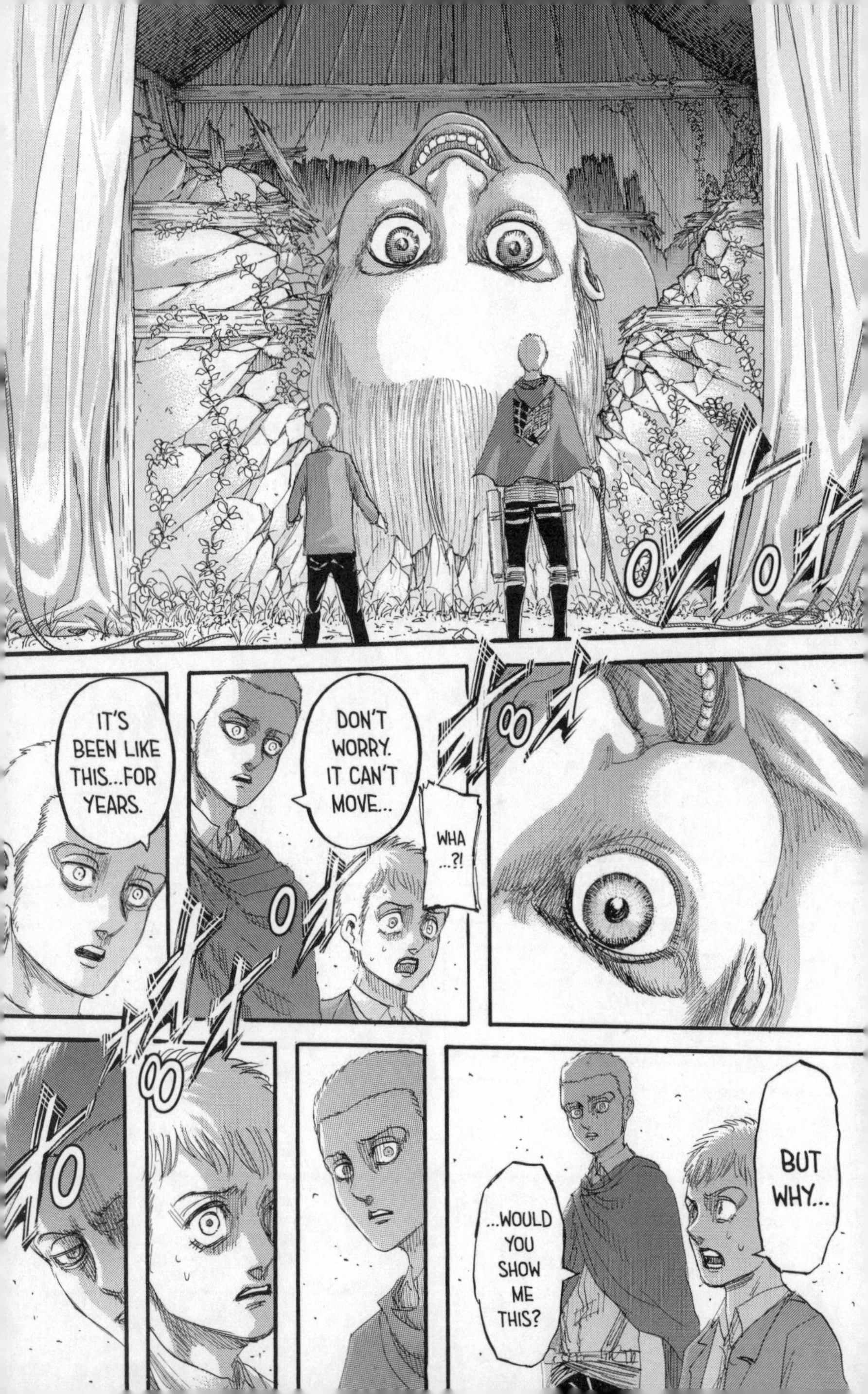
WHA ...?!
DON'T WORRY. IT CAN'T MOVE...
IT'S BEEN LIKE THIS...FOR YEARS.
BUT WHY...
...WOULD YOU SHOW ME THIS?

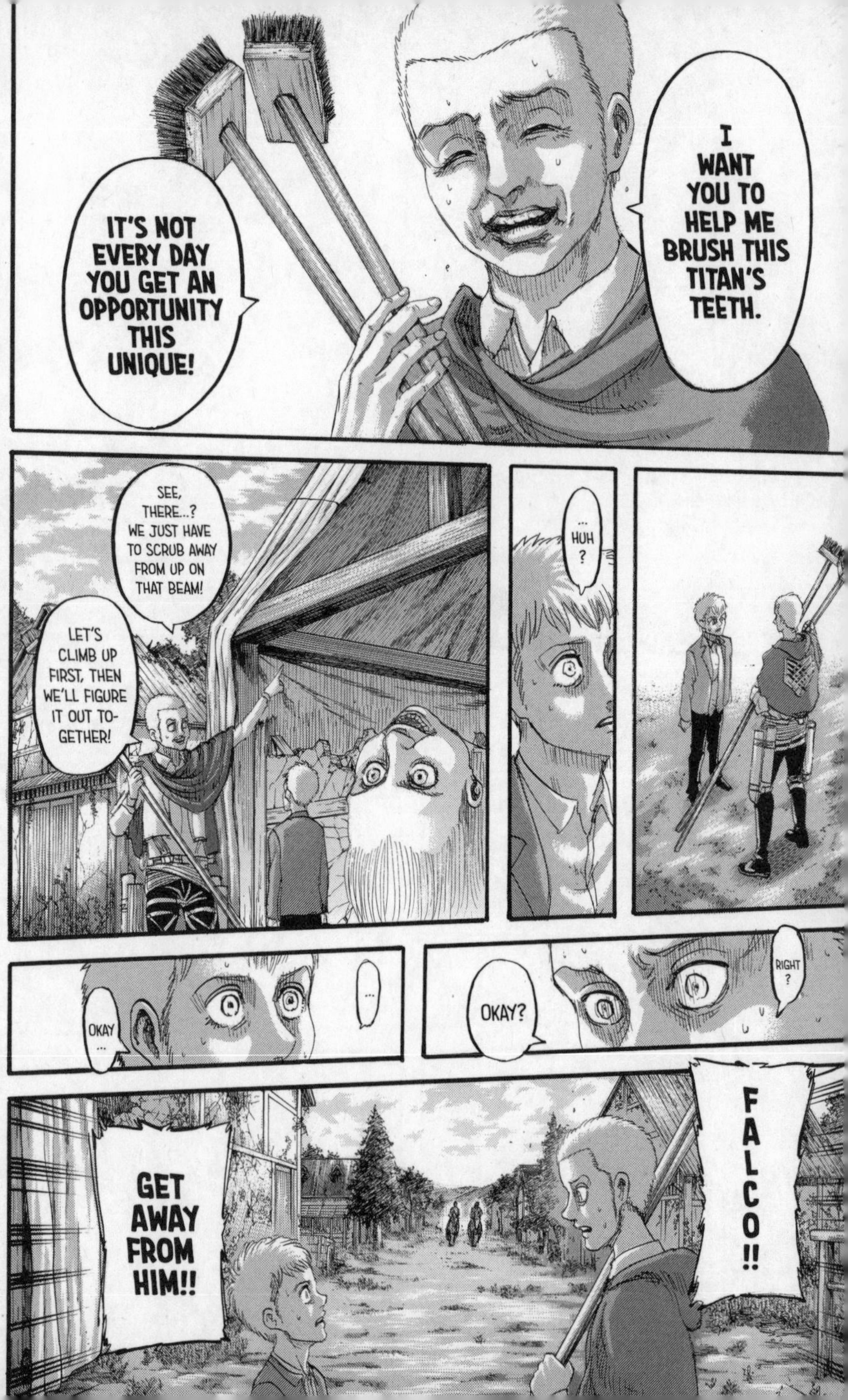
I WANT YOU TO HELP ME BRUSH THIS TITAN'S TEETH.
IT'S NOT EVERY DAY YOU GET AN OPPORTUNITY THIS UNIQUE!
... HUH ?
SEE, THERE...? WE JUST HAVE TO SCRUB AWAY FROM UP ON THAT BEAM!
LET'S CLIMB UP FIRST, THEN WE'LL FIGURE IT OUT TO-GETHER!
RIGHT ?
OKAY?
...
OKAY ...
FALCO!!
GET AWAY FROM HIM!!

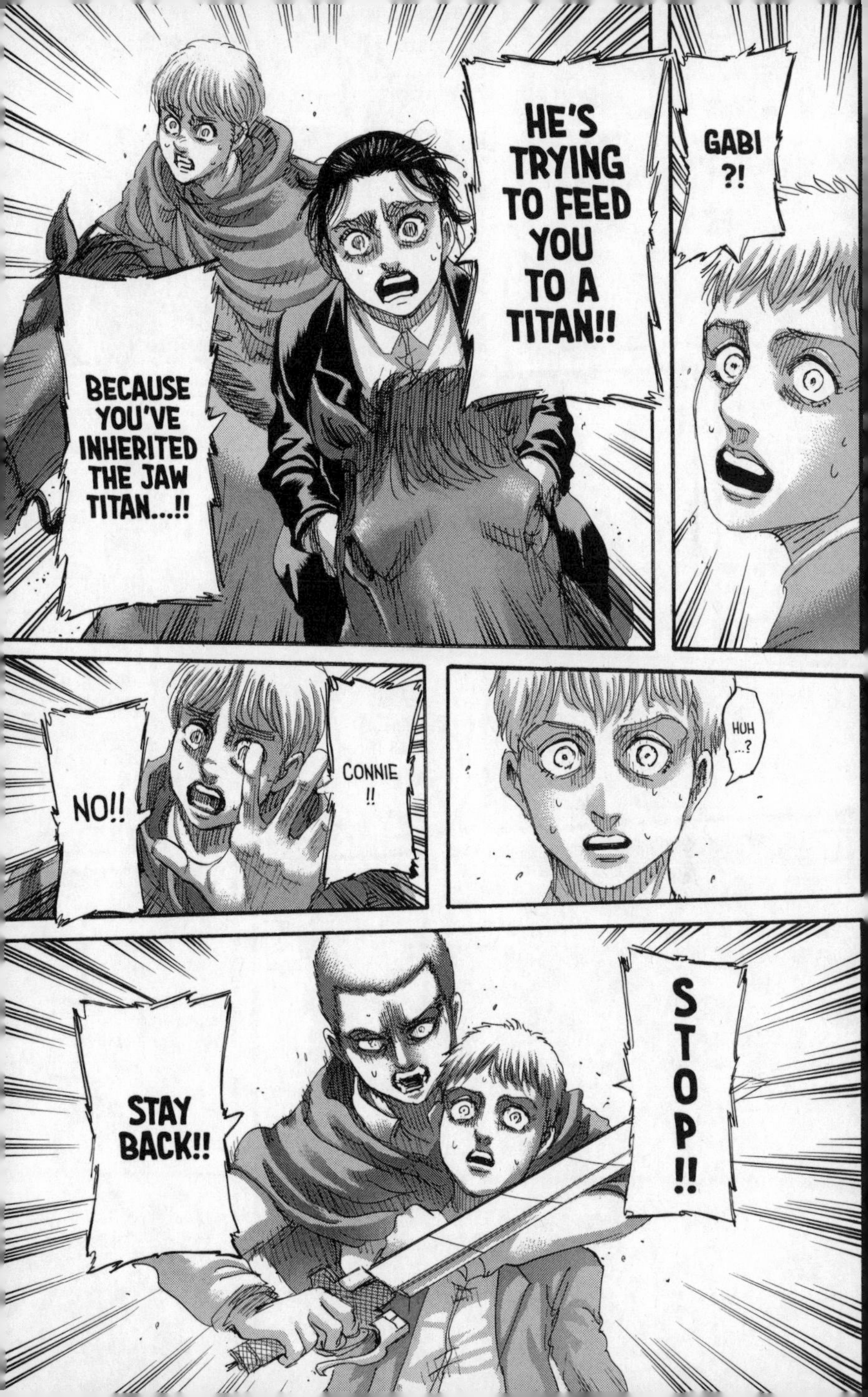
GABI ?!
HE'S TRYING TO FEED YOU TO A TITAN!!
BECAUSE YOU'VE INHERITED THE JAW TITAN...!!
HUH ...?
CONNIE !!
NO!!
STOP!!
STAY BACK!!

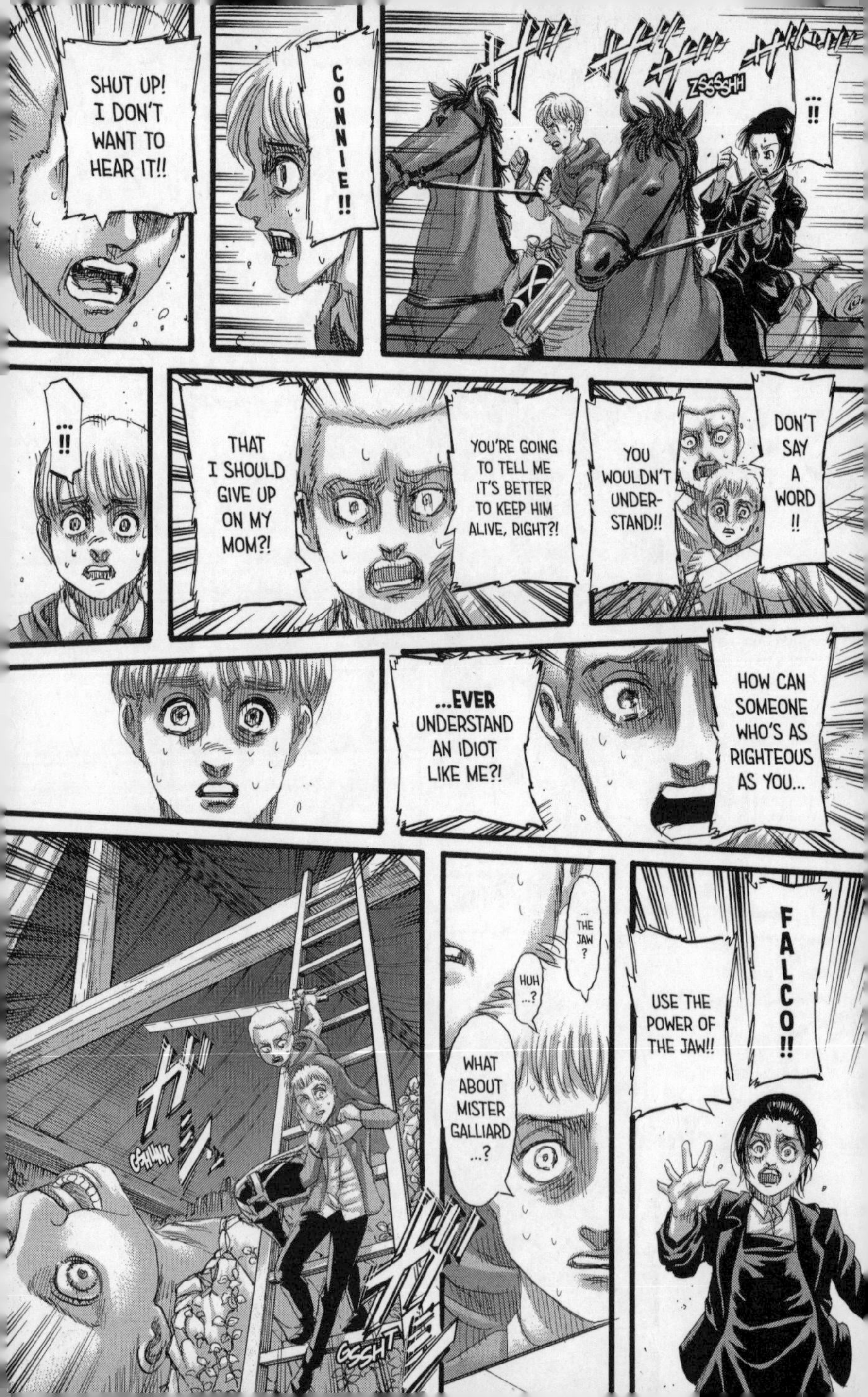
ZSSSSHH
...!!
CONNIE!!
SHUT UP! I DON'T WANT TO HEAR IT!!
DON'T SAY A WORD!!
YOU WOULDN'T UNDER-STAND!!
YOU'RE GOING TO TELL ME IT'S BETTER TO KEEP HIM ALIVE, RIGHT?!
THAT I SHOULD GIVE UP ON MY MOM?!
...!!
HOW CAN SOMEONE WHO'S AS RIGHTEOUS AS YOU...
...EVER UNDERSTAND AN IDIOT LIKE ME?!
FALCO!!
USE THE POWER OF THE JAW!!
...THE JAW?
HUH...?
WHAT ABOUT MISTER GALLIARD...?
GCHUNK
GSSHT

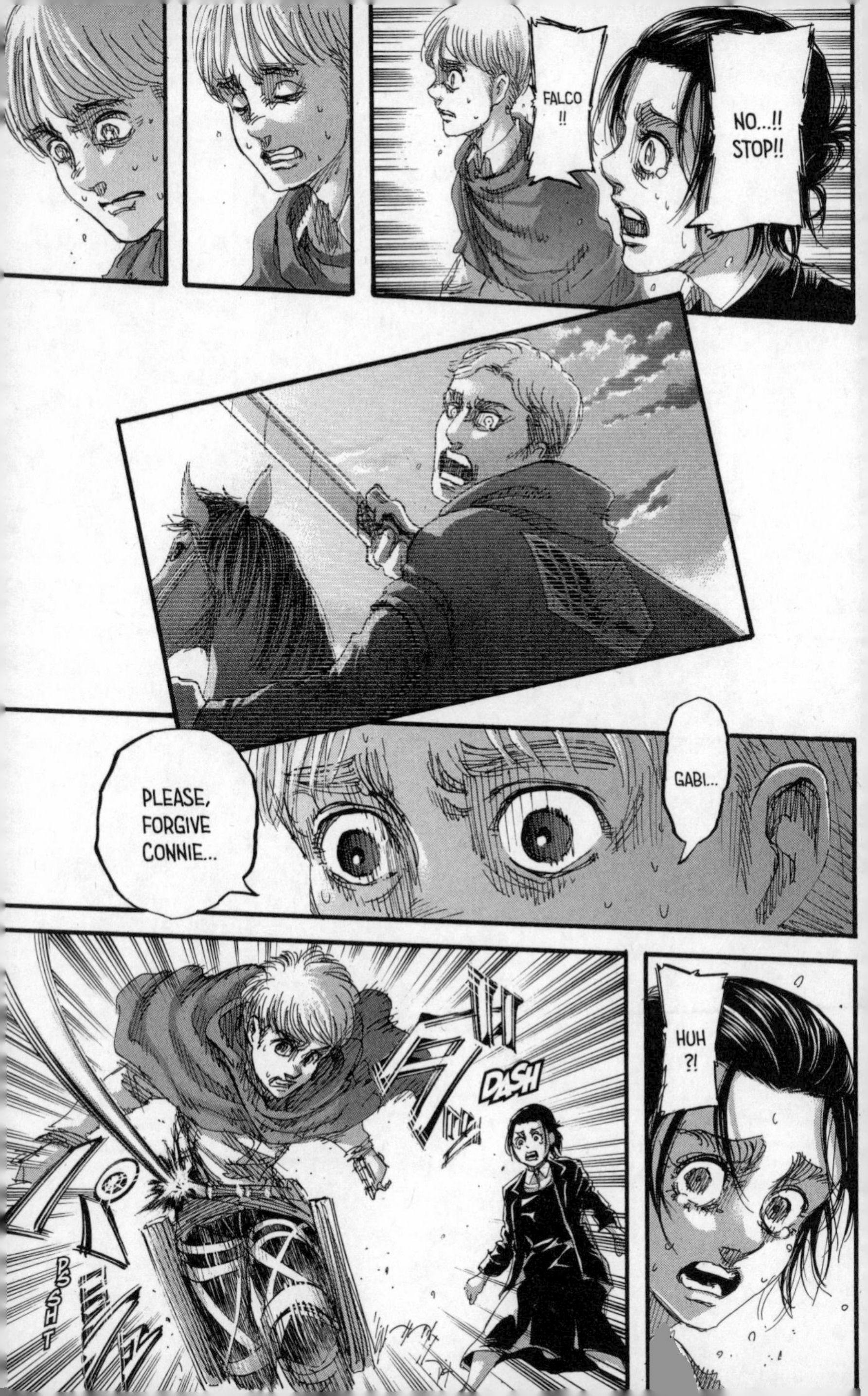
NO...!! STOP!!
FALCO !!
GABI...
PLEASE, FORGIVE CONNIE...
HUH ?!
DASH
PSSHT

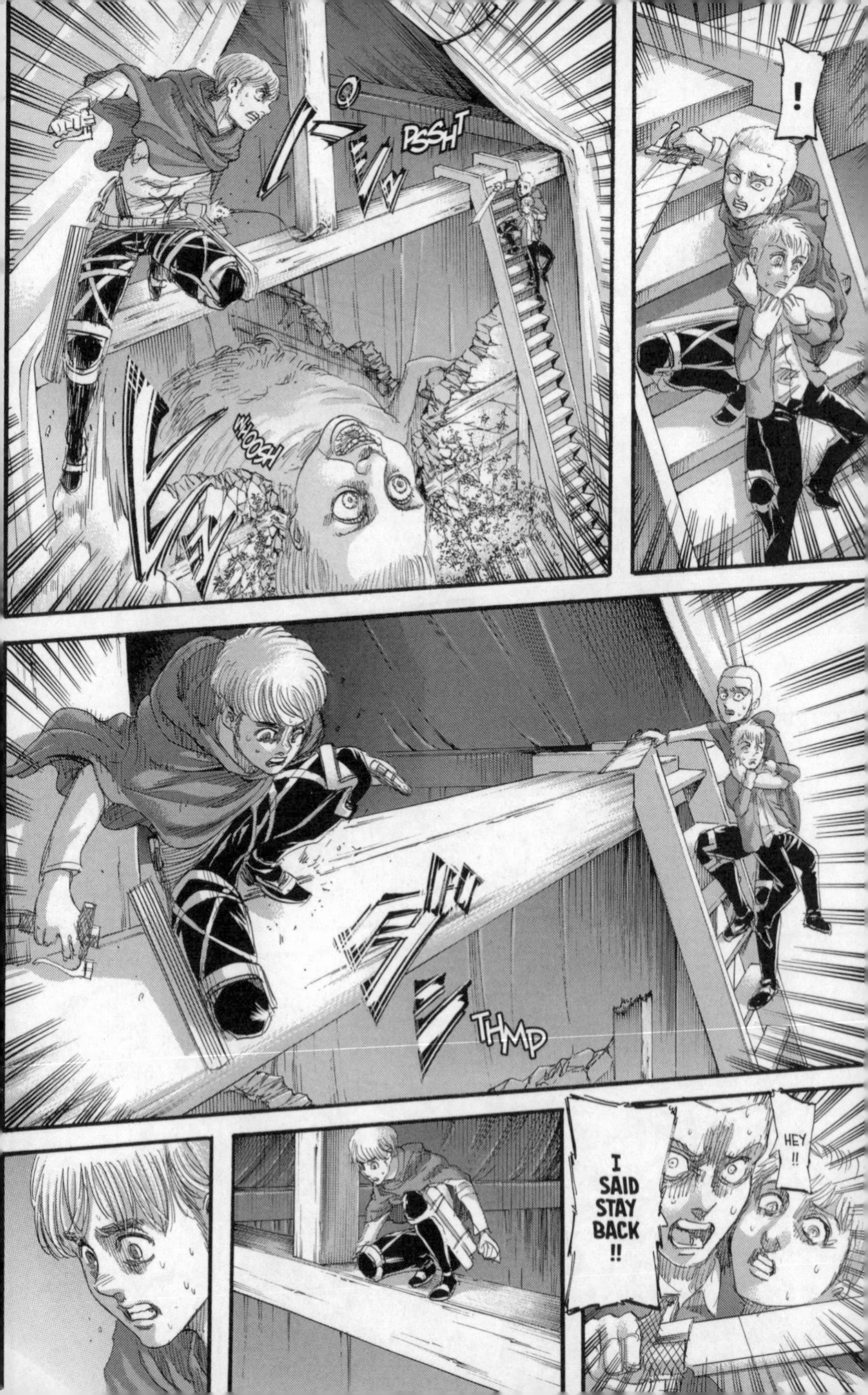
!
PSSHT
WHOOSH
THMP
HEY !!
I SAID STAY BACK !!

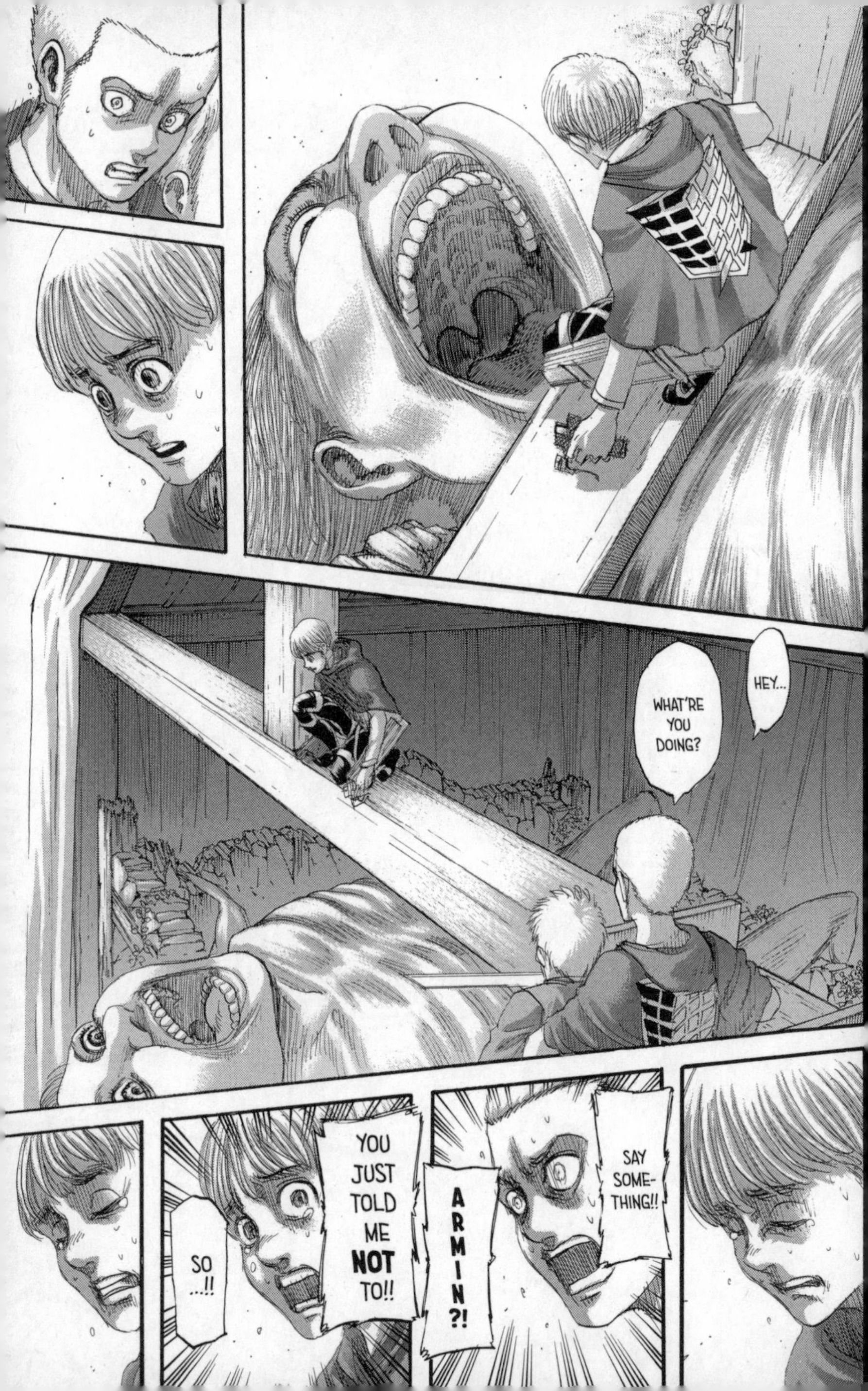
HEY...
WHAT'RE YOU DOING?
SAY SOMETHING!!
ARMIN?!
YOU JUST TOLD ME **NOT** TO!!
SO ...!!

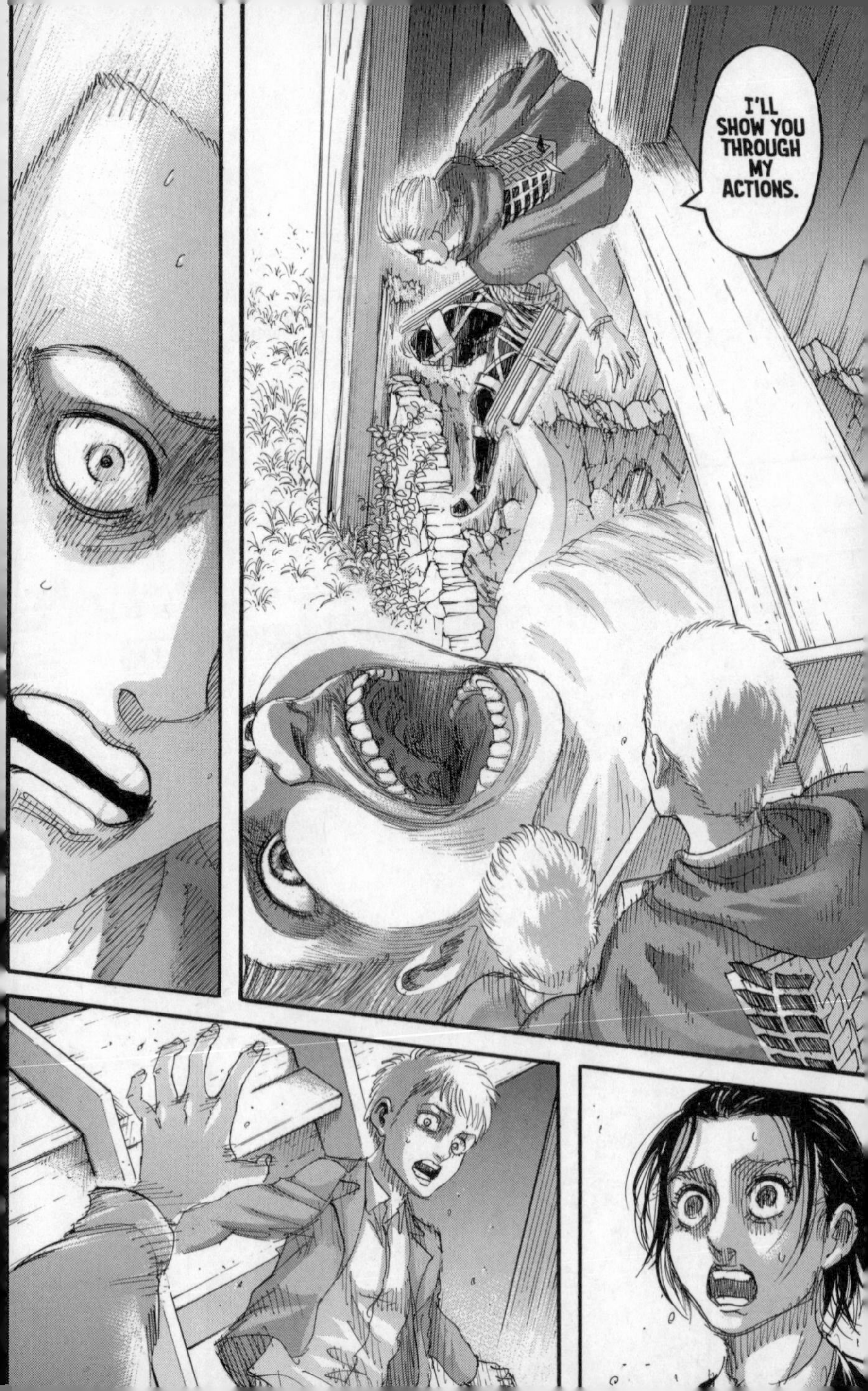
I'LL SHOW YOU THROUGH MY ACTIONS.

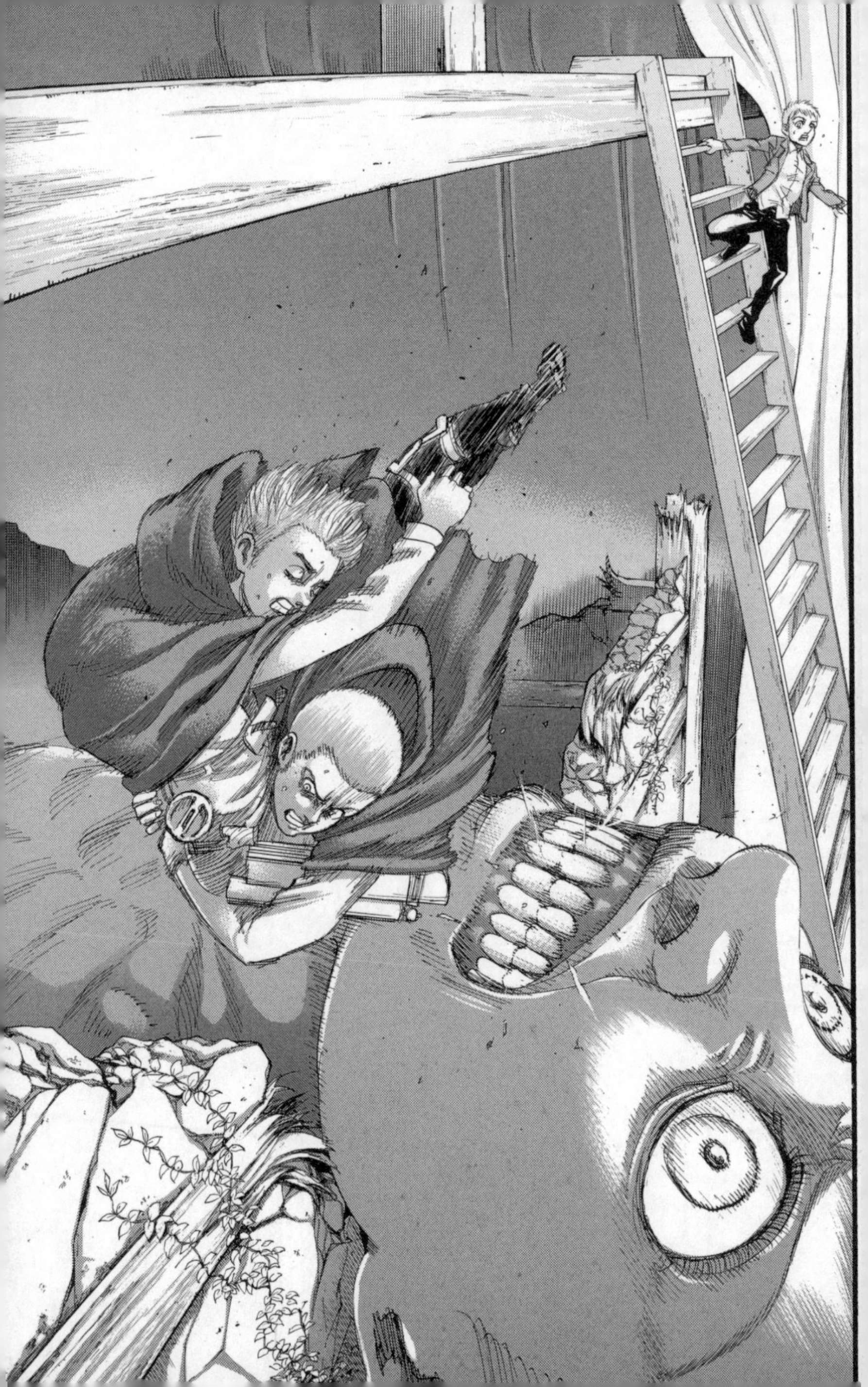

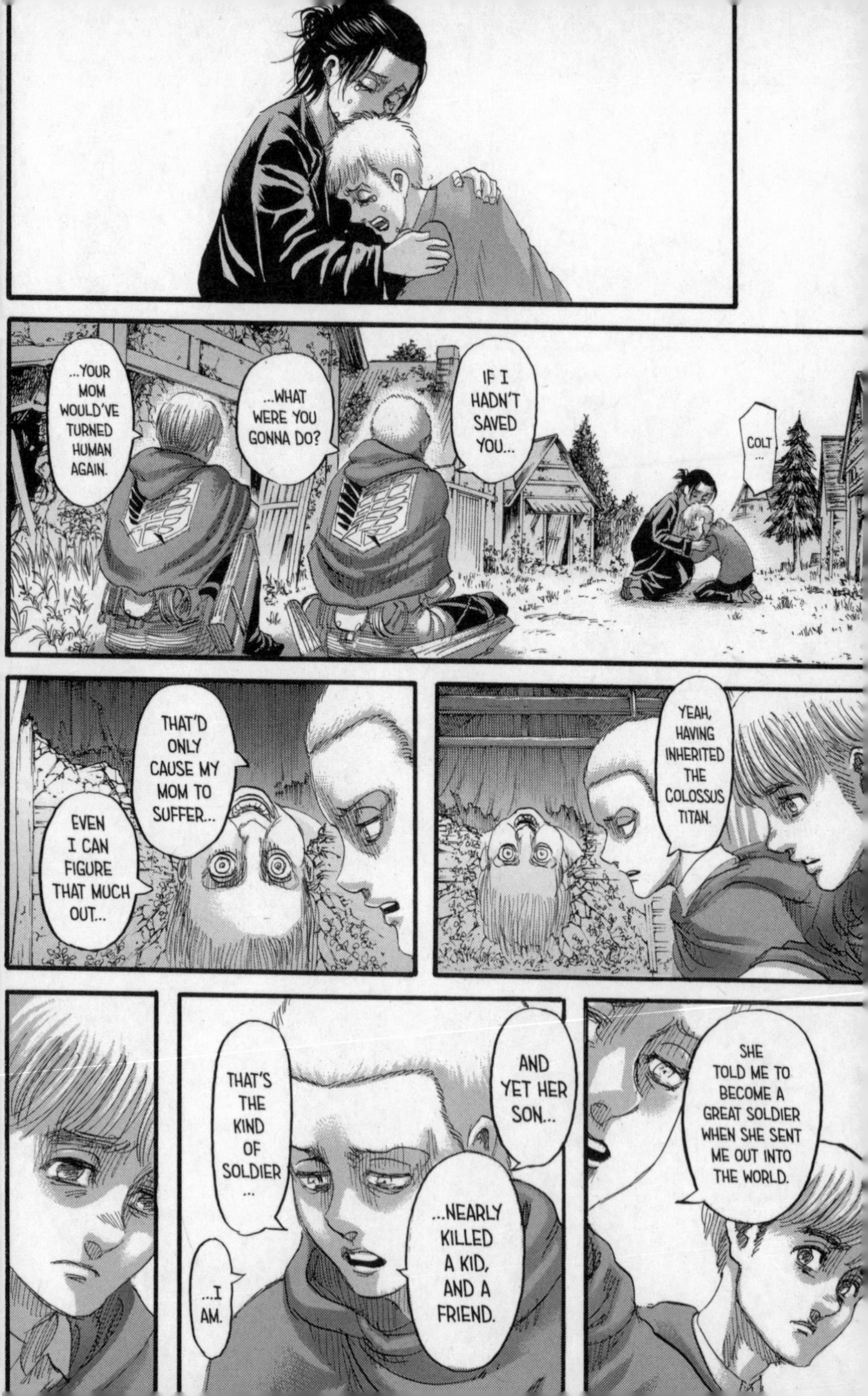
COLT...
IF I HADN'T SAVED YOU...
...WHAT WERE YOU GONNA DO?
...YOUR MOM WOULD'VE TURNED HUMAN AGAIN.
YEAH, HAVING INHERITED THE COLOSSUS TITAN.
THAT'D ONLY CAUSE MY MOM TO SUFFER...
EVEN I CAN FIGURE THAT MUCH OUT...
SHE TOLD ME TO BECOME A GREAT SOLDIER WHEN SHE SENT ME OUT INTO THE WORLD.
AND YET HER SON...
...NEARLY KILLED A KID, AND A FRIEND.
THAT'S THE KIND OF SOLDIER...
...I AM.

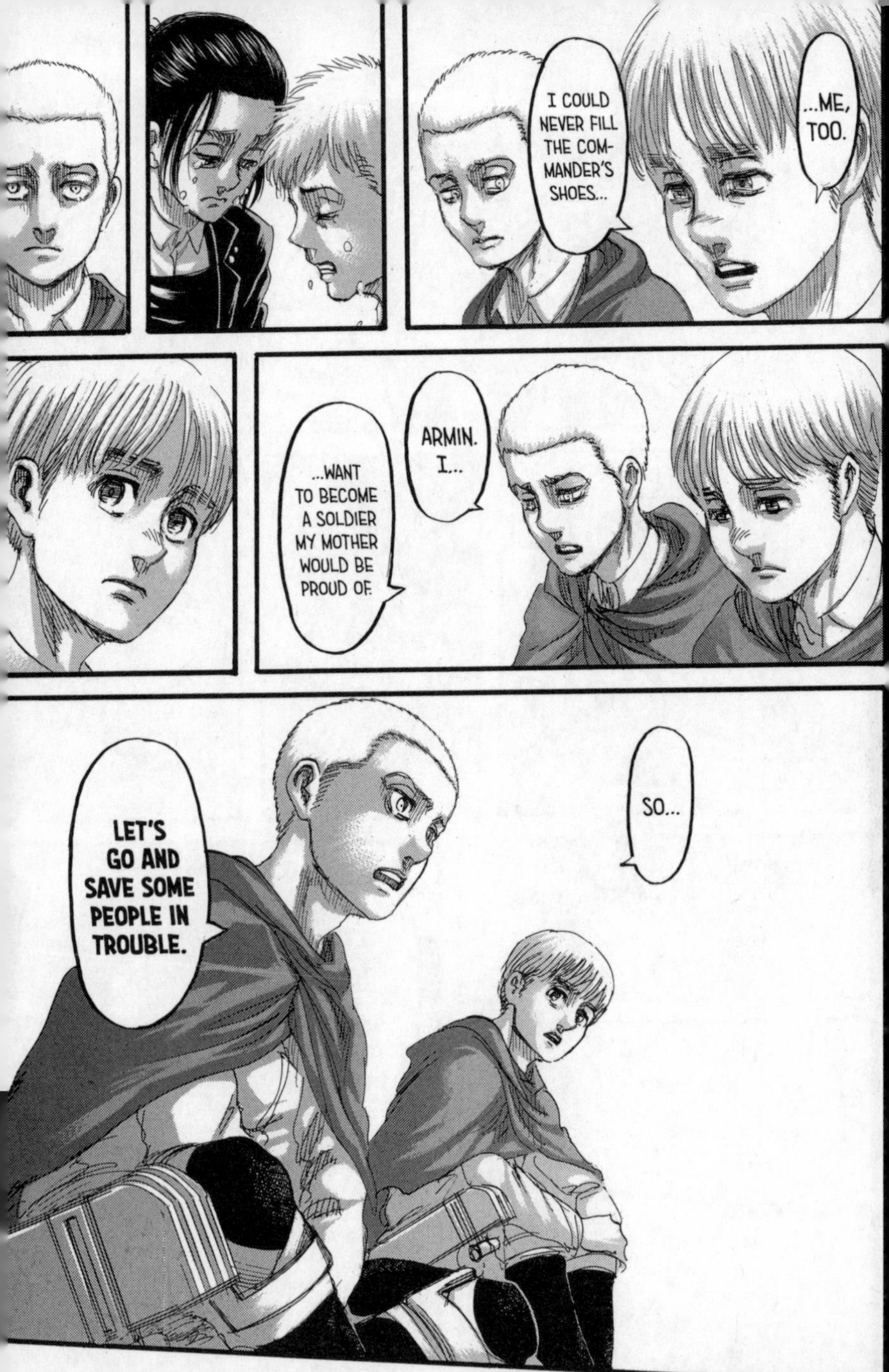
I COULD NEVER FILL THE COMMANDER'S SHOES...
...ME, TOO.
ARMIN. I...
...WANT TO BECOME A SOLDIER MY MOTHER WOULD BE PROUD OF.
SO...
LET'S GO AND SAVE SOME PEOPLE IN TROUBLE.

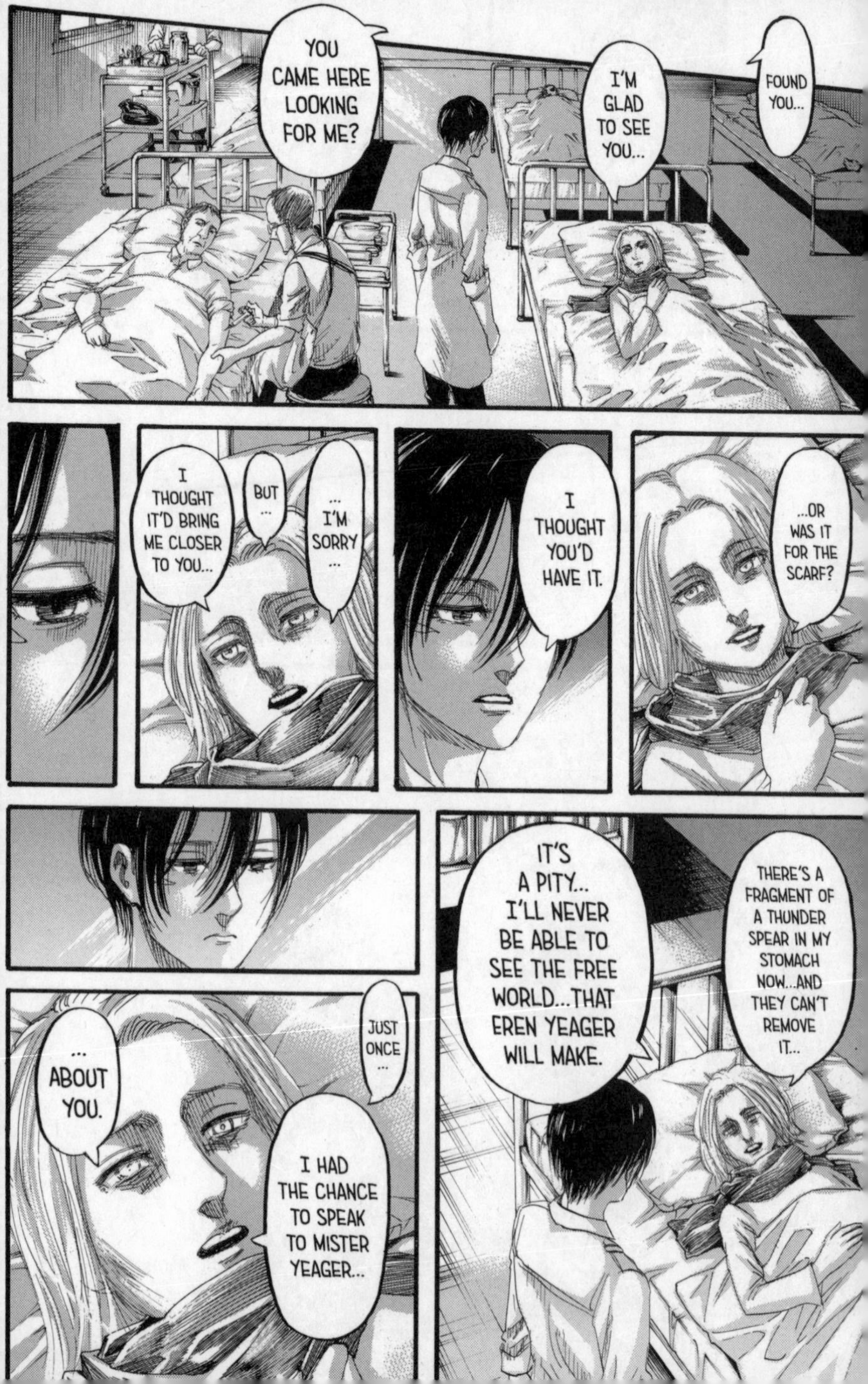
FOUND YOU...
I'M GLAD TO SEE YOU...
YOU CAME HERE LOOKING FOR ME?
...OR WAS IT FOR THE SCARF?
I THOUGHT YOU'D HAVE IT.
... I'M SORRY ...
BUT ...
I THOUGHT IT'D BRING ME CLOSER TO YOU...
THERE'S A FRAGMENT OF A THUNDER SPEAR IN MY STOMACH NOW...AND THEY CAN'T REMOVE IT...
IT'S A PITY... I'LL NEVER BE ABLE TO SEE THE FREE WORLD...THAT EREN YEAGER WILL MAKE.
JUST ONCE ...
I HAD THE CHANCE TO SPEAK TO MISTER YEAGER...
... ABOUT YOU.

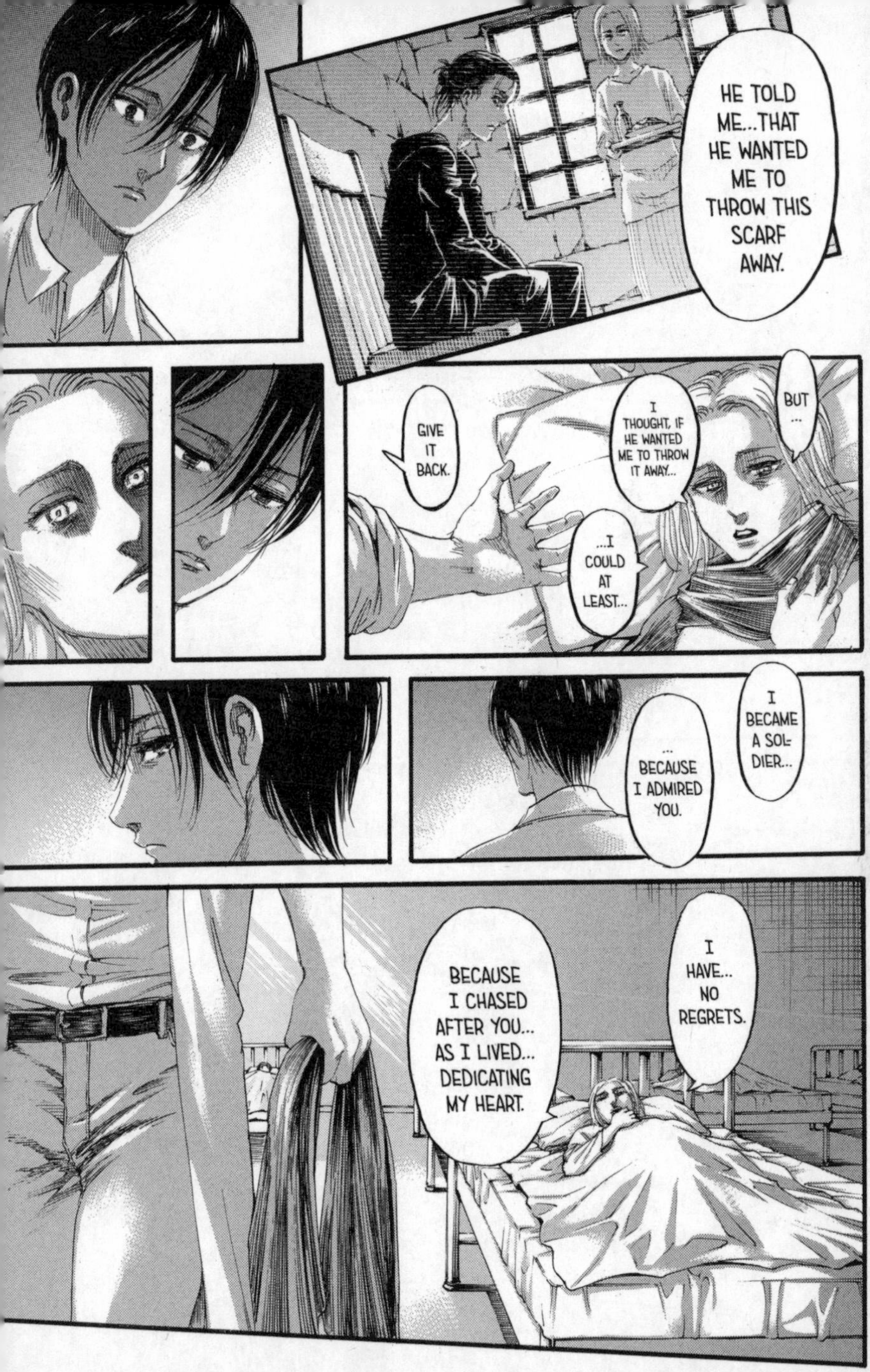
HE TOLD ME...THAT HE WANTED ME TO THROW THIS SCARF AWAY.
BUT ...
I THOUGHT, IF HE WANTED ME TO THROW IT AWAY...
...I COULD AT LEAST...
GIVE IT BACK.
I BECAME A SOLDIER...
...BECAUSE I ADMIRED YOU.
I HAVE... NO REGRETS.
BECAUSE I CHASED AFTER YOU... AS I LIVED... DEDICATING MY HEART.

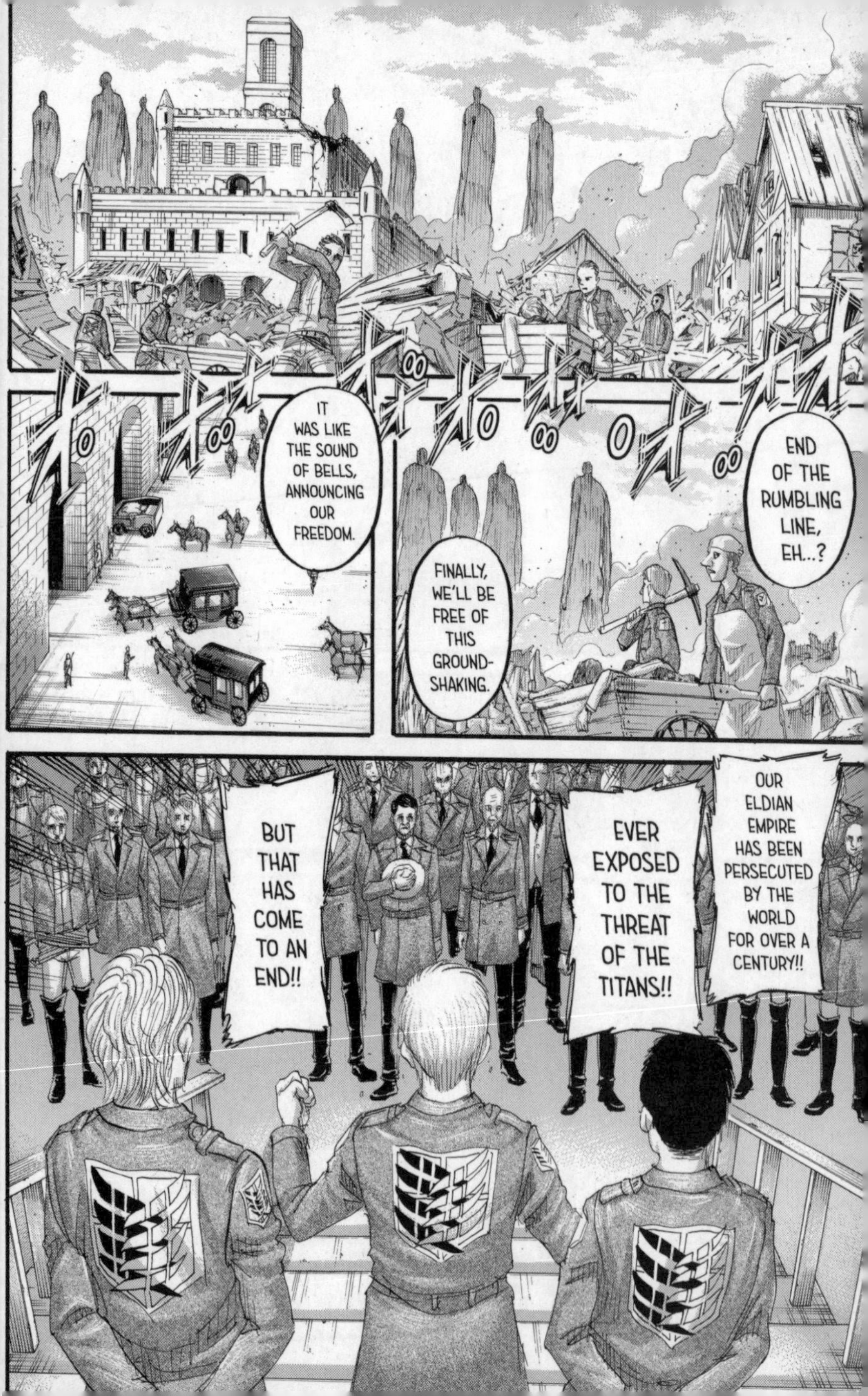
END OF THE RUMBLING LINE, EH...?
FINALLY, WE'LL BE FREE OF THIS GROUND-SHAKING.
IT WAS LIKE THE SOUND OF BELLS, ANNOUNCING OUR FREEDOM.
OUR ELDIAN EMPIRE HAS BEEN PERSECUTED BY THE WORLD FOR OVER A CENTURY!!
EVER EXPOSED TO THE THREAT OF THE TITANS!!
BUT THAT HAS COME TO AN END!!

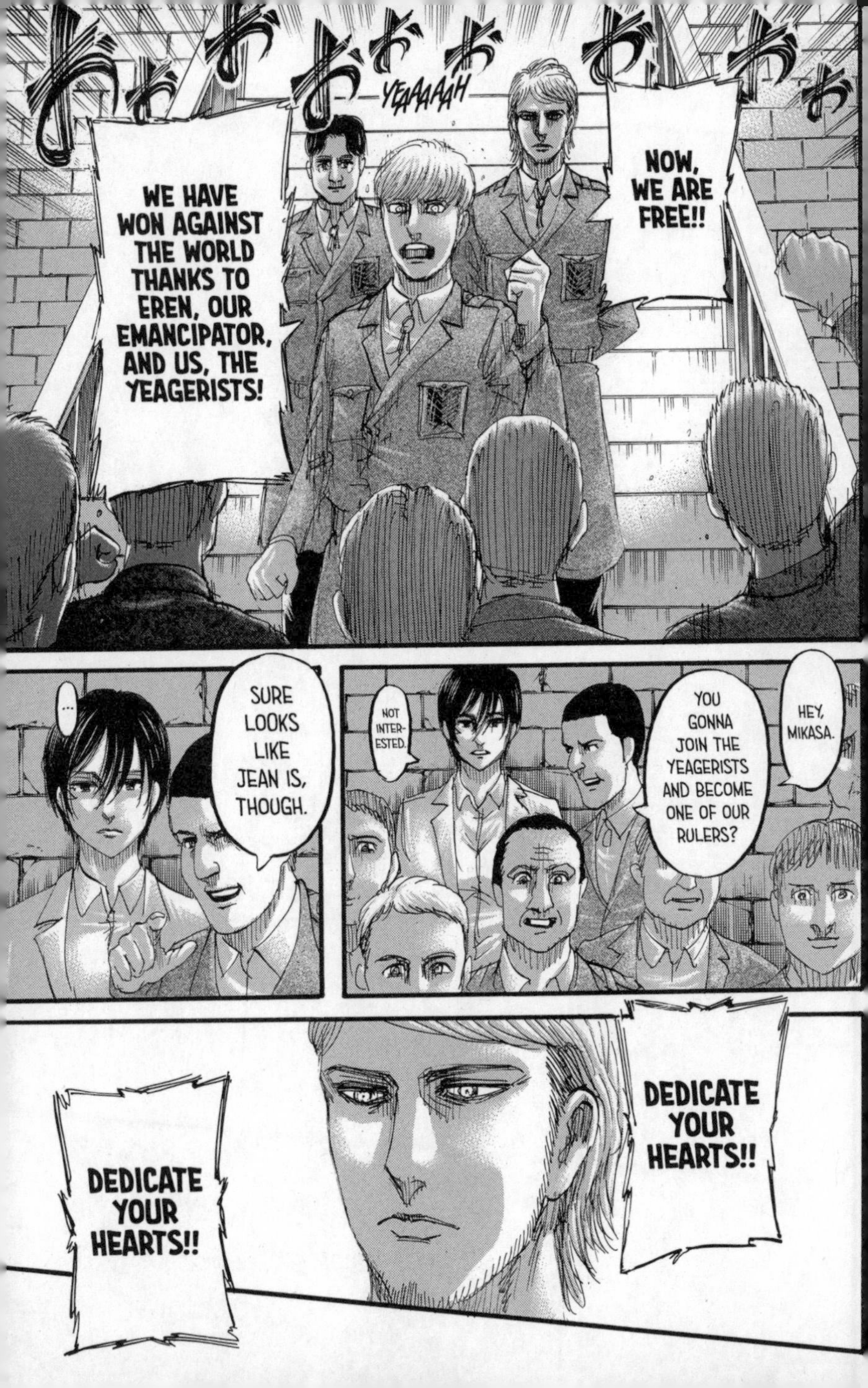
YEAAAAAH
NOW, WE ARE FREE!!
WE HAVE WON AGAINST THE WORLD THANKS TO EREN, OUR EMANCIPATOR, AND US, THE YEAGERISTS!
HEY, MIKASA.
YOU GONNA JOIN THE YEAGERISTS AND BECOME ONE OF OUR RULERS?
NOT INTERESTED.
SURE LOOKS LIKE JEAN IS, THOUGH.
...
DEDICATE YOUR HEARTS!!
DEDICATE YOUR HEARTS!!

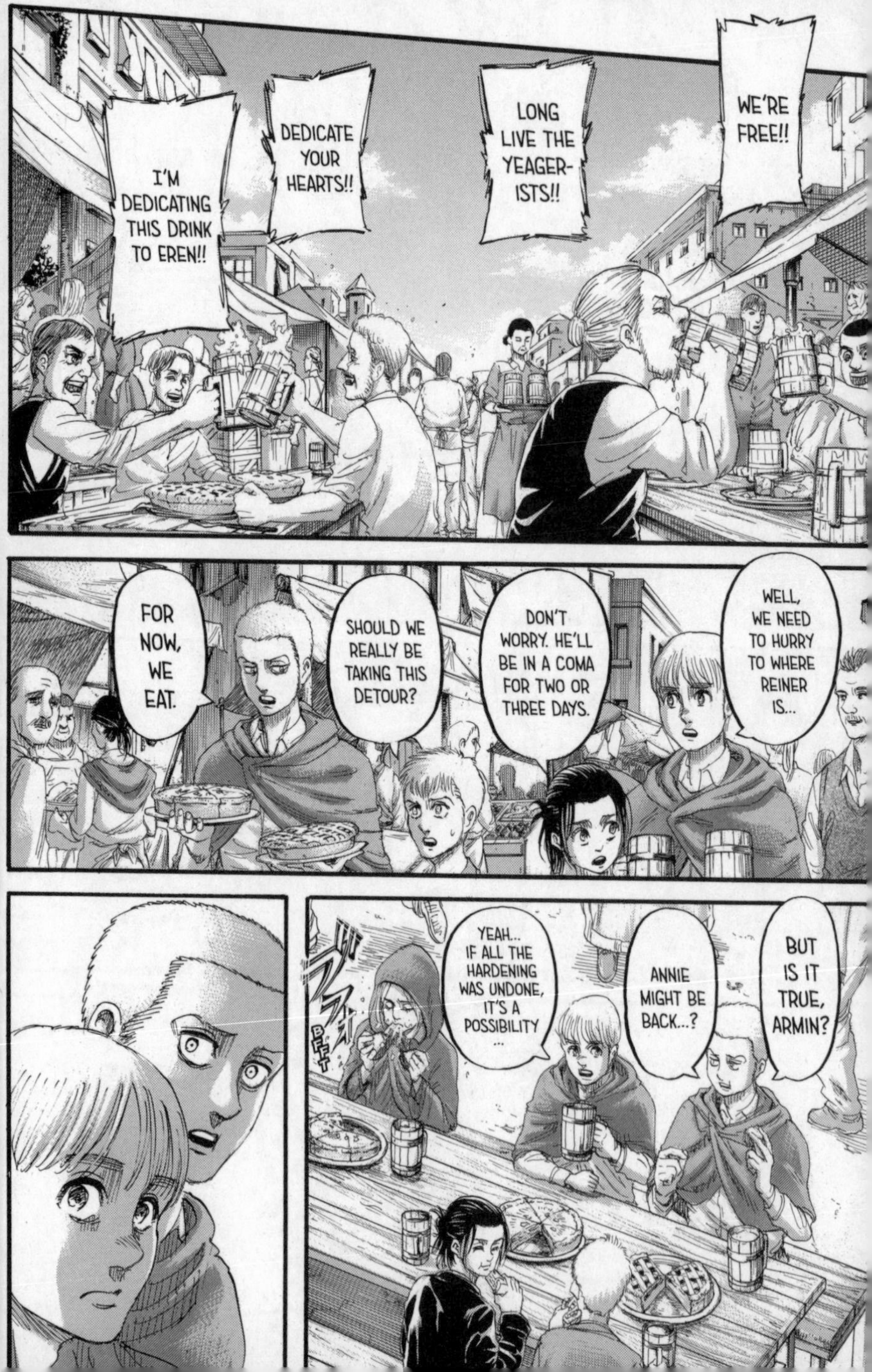
WE'RE FREE!!
LONG LIVE THE YEAGER-ISTS!!
DEDICATE YOUR HEARTS!!
I'M DEDICATING THIS DRINK TO EREN!!
WELL, WE NEED TO HURRY TO WHERE REINER IS...
DON'T WORRY. HE'LL BE IN A COMA FOR TWO OR THREE DAYS.
SHOULD WE REALLY BE TAKING THIS DETOUR?
FOR NOW, WE EAT.
BUT IS IT TRUE, ARMIN?
ANNIE MIGHT BE BACK...?
YEAH... IF ALL THE HARDENING WAS UNDONE, IT'S A POSSIBILITY...
BFFT

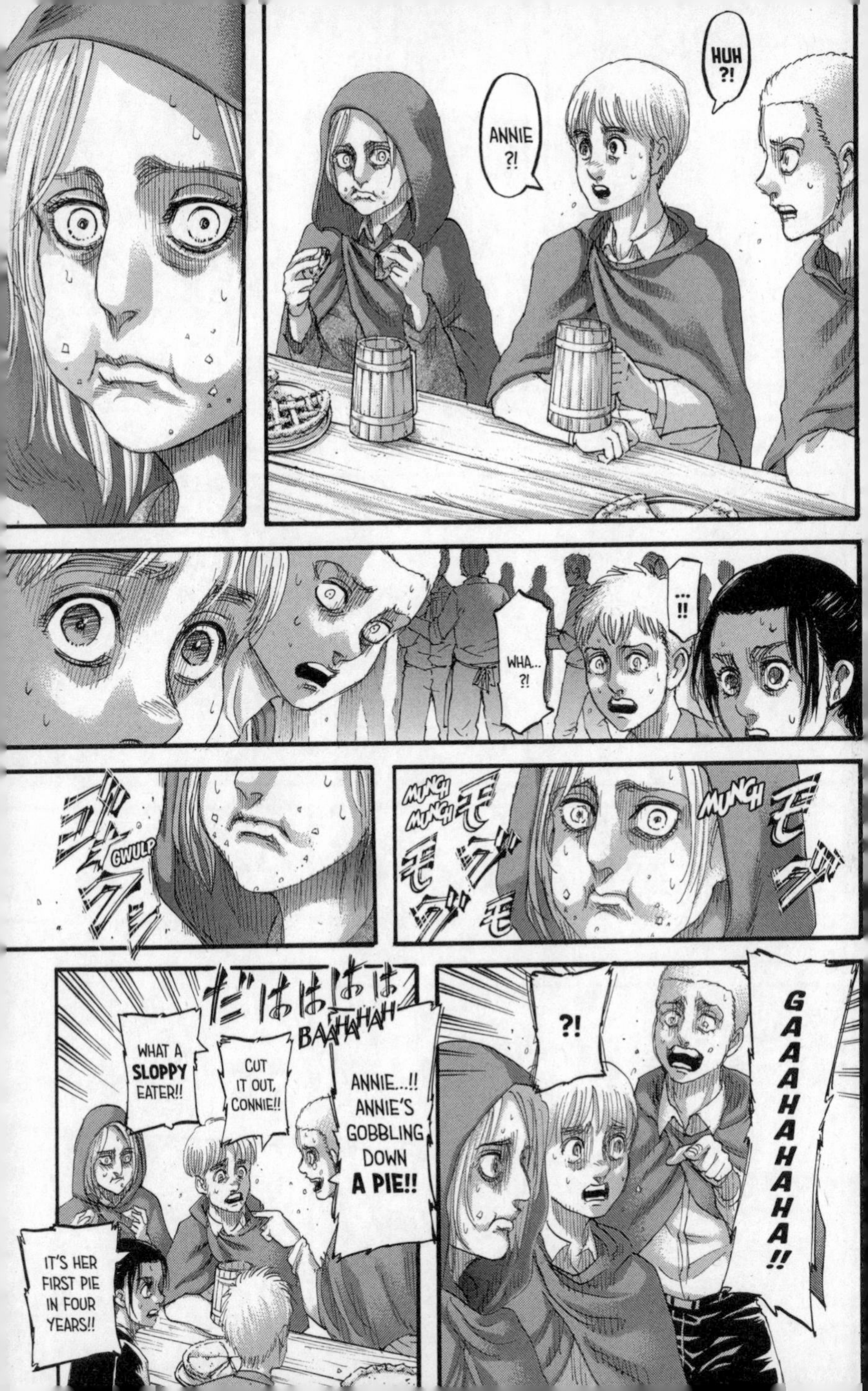
HUH ?!
ANNIE ?!
...!!
WHA... ?!
MUNCH
MUNCH MUNCH
GWULP
GAAAHAHAHAHA!!
?!
だはははは
BAAHAHAHAH
ANNIE...!! ANNIE'S GOBBLING DOWN A PIE!!
CUT IT OUT, CONNIE!!
WHAT A SLOPPY EATER!!
IT'S HER FIRST PIE IN FOUR YEARS!!

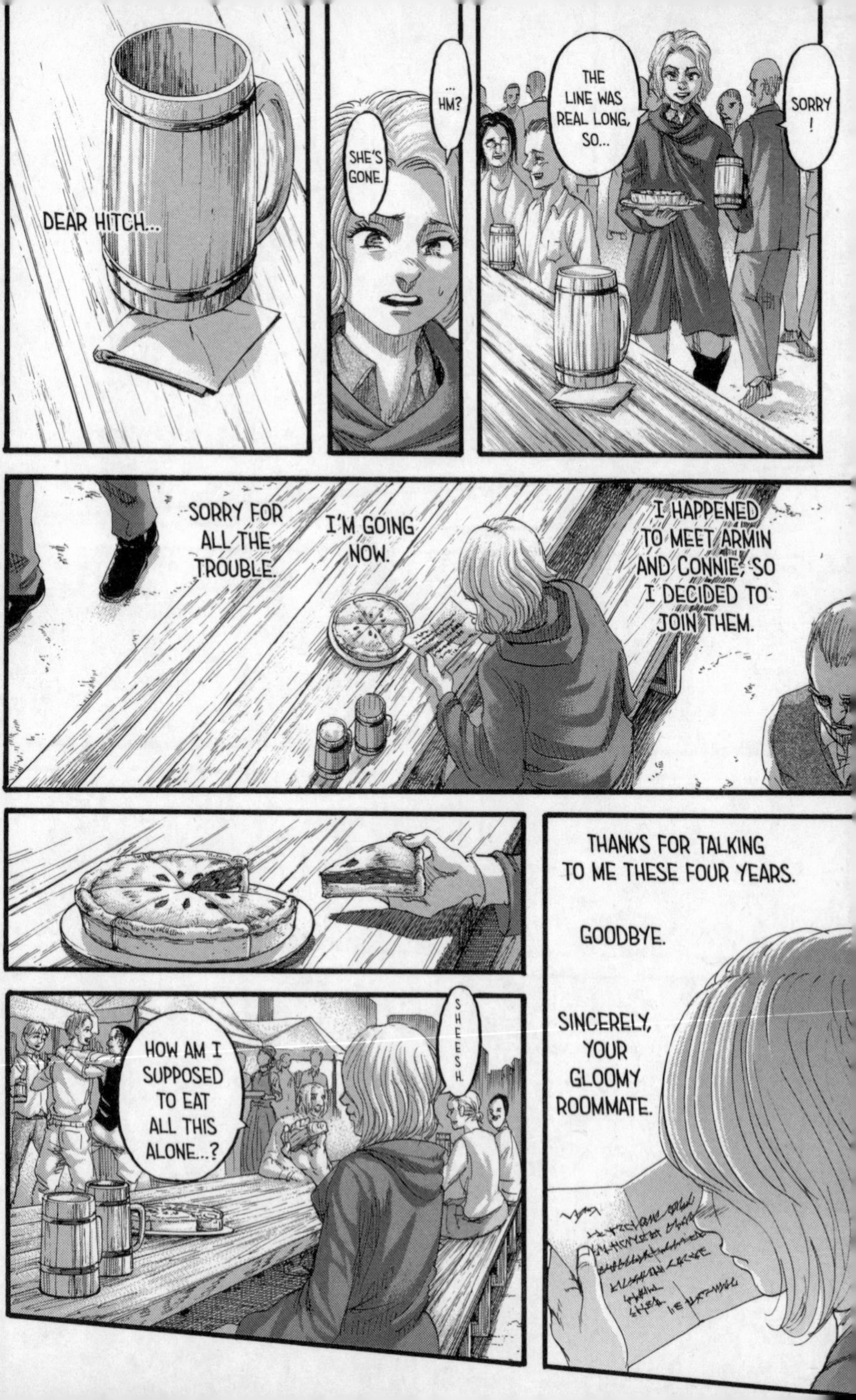
SORRY!
THE LINE WAS REAL LONG, SO...
...HM?
SHE'S GONE.
DEAR HITCH...
I HAPPENED TO MEET ARMIN AND CONNIE, SO I DECIDED TO JOIN THEM.
I'M GOING NOW.
SORRY FOR ALL THE TROUBLE.
THANKS FOR TALKING TO ME THESE FOUR YEARS.
GOODBYE.
SINCERELY, YOUR GLOOMY ROOMMATE.
SHEESH.
HOW AM I SUPPOSED TO EAT ALL THIS ALONE...?

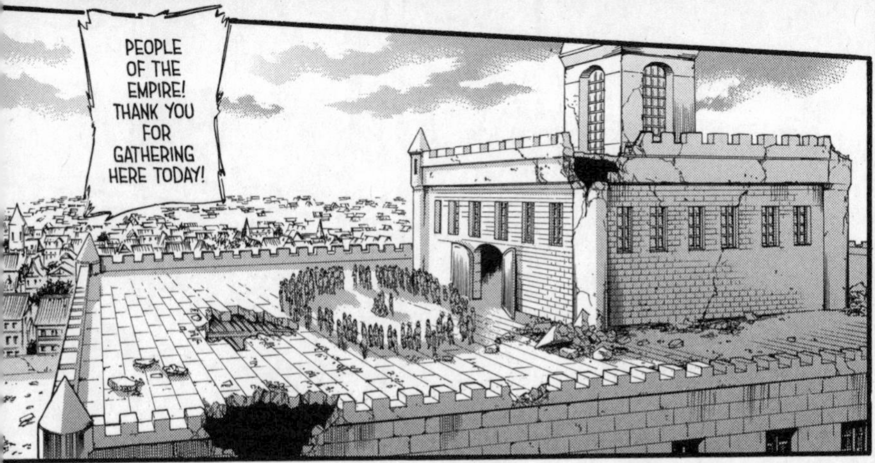
PEOPLE OF THE EMPIRE! THANK YOU FOR GATHERING HERE TODAY!

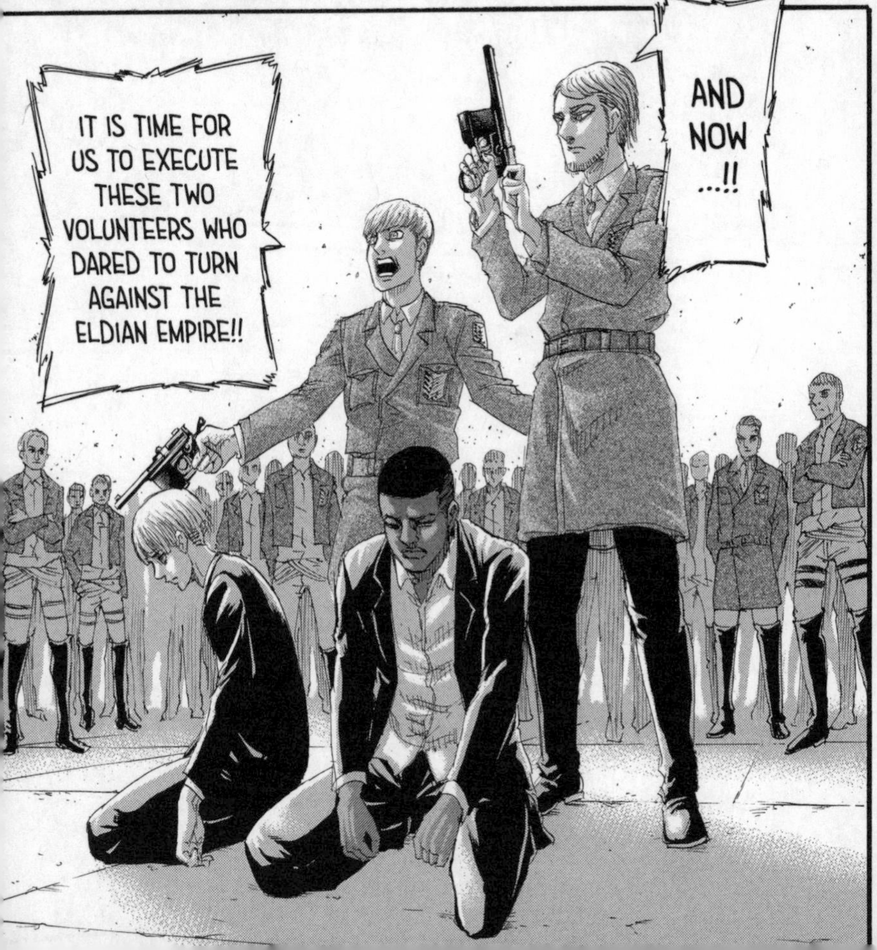
AND NOW …!!
IT IS TIME FOR US TO EXECUTE THESE TWO VOLUNTEERS WHO DARED TO TURN AGAINST THE ELDIAN EMPIRE!!

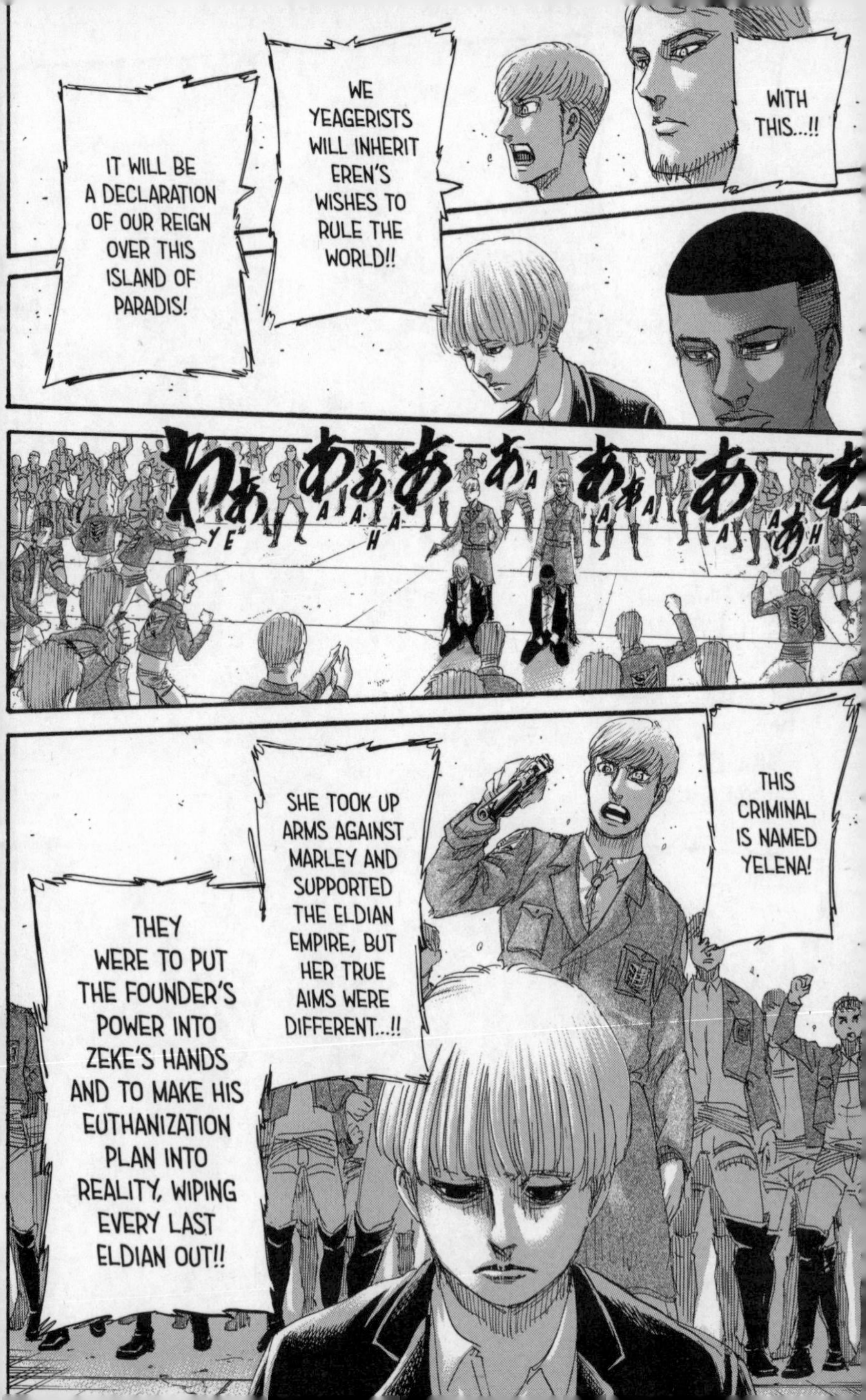
WITH THIS...!!
WE YEAGERISTS WILL INHERIT EREN'S WISHES TO RULE THE WORLD!!
IT WILL BE A DECLARATION OF OUR REIGN OVER THIS ISLAND OF PARADIS!
わぁあぁああ
YEAAAAH
THIS CRIMINAL IS NAMED YELENA!
SHE TOOK UP ARMS AGAINST MARLEY AND SUPPORTED THE ELDIAN EMPIRE, BUT HER TRUE AIMS WERE DIFFERENT...!!
THEY WERE TO PUT THE FOUNDER'S POWER INTO ZEKE'S HANDS AND TO MAKE HIS EUTHANIZATION PLAN INTO REALITY, WIPING EVERY LAST ELDIAN OUT!!

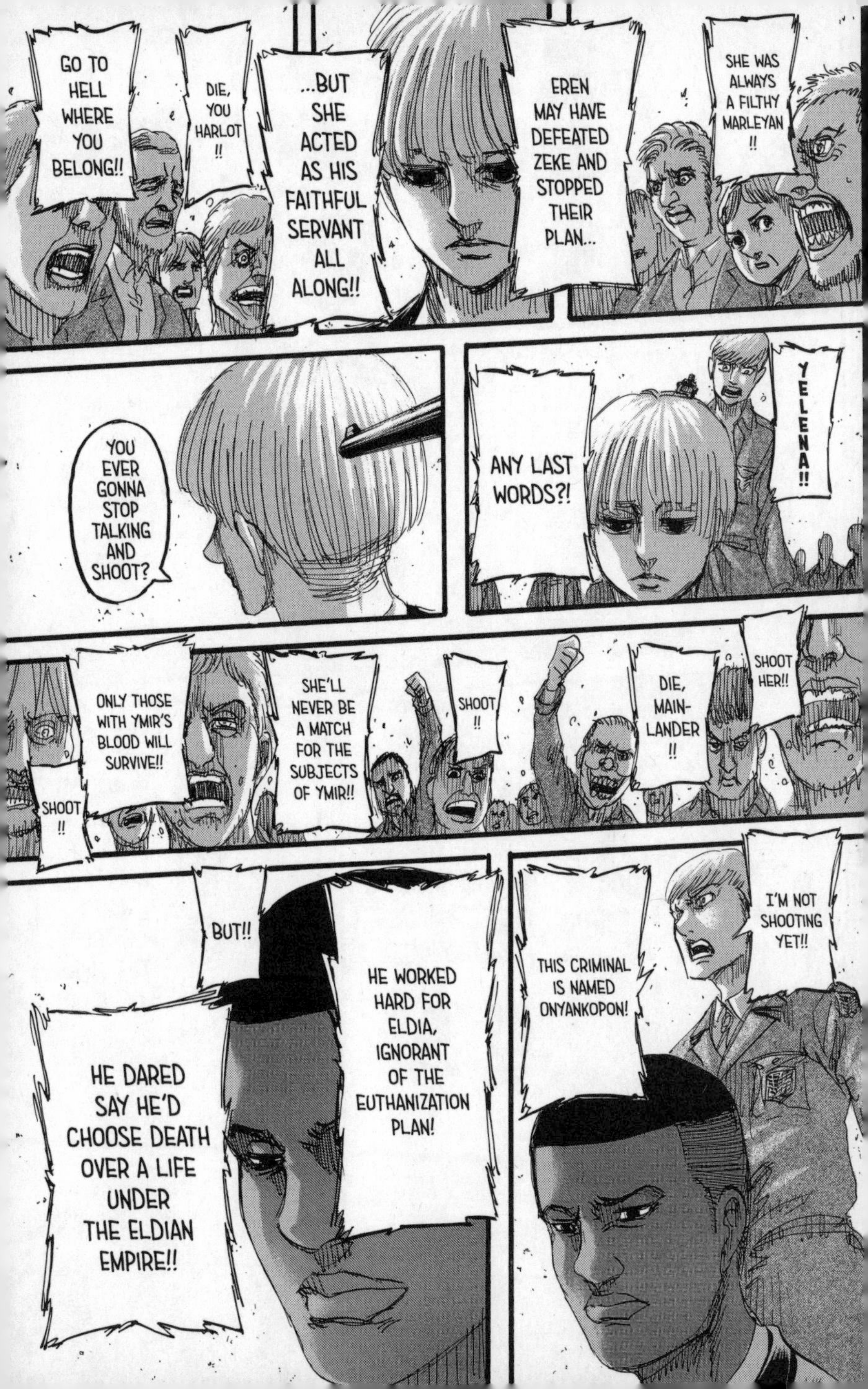
SHE WAS ALWAYS A FILTHY MARLEYAN!!
EREN MAY HAVE DEFEATED ZEKE AND STOPPED THEIR PLAN...
...BUT SHE ACTED AS HIS FAITHFUL SERVANT ALL ALONG!!
DIE, YOU HARLOT!!
GO TO HELL WHERE YOU BELONG!!
YELENA!!
ANY LAST WORDS?!
YOU EVER GONNA STOP TALKING AND SHOOT?
SHOOT HER!!
DIE, MAINLANDER!!
SHOOT!!
SHE'LL NEVER BE A MATCH FOR THE SUBJECTS OF YMIR!!
ONLY THOSE WITH YMIR'S BLOOD WILL SURVIVE!!
SHOOT!!
I'M NOT SHOOTING YET!!
THIS CRIMINAL IS NAMED ONYANKOPON!
HE WORKED HARD FOR ELDIA, IGNORANT OF THE EUTHANIZATION PLAN!
BUT!!
HE DARED SAY HE'D CHOOSE DEATH OVER A LIFE UNDER THE ELDIAN EMPIRE!!

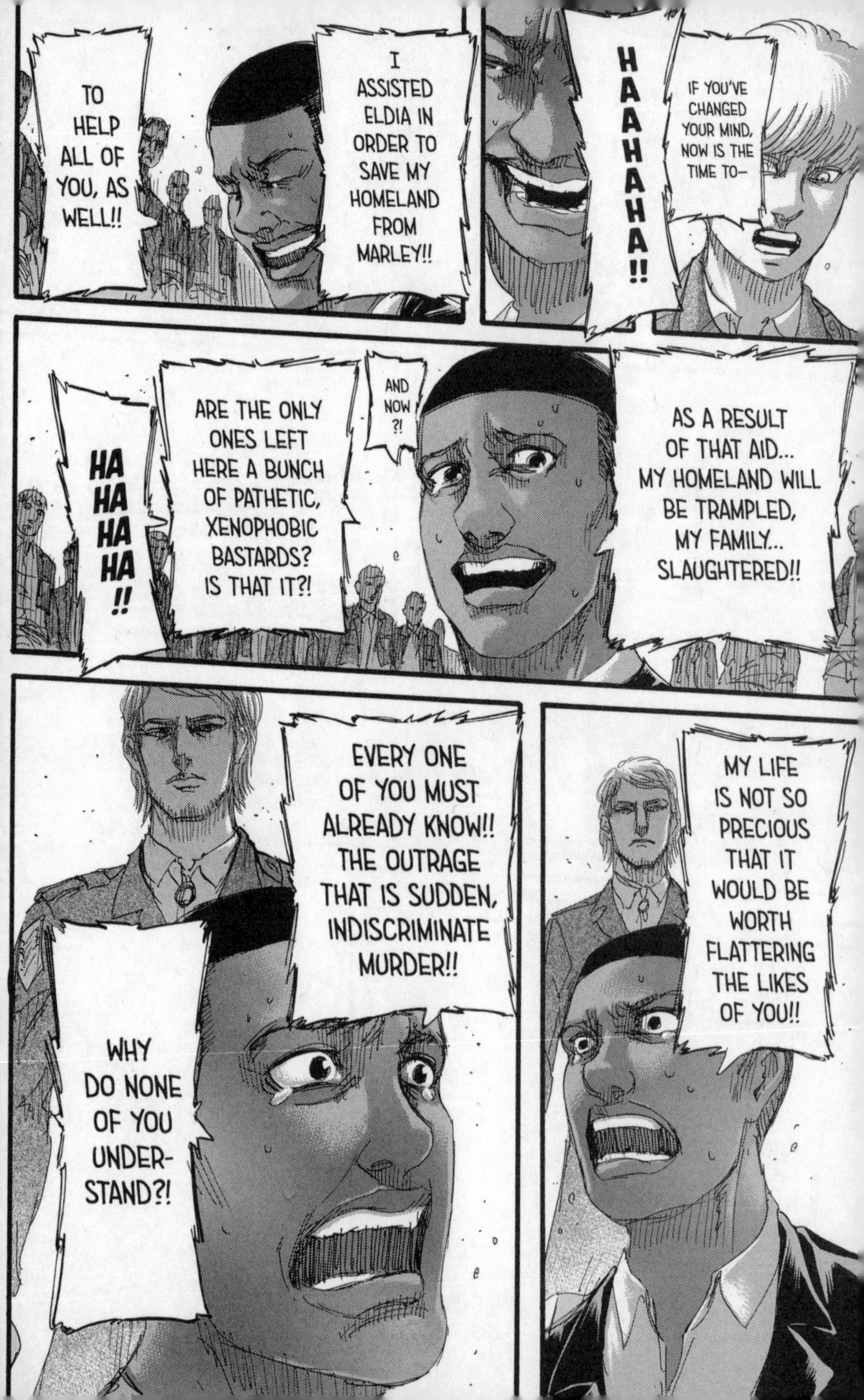
IF YOU'VE CHANGED YOUR MIND, NOW IS THE TIME TO—
HAHAHAHA!!
I ASSISTED ELDIA IN ORDER TO SAVE MY HOMELAND FROM MARLEY!!
TO HELP ALL OF YOU, AS WELL!!
AS A RESULT OF THAT AID... MY HOMELAND WILL BE TRAMPLED, MY FAMILY... SLAUGHTERED!!
AND NOW?!
ARE THE ONLY ONES LEFT HERE A BUNCH OF PATHETIC, XENOPHOBIC BASTARDS? IS THAT IT?!
HA HA HA HA!!
MY LIFE IS NOT SO PRECIOUS THAT IT WOULD BE WORTH FLATTERING THE LIKES OF YOU!!
EVERY ONE OF YOU MUST ALREADY KNOW!! THE OUTRAGE THAT IS SUDDEN, INDISCRIMINATE MURDER!!
WHY DO NONE OF YOU UNDER-STAND?!

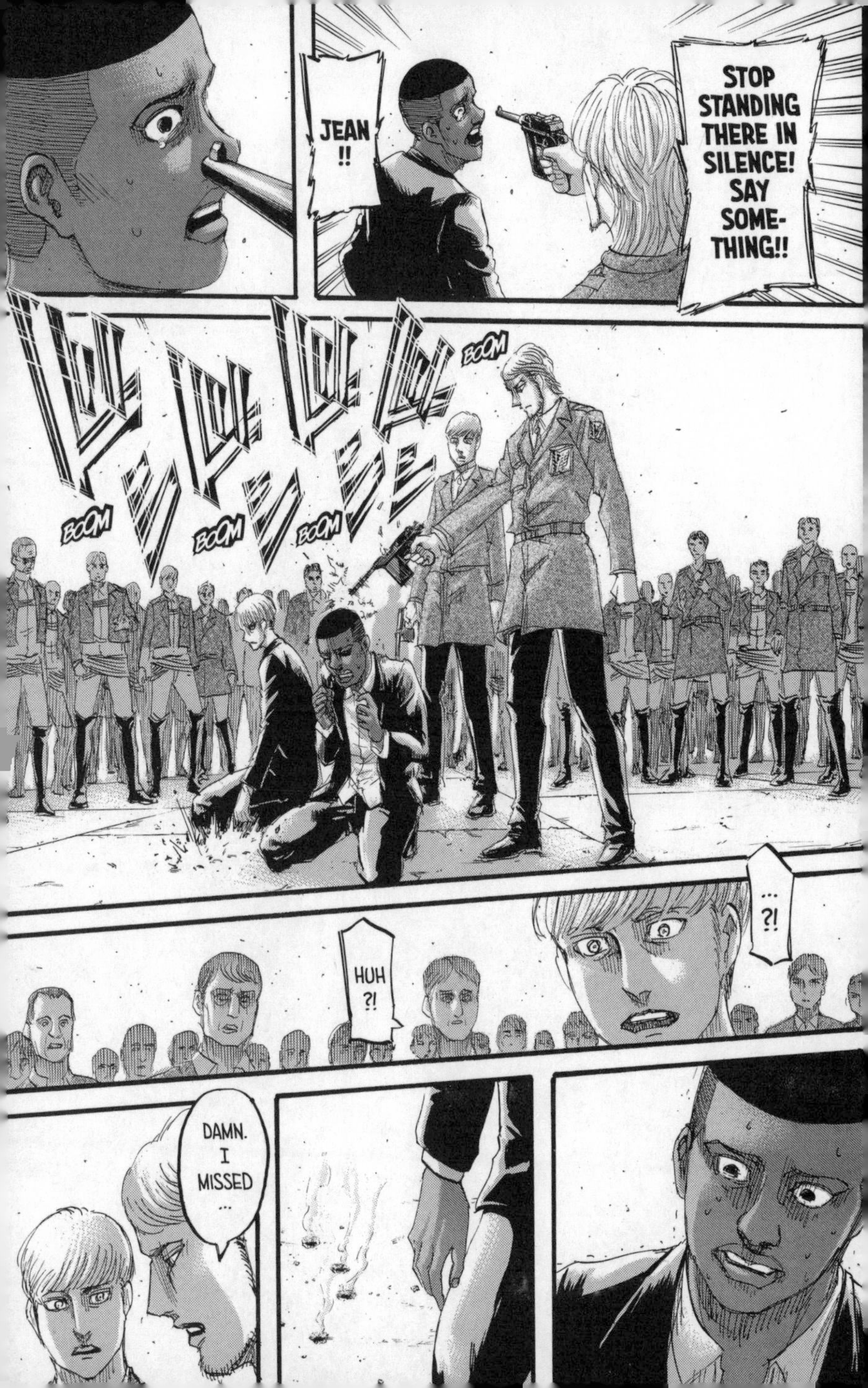
STOP STANDING THERE IN SILENCE! SAY SOME-THING!!
JEAN !!
BOOM
BOOM
BOOM
BOOM
... ?!
HUH ?!
DAMN. I MISSED ...

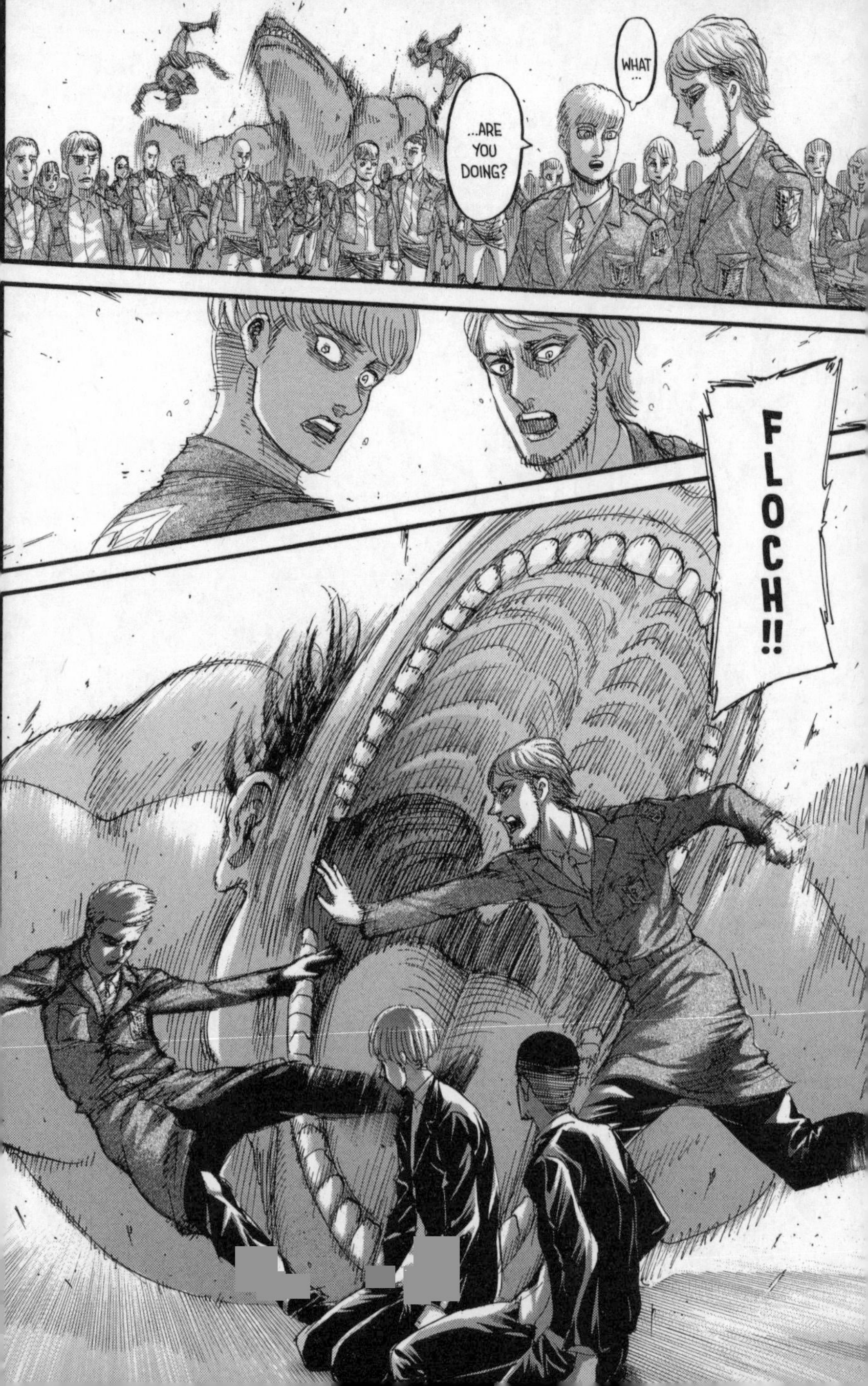
WHAT ...
...ARE YOU DOING?
FLOCH!!

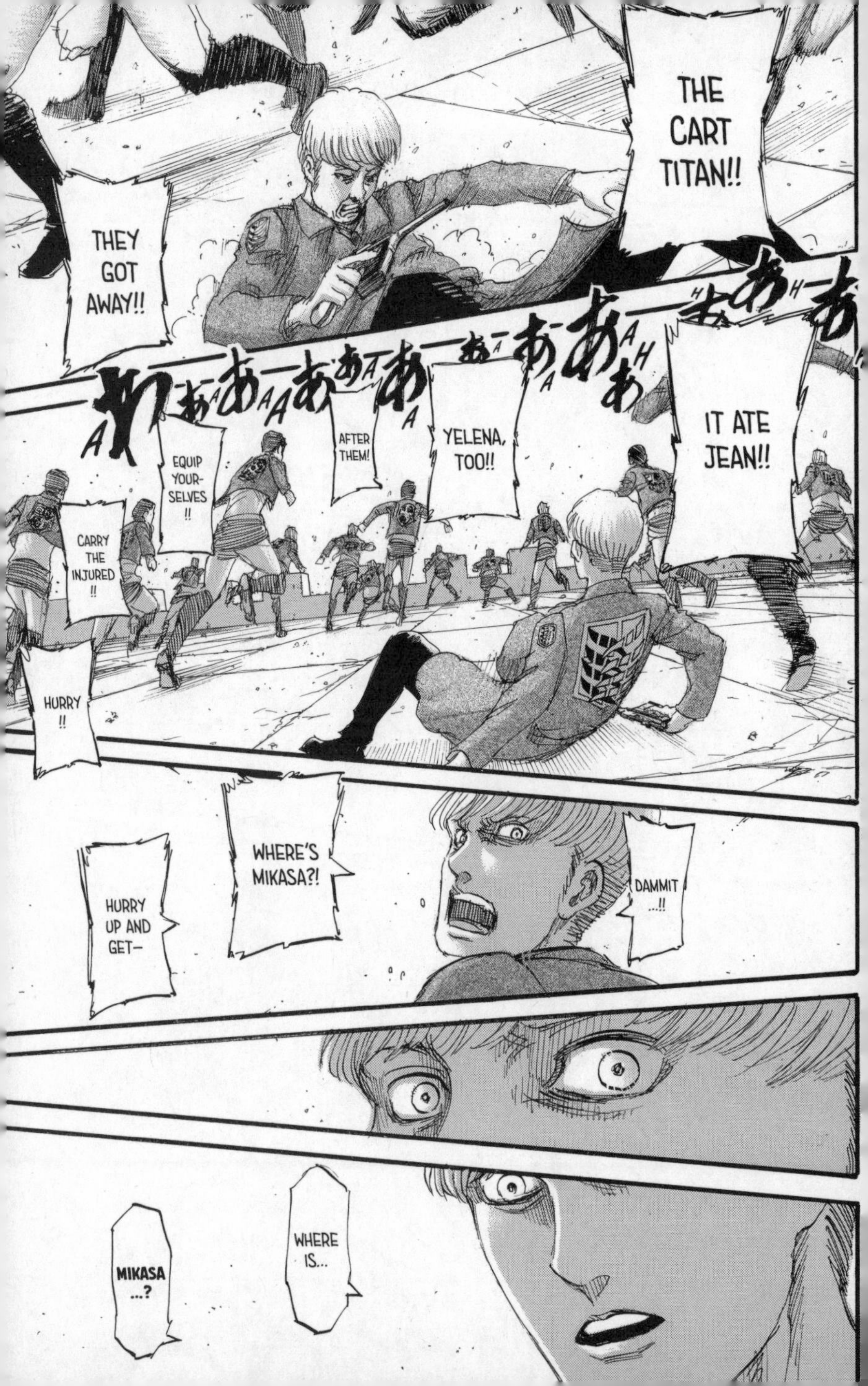
THE CART TITAN!!
THEY GOT AWAY!!
IT ATE JEAN!!
YELENA, TOO!!
AFTER THEM!
EQUIP YOURSELVES!!
CARRY THE INJURED!!
HURRY!!
DAMMIT ...!!
WHERE'S MIKASA?!
HURRY UP AND GET—
WHERE IS...
MIKASA ...?

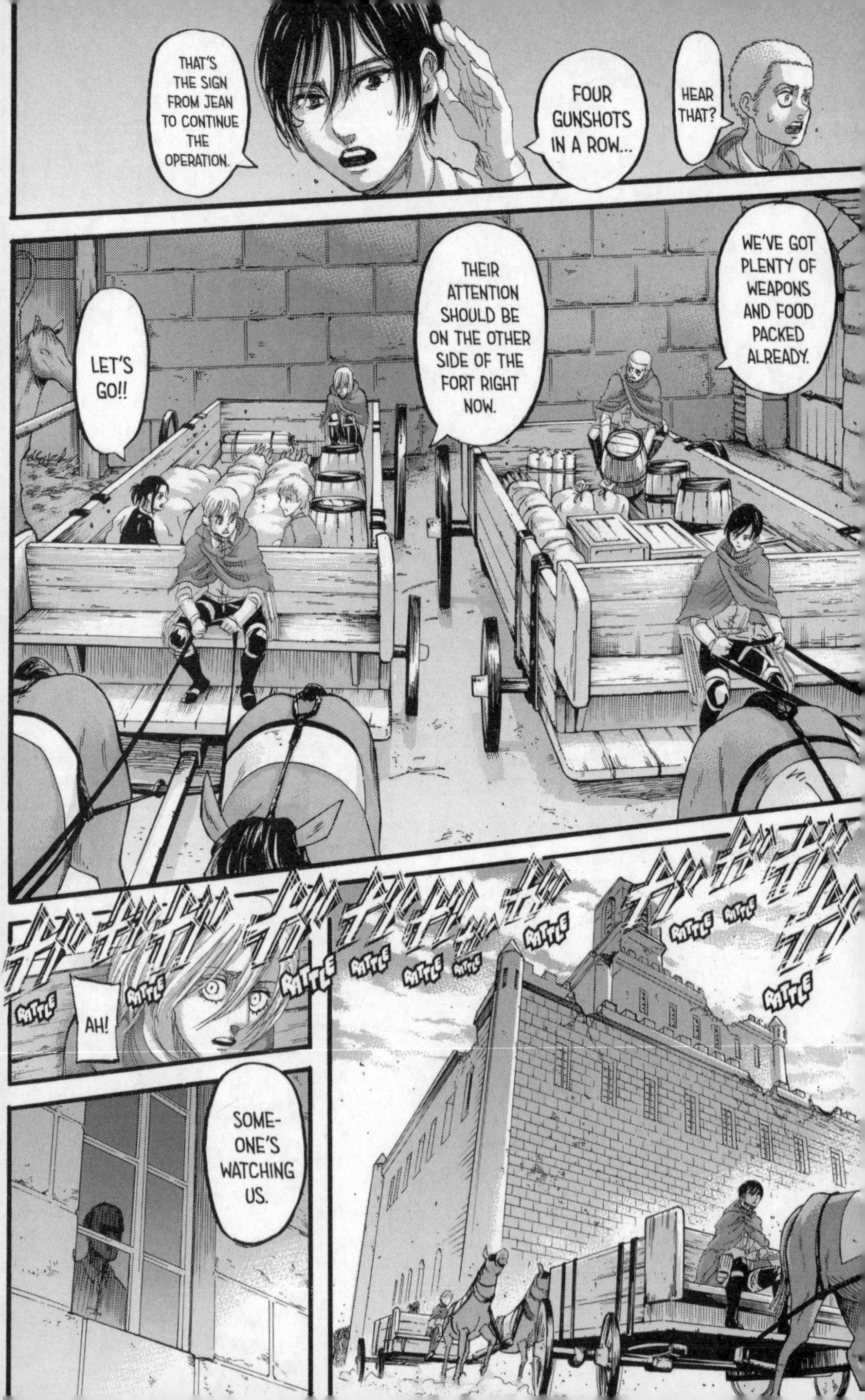
HEAR THAT?
FOUR GUNSHOTS IN A ROW...
THAT'S THE SIGN FROM JEAN TO CONTINUE THE OPERATION.
WE'VE GOT PLENTY OF WEAPONS AND FOOD PACKED ALREADY.
THEIR ATTENTION SHOULD BE ON THE OTHER SIDE OF THE FORT RIGHT NOW.
LET'S GO!!
RATTLE RATTLE RATTLE RATTLE RATTLE RATTLE RATTLE RATTLE RATTLE
AH!
RATTLE RATTLE
SOME-ONE'S WATCHING US.

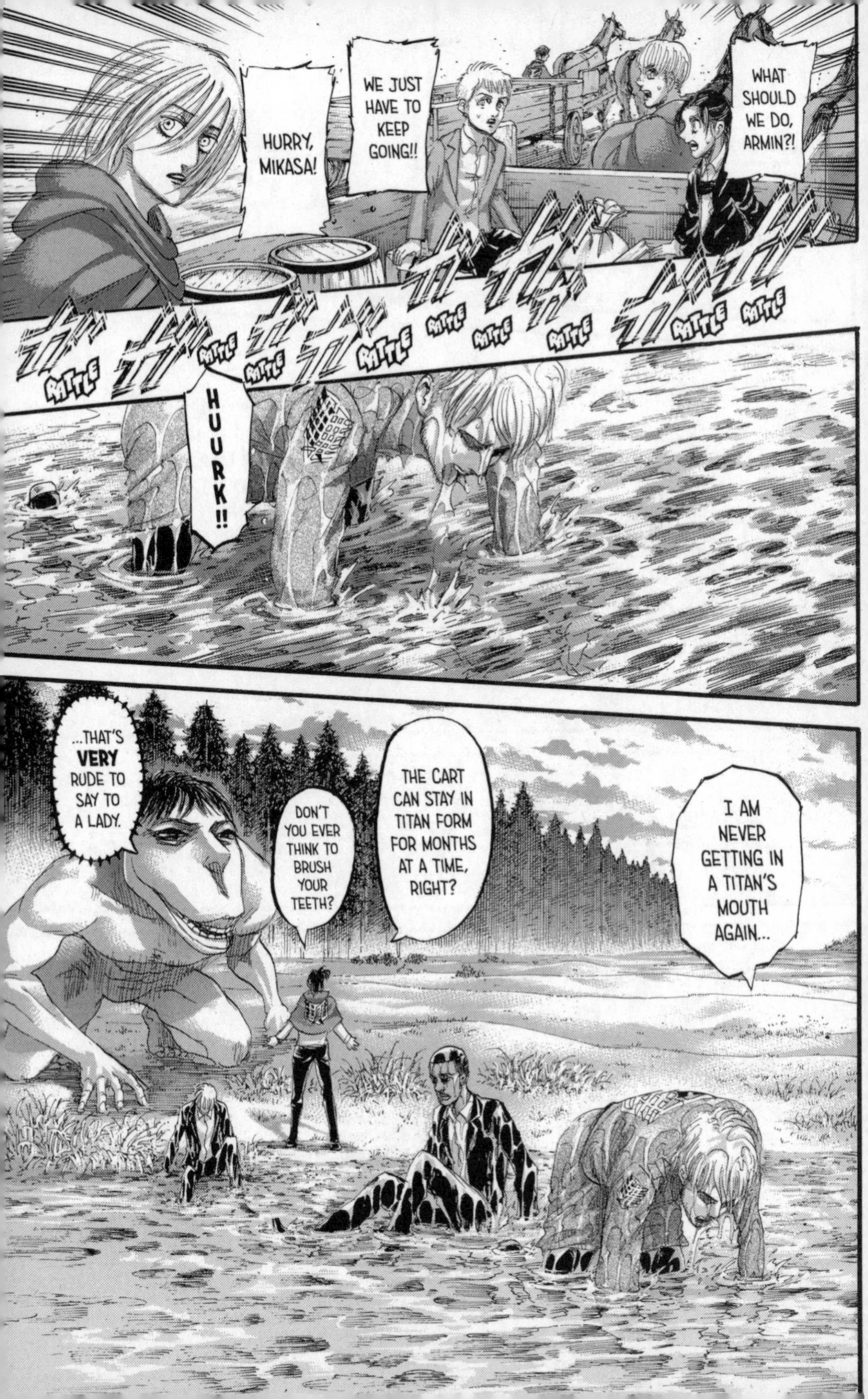
WHAT SHOULD WE DO, ARMIN?!
WE JUST HAVE TO KEEP GOING!!
HURRY, MIKASA!
RATTLE RATTLE RATTLE RATTLE RATTLE RATTLE RATTLE RATTLE RATTLE
HUURK!!
I AM NEVER GETTING IN A TITAN'S MOUTH AGAIN...
THE CART CAN STAY IN TITAN FORM FOR MONTHS AT A TIME, RIGHT?
DON'T YOU EVER THINK TO BRUSH YOUR TEETH?
...THAT'S **VERY** RUDE TO SAY TO A LADY.

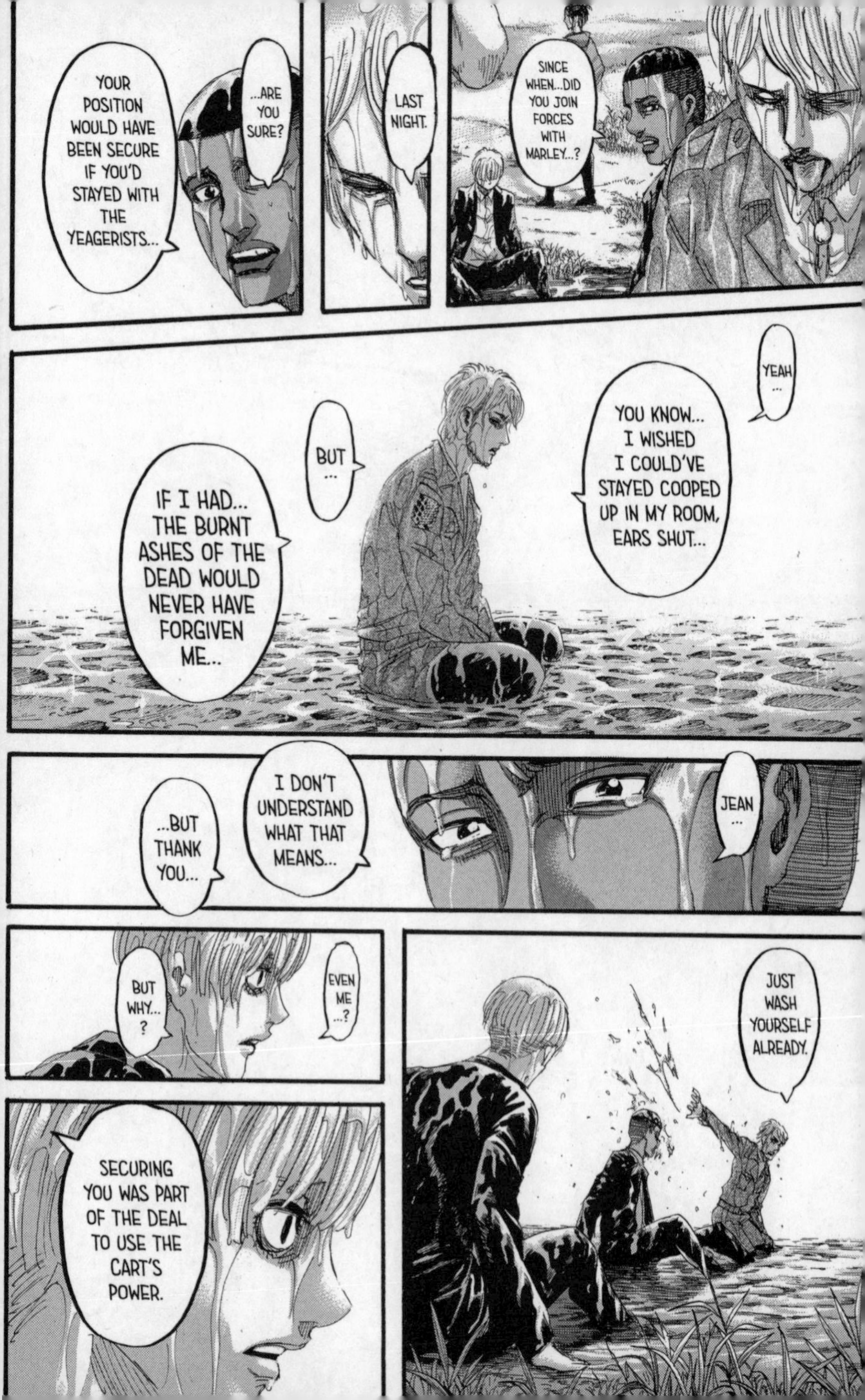
SINCE WHEN...DID YOU JOIN FORCES WITH MARLEY...?
LAST NIGHT.
...ARE YOU SURE?
YOUR POSITION WOULD HAVE BEEN SECURE IF YOU'D STAYED WITH THE YEAGERISTS...
YEAH...
YOU KNOW... I WISHED I COULD'VE STAYED COOPED UP IN MY ROOM, EARS SHUT...
BUT...
IF I HAD... THE BURNT ASHES OF THE DEAD WOULD NEVER HAVE FORGIVEN ME...
JEAN...
I DON'T UNDERSTAND WHAT THAT MEANS...
...BUT THANK YOU...
JUST WASH YOURSELF ALREADY.
EVEN ME...?
BUT WHY...?
SECURING YOU WAS PART OF THE DEAL TO USE THE CART'S POWER.

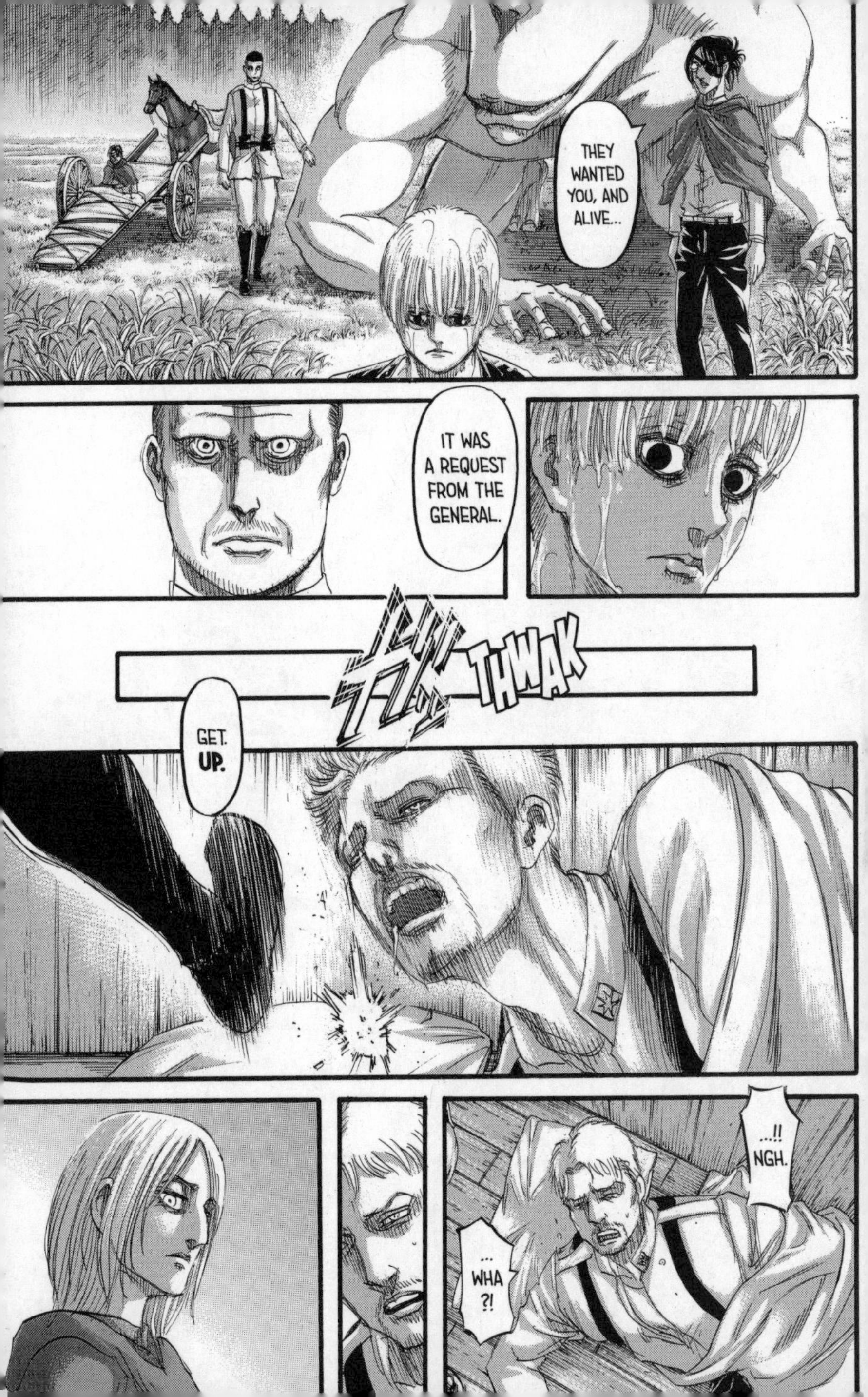
THEY WANTED YOU, AND ALIVE...
IT WAS A REQUEST FROM THE GENERAL.
THWAK
GET. UP.
...!! NGH.
... WHA ?!

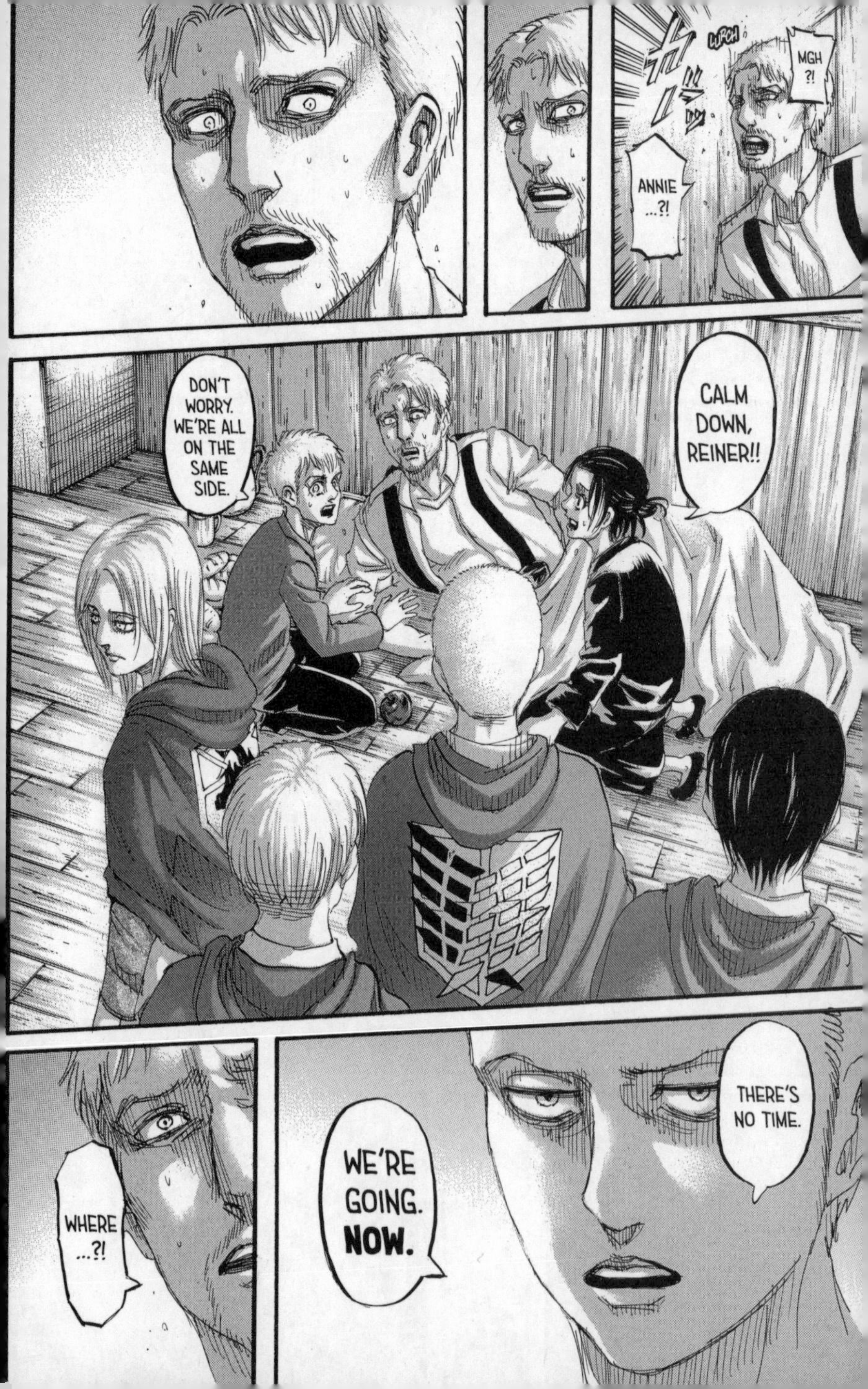
MGH ?!
LURCH
ANNIE ...?!
CALM DOWN, REINER!!
DON'T WORRY. WE'RE ALL ON THE SAME SIDE.
THERE'S NO TIME.
WE'RE GOING. **NOW.**
WHERE ...?!

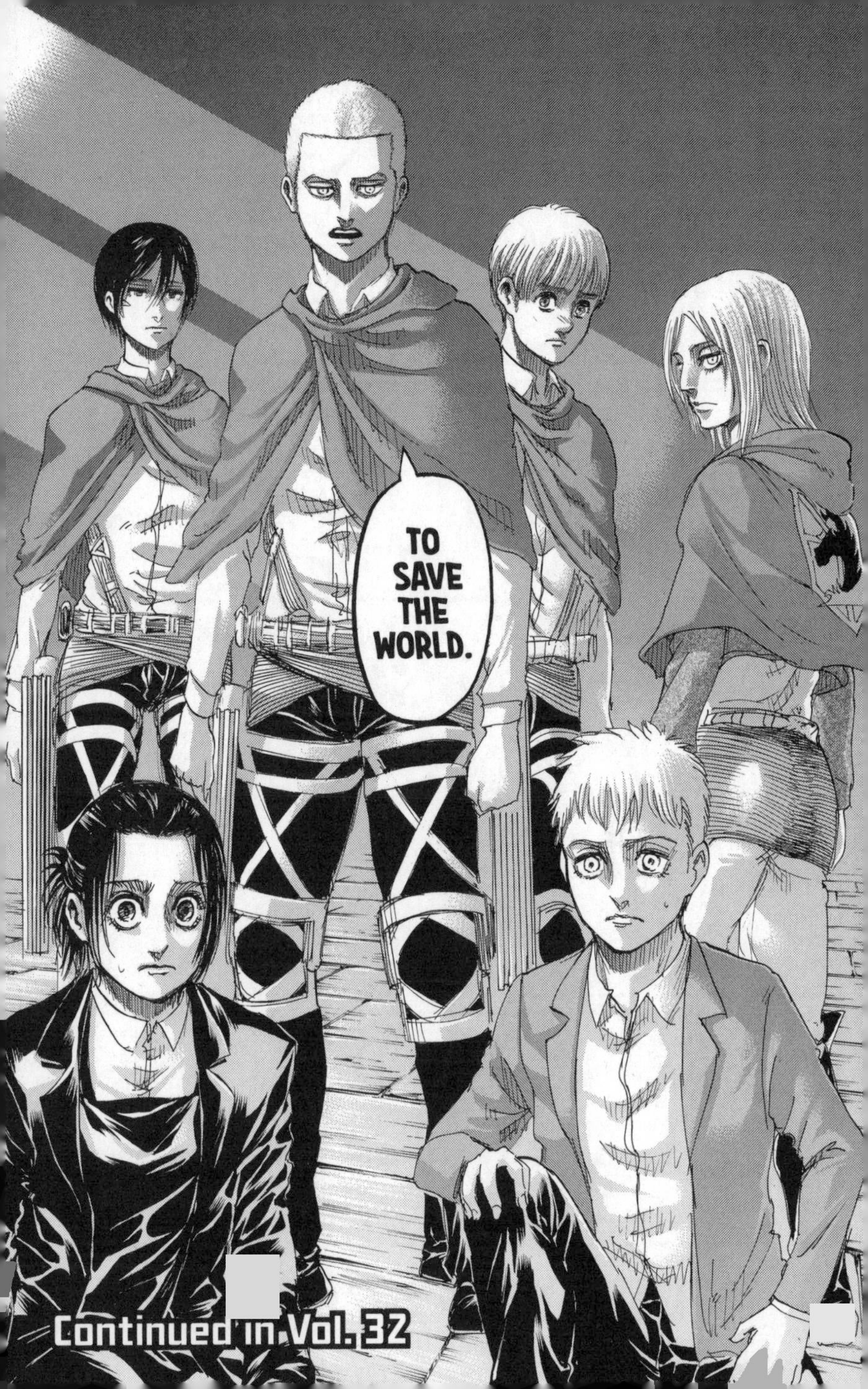
TO SAVE THE WORLD.

Continued in Vol. 32

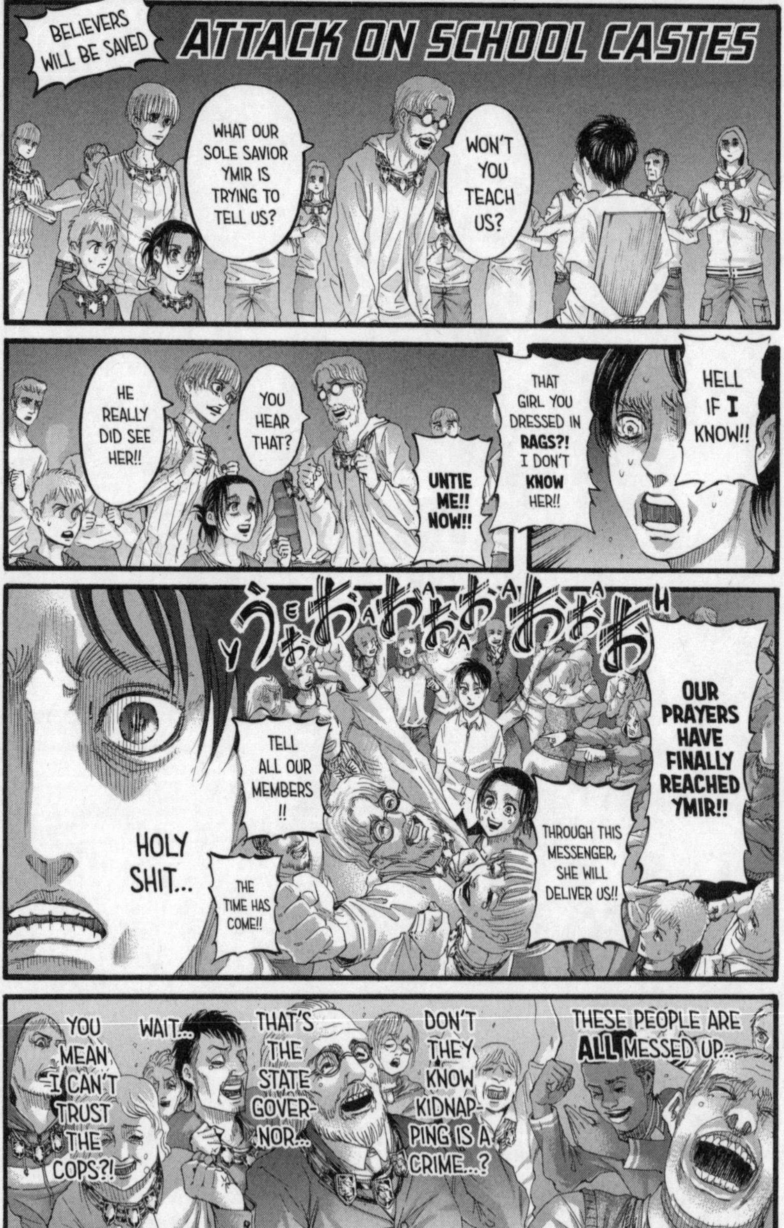
ATTACK ON SCHOOL CASTES
BELIEVERS WILL BE SAVED
WON'T YOU TEACH US?
WHAT OUR SOLE SAVIOR YMIR IS TRYING TO TELL US?
HELL IF I KNOW!!
THAT GIRL YOU DRESSED IN RAGS?! I DON'T KNOW HER!!
UNTIE ME!! NOW!!
YOU HEAR THAT?
HE REALLY DID SEE HER!!
YEAAAAAH
OUR PRAYERS HAVE FINALLY REACHED YMIR!!
THROUGH THIS MESSENGER, SHE WILL DELIVER US!!
TELL ALL OUR MEMBERS !!
THE TIME HAS COME!!
HOLY SHIT...
THESE PEOPLE ARE ALL MESSED UP...
DON'T THEY KNOW KIDNAPPING IS A CRIME...?
THAT'S THE STATE GOVERNOR...
WAIT...
YOU MEAN I CAN'T TRUST THE COPS?!

COMING SOON!

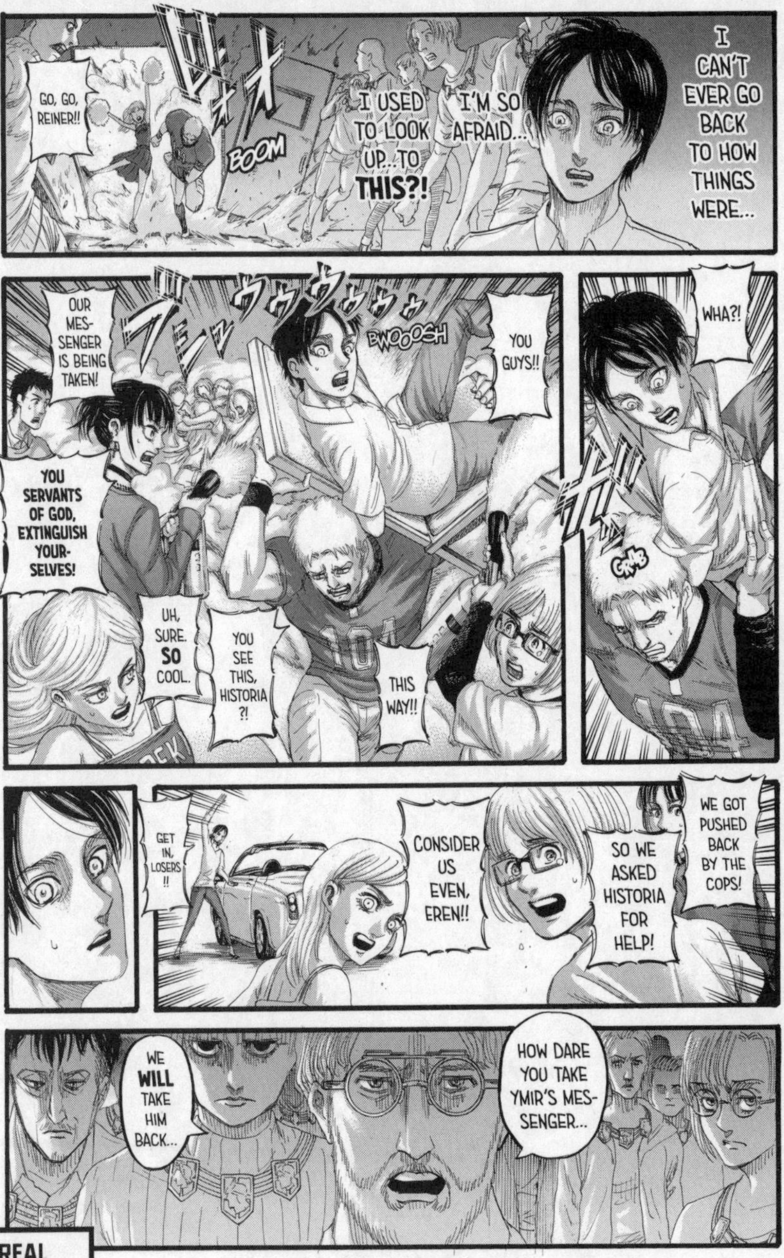
I CAN'T EVER GO BACK TO HOW THINGS WERE...
I'M SO AFRAID...
I USED TO LOOK UP... TO **THIS?!**
BOOM
GO, GO, REINER!!
WHA?!
GRAB
YOU GUYS!!
BWOOOSH
OUR MES-SENGER IS BEING TAKEN!
YOU SERVANTS OF GOD, EXTINGUISH YOUR-SELVES!
THIS WAY!!
YOU SEE THIS, HISTORIA ?!
UH, SURE. **SO** COOL.
WE GOT PUSHED BACK BY THE COPS!
SO WE ASKED HISTORIA FOR HELP!
CONSIDER US EVEN, EREN!!
GET IN, LOSERS !!
HOW DARE YOU TAKE YMIR'S MES-SENGER...
WE **WILL** TAKE HIM BACK...

***REAL PREVIEW IS ON THE FOLLOWING PAGE!**

VOLUME 32

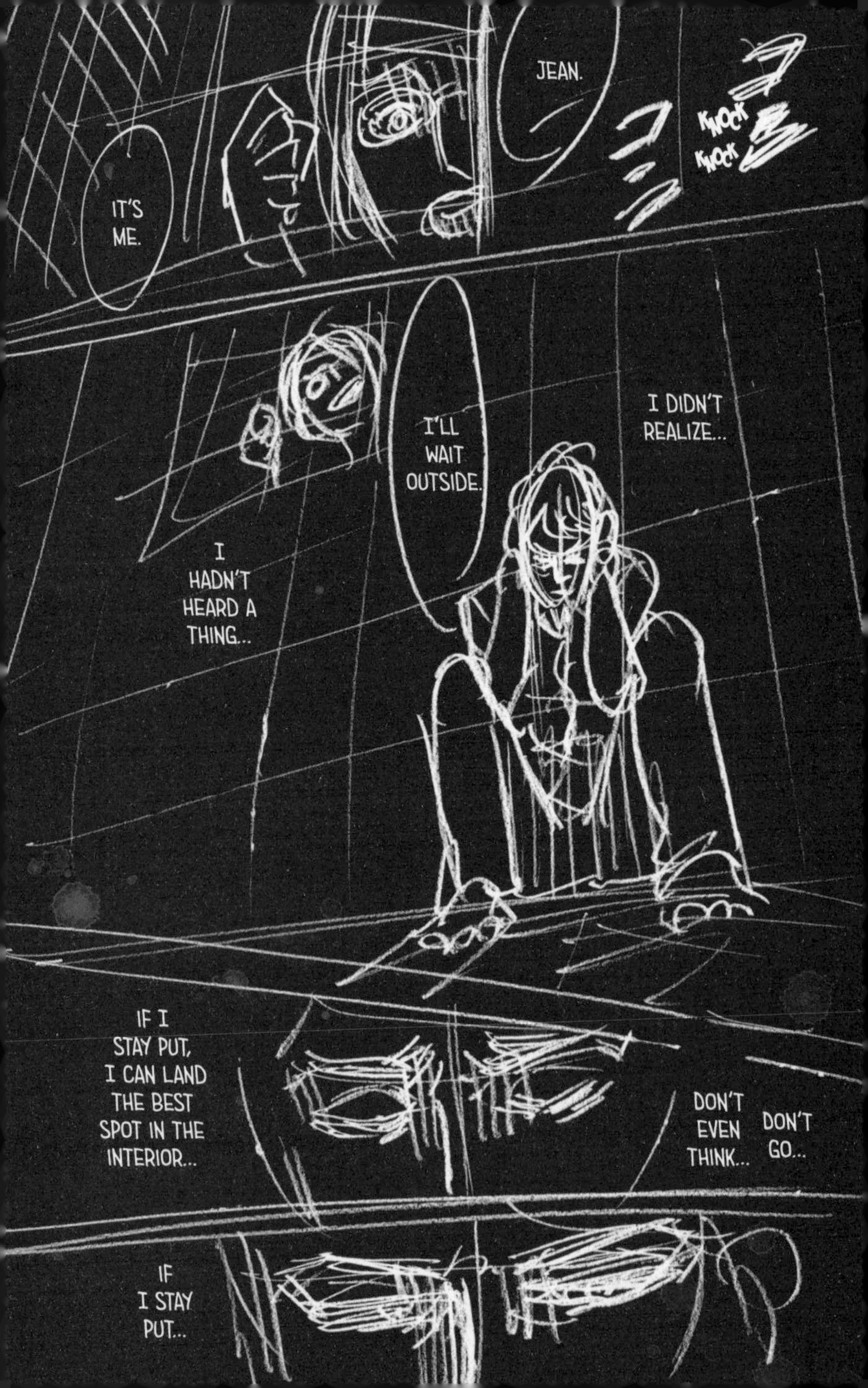
KNOCK
KNOCK
JEAN.
IT'S ME.
I DIDN'T REALIZE...
I'LL WAIT OUTSIDE.
I HADN'T HEARD A THING...
DON'T GO...
DON'T EVEN THINK...
IF I STAY PUT, I CAN LAND THE BEST SPOT IN THE INTERIOR...
IF I STAY PUT...

VOLUME 32 COMING SOON!

PEOPLE ARE
PRESSED FOR
A DECISION.

NO MATTER THE
OUTCOME, THEY
MUST CHOOSE.

A Kodansha Comics Trade Paperback Original
Attack on Titan 31 copyright © 2020 Hajime Isayama
English translation copyright © 2020 Hajime Isayama

All rights reserved.

Published in the United States by Kodansha Comics, an imprint of Kodansha USA Publishing, LLC, New York.

Publication rights for this English edition arranged through Kodansha Ltd., Tokyo.

First published in Japan in 2020 by Kodansha Ltd., Tokyo as *Shingeki no kyojin*, volume 31.

ISBN 978-1-63236-979-6

Original cover design by Takashi Shimoyama/Manami Fukunaga (Red Rooster)

Printed in the United States of America.

www.kodanshacomics.com

9 8 7 6 5
Translation: Ko Ransom
Lettering: Dezi Sienty
Editing: Haruko Hashimoto
Kodansha Comics edition cover design by Phil Balsman

Publisher: Kiichiro Sugawara

Director of publishing services: Ben Applegate
Associate director of operations: Stephen Pakula
Publishing services managing editor: Noelle Webster
Assistant production manager: Emi Lotto, Angela Zurlo